The
Brazilian Legislature
and Political System

Recent Titles in
Contributions in Political Science

THE
BRAZILIAN LEGISLATURE
AND POLITICAL SYSTEM

ABDO I. BAAKLINI

Contributions in Political Science, Number 298
Bernard K. Johnpoll, Series Editor

GREENWOOD PRESS
Westport, Connecticut • London

Library of Congress Cataloging-in-Publication Data

Baaklini, Abdo I.
   The Brazilian legislature and political system / Abdo I. Baaklini.
     p. cm.—(Contributions in political science, ISSN 0147-1066
; no. 298)
   Includes bibliographical references and index.
   ISBN 0-313-28450-4 (alk. paper)
   1. Brazil. Congresso Nacional. 2. Brazil. Congresso Nacional—
Officials and employees. 3. Brazil—Politics and
government—1964-1985. 4. Brazil—Politics and government—1985-
I. Title. II. Series.
JL2454.B3 1992
  328.81—dc20   91-44633

British Library Cataloguing in Publication Data is available.

Library of Congress Catalog Card Number: 91-44633
ISBN: 0-313-28450-4
ISSN: 0147-1066

First published in 1992

Greenwood Press, 88 Post Road West, Westport, CT 06881
An imprint of Greenwood Publishing Group, Inc.

Printed in the United States of America

The paper used in this book complies with the
Permanent Paper Standard issued by the National
Information Standards Organization (Z39.48-1984).

10 9 8 7 6 5 4 3 2 1

*To my sons
Farid and Iskandar*

Contents

Tables and Figure

TABLES

FIGURE

Acknowledgments

The past two decades of close involvement in the study of Brazilian politics and political institutions have left me indebted to many people in many ways. Under a United States Agency for International Development sponsored program of assistance to the Brazilian Congress in the 1970s, and through two Fulbright program grants (one in the summer of 1985 and the other for six months in 1988), I had the opportunity to travel to and spend several months in Brazil working with hundreds of Brazilian legislators and their staffs, at both the federal and state levels. These people proved to be the best mentors to the intricacies and subtleties of Brazilian politics. I am sure many of them will notice their insights scattered throughout this book.

In this short space, I can only acknowledge a few of the many outstanding individuals, who without their help and assistance this project would not have been possible. Eduardo Jorge Caldas Pereira introduced me to the study of Brazilian Congress in the early 1970s and has been my guide and mentor ever since. He assisted in the collection of data and reviewed the entire manuscript more than once, introducing significant changes that enabled me to avoid many errors of fact and judgment. Antonio Carlos Pojo de Rego collaborated with me on several research projects while he was a graduate student at the University at Albany, State University of New York, and his contributions are cited throughout the book. Aldo Zagonel dos Santos systematized the many tables throughout the book, built the index, organized the bibliography, and performed numerous other editorial jobs. Lourival Zagonel dos Santos, Paulo Affonso, Flávio Marcílio, and José Carlos all in their own ways made it possible for me to collect the data needed for this book. Rosinethe Soares helped in the collection of bills considered by the Chamber of Deputies in the 1970s and 1980s, and Oswaldo Sanches helped in the analysis and classification of those bills.

On the academic side, I am deeply indebted to David Fleischer, whose advice, guidance, and comments were always insightful and a special source of inspiration for my work. Professor Fleischer was kind enough to review the entire manuscript and make significant suggestions which were incorporated into the final version. The works of Thomas Skidmore, Alfred Stepan, Bolivar Lamounier, Guillermo O'Donnell and Senator Fernando Henrique Cardoso were all of special relevance to this research.

For the production of this book, I am grateful to Mildred Vasan and Lynn Flint of the Greenwood Press for their excellent editorial assistance, and to Linda Gould and her two assistants, Beatriz Lacerda and Jorge Bela, from the Center for Legislative Development at the University at Albany, for coordinating and producing the final manuscript.

Abbreviations

APPD:	Associação dos Profissionais em Processamento de Dados (Professional Association of Data Processors)
ARENA:	Aliança Renovadora Nacional (Alliance for National Renovation)
BNDE:	Banco Nacional do Desenvolvimento Econômico (National Bank for Economic Development)
BSEN:	Biografia dos Senadores (Members' Biographies)
CAPRE:	Coordenadoria das Atividades de Processamento Eletrônico (Coordinating Commission for Electronic Processing Activities)
CEDESEN:	Centro de Desenvolvimento de Recursos Humanos do Senado Federal (Staff Development and Training Center of the Federal Senate)
CEGRAF:	Centro Gráfico do Senado Federal (Printing Shop of the Federal Senate)
CLT:	Consolidação das Leis do Trabalho (Consolidation of the Labor Legislation)
COBRA:	Computadores e Sistemas Brasileiros (Brazilian Computers and Systems)
CONCEX:	Conselho Nacional do Comércio Exterior (Foreign Commerce Council)
CONIN:	Conselho Nacional de Informática e Automação (National Council on Informatics and Automation)
CPI:	Comissão Parlamentar de Inquérito (Parlimentary Inquiry Committee)
CSN:	Conselho de Segurança Nacional (National Security Council)
DAI:	Funções de Direção e Assistência Intermediárias (Intermediate Administrative and Assisting Functions)
DAS:	Funções de Direção e Assessoramento Superiores (Superior Administrative and Advisory Functions)
DASP:	Departamento Administrativo do Serviço Público (Public Service Administrative Department)
EMFA:	Estado Maior das Forças Armadas (General Staff of the Armed Forces)
ESG:	Escola Superior de Guerra (Superior War College)
FAS:	Funções de Assessoramento Superior (Superior Advisory Functions)
FC:	Funções Comissionadas (Comissioned Functions)
IBGE:	Instituto Brasileiro de Geografia e Estatística (Brazilian Geographic and Statistical Institute)
IBM:	International Business Machines
INCRA:	Instituto Nacional de Colonização e Reforma Agrária (National Institute for Colonization and Agrarian Reform)
INPI:	Instituto Nacional de Propriedade Industrial (National Institute for Industrial Property)
MDB:	Movimento Democrático Brasileiro (Brazilian Democratic Movement)

MNC:	Multinational Corporation
MUP:	Movimento de Unidade Progressista (Movement for the Unity of the Progressives)
NCA:	National Constituent Assembly
OAB:	Ordem dos Advogados do Brasil (Brazilian Bar Association)
PCB:	Partido Comunista Brasileiro (Brazilian Communist Party)
PC do B:	Communist Party of Brazil
PDC:	Partido Democrata Cristão (Christian Democratic Party)
PDS:	Partido Democrático Social (Democratic Social Party)
PDT:	Partido Democrático Trabalhista (Democratic Labor Party)
PFL:	Partido da Frente Liberal (Front Liberal Party)
PL:	Partido Liberal (Liberal Party)
PMDB:	Partido do Movimento Democrático Brasileiro (Party of the Brazilian Democratic Movement)
PP:	Partido Popular (Popular Party)
PRN:	Partido da Reconstrução Nacional (National Reconstruction Party)
PRODASEN:	Centro de Informática e Processamento de Dados do Senado Federal (Center for Data Processing of the Federal Senate)
PSB:	Partido Socialista do Brasil (Socialist Party of Brazil)
PSDB:	Partido da Social Democracia Brasileira (Brazilian Social Democratic Party)
PSP:	Partido Social Progressista (Social Progressive Party)
PT:	Partido dos Trabalhadores (Worker's Party)
PTB:	Partido Trabalhista Brasileiro (Brazilian Labor Party)
SAI:	Sistema Administrativo Integrado (Integrated Administrative System)
SBC:	Sociedade Brasileira de Computação (Brazilian Society for Computer Affairs)
SDI:	Sistema de Disseminaçãos Informações (Information Dissemination System)
SEI:	Secretaria Especial de Informática (Special Informatics Secretariat)
SEP:	Sistema de Endereçamento Parlamentar (Parliamentary Address System)
SEPLAN:	Secretaria de Planejamento (Planning Secretariat)
SICON:	Sistema de Informações de Congresso (Congressional Information System)
SNI:	Serviço Nacional de Informações (National Information Service)
STF:	Supremo Tribunal Federal (Supreme Federal Court)
STM:	Superior Tribunal Militar (Superior Military Court)
TCU:	Tribunal de Contas da União (Accounting Court of the Union)
TSE:	Tribunal Superior Eleitoral (Superior Electoral Court)
TST:	Tribunal Superior do Trabalho (Superior Labor Court)
UDN:	União Democrática Nacional (National Democratic Union)
UDR:	União Democrática Rural (Rural Democratic Union)

Preface

Brazil, unlike Argentina, the Philippines, and other military-authoritarian regimes, made a gradual and peaceful transition to democracy. This phenomenon intrigues scholars and political analysts. How did Brazil's bureaucratic, authoritarian regime extricate itself from power without serious disruptions to itself and to the country? What was the role of the National Congress of Brazil in this peaceful transition?

The academic literature in English and Portuguese has elaborated on the economic and political characteristics of this transition. Some authors trace the beginning of the transition as far back as 1974, to the time of President Ernesto Geisel's inauguration. Others believe it began later, in 1979, with President João Figueiredo, assisted by his Chief of Staff, General Golbery do Couto e Silva, as conductors of the process that became known as *abertura*, or political opening, that eventually led to the departure of the military from power. The emphasis of these studies has been on the economic dilemmas the regime faced. Many argue that what forced the regime to hasten its departure was the worsening of the economic conditions. Others highlight the role of the civil society, such as the political parties, the labor unions, the church, the Brazilian Bar Association, and other civic and professional associations. However, the role of the Congress in this process is often neglected or misunderstood.

Observers of the Congress during this period are divided on its importance in easing the transition to democracy. Some feel that, during the military regime, the Congress was dominated by the regime; that it was allowed to exist only as a symbol of the regime's purported role as guardian of the constitution and the democratic order against its leftist enemies. The Congress, according to this logic, was supposed to ensure a modicum of legitimacy for the regime. Its role was that of a minimal legislature, including its role in the transition to democracy. Other observers omit any mention of the Congress in connection with this transition.

Characterized as a minimal legislature, the Congress of Brazil did not attract scholarly interest. Although some research has been done on Brazil's constitutional issues, electoral laws, political representation, and political parties, little has been written on the Congress as an institution. How was the Congress transformed by the authoritarian regime? What roles was it supposed to play? What roles did it actually play? What resources were available to it during the authoritarian regime? These and a host of similar questions were left unexplored.

The presidential system of government in Brazil produced many tensions and crises between the President and the Congress. These problems affected negatively the evolution and character of the political parties and led to a bureaucratic political system. The authoritarian regime that assumed power in 1964 tried, among other things, to resolve some of the intrinsic and extrinsic problems associated with the presidential system of government. In this book, we examine the attempts of the authoritarian regime to transform the political system, with emphasis on the relationship between the President and the Congress. The nature of this transformation and the work of the Congress between 1964 and 1988 are covered in detail. Finally, we discuss the role of the Congress in mediating the return to an open, competitive multiparty system.

The Introduction sketches the historical evolution of the presidential system of government in Brazil, the characteristics of the political parties it created, and the bureaucracy it produced. Chapter 1 discusses how the military regime that assumed power in 1964 attempted to reformulate the political system by changing the nature of the political parties, the bureaucracy, and the Congress in order to avoid some of the contradictions inherent in the presidential system of government. Chapter 2 details the impact of these changes on congressional leadership and elaborates on the ability of the Congress to discharge its constitutional mandates. Chapter 3 discusses the evolution and structure of congressional staff in its attempt to modernize the information capabilities of the Congress. It also details the development of the Centro de Informática e Processamento de Dados do Senado Federal (Prodasen—Center for Data Processing of the Federal Senate of Brazil) and discusses the type of data bases Prodasen developed to assist the Congress. Chapter 4 evaluates the work of the staff and its orientation toward the Congress, its members, and politics in general. In Chapter 5 we outline in detail the type and volume of work the Congress performed between 1964 and 1986, and we analyze the importance of this work in paving the way toward the return to a democratic form of government. Chapter 6 illustrates how the Congress attempted to formulate alternative policy proposals to those the regime was formulating and implementing. In order to further elaborate on the congressional policy making role, we also discuss one such policy in detail, the *Política Nacional de Informática*, or National Informatics Policy. Chapter 7 examines how the Congress structured itself to draft the new constitution, a process that lasted nearly two years, and which resulted in the promulgation of the Constitution of 1988. In Chapter 8 we assess the main characteristics of this new constitution, and we discuss how the Congress emerged as an autonomous institution and an equal partner to the executive. Chapter 8 also illustrates how the objectives pursued by the opposition within the Congress during the authoritarian regime became embodied in the new constitution. Chapter 9 integrates the various findings of the book and assesses the performance of the Congress and the presidential system of government in Brazil.

Most of the data in this book was collected by the author during twenty years of fieldwork in the Congress of Brazil. For example, the data on the congressional staff, which is examined in Chapters 3 and 4, was collected through surveys conducted in 1981 and 1986, and through extensive interviews with both Federal Senate and Chamber of Deputies staff, beginning as far back as 1972, until 1989.

Another such example is the extensive data set used in Chapter 5. This data was developed by the author as a result of a detailed analysis of the *Diário do Congresso Nacional*, or Congressional Record, and of the data bases existent in Prodasen. In order to describe the work of the Congress during the authoritarian regime, we have included in Chapter 5 a statistical analysis of legislation introduced between 1960 and 1986, to demonstrate the role of the committees and the President-Congress relation. Also in Chapter 5, we introduce several new criteria that are useful for evaluating the work of a minimal legislature functioning under an authoritarian system. In addition to bills that were approved or rejected, we examine various strategies that the Congress used to embarrass and criticize the executive. Later, in Chapter 6, we explore the analysis of the content of thousands of bills introduced between 1972 and 1988, in order to explain how the Congress, under the military regime, developed and propagated the political and economic vision that eventually became part of the new constitutional order established in 1988.

These transformations and adaptations and the detailed analysis of the work of the Congress influenced the way Congress conducted its business. Chapters 6, 7, and 8, for example, describe how the Congress functioned in three important areas: the budget, the industrial policy, and the drafting of a new constitution. A part of Chapter 6 discusses the way the Congress dealt with the budget. The budget, under the authoritarian regime, was to a large extent the prerogative of the executive. The Congress was supposed to be excluded from budget negotiations. Discussing the role of Congress in the budget process represents congressional action in an exclusionary executive area. Brazil's industrial policy known as National Informatics Policy became the driving force of the regime's push to acquire and develop high technology industry. This policy initially was the domain of the President, but it eventually became a legislative concern. Informatics policy represented congressional action in an area of the President's concern. It illustrates how the legislature was able to act in policy areas that required specialized information. Finally, the Congress, as a National Constituent Assembly, worked under its own rules and regulations and enjoyed almost total autonomy from the President. The role of the Congress in drafting the constitution is particularly important for several reasons. Few constitutions have been drafted the way Brazil's Constitution of 1988 was, in an open and participatory manner. Since the new constitution represents a compromise between the departing regime and the civilian regime, it enables us to assess the extent to which it also represented the vision articulated by the Congress discussed in Chapter 6. Understanding the articles of the new constitution and the nature of the political, economic, and social order Congress adopted is also important to the understanding of present-day Brazil and the challenges it faces and will likely face.

We believe this book to be relevant to several groups of scholars and public policymakers. Those concerned with legislative studies will find the material on the National Congress of Brazil not only new but challenging the prevailing wisdom regarding the role and importance of a minimal legislature. In the same manner, those concerned with comparative government and government institutions will find the emphasis on the presidential system of government and its problems worthy of close attention, since some fundamental questions are raised about the relationship between the structure of government and government stability. With respect to those concerned with the process of transition to democracy, whether from rightist or leftist authoritarian regimes, this book will contribute to the discussion of how a legislature can be a bridge between old and new regimes. Finally, this book attempts to fill a gap for those concerned with the study of Brazilian politics.

NOTES

1. The transition from authoritarianism to democracy has been the topic of heated debate among Latin American specialists. The Brazilian transition has been of special interest, since it was gradual and peaceful. For a review of this literature, see Guillermo O'Donnell, Phillippe C. Schmitter, and Laurence Whitehead (eds.), *Transitions from Authoritarian Rule: Latin America* (Baltimore: Johns Hopkins University Press, 1986); Riordan Roett, "The Transition to Democratic Government in Brazil," *World Politics*, 38, no. 2 (January 1986), pp. 371-82; Riordan Roett and Scott D. Tollefson, "The Transition to Democracy in Brazil," *Current History* (January 1986), pp. 21-24; Eli Diniz, "A Transição Política no Brasil: Uma Reavaliacao da Dinâmica da Abertura," *Dados* 28, no. 3 (1985), pp. 329-46; Karen Remmer, "Redemocratization and the Impact of Authoritarian Rule in Latin America," *Comparative Politics*, 17, no. 3,

(April 1985), pp. 253-75; Bolivar Lamounier, "Opening Through Elections: Will the Brazilian Case Become a Paradigm?" *Government and Opposition*, 19, no. 2, (Spring 1984), pp. 167-77; Samuel P. Huntington, "Will More Countries Become Democratic?" *Political Science Quarterly*, no. 2 (Summer 1984), pp. 193-218; and Robert Wesson and David Fleischer, *Brazil in Transition* (New York: Praeger, 1983).

2. The comparative study of legislatures and the study of legislatures in developing countries became the concern of some scholars in the 1970s. The leading book influencing the study of legislatures outside the United States was John C. Wahkle et al., *The Legislative System* (New York: John Wiley & Sons, 1962). For a discussion on the concept of a minimal legislature, see Michael L. Mezey, "The Functions of Legislatures in the Third World," *Legislative Studies Quarterly*, no. 8 (November 1983), pp. 511-50. For other such studies, see Gerhard Loewenberg and Samuel Patterson, *Comparing Legislatures* (Boston: Little, Brown & Co., 1979); Abdo I. Baaklini, "Legislatures in New Nations: Toward a New Perspective," *Polity*, no. 8 (1976), pp. 558-80; Abdo I. Baaklini, *Legislatures and Political Development: Lebanon, 1840-1972* (Beverly Hills: Sage Publications, 1974); Jean Blondel, *Comparative Legislatures* (Englewood Cliffs, N.J.: Prentice Hall, 1973); Allan Kornberg (ed.), *Legislatures in Comparative Perspective* (New York: David McKay, 1973); Herbert Hirsch and M. Donald Hancock (eds.), *Comparative Legislative Systems: A Reader in Theory and Research* (New York: The Free Press, 1971); and Allan Kornberg and Lloyd D. Musolf (eds.), *Legislatures in Developmental Perspective* (Durham, N.C.: Duke University Press, 1970).

The
Brazilian Legislature
and Political System

Introduction. Brazilian Presidentialism in Historical Perspective

Since its independence from Portugal in 1822, Brazil has had periods of relative stability and high instability. Until 1964, Brazil had experienced four distinct political periods: the Imperial period, the First Republic period, the New State period, and the Competitive period.[1]

The Imperial Period (1822-1889)

From 1822, the date of Brazilian independence from Portugal, until 1889, the date of the proclamation of the Republic, Brazil was ruled by a constitutional monarchy. The Emperor acted as the head of state and assumed all the prerogatives connected with that office. He had the "poder moderador," which enabled him to moderate among the contending political forces and in a sense act as a stabilizing factor. Political parties, in the modern sense, were nonexistent, and legislatures acted merely as advisory councils. Participation in elections was limited to the nobility and to the few members of the propertied class.

During the first phase a number of political disturbances led Pedro I to resign the regency in 1831. Yet relative to other periods, the Imperial period can be characterized as having had a relatively high degree of institutional stability. This relative stability was broken in 1889 with the establishment of the Republic and the adoption of a presidential system of government modeled after that of the United States.[2]

The First Republic Period (1889-1930)

During the First Republic (Old Republic) period, the landed classes continued to dominate Brazilian politics. Although slavery was abolished in 1888, those freed were not given political rights unless they were literate. Along with the propertied class, the church and senior military officers dominated the political scene.[3] Presidential elections were highly influenced by the state governors, in particular the governors of the states of Rio de Janeiro, São Paulo, and Minas Gerais who exercised great influence in choosing the President.[4] The Constitution of 1891 endorsed liberal positivism ideals, giving the government a very limited role in the social and economic realms. Whatever limited powers the government possessed were exercised by the state and local governments rather than by the federal government. In the absence of organized national political parties, landed local classes dominated the electoral process.[5] Because of restrictive electoral laws, less that 5 percent of the total population participated in the elections. The coffee barons, the Brazilian term for the big coffee producers, emerged as the economic elite, and immigrant labor began to supplant slave labor. During this period, political conflict under the presidential system of government was not between the President and the legislature, or the President and the political parties, but between the President and the state governors. The military elite and the aristocratic elite overlapped.

Between 1822 and 1930, Brazil had only two constitutions, each with major constitutional amendments.[6] Combined, these two periods, in spite of several political impasses, represent the highest degree of relative institutional stability that Brazil has attained.

Four factors account for the relative stability of the Old Republic period. First, participation in elections was restricted to the elite; second, the role of the government was limited to the essential law-and-order function; third, whatever power the government possessed was located at state and local levels, rather than at the federal level; and fourth, there were no strong national political parties, nor a mass electorate.[7]

The domination of the electoral process by the elite guaranteed their social and economic interests at the state level, and in the private sector. Wealth was in private hands, and private initiatives were dominant. Mass politics, or what is known in South America as populism, and its many demands from the political system had not yet surfaced.[8] In the absence of mass national political parties, which normally mobilize the disenfranchised, the legislature represented the same economic interests as the executive, and, therefore, the executive-legislative conflict that characterizes many modern presidential systems of government was avoided.

During the First Republic, the limited role of the government, and its decentralized feature, prevented the emergence of a strong President and the winner-take-all syndrome associated with many of today's presidential systems of government. The winning of the presidency by one group of elites did not prevent the defeated group from continuing to secure its interest either at the state level or in the private domain. Those who lost kept their economic and political bases intact and were later able to wage a campaign for the next presidential election.

The New State Period (1930-1945)

Between 1930 and 1945, Brazil witnessed extreme institutional and political instabilities and fundamental changes in the role of the government and the nature of the federal system. In 1930, a revolt led by dissatisfied governors and military brought to power Getúlio Vargas. In 1932, pro-constitutionalists in São Paulo attempted to unseat Vargas, because of his failure to reinstitutionalize liberal political reforms, but they failed. In 1934 a constitution was drafted. In 1935, with the support of a right-wing group of officers and their civilian supporters known as *Integralistas* (a pro-fascist group), Vargas managed to suppress an ill-conceived communist insurgency. In 1937, having outmaneuvered his opponents to the right and to the left, Vargas began to create what he called the *Estado Novo*, or the New State. In 1938, he suppressed an attempted coup organized by the *Integralistas*, thus putting himself in the center of the political spectrum, a position he maintained until his deposition in 1945.[9]

The New State period witnessed legislation in the economic and social spheres initiated by Vargas, which transformed the federal government into the main political and economic actor. Vargas understood that the old elitist politics of the few could not sustain the strong governmental role that was needed to bring the country together and to initiate long-overdue development programs. Although Vargas worked hard to protect Brazilian coffee producers by providing them with subsidies and protective legislation, he sought to mobilize the emerging urban labor force as a basis for his political power against threats to his regime from both the left and the right. He created the Ministries of Labor and Education, adopted a new labor law to protect workers and ensure their right to have their own labor unions, and established social security laws. At the same time he sought to reduce Brazil's dependency on the export of coffee by encouraging the exploration of mineral and other natural resources, including oil and hydroelectric energy. He even adopted functional representation for the Chamber of Deputies, reserving a number of seats for the workers.[10]

By 1945, Vargas's *Estado Novo* had radically changed the way politics was conducted in Brazil in four major ways, with significant implications to the durability of the presidential system of government.

Vargas's reforms and programs transformed the federal government's role in the socioeconomic realm. The federal government became the hub of society and of the economy. The role of state and local governments was irrevocably diminished, even as suppliers of goods and services. The decentralized federal system of government, which Brazil enjoyed until 1930, gave way to a more centralized system. Major aspects of public policies that directly affect the day-to-day life of the citizens were decided at the federal capital in Rio de Janeiro. This meant that those who lost the presidential election were less likely to survive and compete in the next election. Controlling a state government carried less political weight, since the state became dependent on the resources from the central government for the implementation of its social and economic services to the citizens. The governor's role as a counterbalance to the President during the Old Republic was undermined. From then on, the presidency became the undisputed power center of the entire political system.

Another way the Vargas era changed Brazil's political system was in the emergence of the institution of the armed forces as the arbiter of political succession and the guardian of the constitution.[11] Although in the First Republic the officers played a role in the presidential succession, the federal military establishment as an institution was weak. Under Vargas the centralization of the government took place not only in the socioeconomic arena, but also in the military arena. Until 1930, each state had its own militia. Militias in some states, such as Rio Grande do Sul, São Paulo, and Minas Gerais, were stronger than the central armed forces. The militia, which was under the command of the state governor, gave the governor a decided advantage in times of crisis, vis-à-vis the central government.

Vargas's *Estado Novo* weakened the state militia and strengthened the central armed forces. The officers became closer to the central authorities and began to assume the role of arbiters of political conflict. As guardians of the centralized government, they sometimes were open advocates of policies and programs that were at variance with the political authorities of the time. Indeed, after World War II, they played a prominent role in forcing Vargas out of power and in the establishment of the liberal democracy of the Constitution of 1946.

Another change brought about by the Vargas era was the emergence of the urban masses as a major force in presidential elections. The unorganized urban masses became the target of populist politicians seeking office. Vargas himself, in addition to using the military to ward off his challengers, resorted to populist programs to mobilize the support of the urban masses. Future presidential candidates could only be elected with the support of the urban population. Once elected, however, they found themselves unable to satisfy the populist demands. Populist programs and policies were resisted by factions with political ties to the armed forces and, to a lesser extent, within the Congress. The present dilemma of Brazilian presidents was created: To be elected and to acquire political legitimacy, a contemporary presidential candidate needs the support of the urban poor. To remain in power the President needs the support of the armed forces. To have programs and policies approved, the President needs the support of the Congress. Given the conflicting and sometimes irreconcilable interests among these groups, political impasses between the President and the Congress often occurred.

The Competitive Period (1946-1964)

From 1946 until the military coup of 1964, Brazil had a liberal presidential system of government with a multiparty system as the basis for contesting elections. The Vargas regime represented an authoritarian presidential system of government. With the liberal Constitution of 1946, the power of the President was circumscribed and political parties and the Congress played a more prominent role. It is during this period that the presidential system of government demonstrated its fragility and precariousness.[12] In spite of the declared political and economic liberalism advocated by the Constitution of 1946, the first elected President, General Eurico Gaspar Dutra, used a clause in the constitution that banned antidemocratic forces from openly competing in elections in order to declare the Brazilian Communist Party (Partido Comunista Brasileiro, PCB) illegal and to reshuffle unions accused of being under Communist sway. In 1951, Vargas returned to power, this time through direct election, by forming a temporary alliance between his party, the Brazilian Labor Party (Partido Trabalhista Brasileiro, PTB), the São Paulo's populist Ademar de Barros, of the Social Progressive Party (Partido Social Progressista, PSP), elements of the Social Democratic Party (Partido Social Democrático, PSD), and, in some states, the National Democratic Union (União Democrática Nacional, UDN) against both the hard-liners and liberals of the armed forces who dreaded his return and feared that he would exact retribution for his overthrow in 1945. When a coup led by army officers demanded his resignation in 1954, Vargas committed suicide rather than surrender. In 1955, the attempt of the armed forces to elect Juarez Távora, their candidate for the presidency, failed. After many maneuvers by the Armed Forced within the Congress and the military, Juscelino Kubitschek, the elected President, was allowed to assume the presidency in January 1956.[13] In August 1961, Kubitschek's successor, Jânio Quadros, resigned, claiming unspecified pressure.[14] His Vice-President, João Goulart, was allowed to assume power only after he agreed to rule under a parliamentary system of government. Parliamentarism was revoked by a popular referendum in January 1963. In 1964 a coup d'état deposed Goulart and sent him into exile.

Why did the presidential system of government prove unworkable during this period in spite of its liberal character and the political guarantees of the Constitution of 1946? Some have argued that, for a presidential system of government to function democratically, a coherent two-party system is needed. A multiparty system, it was suggested, cannot give the President the support he needs. Every agreement becomes a major obstacle requiring extensive time, energy, and resources to be surmounted, thus leading to procrastination and inaction, if not to an impasse. A two-party system, however, although it may be able to give the President the support he needs, is very difficult to sustain. The opposition may control the majority in the Congress, setting the stage for executive-legislative confrontation. Otherwise, to maintain a pro-executive majority the President would have to manipulate the elections to prevent the opposition from becoming the majority. In the case of a hegemonic majority party, sustained in power through executive manipulation, the opposition party may cease to exist or may atrophy. An authoritarian system, one may argue, emerges in order to maintain the stability of the presidential system of government. The collapse of the competitive period in Brazil seems to corroborate this mode of analysis.

Political Parties and the Presidential System of Government

According to Bolivar Lamounier and Rachel Meneguello, a major characteristic of political parties in Brazil is a lack of historical roots and continuity.[15] Political parties, Lamounier suggests, have passed through seven stages of transformation: (a) 1837-1889, liberals versus conservatives; (b) one state-oriented party, the Republican party in the First Republic until the revolution of 1930; (c) the embryonic multiparty system until the coup of 1937; (d) a multiparty system that was well organized, from 1945 until 1965, when abolished by the Institutional Act No. 2; (e) a two-party system between 1965 until 1979; (f) controlled return to a multiparty system that began in 1980 and culminated with Constitutional Amendment No. 25 of May 1985, which removed many of the restrictions imposed by the military against parties, including the legalization of Communist parties. In each period the party system was broken up by central authorities. Lamounier further characterizes Brazilian political parties as undisciplined, fractured along state lines, organized around individuals rather than ideals and programs, artificial, and unauthentic.

Some scholars attribute party disintegration in Brazil to the bureaucratic-familial structure of its government. Political parties disintegrate, it was argued, because they are not able to maintain members' interest by using the state's resources, and, therefore, break with civil order. It was also argued that the political parties in Brazil produce narrow party identification and loyalty. Some blamed Brazil's Portuguese heritage and colonial past; others blamed the predominant role of both the bureaucracy and the landlords in the Brazilian society.[16] The electoral system is often cited as a further contributing factor to the weakening of the party system in Brazil. Unlike the United States, the presidential system of government and the election of the President in Brazil did not produce a national party organization. The enormous size of Brazil and its federal system also failed to produce national parties.

From 1945 to 1964, parties in the contemporary sense did emerge, only to face a series of crises between 1961 to 1964: the radicalization of the right and the left; Goulart's ambiguity about his successor and his frequent disregard for constitutional norms; the effect of the Cuban Revolution; and the U.S. support of rightist forces and economic pressure against Brazil all may help to explain the 1961-1964 crises. Some see the military coup of 1964 as a logical consequence of the economic contradiction and the social and cultural transformation of the Brazilian society. Others blame it on the failure of the political parties to perform their function of interest articulation. This interpretation also viewed the coup as a consequence of the party system's failure to resolve the conflict between the progressive forces and the conservative ones.[17]

Those who attributed the weaknesses of political parties to political rather than socioeconomic reasons blamed the electoral laws that were adopted by the various regimes. Electoral laws, they argued, had an impact on political recruitment and regional and socioeconomic representation. The electoral system did not reflect the political forces in the country; it accentuated the conflict between the modern and traditional sectors. The modern sectors of the Southeast and the South were always underrepresented, if compared to the North and the Northeast where the traditional oligarchies live. In this regard, many authors argued that the electoral system gave advantage to the rural states, against the more populous states, and, therefore, increased the number of conservative candidates. The system created a conflict between the legislature, which was usually more conservative, and the President, elected by popular vote, where the urban population exerted a larger influence than the rural population. This made the President more responsive to urban needs and the legislature more responsive to rural needs. A conflict of priorities between the President and the legislature often followed.[18]

Lamounier concluded that Brazil's weak party system had different explanations, depending on the historical conditions.[19] Many of the factors that contribute to a weak party system are, however, associated with the presidential system of government. The centralization-of-power phenomenon is directly related to presidential ambitions to dominate all resources in society. It is also associated with the presidential winner-take-all attitude. From that perspective, state and local governments have to be eliminated as competitors. Similarly, weak political parties are also needed to keep the legislature from challenging presidential authority. Finally, the presidential system of government fosters the legislative-executive conflict when a President elected at large is called upon to represent the entire nation, versus a Congress elected at the state level that is expected to concern itself with distributive politics and particularized needs.

Thus, during the period of the liberal constitution, from 1946 to 1964, three major political parties dominated the legislative scene: the PSD, representing the middle class and rural elites; the UDN, representing the emerging professional and business interest in the cities and rural areas; and the PTB, representing the bureaucracy and organized urban labor. Smaller parties from the right and the left were also represented in the legislature. During the first dozen years of this period, the PSD was the largest party, and it provided, along with some of the smaller parties, some stability within the legislature. However, toward the late fifties, the PSD began to lose its ability to formulate a majority coalition. Both the PTB on the left and the UDN on the right were gaining power at the expense of the PSD. Yet no single political party was strong enough to assume leadership in the legislature. Deputies and senators were elected in accordance with an electoral system that rewarded the small states and the agriculture section of the country as opposed to the most populous states and the urban population. Therefore, some segments of the population or some regions of the country had more representation in Congress than others. The one-man, one-vote principle guided presidential elections only. As was the case in Chile and Colombia,[20] the coalitions that were formulated prior to the presidential election broke up once the election was completed. Once elected, in the absence of a majority party to support them in the legislative arena, presidents followed a dual strategy to survive legislative battles. In control of the government apparatus and its huge resources, they resorted to the politics of trading favors with those who supported them and denying those same favors to those who opposed them. This open favoritism cost presidents their legitimacy as guardians of the constitution and impartial arbitrators of conflict, and undermined their claim to represent the nation.[21]

Since presidents lacked the support of a dominant party within the Congress, they used favors and threats to keep political parties in the Congress in a state of upheaval. The nature of political parties in Brazil facilitated this method. Unlike the party system in Chile, political parties in Brazil are fractured, discontinuous, and in a state of continuous flux. Political parties lack clear ideologies, and party support usually disintegrates as soon as the elections are over. Furthermore, presidential power and resources are dangled in front of individual members of the legislature to ensure their support.

Although even weak presidents continued to score victories in their confrontations with the legislature, the introduction of nonlegislative players into the equation complicated matters and produced deadlock and legislative paralysis.

Even with their enormous resources, presidents were limited in their ability to woo members of the Congress.[22] Every bill became a battle that the legislators used to extract major favors. The mobilization of legislators by the presidents or their aides helped undermine the authority of party leaders over the members. Electoral laws where congressmen were elected through their own efforts and through the temporary preelection coalition they forged worked to further weaken the party leaders. Although the weakening of party leaders served the interest of the President in the short run, it created problems for him over time, since he was unable to depend on strong party leaders to do his bidding in time of crisis. Building a winning coalition in the legislature soon ran its course. The anticipation of a coming election forced many of those seeking reelection to position themselves in opposition to the President, who, as in the case of many Latin American democracies, could not seek a second term. If the President hoped to influence the upcoming election he had to sponsor legislation favored by the urban masses that elected him. If he followed this strategy in alliance with the progressive members of the legislature, he found himself at odds with a conservative alliance of landlords, business people, and the armed forces. This strategy won him popular support but put him at a standstill with the legislature; if he was able to tip the balance in his favor in the legislature, a military intervention became a possibility. If he allied himself with the conservative elements in the legislature and secured the support of the military, he gained in security but lost in popularity and legitimacy.[23]

Beginning with Vargas, Brazil's presidents found themselves following populist policies by the end of their terms, despite the positions of conservatives in the legislature and in the military. Vargas committed suicide rather than bow to the military's subsequent demands for his resignation. Kubitschek faced two attempted coups by some radical military officers, but was able to work with the Congress that was dominated by his party in association with PTB. Quadros resigned, and Goulart was deposed and exiled. With the exception of Kubitschek, presidents during this period were unable to work out their differences with the legislature because they had managed to destroy the leadership of both the political parties and the legislature so as to serve their own shortsighted interests. They were unable to find an interlocutor with enough power and authority in the legislature or in the parties to break this deadlock. Congressional paralysis in Brazil, however, had other structural causes, which we shall address later in Chapter 2.

Presidentialism and Bureaucracy in Brazil

To control the bureaucracy (civilian and military), presidents sought the appointment of their supporters, who were often more politically connected than professionally qualified. In a political system such as Brazil's, where the political class was divided and where the democratic order was quite often broken, bureaucrats became the de facto government. Bureaucrats used their positions and tenures to pursue policies and implement programs beneficial to their corporate interests. The alliance of the military and civilian bureaucracies was a formidable force. When united, and in the absence of a legitimate popularly supported government, bureaucrats often seized power and ruled directly or through surrogate civilian organizations. The Brazilian military, since the early days of the Republic, has guarded its corporate autonomy against civilian encroachments, protected its privileges, anointed itself as guardian of the constitutional order, and, during most of Brazil's history since independence, has been involved in ruling the country directly or indirectly.[24] The bureaucratic experience of Brazil can be divided into four periods: the first period includes the Imperial and the Old Republic periods, from 1822 until 1930; the second covers the New State period, from 1930 to 1945; the third coincides with the Competitive period, from 1945 until 1964; and the fourth is the Bureaucratic-Authoritarian period, from 1964 until 1988. This last period, from the coup of 1964 until the promulgation of the Constitution of 1988 will be discussed in Chapter 1.

The Imperial and Old Republic Periods (1822-1930)

When Brazil became independent in 1822 under Don Pedro, its bureaucratic structure changed very little. While Don Pedro was still a Regent, his cabinet was composed of four ministries: the first encompassed Imperial Court, Justice, and Foreign Affairs; the other three ministries were Finance, War, and Navy. After Brazil's independence, Don Pedro granted ministerial status to each of the three subdivisions of his first ministry. The other three ministries remained unchanged. This arrangement continued until 1860, when Don Pedro II, who assumed power in 1841, created the Ministries of Agriculture, Commerce, and Public Works.

With the abolition of the monarchy in 1889 and the establishment of the Republic, the Ministry of Imperial Court was abolished, and the Ministry of Education, Post, and Telegraph was created.[25].

During this period the Emperor practiced the strategy of "circulating the elite." For example, although between 1822 and 1889 only two emperors ruled Brazil, legislative elections not only provided the elite with the opportunity to compete, but created enough conflict among them that the Emperor was forced to either dissolve the Chamber of Deputies or, as was frequently the case, to reshuffle his cabinet to reflect the new power balance among the elite. Cléa Sarmento, in her analysis of cabinet turnovers between 1822 and 1889, found a high degree of political-administrative instability as reflected by the ministerial rotation rate, which was calculated by comparing the ministerial rotation and the duration of the period of the government. With few exceptions, government stability was about 0.27.[26]

Appointment to public service during this period was not based on any merit criteria. Courtiers and supporters of the Emperor, relatives and friends of the members of the political class, which was controlled predominately by the aristocratic families, and owners of plantations and ranches dominated both the civil and military service. The political and bureaucratic elite belonged to the same classes and families. Slaves and, after 1889, immigrant laborers provided the elite with enough income to make it easier to resolve their conflicts within the rules of the game. Furthermore, the limited role of the government at the federal, state, and local levels made it possible to limit the size of the bureaucracy. Public service provided its members with income and tenure, but its primary attraction was power, prestige, and status—a public servant belonged to the ruling class. Since the economy of the country was controlled by uncoordinated regional markets, there was not a compelling need for a sophisticated bureaucracy. Yet toward the end of the nineteenth century, with the creation of ministries such as Agriculture, Commerce, and Public Works, as well as Education, Post and Telegraph, public service recruitment was extended to individuals from low- and middle-class backgrounds who had the needed skills. Thus, according to Alberto Guerreiro Ramos, the administration during this period served as a mechanism to co-opt the emerging educated middle class and therefore helped avoid transforming the middle class into a subversive one. The clientelism and corruption that pervaded the appointment and the work of the public service, according to Ramos, contributed to the formation of a middle class that played an important role in the economic, political, and cultural life of Brazil. Indeed, the emergence of this class was at the base of the collapse of the Old Republic and the emergence of the *Estado Novo* of Getúlio Vargas.[27]

The New State Period (1930-1945)

The 1930s brought important changes to the polity and economy of the country. The hegemony of the governing elites that maintained the tenuous calm between the political institutions and the bureaucracy collapsed. A new elite with nationalistic vision came to power, with the express goal of creating a unified government of the various disparate regions that made up Brazil. The world depression of the 1930s and the collapse of prices of primary products, such as coffee and other agricultural products and raw minerals, weakened the local Brazilian aristocracy and led to the emergence of a new entrepreneurial middle class to promote import substitution industries. Ministerial changes were conducted, which resulted in the creation of new Ministries of Labor, Industry and Commerce, plus Education and Health. New government monopolies, public corporations, and joint public and private ventures were created to lead the way for economic development and national control of Brazilian natural resources. For all these new functions, a professional, differentiated, and efficient public service was needed.

Vargas became preoccupied with the creation of this professional and competent bureaucracy even before the foundation of his *Estado Novo*. In 1931, a centralized purchasing commission was created to regulate purchasing practices of the federal government and eliminate waste and corrupt practices. Another commission was created to classify federal civil service jobs. A third commission was to increase the efficiency and productivity of the civil service, and, in 1936, a fourth commission was charged with reducing and rationalizing the size of the bureaucracy.

Vargas's most notable attempt to professionalize and rationalize the civil service was the creation of the Departamento Administrativo do Serviço Público (DASP, Public Service Administrative Department) in 1938, which was overseen directly by the President and charged with public sector planning, organizing, budgeting, documenting, administering personnel, supplies and material, and human relations.[28]

In spite of its prestige and power, DASP failed to meet its challenge of creating a merit-based professional bureaucracy. The public sector continued its rapid expansion with little regard to merit principles. In addition to the direct administration, a number of public authorities such as the Banco Nacional do Desenvolvimento Econômico (BNDE, National Bank for Economic Development) and the Conselho do Desenvolvimento (Development Council) were created to perform functions that the weak private sector was unable or unwilling to perform. Finally, the need to accommodate supporters of significant political actors by providing them with government jobs undermined DASP's ability to attain a purely merit-based professional bureaucracy. According to DASP, of the more than 300,000 federal employees in the direct and indirect civil service in 1958, only 28,406 were recruited through competitive examinations; the rest were admitted through noncompetitive methods, such as the politics of clientelism.[29]

During the New State period, bureaucracy attained its three essential characteristics: It was tenured, its members depended on their income for their survival, and it reached a high degree of interdependence, thereby bestowing on it the attributes of a class. In view of the weakness of political parties and the private sector, public bureaucracy, through its military and civilian parts, became the dominant ruling class. It was able to co-opt or neutralize political opposition from both the left and the right. Labor legislation ensured that the growing urban union movement remained subservient to the bureaucracy. Union dues were collected and distributed by the bureaucracy to union leaders it supported. Conflict was arbitrated by a structure of labor courts, culminating with the Tribunal Superior do Trabalho (TST, Superior Labor Court), and by applying labor laws drafted and enacted by the bureaucracy.

The Competitive Period (1946-1964)

The return to competitive politics after World War II was an attempt by certain forces within the military and civilian bureaucracies, in alliance with political parties, to democratize the government and open it for more participation by the expanding middle class. In spite of Vargas's attempt to rationalize the bureaucracy, various reports concluded that it remained an inadequate instrument to lead the process of economic and social modernization. Disenfranchised urban workers and the growing ranks of the unemployed were demanding that the bureaucratic system open up to accommodate some of their demands. Internal and external political and economic pressures converged to produce the liberal constitutional order established in 1946. A presidential system of government working alongside an elected Congress was reinstated.

Public bureaucracy continued to expand during this period. The number of people working in the civilian direct and indirect administrations rose from a mere 150,000 in 1947 to 300,000 in 1959. In 1962, another 100,000 workers were added to the public rolls. Toward the end of this period, in 1963, those in the public service reached 675,554 employees, working in ten ministries and numerous public authorities and joint ventures. Their share of the Gross National Product (GNP) rose from 6.7 percent in 1960 to 7.5 percent in 1961, and to 8.3 percent in 1963.

DASP continued its efforts. In 1944, the Fundação Getúlio Vargas (Getúlio Vargas Foundation) was created, and in 1952 its School of Public Administration was established. Also, beginning in 1946, the Faculty of Economics of the University of São Paulo was created. These two schools played a very important role in the formation and training of high-level civil servants. During this period, the Escola Superior de Guerra (ESG, Superior War College) was established to provide military and civilian leaders with training in national security and economic development. Of the more than 152 cabinet ministers who occupied cabinet posts during this period, ninety-one of them (59.9 percent) had legislative experience either at the federal or at the state levels, three (2 percent) had military backgrounds, five (3.3 percent) came from the bureaucracy, and thirty-nine (25.7 percent) came from other professional and economic backgrounds. There was no information on the backgrounds of fourteen (9.2 percent) of the ministers. During this period 191 ministers served a total of 219 months, indicating a high degree of government instability and transient turnover. Successive presidents and their transient allies failed to bring the bureaucracy under effective political control. Clientelism in appointments continued unabated, and corruption was pervasive. The goal of a merit-based professional bureaucracy remained elusive. All that presidential politics was able to achieve was the rapid growth in the size and power of the bureaucracy and its penetration to all spheres of Brazilian life.

NOTES

1. For the logic behind this classification, see Senator Marco Maciel's pronouncement at the Associação dos Advogados do Brasil (OAB, Brazilian Bar Association), in São Paulo on June 13, 1988. See also Marco Maciel, Por que a Crise é Contemporânea? (Brasília: Senado Federal, 1987); and Sylvio Romero, "Parlamentarismo e Presidencialismo na República Brasileira," *Revista de Ciência Política*, 27, no. 3 (December 1984), pp. 129-72.

2. For a historical account of this period, and for the role of the various institutions, see Francisco Iglesias, *Constituintes e Constituições Brasileiras* (São Paulo: Brasiliense, 1986); Vicente Ferrer Correia Lima, *O Congresso Nacional nos Períodos Presidenciais da República Brasileira* (1984); Robert Wesson and David V. Fleischer, *Brazil in Transition* (New York: Praeger, 1983); Ernest Hambloch, *Sua Majestade, O Presidente do Brasil: Um Estudo do Brasil Constitucional: 1889-1934* (Brasília: Universidade de Brasília, 1981); Paulino Jacques, "Do Relacionamento dos Poderes Políticos na Constituição do Império," *Revista de Informação Legislativa*, 11, no. 41 (January/March 1974), pp. 5-16; Collares Moreira, "A Câmara e o Regime Eleitoral no Império e na República," *Estudos Legislativos*, 1, no. 1 (January/June 1973), pp. 71-133; Raymundo Faoro, *Os Donos do Poder* (Porto Alegre: Editora Globo, 1958); and Felisbelo Freire, *História Constitucional da República dos Estados Unidos do Brasil*, 2d ed. (Rio de Janeiro: Aldina, 1894).

3. For a review of the history of the Old Republic and of the role of the colonels, see José Maria Bello, *História da República: 1889-1954* (Stanford, Calif.: Stanford University Press, 1966); and Victor Nunes Leal, *Coronelismo, Enxada e Voto: O Município e o Regime Representativo no Brasil* (Rio de Janeiro: 1984).

4. For the rationale behind this statement, see Thomas E. Skidmore, *Politics in Brazil: 1930-1964, An Experiment in Democracy* (New York: Oxford University Press, 1967).

5. For an examination of the problems involving Brazilian political parties, see David V. Fleischer (ed.), *Os Partidos Políticos no Brasil* (Brasília: Universidade de Brasília, 1981); Vamireh Chacon, *História dos Partidos Brasileiros* (Brasília: Universidade de Brasília, 1981); Maria D'Alva Gil Kinzo, *Representação Política e Sistema Eleitoral no Brasil* (São Paulo: Editora Símbolo, 1980); Carlos Guilherme Mota, *Estado e Partidos no Brasil, 1930-1964* (São Paulo: Alfa-Omega, 1976); and Maria do Carmo Campello de Souza, "O Processo Político-Partidário na Primeira República," Carlos Guilherme Mota (ed.), *Brasil em Perspectiva*, 3d ed. (São Paulo: Difel, 1971).

6. See Vamireh Chacon, *Vida e Morte das Constituições Brasileiras* (Rio de Janeiro: Forense, 1987); and James L. Busey, "Brazil's Reputation for Political Stability," *Western Political Science Quarterly*, 18, no. 4 (December 1964), pp. 866-80.

7. These are some of the factors identified as para-constitutional variables associated with the survival of the presidential system of government in the United States, as argued by Fred Riggs, "The American Presidentialist Case" (a paper presented at the International Political Science Association meeting in Washington, D.C., August 1988).

8. The phenomenon of populism, and its impact on the political stability of Brazil and other Latin American countries, has attracted the attention of many scholars. For a review of this phenomenon, see Robert Wesson, "Populism and Military Coups," Wesson (ed.), *New Military Politics in Latin America* (New York: Praeger, 1982), pp. 17-34; Peter Flynn, *Brazil: A Political Analysis* (Boulder, Colo.: Westview Press, 1978); Vamireh Chacon, *Estado e Povo no Brasil: As Experiências do Estado Novo e da Democracia Populista, 1937-1964* (Brasília: Câmara dos Deputados, 1977); and Octávio Ianni, *Crisis in Brasil* (New York: Columbia University Press, 1970).

9. For a good review of the political and economic development during this period, see Skidmore, *Politics in Brazil*, op. cit., chap. 1 and 2; Luiz Carlos Bresser Pereira, *Desenvolvimento e Crise no Brasil, entre 1930-1967* (Rio de Janeiro: Zahar, 1968); and Edgar Carone, *Revoluções do Brasil Contemporâneo, 1922-1938* (São Paulo: 1965).

10. See Celso Furtado, *The Economic Growth of Brazil* (Berkeley and Los Angeles: University of California Press, 1963).

12   The Brazilian Legislature and Political System

11. The classic work on the role of the military in Brazilian politics is Alfred Stepan, *Military in Politics: Changing Patterns in Brazil* (Princeton, N.J.: Princeton University Press, 1975). For a critique of Stepan's thesis, see John Markoff and Silvio R. Duncan Baretta, "Professional Ideology and Military Activism in Brazil: Critique of a Thesis of Alfred Stepan," *Comparative Politics*, 17, No. 2 (January 1985), pp. 175-91; and Edmundo Campos Coelho, "A Instituição Militar no Brasil," *Boletim Informativo e Bibliográfico de Ciências Sociais*, no. 19 (1st Semester 1985), pp. 5-19.

12. For a good analysis of this period, see Lúcia Hippólito, *De Raposas e Reformistas: O PSD e a Experiência Democrática Brasileira, 1945-1964* (Rio de Janeiro: Paz e Terra, 1985); Olavo Brasil de Lima, Jr., *Os Partidos Políticos Brasileiros: A Experiência Federal e Regional: 1945-1964* (Rio de Janeiro: Graal, 1983); Maria Victória de Mesquita Benevides, *A UDN e o Udenismo: Ambiguidades do Liberalismo Brasileiro, 1945-1965* (Rio de Janeiro: Paz e Terra, 1981); and Nathanial Leff, *Economic Policy-Making and Development in Brazil, 1947-1964* (New York: John Wiley & Sons, 1968).

13. Because of the enormous popularity of Kubitschek, the presidential system seemed to work smoothly. However, under his successors the impasses between the Congress and the President became acute.

14. The conditions that led to the Quadros resignation are still a topic of controversy. It is believed that Quadros was trying to enlist the support of the military against the Congress who was not supporting Quadros in many of his legislative programs. Since he thought that his Vice-President Goulart was not acceptable to the military, threatening to resign was expected to bring the military to his aid. Indeed the military tried to prevent Goulart from assuming power and agreed to allow him to ascend to the presidency only after limiting the power of the presidency by introducing the parliamentary system of government.

15. Bolivar Lamounier and Rachel Meneguello, *Partidos Políticos e Consolidação Democrática: O Caso Brasileiro* (São Paulo: Brasiliense, 1986). See also Netto Cotrim and Alberto Bitencourt, "Natureza Jurídica dos Partidos Políticos Brasileiros," *Revista de Informação Legislativa*, no. 13 (January/March 1976), pp. 63-74.

16. See Adelina Maria Novaes e Cruz et al. (eds.), Impasse na Democracia Brasileira, 1951-1955: *Coletânea de Documentos* (Rio de Janeiro: Fundação Getúlio Vargas, 1983); Olavo Brasil de Lima, Jr., "Evolução e Crise do Sistema Partidário Brasileiro: As Eleições Legislativas Estaduais de 1947 a 1962," *Dados*, no. 17 (1978), pp. 29-52; and Simon Schwartzman, "As Eleições e o Problema Institucional," *Dados*, no. 14 (1977), pp. 447-72.

17. In the early 1960s, according to this logic, PSD disintegrated under the pressure of its left (the Ala Moca movement, which included Ulysses Guimarães and Renato Archer—both important leaders of the future PMDB) and the agrarian reform. This led to a vacuum in the center and a polarization between the PTB and the UDN. Thus, the 1964 crisis was interpreted as a consequence of (1) the exhaustion of the economic model based on income substitution; (2) a conflict between modern and traditional forces; (3) party disintegration, because the parties did not have access to the existing resources and, therefore, could not perform their functions of aggregation and mediation; (4) the result of the disappearance of the center of the political spectrum, which led to polarization.

18. The archaic electoral system, Schwartzman argued, led to the margining of the emerging economic and urban classes, especially in São Paulo. Because the legislature was no longer viewed as representative, other institutions began encroaching on its prerogatives and assuming legislative roles (e.g., the Conselho Monetário Nacional—National Monetary Council).

19. See Bolivar Lamounier and Maria D'Alva Gil Kinzo, *Partidos Políticos, Representação e Processo Eleitoral no Brasil: 1945-1978* (Rio de Janeiro: Associação Nacional de Pós-Graduação e Pesquisa em Ciências Sociais, 1978). For further elaboration on political parties in Brazil, see Fleischer (ed.), *Os Partidos Políticos no Brasil*, op. cit.; Joaquim José Felizardo and Mateus Schmidt, *Partidos Políticos e Eleições no Brasil* (Petrópolis: Vozes, 1982); Kinzo, *Representação Política e Sistema Eleitoral no Brasil*, op. cit.; Michael Wallerstein, "The Collapse of Democracy in Brazil: Its Economic Determinants," *Latin American Research Review*, 15, no. 3 (1980), pp. 3-40; Margaret S. Jenks, "Political Parties in Authoritarian Brazil" (Ph.D. diss., Duke University, 1979); Maria do Carmo Carvalho Campello de Souza, *Estados e Partidos*

Políticos no Brasil, 1930 a 1964 (São Paulo: Alfa-Omega, 1976); Bolivar Lamounier and Fernando Henrique Cardoso, Os Partidos e as Eleições no Brasil (Rio de Janeiro: Paz e Terra, 1975); and Paulo Roberto Motta, *Movimentos Partidários no Brasil* (Rio de Janeiro: Fundação Getúlio Vargas, 1971).

20. Arturo Valenzuela, "Party Politics and the Failure of Presidentialism in Chile: A Proposal for a Parliamentary Form of Government"; and Jonathan Hartlyn, "Presidentialism and Colombian Politics" (papers presented at the International Political Science Association meeting in Washington, D.C., August 1988). The Argentinean case was presented in the same meeting by N. Guillermo Molinelli, "President-Congress Relations in Argentina: 1960-1980."

21. This point was emphasized in the same meeting by Juan Linz, "Democracy: Presidential or Parliamentary? Does It Make a Difference?"

22. See Barry Ames, *Political Survival* (Berkeley and Los Angeles: University of California Press, 1987).

23. Wanderley Guilherme dos Santos, "The Calculus of Conflict: Impasse in Brazilian Politics and the Crisis of 1964" (Ph.D. diss., Stanford University, March 1979).

24. Since the bureaucracy's emergence as a prominent institution, its study in the United States has been dominated by two general theoretical conceptions: (1) that it is an instrument to the realization of societal goals; and (2) that it is a neutral instrument, separate from politics.

To view bureaucracy as an instrument means to believe that societal goals are determined by those officially in power, and that the bureaucracy merely implements those goals. According to the Marxists, in capitalist societies the bureaucracy is under the domination of the capitalist class. On the other hand, for the non-Marxists, bureaucracy is under the control of legitimate representatives of the people. In the American conception, the state is not an instrument of a class but a conglomeration of many interests. In this case, pluralism replaces a privileged class as the dominant driving force, informing and controlling the behavior of the bureaucrats. Whether an instrument of a dominant class, or of a pluralistic democratic government, bureaucracy is, nevertheless, a means toward ends that are defined by other than the bureaucracy itself.

The American conception of bureaucracy as a neutral instrument is necessary to fit the theory of representative government. Thus, the myth of the politics administration dichotomy was born. According to this conception, bureaucracy is, or should be, a neutral instrument. To ensure its neutrality, appointment should be made on the basis of merit and should be nonpartisan. Those appointed should also be protected against partisan influence through measures such as tenure, restriction of their political activities, and instillation of a sense of public mission and professionalism. Control over the bureaucracy should be exercised by elected officials through formal and informal means, including the appointment of intermediate trusted supporters. Fred Riggs, "Bureaucratic Politics in the U.S.: Benchmarks for Comparison," *Governance*, 6, no. 4 (October 1988), pp. 343-79, calls this group of supporters the transients, under a presidential system of government. At least in theory, a transient should remain in his or her position only as long as his or her boss remains in power. A new president means new transients to carry forward new goals.

With few exceptions, the literature on development views bureaucracy as the most effective means of achieving societal goals. Bureaucracy is also viewed as the vehicle to achieve both economic and social development, which are considered prerequisites for political development. All of these terms are defined within the context of the historical experiences of the Western industrial societies. Thus, for an orderly and peaceful development, what was needed in developing countries was a neutral, merit-oriented bureaucracy, along the Webberian rational legal type. Therefore, it was no surprise that U.S. and other international Western technical assistance programs to developing countries emphasized the building of government bureaucracies.

From within the conception of bureaucratic neutrality, government action and scholarly concerns focused on the best ways of building such a bureaucracy, and of ensuring it to be an effective instrument, indeed separate from politics. On the other hand, the conception of bureaucracy as a power structure, pursuing goals of its own and utilizing means it considers appropriate to fulfill its corporate interests and survival, was de-emphasized. Indeed, the conception of bureaucracy (both civilian and military) as neutral and instrumental helped to legitimize the dominant role that bureaucrats came to play in many developing countries during the past four decades.

Yet, to view bureaucracy as a power structure pursuing its own goals does not imply that bureaucracy performs the same roles, and uses the same means in every society. As Riggs has argued, the study of comparative governments could benefit from the focus on bureaucracy, its roles, its instruments, and its interaction with other institutions in society, such as the private sector, political parties, labor unions, and other organized, as well as unorganized, groups.

25. See Edgar Carone, *A República Velha*, 4th ed. (São Paulo: Difel, 1983).

26. See Cléa Sarmento, "Estabilidade Governamental e Rotatividade de Elites Políticas no Brasil Imperial," *Dados*, 29, no. 2 (1986), pp. 139-75.

27. See Alberto Guerreiro Ramos, *A Crise do Poder no Brasil: Problemas da Revolução Nacional Brasileira* (Rio de Janeiro: Zahar, 1961).

28. See J. Reis, "Política de Pessoal do Serviço Público," *Ciência e Cultura*, 31, no. 5 (May 1979), pp. 505-14; James M. Malloy (ed.), *Authoritarianism and Corporatism in Latin America* (Pittsburgh, Pa.: University of Pittsburgh Press, 1977); Kenneth Paul Erickson, *The Brazilian Corporative State and Working-Class Politics* (Berkeley and Los Angeles: University of California Press, 1977); Beatriz M. de Souza Wahrlich, "Reforma Administrativa Federal Brasileira: Passado e Presente," *Revista de Administração Pública*, 2, no. 8 (April/June 1974), pp. 27-75; Laurence S. Graham, *Civil Service Reform in Brazil* (Austin: University of Texas Press, 1968); Robert T. Daland, *Brazilian Planning: Development Politics and Administration* (Chapel Hill: The University of North Carolina Press, 1967); and Alberto Guerreiro Ramos, *Administração e Estratégia do Desenvolvimento: Elementos de uma Sociologia Especial de Administração* (Rio de Janeiro: Fundação Getúlio Vargas, 1966).

29. *Jornal do Brasil* (December 22, 1989), p. 26. See also Edson de Oliveira Nunes, "Legislativo, Política e Recrutamento de Elites no Brasil," *Dados*, no. 17 (1978), pp. 53-78.

Chapter 1

From Presidentialism
to Authoritarianism

Instabilities associated with the presidential system of government, and the chronic crises between a popularly elected President and a legislature whose electoral interests were often at odds with that of the President, precipitated the military coup of 1964 that toppled the government of President João Goulart.[1] The group of military officers that assumed power shared a general common ideology but lacked any definite program of action. As soon as the new regime assumed power, it faced the challenge of translating its ideology into policies, programs, and actions. The formidable obstacles they had to surmount were the various inherent weaknesses and instabilities of the presidential system of government embodied in the Constitution of 1946.

This chapter discusses the ideology of the regime, the constraints within which it had to operate, the instruments it employed, and the results of its attempts to transform and restructure the political system. Particular emphasis is given to the efforts to transform the relationship between the executive and the political parties, and between the executive and the bureaucracy. The transformation of the executive-legislative relations is briefly outlined in this chapter and discussed in subsequent chapters.

The Ideology of the Coup of 1964

The ideology of the authoritarian regime that gained power in 1964 has received extensive analysis, by both Brazilian and foreign scholars, because it was assumed to be the driving force behind the policies adopted and the actions undertaken by the authoritarian regime. The writings of Alfred Stepan in the late 1960s and the subsequent elaboration by Stepan and others[2] provided a detailed analysis of the Doctrine of National Security and Development as taught at the Escola Superior de Guerra (ESG), or Superior War College, and as articulated by one of the most prominent intellectuals of the regime, General Golbery do Couto e Silva.[3]

The Doctrine of National Security and Development accepted many of the assumptions of the Cold War literature but placed special emphasis on the internal dimension. According to Maria Helena Moreira Alves, the doctrine of Golbery encompassed "a theory of war, a theory of international subversion and revolution, a theory of Brazil's role in world politics and its geopolitical potential as a world power, and a particular model of associated dependent economic development that combines Keynesian economics and state capitalism."[4]

The theory of war placed special emphasis on the various types of war and concluded that modern warfare between the superpowers could not be limited war. In view of the huge arsenals of destructive weapons available to both the United States and the Soviet Union, any war was likely to be an outright war, with the potential for total destruction. Even conventional limited wars were likely to escalate into total wars. Golbery concluded, therefore, that it was in the interest of the superpowers to avoid any type of direct confrontation. Instead, they were likely to encourage proxy wars, psychological wars, and support of internal subversions and revolutions. Thus the emphasis in the Doctrine of National Security and Development was placed on the enemy from within—on internal subversions and revolutions.

Because of historical and geopolitical as well as developmental reasons, which were elaborated in the doctrine, the Soviet Union was identified as the power most likely to engage in the encouragement of internal subversions and revolutions in Brazil. The doctrine placed special emphasis on the elements likely to be used in these subversive activities and the methods, both physical and psychological. It also addressed the various ways and means of combating subversion and revolution.

For geopolitical and historical reasons, Brazil, according to the doctrine, was destined to play the role of a world power. Its area was extensive, its resources were immense, and its potential was unlimited. Because of the absence of antagonism with its northern neighbor the United States, Brazil's manifest destiny could be realized in cooperation with the United States. This was especially necessary for the type of economic development model that the doctrine envisioned.

The economic model accepted many of the assumptions postulated by proponents of the theories of economic dependency, with particular regard to the need to import capital and technology from the more advanced nations such as the United States, Europe, and Japan, but it rejected the notion of permanent dependency inherent in the theory. The triple alliance of international capital, national capital, and the economic, political, and military power of the government could result in significant development that, at some point, would become independent development. Under this model, the Brazilian government became the critical actor in attracting international capital and technology, which could be done by ensuring internal law and order and guaranteeing a fair and transferable return on investments. The government could also play a critical role in mobilizing and encouraging national capital, through a series of tax incentives, import and export preferential policies, and investment and fiscal policies. Finally, the government, as the protector of the national interest, could undertake a direct role in critical sectors of the economy, such as energy, transportation, defense industries, communications, natural resources, and banking.

According to Golbery, to realize the Doctrine of National Security and Development the government needed to develop a political strategy, an economic strategy, a psychological strategy, and a military strategy.[5] All of these strategies were intended to neutralize the obstacles and adverse conditions existing in the Brazilian reality. Thus, the political strategy dealt with the relationship between the executive, the legislature, the judiciary, the bureaucracy, and the political parties, and with how to eliminate conflict and impasse, centralize decision making, formulate public policy, and expedite action. The economic strategy dealt with the private and public sectors of the economy and their relationship to the domestic and international markets. The strategy called for the integration of the various regions of the country, specially those least developed, such as the North, Northeast and Centralwest, with those most developed, such as the South and Southeast. Also included were the massive exploitation and settlement of the Amazon region, the expansion of the economy, and the acquisition of science and technology. The psychological strategy would require changes in society, the family, schools and universities, labor unions, the media, the church, and other centers of research, and the formulation of public opinion. Finally, the military strategy was concerned with the security apparatus, military preparedness, armaments, training, and alliances of the three branches of the armed forces: army, navy, and air force.

In trying to restructure the political system, especially the Congress, political parties, elections, the bureaucracy, and the federal system of government, the regime faced its most formidable challenge: how to overcome the inherent political obstacles associated with a presidential system of government in a federal context. Thus the political strategy, in addition to its basic goal of realizing the objectives of the Doctrine of National Security and Development, can be construed as an attempt to resolve some of the contradictions and obstacles associated with a presidential system of government.

CONTRADICTIONS OF THE PRESIDENTIAL SYSTEM OF GOVERNMENT

The Doctrine of National Security and Development outlined goals and orientations but defined no objectives. Initially, the leaders of the 1964 coup gave the impression that their intervention would be limited in scope and duration.[6] Under the pretext of guarding the constitutional and legal order against the designs and conspiracies of Goulart and his populist supporters—a role the Brazilian military had assumed since the Old Republic period—the regime sought to undertake a clean sweep and to eradicate from the system what it considered hostile elements and enemies of the constitutional order. According to this logic, nothing was wrong with the Brazilian political system, only with some individuals who occupied positions of responsibilities, abused their power, and worked to subvert the system and undermine its constitutional basis. Institutional Act No. 1, issued by the military, was supposed to provide a quick fix by purging those members of the Congress, the political parties, the armed forces, the bureaucracy, and state and local governments who threatened the system. It also tried to alter the power relationship between the President and the Congress, in favor of the President.[7]

The more the new military regime tried to deal with the structural problems of the system, the more it discovered that there was no quick fix, and the more it resorted to coercion and arbitrariness. In less than a year, the new regime resolved that, if the goals of the Doctrine of National Security and Development were to be realized, it was necessary to radically transform the structure of the political system in order to produce a new type of relationship among its various parts. The institutionalization of the authoritarian regime became a necessary means for transforming and restructuring the political system.

It is important to put the experience of Brazil in some comparative perspective. The study of political institutions and the impact of political institutions on political behavior have not been, for some time, a favorite topic among political scientists. Recently, however, a group of political scientists under the leadership of Professor Fred Riggs have begun resurrecting the study of political institutions, paying particular attention to the relationship between political structure and political instability.[8] One of their tentative findings indicates a direct relationship in many Third World countries between political instability and the presidential system of government. Riggs summed up the problems of presidentialism in two categories: intrinsic and extrinsic problems.[9]

Under intrinsic problems, Riggs identified four constraints that undermine the stability of the presidential system of government: (1) head of state versus head of government, (2) veto groups rather than opposition, (3) the winner-take-all syndrome, and (4) the fragile political base.

Riggs also identified four extrinsic problems: (1) executive-legislative relations, (2) executive-judicial relations, (3) the party system relations, and (4) bureaucratic relations.

(The following is a reinterpretation of the actions of the military regime between 1964 and 1985 as a means of resolving the problems associated with the presidential system of government in Brazil.)

Intrinsic Problems of the Presidential System of Government

The intrinsic problems of presidential systems of government are associated with the high expectations of both the public and the President and the typically restricted power of the presidency. This contradiction usually leads to severe constitutional constraints on the ability of the president to deliver on what he and the public actually expect of him, which eventually leads either to paralysis or confrontation. In the case of paralysis, the urgent affairs of the government are often left unattended and unresolved. A confrontation is normally resolved through a coup d'état by the military or a popular revolt. If the President emerges victorious, the democratic order is often suspended in favor of an authoritarian, undemocratic regime. If the legislature emerges victorious, the powers of the President are further diminished, and his ability to meet the public expectations are further eroded.

Head of State versus Head of Government

Under the presidential system of government, presidents are expected to play two contradictory roles—head of state versus head of government. As heads of state, they represent the nation and are expected to act as symbols of national unity and purpose. In this role they expect public loyalty and support. In return, the public expects them to be fair and to act as arbitrators. As heads of government, however, they are involved in making controversial public policy decisions and are often involved in partisan strategies. In this role their support varies from one day to the next and they are often criticized by those who politically disagree with them. In reality, it is often difficult to distinguish between the two roles. Legitimate criticisms of presidential policies quite often are viewed as disloyalty and treason. In their attempts to preserve the symbolic value of the office, presidents use repression against their political opponents and try to suffocate legitimate criticism.

During the Brazilian authoritarian regime, beginning in 1964, the distinction between the President's role as head of state and as head of government was blurred. Minor criticisms often brought swift and repressive measures, such as imprisonment, exile, loss of job, cancellation of electoral mandate, and other forms of political, economic, and corporal punishment. The more a President tries to consolidate his prerogatives and power the less he tolerates legitimate criticism—and the harder it becomes to distinguish between his two roles. In a sense, attempting to resolve the extrinsic problems of the presidency accentuates the intrinsic problems.

Veto Groups rather than Opposition

Another intrinsic problem of a presidential system of government is the resulting fracture of political authority and the need to neutralize power centers that are outside the purview of the President. This fracturing of political authority precludes the development of a coherent political opposition that has any realistic prospects of forcing the President to change his policies. Instead, the groups—whether the opposition within the legislature, the judiciary, or the bureaucracy—can only exercise a veto power over presidential proposals, without forcing the executive to adopt their alternate proposals. In the Brazilian context, presidents between 1946 and 1964 continued to hold on to their power long after their political bases eroded. Fundamental changes and adjustments were avoided in favor of provisional measures. To overcome the resistance of these veto groups, presidents had to resort to extra-legal and constitutional means, either to appeal directly to popular support or to use the ever-present threat of the military. In many cases impasse and paralysis were the order of the day.

Through a series of measures aimed at the legislature, the judiciary, the bureaucracy, and state and local governments, the regime succeeded in eliminating all veto groups within the formal structures of government. Opposition to the regime was transferred from the halls of government to the voluntary institutions of the civil society. Church-related groups, universities, student associations, labor unions, the bar association, and neighborhood groups became the focus of political opposition. To purge the veto groups inherent in the presidential system of government under a democratic order, the regime had to resort to authoritarian measures. These measures further isolated the regime from popular support and denied it political legitimacy.[10] Once again, the presidential system of government failed to resolve its intrinsic weaknesses without subverting the democratic order, which it claimed to be attempting to salvage and reinforce.

The Winner-Take-All Syndrome

The office of the President in a presidential system of government is a highly sought-after post. Winners of a presidential race control all the resources of the state. Since the competition is over one position, presidential campaigns are often highly divisive and to the participants represent a zero-sum game. To ensure their success, Brazilian incumbents try to eliminate their opponents by any means available to them, including harassment, manipulation of the election, and outright fraud. Since presidents have monopoly control over the bureaucracy and the various opportunities it offers in terms of employment, benefits, licenses, contracts, and other types of services, winning a presidential election denies the defeated parties access to perks and favors. Since presidents are normally limited to one term in office, they try to exploit their tenure to reward their supporters. Once in power, presidents engage in all sorts of shady deals to channel benefits to their supporters. They behave in a partisan manner, thus further exacerbating the contradiction between their role as head of state and head of government. The more presidents resort to what the opposition sees as corrupt activities to reward their supporters and to arbitrary activities to deny opposition groups their due rights, the more presidential regimes lose legitimacy.

The lack of access to resources, on the other hand, prevents the opposition from maintaining its coherence to contest the next election. Absence of a coherent opposition in turn offers the incumbents the opportunity to manipulate the next election in its favor.

The authoritarian regime, in its attempt to eliminate veto groups within the formal structure of government, engaged in massive electoral engineering and manipulation to the extent that every Brazilian election that was held between 1964 and 1986 was held in accordance with a special electoral law designed to deny the opposition the opportunity to win a majority.[11] Sometimes electoral laws were drafted specifically to eliminate specific candidates that the authoritarian regime did not favor. Opposition candidates were denied the opportunity to win not only at the federal level, but also at the state and local levels. By concentrating all power at the federal level, the role of the states and localities as power centers declined. States and localities had to depend on federal resources to finance their activities. In addition to centralizing resources and decision making at the federal level, the authoritarian regime resorted to the method of indirect election of both governors and one third of the Senate in 1978, to ensure that only its supporters were elected. State capitals and many cities with populations of more than 100,000 were declared security zones, and therefore were prevented from electing their own mayors. The authoritarian regime exacerbated this intrinsic problem by not only giving the President a monopoly over federal resources, but by also trying to extend this monopoly to traditional state and local resources. The more the centralization of resources was in the hands of the President, the more corrupt and the less politically legitimate was the regime.

The Fragile Political Base

In a multiparty political system such as Brazil's, in which a majority party doesn't exist, and the bureaucracy has protected its prerogatives against political encroachments, presidents, upon election, find themselves operating with a fragile political base. In addition to the strategies just discussed, victorious presidents are often elected through a temporary coalition of political forces that have little in common. Over time, the coalition that brought the President to power disintegrates under the exigencies of governing. Congressional members' electoral needs clash with presidential interests. Under a democratic system of government the President can only enact his policies by continuously building a winning coalition. Since presidents lack resources to satisfy the various demands made upon them, the closer it gets to election time, the more it is in the interest of the political parties to distance themselves from the President, and the more difficult it becomes for the President to build winning coalitions. Government's ability to act is paralyzed. The President opts either for inaction or provisional measures, if he opts to work within the legal and constitutional norms. If he decides to break this impasse, the president has to take illegal and arbitrary measures. The various presidential crises between 1946 and 1964 were attempts by Brazilian presidents to surmount such impasses.

The bureaucracy, which is the main power base of the President, faces a similar problem. Lacking any firm political base or the support of a majority political party, presidents are at the mercy of the bureaucracy over which they preside. The first priority of the bureaucracy is to protect its corporate interest by ensuring that its monopoly over material resources and powers of coercion are not threatened. To protect its corporate interests the bureaucracy embodies its rights and privileges in the constitution and in basic laws. Presidents find it difficult to challenge these rights and privileges without violating the law and the constitution. Since presidents cannot fire members of the bureaucracy without prolonged and costly proceedings, they resort to political appointments of transients. In time the transients become permanent, and the new President has to resort to the appointment of new transients who lack the expertise, professionalism, and commitment to public service. A bureaucracy ostensibly created to be an instrument of political development becomes an end in itself and a power base in its own right.

After 1964, the authoritarian regime tried to reign in both the Congress and the bureaucracy only to find that such a goal could not be achieved within constitutional and legal norms. In a sense, the authoritarian regime spent most of its time trying to achieve this elusive goal. In the end, the regime achieved temporary success, but only through undemocratic, arbitrary, and often coercive measures that lacked constitutionality and public support, proving once again that the intrinsic problems of presidential systems of government in Brazil cannot be eliminated democratically. The arbitrary authoritarian measures can achieve temporary relief but only at a high cost in terms of political legitimacy and acceptance.

Extrinsic Problems of the Presidential System of Government

The intrinsic problems of Brazilian presidential systems of government are the necessary by-product of their extrinsic problems. To the extent that presidential systems of government cannot democratically resolve their extrinsic problems, the intrinsic problems are also not resolved. As the authoritarian regime in Brazil found out, resolving the extrinsic problems of the presidential system of government through authoritarian measures can only exacerbate intrinsic problems and deny political legitimacy and necessary support.

The extrinsic problems of presidentialism are rooted in the separation-of-power principle. Constitutions that embody presidential systems of government stress the separation of powers: executive, legislative, and judicial. At least from a constitutional perspective, the executive cannot dissolve the legislature, nor can the legislature dismiss the President through a vote of no confidence, as in the parliamentary system of government. The courts have independent powers and arbitrate conflicts between the executive and the legislature.

In addition to the relationship between the executive and the legislature, and the executive and the judiciary, the presidential system of government poses two other important extrinsic problems: its relationship with the political parties and its relationship with the bureaucracy.

Executive-Legislative Relations

The most critical problem with the presidential system of government is the President's relationship with the Congress. Under the parliamentary system of government, when a head of government loses his support from the parliament, the government resigns and negotiations begin for the creation of a new cabinet. The cabinet, in a sense, combines both the executive and the legislative powers, since it can only continue in power as long as it has the majority support of the parliament. If a cabinet cannot be formulated, the head of state is entitled to dissolve the parliament, and call for a new election, which will lead to the empowerment of a new cabinet. Prolonged impasses and paralysis are thus avoided.

In the presidential system of government, however, the executive can continue in power long after his power base in the Congress has eroded. Conversely, a President enjoying overwhelming popular support cannot force the Congress to accept his policies, since he lacks the ability to dissolve the Congress and call for a new election.

When the military assumed power in 1964, they were determined to change the relationship between the President and the Congress. Within less than a year, they discovered that the relationship could not be changed simply by getting rid of the undesired elements within the Congress. Rather, basic structural and procedural changes would be needed. In undertaking these changes, they were constrained by constitutional and political factors that in the long run prevented them from resolving these contradictions.

Under the pretext that their military intervention was carried out to protect the constitution and the democratic order which was being threatened by Goulart and his supporters, the regime decided to keep the Congress open and to maintain the Constitution of 1946. Under Institutional Act No. 1, the regime gave itself temporary power to undertake measures to get rid of the undesired elements within the Congress and to pass urgent legislation as decree laws to deal with critical political and economic issues in order to stabilize the new regime. Although the preamble of Institutional Act

No. 1 claimed that the new regime received its legitimacy neither from the Congress nor from the Constitution, but from the fact that the revolution was "victorious," throughout its various institutional acts, constitutional amendments, complementary laws, and decree laws, the regime sought to legitimize itself through the Congress and consequently through elections, regardless of how undemocratic and fraudulent the elections may have been. This decision, to maintain at least the appearance that they intended to play the political game in accordance with constitutional and legal norms, forced them to concern themselves with maintaining their support within the Congress.[12] Contesting and winning congressional elections became their top priority. For it was the Congress that would have to ratify the selection of the President, executive bills, decree laws, constitutional amendments, and other measures enacted by the regime.

Surviving politically, however, meant that many of the changes and restructuring introduced by the regime dealt with immediate political concerns, rather than fundamental issues. Changes introduced for the purpose of winning elections or defeating an opponent overshadowed those intended to bring about fundamental changes and were undertaken in an arbitrary manner, thus undermining whatever legitimacy the regime may have enjoyed. The more the regime became concerned with winning elections, the more arbitrary measures it undertook, the less political support it received, and the less capable it became in introducing everlasting fundamental changes. Thus, whatever changes the regime introduced to the executive-legislative relations and to other aspects of the presidential system of government, these changes began to be gradually dismantled during the political opening period to be discussed later. With the Constitution of 1988, most of these changes were replaced with the classic features of a presidential system of government.

The changes that the authoritarian regime introduced to executive-legislative relations can be divided into two kinds: formal and informal. The formal changes involved structural, procedural, and jurisdictional changes. The informal changes involved the relationship between the regime and the leadership of the Congress and the government party.

Structural changes dealt mainly with the way the Congress organized itself for action. In each house of the Congress, these changes covered the term of office of the members of the Comissão Diretora (Mesa), including the president of each house, and the chairmen of standing committees and their respective jurisdiction and prerogatives. Under the guise of democratizing and depoliticizing the congressional process, the members of the Mesas, including their presidents, and the committee chairmen, had their terms limited to two-year, nonrenewable periods. Continuing on an earlier practice, the members of the Mesas, especially the presidents, were put in control of all the internal financial and personnel resources of the two houses and were expected to conduct themselves in a nonpartisan fashion. Party leaders, whose responsibility it was to lead the debate over legislation, were denied control of their needed resources. The net effect of these changes was to avoid the development of powerful, stable, and independent leadership in the Congress. Such strong leadership, if developed, might pose real threats to the hegemony of the President, or could launch an effective campaign over any piece of proposed legislation.[13] The impact of these structural changes is analyzed in great detail in Chapter 3.

Other structural changes of significance included the creation of the Joint Budget Committee to evaluate and approve the budget and other bills of a fiscal nature; the frequent resort to joint sessions of the Congress to consider and approve the budget; and urgent measures or constitutional amendments introduced by the President. The professed justification for these changes was the speeding-up of the legislative process and the elimination of unnecessary delays in areas considered important by the President. Along with these structural changes, the amount of time Congress had to consider proposed measures was limited. This had the effect of both limiting debate and discussion and of limiting the ability of the Congress to play an active role in issues the President considered urgent. The way Congress exercised its limited budgetary power during this period will be discussed in Chapter 6.

Procedural changes that were introduced dealt essentially with the process a bill needs to go through to become law. Here the regime imposed a number of changes aimed at limiting the power of the Congress to challenge presidential initiatives. In addition to the resort to joint congressional sessions, certain bills introduced under "urgent provision" measures had to be acted upon within thirty days (later, the span of time was extended to forty-five days, and, finally, sixty days). If the Congress did not act within the prescribed time, the President could promulgate the measure under the *decurso de prazo*, or time limitation provision.

Another such innovation intended to weaken the opposition in the Congress was the party fidelity provision. When party fidelity was demanded from the party leader, members of the Congress could not vote against their party orientation in the plenary session. To vote differently from their leader implied the loss of their congressional seat. Although the ostensible purpose of this provision was to strengthen the political parties and their leadership within the Congress, it actually forced the Aliança Renovadora Nacional (ARENA, Alliance for National Renovation), the pro-government party, to refrain from voting against presidential sponsored legislation, even if the individual member did not agree with it. This provision was introduced after several ARENA members voted against the President's position in a crucial vote in 1968. At stake, was the President's desire to have the Congress lift the parliamentary immunity of one of its members, Deputy Márcio Moreira Alves. The government's request was defeated by 216 votes, of which ninety-four came from ARENA. As a result of this, the President issued Institutional Act No. 5 and Complementary Act No. 38: Congress was suspended indefinitely.

A corresponding measure to the party fidelity provision enabled party leaders or vice leaders to vote on behalf of all party members in the plenary sessions when voting was by a show of hands rather than through a role call vote. This practice was supposed to facilitate the legislative process, especially in the absence of a quorum. However, in practice, it curbed the independence of the members and ensured a speedy approval for bills the President sponsored.

Jurisdictional changes involved the expansion of public policy areas under the exclusive control of the executive. National security matters and budgetary concerns were two such areas. The president could declare a state of emergency and suspend the Constitution through an executive decree, without the approval of Congress. The President could suspend the Congress, thus eliminating a key aspect of the presidential system of government. The President could dismiss elected members at all levels of government, withhold information from the Congress, suspend habeas corpus, arrest and detain individuals without charges or trials, and remove and suspend judges and members of the Supreme Court. In fiscal matters, the Congress lost the power to change the budget; it could only ratify or reject it. After 1968, congressmen lost their parliamentary immunities and could be prosecuted for ordinary alleged violations. Finally, the Congress was given the power to ratify the election of the President of the Republic after he was informally selected by a group of military generals and commanders, and formally nominated by the convention of the government party. Thus, while the members of the Congress and state legislatures were to be elected by the people, Presidents during the authoritarian regime were to be ratified by the Congress, except in 1978 and 1985, when they were ratified by the specially constituted electoral college.

These expanded powers of the President, especially the power to declare martial law, suspend the Constitution and the Congress, dismiss and take away the political rights of elected representatives (a process called *cassação*, or cessation), and issue decree laws placed severe limitations on congressional capabilities to challenge presidential initiatives. When these formal changes were combined with the informal mechanisms used by the executive to control the Congress and the political parties, and to manipulate the elections and the electoral laws, the principle of separation of powers ceased to exist. The unity of the executive and the legislature was tenuously attained, albeit through undemocratic, coercive, and arbitrary measures.

The informal measures undertaken by the regime to alter the executive-legislative relations involved the strategic manipulation of the formal measures and the use of the enormous political and economic resources that came to be monopolized by the executive to either intimidate or buy off the recalcitrant members of the Congress and to reduce, if not eliminate, potential resistance to initiatives sponsored by the President. The informal measures included manipulation of the elections of the government-supported party leadership, of the members of the Mesas, particularly their presidents, and of the chairmen of the standing committees. The most important method of controlling the Congress was through the manipulation of the electoral laws. New electoral laws were drafted for each election. The main purpose was to ensure that elections, at all levels of government, were won by government-supported candidates, thus preventing the opposition party from becoming the majority. Since these laws were closely tied to the way the regime tried to structure and control political parties, this matter will be discussed in that context.

Executive-Judiciary Relations

Under the presidential system of government, an independent judicial system, with the power to review the constitutionality of the laws, and to arbitrate the power relationship between the executive and the legislative branches of government, is an underlying aspect of the principle of separation of powers. The Brazilian judicial system has traditionally tried to maintain an independent position vis-à-vis both the executive and the legislature. When it tried to overrule what it considered unconstitutional or illegal acts by the executive, it found itself on a collision course with the executive. During the first two years of the authoritarian regime, the courts overruled several measures undertaken by the regime and refused to indict individuals who the military sought to prosecute. In need to assert its hegemony and control, the regime purged and redefined the jurisdiction of the judiciary. Because judges of the Supremo Tribunal Federal (STF, Supreme Federal Court, the highest civil court in Brazil), as well as the judges of other specialized courts, enjoyed immunity and permanency, the regime tried to control the judiciary through indirect measures. First, the regime expanded the number of judges that sat on the STF and appointed to the newly created judgeships supporters of the regime. Later, it reduced the number of judgeships and retired those judges whom it considered unfriendly. Finally, the jurisdiction of the civilian courts was reduced and the role of the military courts was expanded. All national security cases, even those that involved civilians only, were referred to military courts, where the regime had full control. The regime also tried to strengthen the function of the specialized courts, such as the Tribunal Superior Eleitoral (TSE, Superior Electoral Court), the Tribunal Superior do Trabalho (TST, Superior Labor Court), and the Tribunal de Contas da União (TCU, Accounting Tribunal of the Union). The latter, though an arm of the Congress, was in reality under the control of the President. These changes reduced the independence of the judiciary as a separate branch of government and forced it to assume a more docile role.

The Party System and Electoral Laws

In 1965 through Institutional Act No. 2, the authoritarian regime created a two-party system to provide political stability in the country. The hope was that through this mechanism the weak characteristics of the Brazilian party system would be resolved. However, to maintain ARENA in the majority, it was necessary to continuously change the electoral laws and impose restrictions on opposition candidates.

The military used several methods to control elections in favor of the ruling party. The most drastic of these methods included the following:

Sublegenda

The *sublegenda* was adopted for the first time in the municipal and senatorial elections of 1966, based on Article 92 of the Electoral Laws of 1965. It was later institutionalized through the *Sublegenda* Law of June 14, 1968. According to this method, a party could submit as many as three candidates for a mayor or senator's seat. The votes of the three candidates were added. The winning candidate was the one who received most votes from the party that accumulated the most votes. The *sublegenda* method allowed aggregation of votes and prevented party fragmentation. It worked in favor of ARENA by keeping competition within the party, uniting ex-UDN and ex-PSD factions.

Party Fidelity

Another method ostensibly used by the military to fortify the two-party system was the party fidelity provision. A member was not allowed to switch parties, and he could lose his mandate if, by his attitude or vote, he was believed to have acted against the interest of his party (Constitutional Amendment No. 1, of 1969). As mentioned previously, this provision was enacted because many ARENA members voted against their own party in 1968.

Lei Falcão

This law, drafted by the Minister of Justice Armando Falcão, was intended to control electoral campaigns and to restrict the access of the opposition candidates to the media. Another complementary law also stipulated that one-third of the federal senators would be chosen by the state legislatures through an indirect election. Of the twenty-two senators selected through this method in 1978, all but one belonged to the ARENA party. This lone senator came from the state of Rio de Janeiro, where the opposition party, the Movimento Democrático Brasileiro (MDB, Brazilian Democratic Movement), controlled the state legislature and a majority of the local governments and thus the state electoral college. The media and the critics of this law dubbed the senators elected through this process "bionic" senators.

April 1977 Package

This package of laws maintained the indirect electoral process for the selection of governors and bionic senators in 1978. It also augmented the number of deputies from Northeast states where the government party enjoyed an electoral advantage.

Multiparty System

After the elections of 1974 and 1978, which resulted in significant MDB gains at both the state and federal levels, a new law was passed in 1979 allowing the return to the multiparty system, with some restrictions.

Analysts have noted that, as early as the election of 1970, voters who objected to the arbitrary imposition of the two-party system were either casting blank ballots or were intentionally invalidating their ballots, rather than voting for ARENA or MDB.[14] Furthermore, as has been demonstrated, the regime sought to restrain the growth of the opposition party through the manipulation of the electoral laws and elections. These measures allowed ARENA to maintain its absolute majority in both houses of the Congress and in most state legislatures. However, with the results of the election of 1978, there was increasing concern that ARENA would not maintain its majority in the election of 1982. By allowing the return to a multiparty system in 1979, the regime expected to divide the opposition (by tying the ballots and preventing coalitions) and ensure the victory for a new government-sponsored party in the election of 1982.

As a result, with the return to the multiparty system, the new government-sponsored party, the Partido Democrático Social (PDS, Democratic Social Party), ARENA's successor, maintained its absolute majority in the Senate, but lost it in the Chamber. In the state legislatures, PDS succeeded in controlling thirteen out of twenty-three legislatures, with exceptions in the industrial south and southeast regions of the country.

November 1981 Package

This innovation in the electoral laws established the *voto vinculado,* or tying of vote. According to this law, a voter could not vote for one party at the local and state levels and another at the federal level. The voters were required to select the same party, at both the federal and state levels. The regime expected that, by tying the votes directed to state-level candidates with the votes directed to federal-level candidates, government support in the Congress would benefit. A reverse coattails effect where local candidates would "pull in" the top of the ticket was anticipated by the government. The reasoning behind this logic relied on the fact that many state governments and services were highly dependent on resources controlled by the government. The measure also obliged political parties to sponsor candidates at all levels if they were to contest an election in a given state, and outlawed formation of party coalitions for the purpose of contesting elections.

One of the unanticipated consequences of this measure was the unification of the Partido Popular (PP, Popular Party) of Tancredo Neves, with the Partido do Movimento Democrático Brasileiro (PMDB, Party of the Brazilian Democratic Movement). The unification of the PMDB, the successor of the MDB, with the PP, in order to avoid the restrictions imposed by the November 1981 package, undermined the government's ability to realize the anticipated effect of the multiparty system.

Another unintended consequence of this law was the reaction of the voters. By requiring the voter to choose the candidate for federal, state, and local offices from the same party, the regime expected a "reverse coattails" to occur. The support that it enjoyed at the state and local levels was supposed to be carried to the federal level. In the Northeast the strategy worked in favor of the regime. However, in the South Central region PMDB benefitted. State and local opposition candidates were elected on the coattails of the federal candidates. Since voters could not split their vote between parties at the state and federal levels, many chose to vote against the government at all levels.

The return to the multiparty system, within the context of the *abertura,* took place gradually, and, in effect, dismantled most of the regime's arbitrary measures to manipulate the elections and the political parties. The arbitrary manner in which the authoritarian regime tried to restructure the political system so as to provide stability and continuity backfired. The political measures to restructure the party system and to manipulate the electoral laws were denounced by a large segment of the Brazilian society as crude attempts to hold onto power. Rather than producing stability and creating a new political structure, they were denounced by opposition politicians and opinion leaders. These extemporaneous measures helped mobilize large segments of the Brazilian population behind the programs and the candidates of the opposition. Voters responded to these manipulations by either voiding their votes or, when given the opportunity, by supporting opposition candidates. Support for the regime was being eroded while support for the candidates associated with the opposition was being continuously augmented.

The erosion of the regime's support forced it to undertake a series of measures known collectively as the *abertura*. The purpose was to avert a violent break with the authoritarian regime by redemocratizing the political system.[15] Two of the most important measures associated with this political opening were the revocation of Institutional Act No. 5, in December 1978, and the return to a multiparty system, with some restrictions, in December 1979. First, in order to be recognized, each party had to obtain a minimum of 5 percent of the country-wide vote, plus a minimum of 3 percent of the vote from at least nine states. Second, each party had to be substantially organized at state and local levels. Third, Communist parties were banned from the electoral process. These restrictions were removed in Constitutional Amendment No. 25, of May 1985. This amendment also called for the election of a National Constituent Assembly (NCA) and granted the illiterate the right to vote.

In August of 1979, other measures associated with the political opening were passed, including the granting of general amnesty for all political crimes and the return of political exiles. In accordance with the terms of the amnesty, crimes committed by the authoritarian regime against its political opponents were also pardoned. When the NCA was elected in November 1986, the restrictions imposed by the regime on formation of political parties had already been eliminated. The return to the chaotic multiparty system of 1946 was complete, as we shall see when we discuss the work of the NCA.

THE AUTHORITARIAN REGIME AND THE BUREAUCRACY

The Brazilian civil service is composed of three different types of employees: *estatutários*, CLTs, and daily laborers. The *estatutários*, or statutory employees, are tenured employees, and special legal provisions (statutes) regulate their appointment, classification, and tenure. Among other things, they must be hired through competitive examinations. The CLTs are employees hired through the same labor legislation governing employees of the private sector, known collectively as the Consolidação das Leis do Trabalho (CLT), or Consolidation of the Labor Legislation. Formal degrees, qualifications, and skills are the basis for their admission to the public service. The daily laborers are those paid on a daily basis, and, usually, formal education requirements or examinations are not needed for their admission.

The *estatutários* have the most prestigious jobs, since they enjoy permanency and are admitted through competitive exams. In principle, and in accordance with the civil service laws, the Brazilian civil service is merit-oriented. In reality, however, the laws governing recruitment, promotion, and demotion are subverted according to the political needs of the presidential system of government.[16]

The President has extensive powers to fill the more than 100,000 jobs in both direct and indirect administration. Since the bureaucracy is permanent and its rights and guarantees are embodied in the Constitution, a new President is given enormous power which ensures that he and his advisors have the means to see to it that their policies are followed and implemented by the bureaucracy. To staff these positions, the President and his cabinet and senior advisors recruit their friends, from within or outside the bureaucracy.

There are four categories of positions the President and his senior aides can staff: *the funções comissionadas* (FC), the *funções de direção e assessoramento superiores* (DAS), the *funções de assessoramento superior* (FAS), and the *funções de direção e assistência intermediárias* (DAI).[17] The FCs, or commissioned functions, are at the top of the bureaucratic hierarchy, immediately below the cabinet minister. Their holders are the second most prestigious executive officials. In 1988, occupants of these positions received monthly salaries ranging between $2,000 and $3,500 for thirteen months each year, and their numbers ranged between 500 and 700.

The DASs, or superior administrative and advisory staff, are at the top echelon of the administrative class. It is the Brazilian equivalent of the U.S. Senior Executive Service. In 1988, their number was close to 9,000. There are six levels of DAS positions, ranging from DAS-1 to DAS-6, in ascending order. The monthly salaries of employees holding these positions range from $700 to $1,500. Most of the people appointed to occupy these positions are *estatutários* of the civil service.

The FASs, or superior advisory staff, work closely with ministers and other senior government officials located in the nation's capital, Brasília. In reality, however, these employees are spread out all over the country. In 1988, it was estimated that 3,862 members of this category earned a minimum monthly salary of $300, and that another 1,488 earned a monthly income of $1,000.

The *direção e assistência intermediárias* (DAI), or intermediate administrative assistant staff, constitutes the largest category of executive positions occupied by transients. In 1988, approximately 55,115 positions in this category were paid an average monthly salary of $200. Many of the political operatives and supporters who are not highly qualified end up in this category.

Within the context of the Brazilian presidential system of government, these extensive executive prerogatives, instead of working to enable the President to control the bureaucracy, worked to destabilize and demoralize it. Although in principle those who occupy these positions could be from within or outside the bureaucracy, in reality most are from within. The rotation of civil servants in these jobs has no pattern except political convenience. Once the minister, himself a transient, leaves his post, some of those appointed by him may also be asked to leave. Back in their low-paying jobs, those who lost in the shuffle spend their time engaging in intrigues against their colleagues who are now at the top. Through intrigues, they prepare the political ground so that they can climb back to the top with the next President or next Minister. Meantime, those elevated to senior positions are supposed to provide the leadership for the administration, yet they know that it was not their professional skills that qualified them for the new position, but rather their political connections and the favors they exchanged. Thus, the civil service is continuously preoccupied with playing musical chairs. Instead of professionalism that is encouraged, it is clientelism. Those who lose are not dismissed from their jobs; they remain lurking in the corners of the hallways, working to undermine whatever innovations the new administration is likely to introduce. Even those appointed from outside the bureaucracy find it appealing to remain even after their benefactors have left. The security and perks of a civil service job are irresistible in a country where the government dominates and controls the economy. Furthermore, by belonging to the bureaucracy, one changes places from being a victim of its actions to becoming a beneficiary of its largess.

This flexibility has caused the Brazilian bureaucracy to lose its bearing. According to the law, the main distinction between *estatutários* and CLTs is tenure. In practice, the distinctions are reduced to differences in salary and other small benefits, because hardly any of the CLTs are ever dismissed. In reality the CLTs are as permanent as the *estatutários*. Those who make it through the competitive examinations join the service under the CLT laws. With time they become permanent and occupy positions that bear no relationship to what they were originally hired for.[18]

The Structure of the Civil Bureaucracy

The Brazilian civil bureaucracy is divided into direct and indirect administrations. The structure of the positions in the indirect administration and their salary scale varies from one entity to another, depending on the conditions prevailing in similar industries and entities in the private sector. This flexibility was intentionally granted to the public enterprises so as to make them competitive in attracting qualified personnel. Under the political logic of the presidential system of government, the flexibility enjoyed by these public enterprises gave both the bureaucrats and the politicians a free hand to reward their relatives and supporters.[19]

The direct administration, composed of the traditional ministries and the departments associated with the more orthodox functions of the government, is organized and classified in accordance with elaborate legislation, and many of the benefits and privileges to which it is entitled are embodied in the Constitution.

PRESIDENTIAL POLITICS AND BUREAUCRATIC PERFORMANCE

Since 1930, Brazil has experienced two kinds of presidential systems of government: (1) an authoritarian presidentialism, reflected in Getúlio Vargas's *Estado Novo*, between 1930 and 1945, and, more recently, in the military rule between 1964 and 1985; and (2) a liberal presidentialism between 1946 and 1964.

The Authoritarian Presidentialism

Under the authoritarian presidentialism, political parties were banned, restricted, or controlled. Elections were tightly manipulated to produce a majority in support of the government in power. The media was censored, and the organized groups in the civil society were repressed. The Congress lost many of its prerogatives. Legitimate political activities were considered subversive by the regime. It may have been expected that the President and his associates would have absolute control under this type of system, since what is known as "political meddling" was absent. The bureaucracy was expected to operate under its own rules of rationality and legality without the irrationality of politics. The conditions for a merit and professional bureaucracy were supposed to be ideal under such a system. Yet an examination of the executive-bureaucratic relations under the authoritarian presidentialism shows a different picture. Why did the authoritarian presidentialism fail to produce a professional, merit-oriented bureaucracy, as it has often claimed and tried to attain?[20]

Contrary to common assumptions, intrabureaucratic conflict during authoritarian regimes intensified. Since there was no outside arena (such as a powerful legislature) to air out and manage or resolve these conflicts, bureaucratic conflicts were either suppressed or expressed in the form of intrigues or conspiratorial associations and actions. In their extreme forms, these conflicts led to attempted *coups d'état*.[21] To preserve his power base within the bureaucracy, the President can either liquidate the opposition or co-opt it. Although liquidation is sometimes practiced under extraordinary circumstances, the preferred option is normally co-opting. Co-opting involves transforming the bureaucracy into independent fiefdoms. Each feudal lord exercises broad and arbitrary control over his domain and engages in expanding his prerogatives and jurisdictions for self aggrandizement and to keep his subjects satisfied. This situation leads to the expansion of the bureaucracy.[22]

Yet this bureaucratic infighting was carried out in accordance with internal rules, as specified by the Constitution and the legislation that was in effect. Bureaucrats also needed allies in their fights.

For the authoritarian regime to maintain its legitimacy it had to maintain the facade of an election and the presence of the Congress. To maintain its supporters in power, the regime adopted the goals of development, which required an energized and expanded bureaucracy. Yet the logic of political survival dictated that the bureaucracy and its civilian allies be satisfied, hence the use of bureaucracy to reward supporters both within and outside the bureaucracy. This was done by expanding the bureaucracy and keeping the bureaucratic elites permanently employed and in constant circulation.

The transients employed by a President under the authoritarian regime to perform those tasks were themselves either bureaucrats or technocrats with little political base. Although their degree of stability in office was a little higher than the transients employed under the liberal presidentialism, their political base outside the bureaucracy was quite limited. This lack of political power undermined their ability to reign over the bureaucracy. Although the Congress was considered a weak legislature, it was the other source of political control over the bureaucracy. However, the restrictions that were placed by the authoritarian presidentialism over congressional structure, operations, and jurisdictions made congressional oversight of the bureaucracy difficult. To maintain their support among the electorate, politicians needed the patronage and the services that only the bureaucracy could provide. Rather than engaging in futile attempts to control the bureaucracy, congressmen opted to seek favors from the bureaucracy. The Congress traded the control of public policy for tangible personal and electoral benefits. The more the Congress engaged in this trade-off, the more it lost control over the bureaucracy. Even when the Congress had the information, it did not have the power or the interest to control the bureaucracy. Yet this trade-off was limited. Under the authoritarian presidentialism, instead of the politicians being the main source of political appointments, the bureaucrats become the main conduit for political appointments.[23]

Bureaucrats became aware of opportunities for employment before the politicians. Their permanency gave them a superior advantage over the politicians allowing them to manipulate the rules and regulations so as to ensure their relatives and friends the security of bureaucratic jobs. Although the press in Brazil and the concerned public often highlighted the clientelism of the politicians, little was mentioned of the more pervasive clientelism perpetrated by the bureaucrats themselves.

The Liberal Presidentialism

The main characteristics of the liberal presidentialism were open and free elections, a competitive multiparty system, a free press, and the rule of law. Presidents came to power as a result of a successful coalition of diverse political forces. Because of the weaknesses and instabilities of political parties in Brazil, few parties were able to attain a majority status within the Congress. Once the President was elected, the coalition that brought him to power began to disintegrate under the exigencies of competition for resources and favors. Sometimes, even the President's party found it politically disadvantageous to continue its close association with his policies. To win congressional approvals for his programs, a President had to be willing and able to forge a majority on every issue that he presented for legislative consideration. This was a task that required time and patience and an exchange of favors. In return for congressional support, members of Congress were appointed to the President's cabinet or were given favors.[24]

In the liberal presidentialism, the presidential cabinet appointees entrusted to supervise the bureaucracy were usually a diverse group of politicians, bureaucrats, and independent professionals. They were appointed to the cabinet more for the groups they represented or the favors they had given or were likely to give to the President than for their allegiance and agreement with the policies of the President.

Once appointed, cabinet members sought to maximize their political and personal advantages. The bureaucracy served as the mechanism for the President to construct his majority coalition and for those appointed to reward their friends and supporters. For every favor the bureaucracy granted, it extracted a corresponding favor. The favors utilized by the transients to reward their relatives and supporters were soon spread out to all members of the bureaucracy.

Being tenured, bureaucrats were more informed of the opportunities for graft and often more used to it. The transients who used the bureaucracy for the same purpose were in no position to grandstand and moralize about graft and favoritism. That function was constitutionally reserved for the press and for the opposition in the Congress. Unfortunately for the Congress, even when it tried to exercise this function, its structure and its informational resources limited it to speeches and denouncements. The violators escaped prosecution, and rarely were they brought to justice.

The history of the various Comissões Parlamentares de Inquérito (CPIs, Parliamentary Inquiry Committees) attests to this generalization. In spite of the zeal by which these investigative committees pursued their work, they often disbanded before they had a chance to present their reports, because by law a committee can exist for only up to 120 days (renewable). The resources the CPIs needed to carry out their work were controlled by the Mesas of the respective houses. Since members of the Mesas, particularly their presidents, were usually supporters of the President of the Republic they tried to scuttle the work of the CPIs. Because the legislators' terms in CPI committees were terminated they were unable to follow-up on their recommendations. Finally, members of the CPIs received inordinate pressures from the executive, including threats that their own questionable behavior, which was available to the executive in secret files, would be made public.

On rare occasions when the legislature did challenge and defy the President, the stage was set for a confrontation that either led to an impasse and paralysis or was resolved when the President appealed for the support of the bureaucracy, especially its military wing.

The coup of 1964 against the established constitutional order can be understood within the above context, as an example of a bureaucracy defending its security and dominance against what it perceived as the encroachment of the political regime and its leftist allies among the population. Using the pretext that President Goulart had encouraged military insubordination and had undermined discipline and moral, and fearing that the popular demands for goods and services to be provided by the government would impoverish the bureaucracy and lead to financial collapse, the military moved and toppled the President. The military's actions were supported by the civilian bureaucrats, the landlords among the politicians, and the business community. These groups feared that the populist policies of the government would lead the country to economic ruin, social upheaval, and political chaos. For twenty years, the main preoccupation of this bureaucratic-authoritarian regime was the attainment of social and political stability as a precondition for economic growth.

The military bureaucracy was given the task of maintaining law and order and ensuring stability, while the civilian bureaucracy was to run the national economy. Bureaucratic reform became a top priority of the new regime. As had been the case since 1934, administrative reforms became a constitutional concern. The Constitution of 1967, in Article 104, included a new provision that allowed the bureaucracy to bypass existing recruitment requirements by hiring through the labor laws in force for the private sector, the *Consolidação das Leis do Trabalho* (CLT). Indeed, this allowed the hiring of temporary and contractual workers without the need of competitive examinations. In 1970, the regime embarked on a major restructuring of the public sector—after it arrogated to itself (through institutional acts, constitutional amendments, and decree laws) the sole responsibility of creating and abolishing administrative institutions, defining and changing their functions, and establishing their personnel and budgetary needs. The bureaucracy was in full control of its own destiny as well as the destiny of the society.

The bureaucracy was also in an expansionist mood. The number of ministries increased from ten in 1963 to fifteen in 1967 and to twenty-seven in 1984. By the end of this period, the number of government-owned entities, such as companies, monopolies, foundations, and joint ventures, was more than 400. Advisory councils increased from seventeen to fifty-five and were employing more than 600 counselors. The number of civil servants employed in the direct and indirect administration doubled, from 675,554 in 1963 to 1.3 million in 1985.

Between 1964 and 1979, four presidents came to power. During a period of almost thirteen years, ninety-nine transients were rotated among sixty-eight cabinet posts.[25] During the Authoritarian period, 29.3 percent of the transients had legislative experience. On the other hand, transients with legislative experience during the Competitive period reached 59.9 percent. Transients with a professional and private sector background rose from 25.7 percent in the Competitive period to 52 percent during the Authoritarian period. In a similar manner, transients with military experience rose from 2 to 10.7 percent, and those with bureaucratic background rose from 3.3 to 5.3 percent. Although the degree of continuity of those occupying ministerial posts during the Authoritarian period showed some improvement as compared with the Competitive period, their ability to reign in the bureaucracy was minimal, since they were appointed and dismissed by the ruling bureaucrats. Bureaucrats wrote the law, interpreted and implemented it, and evaluated their actions. Whatever rationality and legality the bureaucracy displayed, was due to internal constraints and the presence of a Congress that continued to exercise its function of criticism, debate, proposing legislation, and acting on legislation presented to it by the bureaucracy. Frequent outbursts by various civilian groups outside the bureaucracy were silenced or ignored.

The ability of the bureaucracy to manage its own internal conflicts began to show signs of strain. In 1979, the creation of the Ministry of Debureaucratization did little to ease the tension within the bureaucracy and between the bureaucrats and the public. When the economic performance of the country began to decline, bureaucratic conflict increased, and the acquiescence of civil society was replaced with defiance. Labor unions, professional groups, and the Catholic Church led the way. Every election sent a message to the bureaucrats that society was growing impatient with their rule. Through a prolonged and gradual process of released tension and political openness, the bureaucrats accepted the idea of sharing power with other members of the civil society. In 1985, a new civilian bureaucratic regime was inaugurated. In 1986, new elections were held for the Congress, which was charged with writing the new constitution. Finally, in 1988, the new constitution was promulgated.

The return to a civilian form of government did not end the rule of the bureaucrats. Indeed, their number and function continued to expand. By the end of 1988 the number of ministries had risen to twenty-nine. The indirect administration had about 513 entities with 22,000 offices throughout the country. Between 1985 and 1988, the number of civilian bureaucrats in the direct administration, public enterprises, and government monopolies rose from 1.3 million to 1.5 million.

While the power of the Congress was restored and augmented in accordance with the Constitution of 1988, bureaucratic prerogatives and privileges were guaranteed and even augmented. Those who had served in temporary positions were given permanent status. The right to unionize was recognized and guaranteed. Even the right to strike was extended to most public employees. Dismissal from work could only take place in accordance with the provisions of the Constitution and the prevailing labor laws. In less than four years, President José Sarney reshuffled his cabinet three times, created and abolished whole ministries, and increased the public civil service rolls by 200,000. Although the percentage of transients with legislative backgrounds increased during this period, their job permanency decreased. Political parties, as a result of their weaknesses, were incapable of controlling these transients, even when those transients had the same party affiliation. Instead, presidential politics once again, by using government appointments and programs, managed to undermine not only the opposition parties, but even the party coalition that was supposed to be in power. To the public's perception of the bureaucracy as being arrogant, authoritarian, and elitist, under the new civilian regime were added other characteristics, such as inefficient, clientelist, and populist. Presidentialism, both the authoritarian and liberal, failed to create a professional and efficient bureaucracy under acceptable political control. What had been created, especially since the *Estado Novo*, was a tenured, salaried, and interdependent bureaucracy at the helm of political power.

Parliamentarism and the Control of the Bureaucracy

General agreement exists among Brazilian and international observers and policymakers concerned with the performance and control of public policy in Brazil that the system failed to perform two important functions: (1) to develop a professional and efficient bureaucracy and (2) to politically control the bureaucracy. Although some would argue that political control is a necessary prerequisite for an efficient and professional bureaucracy, historically, the Brazilian presidential system of government has tried to maximize presidential control at the expense of professional and efficient bureaucracy. The authoritarian regime that followed the coup of 1964 promised but failed to produce a politically neutral and efficient professional bureaucracy. Its reliance on, and alliance with, the techno-bureaucrats made the bureaucracy an autonomous, self-regulating political system, but failed to professionalize or rationalize its operations.

A debate still rages over how to achieve the goals of a professional and politically controlled bureaucracy. Some argue that a modified presidential system of government is the best way to create a professional bureaucracy. Others argue that, given the nature of Brazilian political parties and the economic system, parliamentarism is the only avenue toward a professional politically controlled bureaucracy.

Supporters of a presidential system of government argue that presidentialism, with all its weaknesses, is still the best way to provide a unified and timely direction to the sprawling, disjointed, overlapping bureaucratic institutions and entities. There is little support for authoritarian presidentialism as the best way to rationalize the bureaucracy. Many believe, however, that a presidential system of government, with all its guarantees of liberal democracy, may be the right answer. In this view, the failures of the attempted liberal presidentialisms were not inherent in the system but in the weak and incoherent political parties and their behavior within the Congress. Indeed, the negative image of politicians and the initial appeals of authoritarian regimes, according to this view, are due to the failure of the Congress to properly oversee the bureaucracy and to develop it along professional lines. Clientelism and nepotism are words reserved to describe the bureaucracy that emerged as a result of the meddling of the politicians under the liberal presidentialism.

What is missing from this analysis, however, is a recognition that perhaps the presidential system of government dictates to some extent the nature of the parties that are likely to emerge and the role that the bureaucracy plays. Within the presidential system of government, with its separation of powers, as Riggs has argued, a strong and disciplined party is an invitation for an impasse between the executive and the legislature. The weak party system is perhaps one of the reasons that the presidential system of government in the United States has been able to survive. Presidential politics, with its need for electoral alliances and viable congressional majorities, necessitates political accommodations and trade-offs. Bureaucratic favors are the currency of this system.

Advocates of a parliamentary system of government recognize that bureaucracy has played and will continue to play a leading political role. The question is not how to create a neutral bureaucracy, but how to synchronize the roles of the bureaucrats and the politicians.[26] What is needed, according to advocates of parliamentarism, is the unity of politics and administration, not the artificial separation. This is achieved by uniting the executive and the legislative powers rather than separating them. If there is a majority political party, as in the present-day United Kingdom, that party dominates both the executive and the legislature. Policy decisions are reserved for a coherent cabinet, while the implementation of those policies are reserved for a professional bureaucracy that has no alternative but to submit to the decisions reached by the cabinet. Since the cabinet is coherent and in full control of the parliament, bureaucrats are in no position to mobilize their constituencies and forge an alliance with a congressional committee or subcommittee, as in the United States.

What if there is no one-party dominated cabinet? Can parliamentarism still work? Given the party characteristics of the Brazilian political system, at least for the foreseeable future, parliamentary cabinet governments are likely to be coalition governments and most likely unstable coalition governments along the lines of the recent Italian model. Can a coalition government create a unity of purpose between administration and politics? Or would it lead to the compartmentalization of the bureaucracy? Advocates of parliamentarism admit that the problems that a weak coalition government would face are formidable and, unless properly handled, would lead to a bureaucracy without leadership. The frequent changes among the coalition partners would force the cabinet members to master the art of political negotiations, with little professional experience in the function of the ministry they are likely to head. This forces the politicians to rely on a professional, permanent bureaucracy along the lines of the European, rather than the American, model. Under this arrangement, political negotiation over public policy takes place where it should, within the Congress. Members of the cabinet, in need of legislative support to stay in power, defend and negotiate their policies along party coalition lines. A professional, permanent bureaucracy, rather than the existing spoils system, would be needed if parliamentarism is to succeed. Thus it is argued that while presidentialism would necessarily bring about a nonprofessional, politically uncontrolled bureaucracy, parliamentarism, by necessity, would promote the unity between administration and politics and between the executive and the legislature. This unity would necessarily promote the development of a professional bureaucracy, since it is in the interest of the executive who is in control of the legislature to be served by a professional and efficient bureaucracy, rather than by nonprofessional, inefficient transients. The hope is that professionalism within the bureaucracy would develop along the lines of the French model, where, in spite of the frequent cabinet changes, the bureaucracy continues to perform adequately.

NOTES

1. Many interpretations have been proffered as to the causes of the 1964 coup. There is general agreement that the impasse between the president and the Congress, along with the maneuvers that each followed to win supporters, precipitated the coup. However, there is disagreement on what caused the impasse. The nature of the political parties, the military, and other national and international security factors are some of the causes pointed to by several researchers. However, institutional factors, such as the nature of the presidential system, are hardly emphasized. For a sample of interpretations concerning the coup, see Affonso Almino, *Raízes do Golpe: Da Crise da Legalidade ao Parlamentarismo, 1961-1963* (São Paulo: Marco Zero, 1988); Wanderley Guilherme dos Santos, *Sessenta e Quatro: Anatomia da Crise* (São Paulo: Vértice, 1986); Riordan Roett, *Brazil: Politics in a Patrimonial Society* (New York: Praeger, 1984); René Armand Dreifuss, *1964: A Conquista do Estado* (Petrópolis: Vozes, 1981); Peter Flynn, *Brazil*, op. cit.; Moniz Bandeira, *O Governo João Goulart: As Lutas Sociais no Brasil, 1961-1964* (Rio de Janeiro: Civilização Brasileira, 1977); Phillippe C. Schmitter, *Interest Groups, Conflict, and Political Change in Brazil* (Stanford, Calif.: Stanford University Press, 1971); Ronald M. Schneider, *The Political System of Brazil: Emergence of a "Modernizing" Authoritarian Regime, 1964-1970* (New York: Columbia University Press, 1971); Thomas E. Skidmore, *Politics in Brazil*, op. cit.; Afonso Arinos de Mello Franco, *Evolução da Crise Brasileira* (São Paulo: Companhia Editora Nacional, 1965); Miguel Reale, *Imperativos da Revolução de Março* (São Paulo: Livraria Martins Editora, 1965); Alberto Dines et al., *Os Idos de Março e a Queda em Abril* (Rio de Janeiro: José Alvaro, 1964); Oliveiros S. Ferreira, *As Forças Armadas e o Desafio da Revolução* (Rio de Janeiro: Edição GRD, 1964); and Fernando Pedreira, *Março 31: Civis e Militares no Processo de Crise Brasileira* (Rio de Janeiro: José Alvaro Editora, 1964).

2. Brazil's authoritarian period, between 1964 and 1985, set a pattern of study in terms of development theories, the role of the military as a modernizing force, and economic and industrial policies under an authoritarian regime. This period of Brazilian history was the one most studied by social scientists, both in Brazil and outside. A sample of this literature is Thomas E. Skidmore, *The Politics of Military Rule in Brazil, 1964-1985* (New York: Oxford University Press, 1988); David Collier, "Overview of the Bureaucratic-Authoritarian Model," and "The Bureaucratic-Authoritarian Model: Synthesis and Priorities for Future Research," in Collier (ed.),

The New Authoritarianism in Latin America (Princeton, N.J.: Princeton University Press, 1979), pp. 19-32 and 363-97, respectively; Albert O. Hirschman, "The Turn to Authoritarianism in Latin America and the Search for Its Economic Determinants," in Collier (ed.), ibid.; Alexandre de Souza Costa Barros, "The Brazilian Military: Professional Socialization, Political Performance, and State Building" (Ph.D. diss., University of Chicago, 1978); Wanderley Guilherme dos Santos, *Poder e Política: Crônica do Autoritarismo Brasileiro* (Rio de Janeiro: Forense, 1978); Georges-André Fiechter, *Brazil Since 1964: Modernization under a Military Regime* (New York: John Wiley & Sons, 1975); Alfred Stepan, *Military in Politics*, op. cit.; Guillermo A. O'Donnell, *Modernization and Bureaucratic-Authoritarianism: Studies in South American Politics* (Berkeley, Calif.: Institute of International Studies, 1973); Alfred Stepan, "The New Professionalism of Internal Warfare and Military Role Expansion," Stepan (ed.), *Authoritarian Brazil: Origins, Policies, and Future* (New Haven, Conn.: Yale University Press, 1973), pp. 47-68; Guillermo A. O'Donnell, *Modernization and Bureaucratic-Authoritarianism* (Berkeley and Los Angeles: University of California Press, 1967); and Cândido de Almeida Mendes, "Sistema Político e Modelos de Poder no Brasil," *Dados*, 1 (2d Semester, 1966), pp. 7-41. The theoretical justification for the need for a strong modernizing control, able to create order, was provided by Samuel P. Huntington, *Political Order in Changing Societies* (New Haven, Conn.: Yale University Press, 1968).

3. See Golbery do Couto e Silva, *Conjuntura Política Nacional, O Poder Executivo e a Geopolítica do Brasil* (Brasília: Editora Universidade de Brasília, 1981); and Elmar Bones, "Golbery: Silêncio e Poder," *Tribuna da Imprensa* (October 2 and 3, 1978), p. 9.

4. Maria Helena Moreira Alves, *State and Opposition in Military Brazil* (Austin: University of Texas Press, 1985), p. 8.

5. See Golbery do Couto e Silva, *Conjuntura Política Nacional*, op. cit., p. 26.

6. The memories of General Cordeiro de Farias, one of the leaders of the coup who later became disenchanted with it, provide a good illustration of the goals of a large segment of the armed forces with regard to the coup. See Olympio Mourão Filho, *Memórias: A Verdade de um Revolucionário* (Porto Alegre: L & PM, 1978).

7. For the constitutionality of the institutional acts, see Jessé Torres Pereira, Jr., "Os Atos Institucionais em Face do Direito Administrativo," *Revista Brasileira de Estudos Políticos*, 47 (July 1978), pp. 77-114. For the full text of all institutional and complementary acts, see *Legislação Constitucional e Complementar* (Brasília: Senado Federal, 1972).

8. The North America Network (NAN) consists of a group of political scientists from several universities, whose research has emphasized the role of institutions in the survivability of democratic governments. NAN has sponsored several panels at the International Political Science Association (IPSA), American Political Science Association (APSA), and American Society for Public Administration (ASPA) meetings, where the nature of the presidential system, the role of the legislature, and the control of the bureaucracy in presidential systems of government have been examined.

9. In 1988, Fred Riggs suggested this concept in a memo sent to NAN members.

10. The regime's attempt to suppress its opponents through coercion and violence is well documented in Maria Helena Moreira Alves, *State and Opposition in Military Brazil*, op. cit.; and Joan Dassin (ed.), *Torture in Brazil* (New York: Random House, 1986).

11. The election process under the authoritarian regime, especially the constant change in the rules, crested much interest for scholars. A sample of this literature is David V. Fleischer, "Constitutional and Electoral Engineering in Brazil: A Double Edged Sword, 1964-1982," Interamerican Economic Affairs, 37 (1984), pp. 3-36; Raimundo Pereira, Alvaro Caropreso, and José Carlos Ruy, *Eleições no Brasil Pós-64* (São Paulo: Global, 1984); João Almino, *Democratas Autoritários* (São Paulo: Brasiliense, 1980); David V. Fleischer, "A Evolução do Bipartidarismo Brasileiro, 1966-1979," *Revista Brasileira de Estudos Políticos* (July 1980), pp. 155-85; and Wanderley Guilherme dos Santos, "Eleição, Representação, Política Substantiva," *Dados*, 8 (1971). An example of the electoral rules can be found in *Legislação Eleitoral e Partidária: Instruções do TSE para as Eleições de 1982*, 4th ed. (Brasília: Senado Federal, 1982).

12. For the various theories regarding why the military decided to keep the Congress open after the 1964 coup, see Gláucio Ary Dillon Soares, "Elections and the Redemocratization of Brazil," Paul W. Drake and Eduardo Silva (eds.), *Elections and Democratization in Latin America, 1980-1985* (San Diego: University of California, Center for Iberian and Latin American Studies, 1986), pp. 273-98.

13. Unfortunately, all these provisions were maintained in the 1988 constitution.

14. Since voting is obligatory in accordance with the electoral laws, members of the opposition to the regime could not exercise their right to abstain, thus they resorted to the blank-and-void ballots.

15. The *abertura* has been the subject of extensive study. However, there is wide disagreement as to when it started and what caused it to happen. It is not the objective of this book to review the various interpretations, or to determine which are more likely to be correct. For an overview of the bibliography concerning this topic, see Skidmore, *The Politics of Military Rule*, op. cit.; Enrique A. Baloyra, "From Moment to Moment: The Political Transition in Brazil, 1977-1981," Selcher (ed.), *Political Liberalization*, op. cit., pp. 9-53; David V. Fleischer, "Brazil at the Crossroads: The Elections of 1982 and 1985," Drake and Silva (eds.), *Elections and Democratization*, op. cit.; pp. 299-327; Bolivar Lamounier and Alkimar R. Moura, "Economic Policy and Political Opening in Brazil," Jonathan Hartlyn and Samuel A. Morley (eds.), *Latin American Political Economy* (Boulder, Colo.: Westview Press, 1986), pp. 165-96; Alves, *State and Opposition,* op. cit.; Bolivar Lamounier, "Apontamentos sobre a Questão Democrática Brasileira," Alain Rouquié et al., (eds.), *Como Renascem as Democracias* (São Paulo: Brasiliense, 1985), pp. 104-40; Walter de Goes and Aspasia Camargo, O Drama da Sucessão e a Crise do Regime (Rio de Janeiro: Nova Fronteira, 1984); Eli Diniz, "O Empresariado e a Nova Conjuntura," Bolivar Lamounier, "As Eleições de 1982 e a Abertura Política em Perspectiva," and André Lara Rezende, Luciano Coutinho, Alkimar R. Moura, Pércio Arida, Walter de Goes, Maria do Carmo C. Souza, and Bolivar Lamounier, "A Crise Econômica e os Modelos Alternativos," Hélgio Trindade (ed.), *Brasil em Perspectiva: Dilemas da Abertura Política* (Porto Alegre: Sulina, 1982), pp. 31-60; Marcus Faria Figueiredo and José Antonio Borges Cheibub, "A Abertura Política de 1973 a 1981: Quem Disse o Que, Quando—Inventário de um Debate," *BIB*, 14 (1982), pp. 22-61; David V. Fleischer, "Parties, Elections, and 'Abertura' in Brazil," Wesson (ed.), *New Military Politics*, op. cit., pp. 79-96; Bernardo Bucinski, *Abertura, A História de uma Crise* (São Paulo: Editora Brasil Debates, 1982); Jan Knippers Black, "The Military and Political Decompression in Brazil," *Armed Forces and Society*, 6 (Summer 1980), pp. 625-638; Fernando Henrique Cardoso, "On the Characterization of Authoritarian Regimes in Latin America," Collier (ed.), *The New Authoritarianism*, op. cit., pp. 33-57; and Wanderley Guilherme dos Santos, *Estratégias de Descompressão Política* (Brasília: Instituto de Pesquisas, Estudos e Assessoria do Congresso—IPEAC, 1973).

16. For an insight into the hiring and promotion practices in the Brazilian bureaucracy, see *Reforma Administrativa: Organização da Administração Federal*, 4th ed. (Brasília: Senado Federal, 1984); Reis, "Política de Pessoal", *Ciência e Cultura*, op. cit.; and *Reforma Administrativa do Governo Federal*, 10th ed. (Editora Atlas, 1977).

17. See Dércio G. Munhoz, "A Política Salarial do Setor Público," *Folha de São Paulo* (February 14, 1978), p. 3.

18. In 1988, when the new Constitution was promulgated, it stipulated that those employees who had been in provisional status for less than five years would lose their jobs. More than 95,000 employees were scheduled for dismissals. This even applied to those who had joined through the competitive route. Once appointed, they managed, through executive flexibility, to occupy positions unrelated to their original jobs. It is not uncommon to find a former clerk or secretary occupying a DAS position.

19. The insistence of the World Bank that many of these public entities be sold to the private sector should be understood from this perspective. It is not the operations they are engaged in are unprofitable. The reason they are unprofitable is that they are poorly managed and run. Over time, they have become sinecure for families, friends, and supporters. Once appointed, an employee is practically guaranteed life employment with all the privileges and the graft opportunities it brings with it. Promotions and demotions are not based on qualifications but on

who happens to be in power.

20. This claim was made by Robert T. Daland, "Development Administration and the Brazilian Political System," *Western Political Science Quarterly*, 12, no. 2 (June 1968), pp. 25-39.

21. For the interbureaucratic conflict among the various factions of the military, see Carlos Chagas, *A Guerra das Estrelas, 1964-1984: Os Bastidores das Sucessões Presidenciais* (Porto Alegre: L & PM, 1985). In chapter eight, we discuss in some detail the intrabureaucratic conflict over one policy, that of the hardware and software computer industry and information systems.

22. The size of the bureaucracy doubled between 1964 and 1985, from 670,000 to 1.3 million people.

23. The results of surveys among employees of the Congress, conducted by the author in 1981 and 1986, revealed that most political appointments, even within the bureaucracy of the Congress, was mediated through congressional staff, rather than the congressmen themselves.

24. If a congressman is appointed to a cabinet post, he can resign temporarily from his seat, which is then occupied by his suplente—a type of vice-congressman. Alternately, if he decides to return to Congress, or if he is dismissed by the president from his cabinet post, he reassumes his seat.

25. See Nunes, "Legislativo, Política e Recrutamento de Elites," *Dados*, op. cit. (1978).

26. For an excellent expose of the parliamentary system of government as the solution to professionalize and politically control the bureaucracy, see the three articles by Cornélio Octavio Pinheiro Pimenta, published by *Revista de Ciência Política*: "Parlamentarismo e Profissionalização do Administrador Público," ibid., 27, no. 1 (1986), pp. 82-93; "Parlamentarismo, Presidencialismo e Interesse Público," ibid., 28, no. 1 (April 1985), pp. 32-8; and "Parlamentarismo e Administração Pública," ibid., 27, no. 1 (April 1984), pp. 70-5.

Chapter 2

Congressional Leadership
in Brazil, 1970–1986

Through the manipulation of electoral laws and the intimidation of voters, the government party was assured the majority in Congress throughout the authoritarian regime, until the election of 1982. The challenge facing the military was how to keep the majority party intact and supportive of government policies within the Congress once the elections were won. Political coalitions were known to disintegrate once elections were over. Members of government-supported parties were also known to desert their parties and vote against government policies. Between 1966 and 1968, in spite of measures taken by the authoritarian regime to silence its critics, MDB members were occasionally joined by ARENA members to defeat proposals presented by the government. Managing the work within the Congress to ensure a compliant and docile political majority that supported the government became one of the regime's preoccupations.

Members of the regime, especially its hard-liners, distrusted politicians after the election of 1965, when two governors were elected in defiance of military objections. The bold attitude of the Congress in supporting one of its members in 1968 against government attempts to revoke his mandate and prosecute him heightened the regime's mistrust against all politicians. The Congress was suspended, and a new Constitution that included all the amendments contained in the 1967 Constitution was imposed on the reconvened Congress in 1970. Amendment No.1 sought to place permanent constraints on the Congress so that government programs would not be derailed by a viable opposition or veto groups within the Congress.

Politicians from the large industrial states of the Southeast and South were especially unreliable, according to the regime. Opposition to the regime in those states was more pronounced, and over time voting results showed that the voters were in favor of the MDB candidates. The emergence of strong political leadership from those states was to be prevented at all costs. Although, constitutionally, the system of government was to remain presidential, the Congress and political parties within the Congress were expected to behave as in a parliamentary system of government. Power within the Congress needed to be managed so that the government party supported the government and the opposition remained unable to constitute a veto power. Because a weak party system could be strengthened by the way those parties organize themselves within the Congress, the organization of congressional leadership became a concern of the regime. The ideal organization, from the perspective of the regime, was a nonpolitical leadership, whose primary preoccupation would be to manage legislation and ratify government initiatives, rather than to formulate public policy. Since politicians were not to be trusted, leadership within the Congress was to be given to temporary figures who were unable to succeed themselves and whose selection to those leadership positions was highly influenced by the support they received from the military. As such, the regime was periodically able to influence the selection of Congressional leaders, rewarding supporters and excluding potential rivals. A rotating leadership policy proved to be a convenient way to control the Congress.

POSITION AND POWER WITHIN THE NATIONAL CONGRESS

Once elected, a legislature's first task is to organize itself so it can mobilize its resources and focus its energies on the work ahead. Research on the U.S. Congress has documented how the Congress organizes itself and the importance of the leadership and organizational characteristics of Congress to the policy process and influence within the Congress.[1] Party leaders, for example, were found to play an important role in influencing the outcome of congressional actions. Committees and committee chairmen are the cornerstone of congressional life.[2] Leadership continuity enables the U.S. Congress to impose some sort of discipline on its members, encourages specialization and career development, and enhances the ability of the legislature to countercheck the executive. Strong congressional leadership is also important for the development and control of legislative staff and for deciding on priorities for information and legislative agendas and strategies. In short, research on the U.S. Congress has shown that the emergence of congressional leadership and its continuity positively contributes to the strengthening of the Congress in performing its many roles.

Chapter 2 examines three interrelated questions: (1) What type of leadership existed in the National Congress of Brazil?; (2) What role did those leaders play?; and (3) To what extent was the policy of preventing the emergence of a stable leadership successful? (Data on leadership positions in the Federal Senate, between 1972 and 1986, and in the Chamber of Deputies, between 1970 and 1984, were used to ascertain the continuity of leadership in selective positions.[3]

Three types of formal leaders within the National Congress of Brazil were identified: party, institutional, and committee leaders.[4]

Party Leadership

Each political party was entitled to a party leader in each house of Congress in which it was represented by more than five members. Also, the parties were entitled to a number of vice-leaders, according to and in proportion to the number of seats the parties held in each house. The party caucuses elected their leaders every two years, at the beginning of the legislative session. During the authoritarian period, the President had a great deal of influence in selecting the leaders of the pro-government party, both in the Senate and in the Chamber.

Party leaders coordinated the positions of their parties on the issues being debated in each house. Party leaders were also empowered to appoint party nominees for the various memberships and other assignments in select committees or delegations. During plenary debates, party leaders were empowered under the party fidelity legislation to cast their votes on behalf of the party unless a roll call was adopted. Party leaders facilitated communication among party members, mobilized party votes, and helped formulate party positions on pending legislation.

Leaders of the pro-government parties, first ARENA and later PDS, its successor, acted as a communication channel between the President and the party members within the Congress. Their role included the championing and defense of the President's agenda and the mobilization of support behind government programs. In return for maintaining party discipline, pro-government party leaders obtained access to favors and perks available to the executive. Members of the pro-government party lobbied executive agencies regarding the interests of their families, supporters, districts, and states. The leaders of the pro-government party in the Chamber and Senate relayed to the President the general sentiments within the party and the Congress in general. Pro-government leaders articulated the executive electoral strategies and the issues of concern to the states. Their daily interaction with the opposition party and its constituencies enabled them to provide the President with political intelligence, to capitalize on favorable opportunities, and to avoid pitfalls. Indeed, ideas and projects that were circulating in Congress and seemed to enjoy general support were brought to the attention of the President who, by taking advantage of his power of initiative, deprived the opposition of the opportunity to use those issues as their platform during electoral campaigns. In short, pro-government parties and their leaders in the Congress acted as if they existed in a parliamentary system of government: They supported executive programs. However, the party leaders had little influence on executive decisions. Their role was confined to that of lobbyists and political informers.[5]

Initially, members and leaders of MDB were an embattled minority. Through a series of arbitrary measures, the regime dismissed radical members of the MDB from the Congress and stripped their political rights. Some were exiled and others were forced to assume a low profile. The challenge to those who survived was how to coexist with a regime they detested and still hold the allegiance of their voters. MDB congressional leaders curtailed the extremism of their members, in return for some protection against arbitrary dismissal and harassment. Throughout campaign speeches, congressional debates, and legislative proposals, MDB leaders tried to articulate an alternate vision to that of the regime.

Although the internal rules of the Congress did not specifically prohibit the reelection of party leaders, after 1975 few party leaders were reelected to their leadership positions.

In the Senate, during the sixteen-year period between 1970 and 1986, both the pro-government party (first ARENA, then PDS) and the opposition (MDB, then PMDB) held eight leadership elections, one election each every two years. As many as thirteen different senators occupied those sixteen leadership terms. Three senators occupied leadership positions for two consecutive terms: Petrônio Portella (ARENA/Piauí), Franco Montoro (MDB and later PMDB/São Paulo), and Humberto Lucena (PMDB/Paraíba). Therefore, the index of party leadership continuity in the Senate, between 1970 and 1986, was 1.23 (or 16 divided by 13)—an index of 1 signifies absolute discontinuity.[6] If party vice-leaders are included in the analysis of continuity, then the index rises to 1.71 (or 111 divided by 65)—an average of less than two terms (or four years) per leader or vice-leader.

In the Chamber, during the fourteen-year period between 1970 and 1984, a total of twenty-three leadership elections were held across all parties represented—after the return to the multiparty system in 1979, other opposition parties came into existence. ARENA (succeeded by PDS) and MDB (succeeded by PMDB) held seven elections each; the Partido Democrático Trabalhista (PDT), or Democratic Labor Party, and the Partido Trabalhista Brasileiro (PTB) held three elections each; the Partido dos Trabalhadores (PT), or Workers' Party, held two elections; and Partido Popular (PP) held one election. As many as eighteen different deputies occupied these twenty-three leadership terms. Two deputies occupied leadership positions for two consecutive terms: José Bonifácio

(ARENA/Minas Gerais) and Laerte Vieira (MDB/Santa Catarina). Two other deputies occupied leadership positions for two nonconsecutive terms: Freitas Nobre (PMDB/São Paulo) and Nélson Marchezan (PDS/Rio Grande do Sul). Finally, Deputy Alceu Colares (Rio Grande do Sul) occupied the leadership of PTB, and later PDT.[7] Therefore, the index of party leadership continuity in the Chamber, between 1970 and 1984, was 1.28 (or 23 divided by 18). If party vice-leaders are included in the analysis of continuity, then the index rises to 1.53 (or 241 divided by 157)—an average of one- and-one-half terms (or three years) per leader or vice-leader.

In spite of the professed stability of the authoritarian regime, particularly with the feature of a two-party system, leadership was in constant turmoil. The degree of continuity of party leaders and vice-leaders in the Congress was low. The fragmentation of the political parties and their fragilities, which was discussed in Chapter 1, was exacerbated rather than cemented under the authoritarian regime. Since parties were denied the opportunity to develop a stable leadership within the Congress, party fragmentation at the societal level was extended to the formal institutional level. In contrast to the U.S. experience where party fragility and fragmentation at the societal level was cemented through the institution of the Congress, in Brazil the structure of leadership in the Congress led to further fragmentation and instability of political parties. The professed intention of the regime was to democratize the process by providing equal opportunities to elected members so that they could assume leadership positions, and by eliminating corruption and manipulation of the many by the few. Instead, those measures led to the bureaucratization of the Congress, encouraged corruption and opportunism, and destabilized an already fragile political party system.

Regional Distribution of Party Leadership

The regional distribution of party leaders is illustrated in Table 2.1. In the Chamber, the regions of the country whose members occupied party leadership positions were, in descending order: the Southeast (11 terms), the South (8 terms), the Northeast (3 terms), and the Centralwest (1 term). No deputy representing a Northern state held party leadership between 1970 and 1984.

Based on the fact that most opposition (first MDB and later PMDB) deputies were elected in the Southeastern and Southern states—the most developed regions—it was no surprise to find that MDB/PMDB leaders were predominantly from the same regions: Southeast (three terms) and South (three terms). The same did not hold true for the pro-government parties (first ARENA and later PDS). Most ARENA/PDS deputies were elected in the Northeastern and Northern states; however, its leadership was predominantly from the Southeast (four terms) and South (two terms). Only one ARENA/PDS leader was from the Northeast.

In the Senate, the regions whose members occupied party leadership positions were, in descending order: the Southeast (seven terms), the Northeast (five terms), the North (two terms), and the South and Centralwest (one term each). The distribution of party leaders by party and by region reflected the regional strength of each party. Thus, ARENA/PDS leaders were predominantly from the Northeast and North (five terms altogether); and MDB/PMDB leaders were predominantly from the Southeast (five terms).

The pattern of party leadership in the Congress did little to strengthen the formation of nationally based political parties. Leadership instability and regional imbalances reinforced the weaknesses of the political parties.

Table 2.1

**Party Leaders in the National Congress of Brazil
by Region and Party**

		Chamber 1970-1984		Senate 1970-1986
Region:	No.:	Party:	No.:	Party:
North	0	none	2	ARENA, PDS(2)
Centralwest	1	PT(1)	1	ARENA(1)
Northeast	3	ARENA(1) PMDB(1) PP(1)	5	ARENA, PDS(3) MDB, PMDB(2)
Southeast	11	ARENA, PDS(4) MDB, PMDB(3) PTB(2) PDT(1) PT(1)	7	ARENA, PDS(2) MDB, PMDB(5)
South	8	ARENA, PDS(2) MDB, PMDB(3) PDT(2) PT(1)	1	PMDB(1)
Total	23	ARENA, PDS(7) MDB, PMDB(7) PDT(3) PT(3) PTB(2) PP(1)	16	ARENA, PDS(8) MDB, PMDB(8)

Institutional Leadership

The weakening of party leadership was enhanced by another mechanism embodied in the internal rules of the Congress. In their strive for a neutral, objective, and nonpolitical legislature, to fit their developmental rationalistic ideology, the military succeeded in isolating the party leadership from the control of the political, informational, financial, material, and staff resources available to the Congress. Those resources were instead placed under the control of a Committee of Directors named Comissão Diretora—most commonly referred to as the Mesa (Portuguese, for table or board).

The Mesa

The Mesa was entrusted with the institutional leadership of the Congress. Each house had its own Mesa, which was composed of seven members elected by each house separately. Mesa members included a president, two vice-presidents, and four secretaries. Additionally, four other members were elected to replace temporarily or permanently absent members. The Mesa was elected for one nonrenewable two-year term. Its composition reflected the strength of the parties in each house. In the Senate, the president of the Mesa until 1985 belonged to ARENA/PDS. In the Chamber, ARENA/PDS also monopolized the presidency until 1985.

Although the Mesa reflected the political composition of each chamber, it was expected to be neutral in the way it discharged its responsibilities. Collectively, the Mesa functioned as the board of directors of a corporation. It prepared the budget of each house and decided on its developmental priorities (i.e., staff, physical facilities, medical facilities, housing, motor vehicles, security, travel, and other benefits to which the congressmen and permanent legislative staff were entitled).

Regarding the legislative process, the Mesa prepared the daily agenda of legislative business and distributed legislative work among the various committees. Over time each member of the Mesa developed a specific jurisdiction in each house. The two most important positions in the Mesa were the president and the first-secretary.

The president represented the institution and spoke on its behalf both nationally and internationally. The president of the Chamber was second in line of succession to the presidency of the nation, after the vice-president. The president of the Senate presided over joint sessions of the Congress and was third in line of succession to the presidency.

In consultation with the party leaders, the presidents of each house established their chamber's agenda and presided over the sessions. Presidents recognized speakers and enforced discipline during debates. As the presiding officer, the president with the assistance of the Mesa secretary general acted as a parliamentarian in charge of interpreting and enforcing parliamentary rules and the internal rules of each chamber. All actions on behalf of the institution carried the signature of the Mesa president or the first-secretary.

The first-secretary was in charge of the staff and the administration of the entire chamber. His responsibility in each house included the recruitment and supervision of thousands of employees, a fleet of official cars, immense physical facilities including offices, houses, and apartments for the congressmen (as well as for some of the senior permanent staff), medical services, social clubs, allowances, travel, educational benefits, and various contracts for services and construction. In a sense, the first-secretary acted as the executive director of the Mesa, and of the house.

The Mesa commanded tremendous resources that enabled it to emerge as a power base within the Congress and consequently within the country as a whole—that is, until 1964 when the Constitution and the internal rules of each house placed serious constraints on the power of the Mesa. As mentioned previously, Mesa members were limited to nonrenewable two-years terms. Also, their leadership was officially separate from party leadership, under the guise of neutrality and objectivity. The president of Mesa was supposed to be a neutral arbitrator with as little partisan involvement as possible, faithfully supporting executive proposals. Both of these measures worked to undermine the potential of the Mesa as a power center within the National Congress of Brazil.

In spite of these limitations, however, membership in the Mesa was a sought-after privilege. Presidents and first-secretaries were prized positions with high visibility and strong potential for patronage and rewards.

In the Senate, during the sixteen-year period between 1970 and 1986, eight Mesas were elected. Of the eight presidents, only Senator Petrônio Portella (ARENA/Piauí) occupied the presidency twice.[8] The index of continuity was 1.14 (or 8 divided by 7). Three senators served as president of the Senate for only one term. Although not simultaneously, they also served as party leaders of ARENA/PDS: Filinto Müller (ARENA/Mato Grosso), Jarbas Passarinho (PDS/Pará), and Nilo Coelho (ARENA/PDS/Pernambuco).

Accomplished senators considered the presidency a worthwhile goal to pursue. However, it was not the ultimate goal for an energetic senator since it was only a temporary position. For an ambitious and energetic senator or deputy, appointment to an executive position at the ministerial level, or winning the election for governor of a state or mayor of a large city, remained the ultimate career objective. Indeed, the internal rules of the Congress did not discourage elected members from seeking other appointed or elected positions outside the Congress for fear of losing seniority or privileges. On the contrary, experience in other positions was advantageous to the enhancement of one's career within the Congress. Nevertheless, the presidency remained a highly competitive position. Only seven senators were able to occupy the eight positions between 1970 and 1986, a continuity index of 1.1.

The first-secretary of the Mesa was a position with a strong potential for patronage. In the Senate, none of the first-secretaries during this period held the position more than once. This was the least stable of the leadership positions in the Congress—a continuity index of 1.00 or absolute discontinuity. In addition to the seven Mesa positions available at each election, and the eight elections during this period (a total of fifty-six positions), two replacements also occurred (bringing the total of positions to fifty-eight). Of those positions, as many as fifty-one different senators occupied them. This represents a continuity index of only 1.14 (58 divided by 51). Thus, institutional leadership in the Senate was in constant change.

In the Chamber, during the fourteen-year period between 1970 and 1984, presidential continuity was substantially higher because of the tenacity of Deputy Flávio Marcílio (ARENA/PDS/Ceará), who occupied that position for three nonconsecutive two-year terms. His ability to be reelected was related to his good connections with the regime, his Northeastern power base and patronage, and the strong support he received from the secretary-general of the Chamber, Paulo Affonso Martins de Oliveira (who, between 1964 and 1988, was the kingmaker in the Chamber). The index of continuity for the presidency of the Chamber was 1.40 (7 divided by 5).

However, the first-secretary position in the Chamber followed a pattern similar to that of the Senate—a different deputy for each and every term. Once again, a continuity index of 1.00 or total discontinuity. In addition to the seven Mesa positions available at each election, and the seven elections during this period (a total of forty-nine positions), one replacement also occurred (bringing the total of positions to fifty). Of those, as many as forty-five different deputies occupied them. This represents a continuity index of only 1.1 (50 divided by 45). Thus, institutional leadership in the Chamber was in constant change.

Regional and Party Distribution of Institutional Leadership

The regional and party distribution of the institutional leaders of the Congress is illustrated in Table 2.2. In the Senate, there is overwhelming dominance of Northeastern ARENA/PDS senators. MDB/PMDB was represented in the Mesa in accordance with its numerical strength, but not in the most important positions. However, the Southeastern and Southern regions, where 60 percent of the population lived and 70 percent of the gross national product was produced, were poorly represented.

In the Chamber and in the Senate the Northeast was over represented, 40 and 51.7 percent, respectively. In the Senate, during the period between 1970 and 1986, the Southeast and South together occupied only 24.2 percent of the Mesa seats.

Among the parties, ARENA/PDS occupied 58 percent of the Mesa seats in the Chamber and 79 percent in the Senate. On the other hand, MDB/PMDB occupied only 21 percent in the Chamber and 36 percent in the Senate. In the Chamber, smaller parties occupied the remaining 6 percent of the positions.

Table 2.2

**Mesa Members in the National Congress of Brazil
by Region and Party**

Region:	No.:	%:	Party:	No.:	%:	Party:
	Chamber 1970-1984			Senate 1970-1986		
North	1	2.0	PMDB(1)	9	15.5	ARENA(8) PMDB(1)
Northeast	20	40.0	ARENA,PDS(13) PMDB(7)	30	51.7	ARENA,PDS,PFL(26) PMDB(4)
Centralwest	1	2.0	MDB(1)	5	8.6	ARENA,PDS(3) PMDB(2)
Southeast	16	32.0	ARENA,PDS(9) PMDB(5) PP(1) PDT(1)	7	12.1	ARENA,PDS(5) PMDB(2)
South	12	24.0	ARENA,PDS(7) PMDB(4) PDT(1)	7	12.1	ARENA,PDS(5) PMDB(2)
Total	50	100.0	ARENA,PDS(29)	58	100.0	ARENA,PDS, PFL(46) MDB,PMDB(18) MDB,PMDB(12) PDT(2) PP(1)

Committee Leadership

Legislative scholars have long demonstrated that, at least in a presidential system of government, the strength of a legislature is to a large extent tied to the strength of its committee system. What contributes to a strong committee system varies from one institution to another. In the U.S. Congress, Richard F. Fenno, Jr., and others have convincingly argued that the autonomy, specialization, professionalism, continuity, and norms of reciprocity characterize and contribute to a strong committee system.[9]

In the Brazilian context, the hallmark of the congressional system under the military regime was the weakness of its committees. As of 1967, congressmen could only be elected to leadership roles within the same committee for a nonrenewable term of two years. Other measures intended to weaken the committee system included restricting the time available for committee consideration of bills and lack of professional staff and budgets to hire staffs. Party leaders on the floor were empowered to override committee reports, and generally did. Finally, committee chairmen and vice-chairmen were not allocated to the majority party, as is the case in the U.S. Congress; instead, they were allocated among the parties in proportion to their representation within each house. This practice worked to depoliticize the committee and to make it more like a bureaucratic department rather than a political body working to achieve the program of the party in power. It diffused political responsibilities and undermined the ability of the committee to have its recommendations accepted by the plenary. These measures weakened the leadership of committees, kept them in constant rotation, and prevented them from developing subject specialization and expertise. Committees had no power base from which to initiate public policy or to control and check the actions of the executive. Indeed, oversight was entrusted to one specialized committee, and was rarely exercised.

With few exceptions, the degree of continuity within each committee was low. Some of the chairmen were able to come back to committee leadership after 1979, when the country returned to the multiparty system. As members of new parties, former chairmen were able to resume committee chairmanships without violating the rule.

In the Senate, the index of continuity for the chairmanship and vice-chairmanship of individual committees was 1.23. Four committees seemed to have experienced a higher degree of continuity: Constitution and Justice, Education and Culture, Foreign Affairs, and Labor. In the Chamber, the degree of discontinuity in committee chairmanships was even more evident; the index of continuity was 1.13. Because the rules restricted continued leadership on the same committee, an available means of maintaining leadership through the committee system was to change committees. Indeed, if we examine the Senate as an example, chairmanship and vice-chairmanship continuity across committees rises to 2.34 during the same period.

Regional and Party Distribution of Committee Leadership

The regional and party distribution of committee leaders is illustrated in Table 2.3. Committee chairmen were overwhelmingly ARENA/PDS members, and predominantly Northeastern. In the Senate, ARENA/PDS senators held ninety of 125 chairmanships (72 percent); Northeastern senators held fifty-six positions (44.8 percent). This distortion was less pronounced in the Chamber, where ARENA/PDS deputies held sixty-one of 103 positions (nearly 60 percent). Northeastern deputies held only thirty five positions (34 percent); Southeastern deputies held forty-two (41 percent). However, even in this region, ARENA/PDS deputies held twenty-one. Beginning with the election of 1978, PMDB/MDB and other GOPs were better represented in the Chamber than in the Senate.

CONTINUITY AND CHANGE IN CONGRESSIONAL LEADERSHIP

The regional distribution of all types of leaders is illustrated in Table 2.4. In the Senate, of all the leadership positions, the Northeastern senators received 42.7 percent of the positions, compared with the 20.8 percent of the Southeastern senators and the 11.5 percent of the Southern senators. In the chamber, the Northeastern deputies received 33.7 percent of all leadership positions, compared with the 35.7 percent of the Southeastern deputies and the 20.5 percent of the Southern deputies. In the Congress as a whole, 37.4 percent of the leadership positions were occupied by Northeastern members, 29.6 percent by Southeastern members, 16.8 percent by Southern members, 9.2 percent by Northern members, and 7.0 percent by Centralwestern members. The Southeastern and the Southern regions, where the opposition party has traditionally showed strength, were clearly underrepresented in terms of leadership.[10]

Table 2.3

Chairmen of Committees in the National Congress of Brazil by Region and Party

Region:	Chamber 1970-1984			Senate 1970-1986		
	No.:	%:	Party:	No.:	%:	Party:
North	3	2.9	ARENA(2) PMDB(1)	15	12.0	ARENA, PDS(10) MDB, PMDB(5)
Northeast	35	34.0	ARENA,PDS(28) MDB,PMDB(7)	56	44.8	ARENA,PDS(48) MDB,PMDB(5)
Centralwest	6	5.8	PMDB(6)	10	8.0	ARENA,PDS(8) PMDB(2)
Southeast	42	40.8	ARENA,PDS(21) MDB,PMDB(19) PP(1) PT(1)	29	23.2	ARENA,PDS(15) MDB,PMDB(14)
South	17	16.5	ARENA,PDS(10) MDB,PMDB(7)	15	12.0	ARENA,PDS(9) MDB,PMDB(6)
Total	103	100.0	ARENA,PDS(61) MDB,PMDB(40) PT(1) PP(1)	125	100.0	ARENA,PDS(90) MDB,PMDB(35)

Table 2.4

**All Leaders in the National Congress of Brazil
by Region**

	Chamber 1970-1984		Senate 1970-1986		Total	
Region:	No.:	%:	No.:	%:	No.:	%:
North	36	6.0	58	13.8	94	9.2
Northeast	204	33.7	179	42.7	383	37.4
Centralwest	25	4.1	47	11.2	72	7.0
Southeast	216	35.7	87	20.8	303	29.6
South	124	20.5	48	11.5	172	16.8
Total	605	100.0	419	100.0	1,024	100.0

The rotation and instability of congressional leadership and the underrepresentation of the most active and industrialized regions of the country weakened the image of the Congress as a representative institution and undermined its institutional capabilities to participate in the legislative process or to oversee the executive. From the regime's perspective these were good outcomes, since they led to both the partial resolution of one of the most important extrinsic problems of the presidential system of government—the conflict between the Congress and the President—and to the creation of a compliant Congress.

The measures introduced by the regime to weaken the Congress were not without supporters within the Congress. Some justified these measures in terms of their democratic and representational attributes and their benefit to the rank-and-file members. The weakening of congressional leadership allowed some of the newly elected members to assume leadership positions irrespective of their seniority. Some members believed it was in their interest to prevent the emergence of strong and durable leadership. New members felt that the system of rotation suited them better since it did not emphasize seniority. Their chances of assuming leadership positions were greater in the absence of entrenched leadership. Furthermore, a congress without strong leaders makes it easier for the newly elected not only to assume leadership positions internally, but also to deal directly with the executive and exchange their votes for services to themselves and to their constituencies.

Liberal-oriented members—another group within Congress that favored the rotation of leaders—had an inherent distrust of authority since it was associated with authoritarianism, arbitrariness, and corruption. Within the context of the imposed two-party system, any strengthening of congressional leaders meant the strengthening of the pro-government groups, specifically ARENA, and the weakening of the opposition party. As one PMDB member put it, "Before we consider strengthening congressional leaders, we need to ensure that the right ones are in power; otherwise we would be strengthening corruption."[11] Even before the advent of the authoritarian regime, liberal members recalled a time when the leadership of the Congress was concentrated in the hands of politically conservative bosses and how that concentration of power in the hands of the few worked against the interest of liberal causes, such as land reform and other social programs. During the authoritarian regime, liberals were always in the minority; therefore, they had no interest to strengthen a leadership that many of them viewed as reactionary and pro-military. In a Congress that had its roles severely restricted, the need for strong leaders was not perceived as important by the rank and file or the political parties. To make speeches in support or opposition of the government, which was the predominant role pursued by many of the members, leaders were not essential. Indeed it was detrimental, since it imposed restrictions on individual members' activities.

Even conservative politicians who typically favored strong leaders saw in the present system a fertile ground for favoritism and corruption and therefore supported it for the spoils it afforded them. Only when the Congress moved from reacting to policy initiatives of the executive to actively formulating public policy and overseeing the executive, did it begin to feel the need for a stronger leadership to ensure that decisions and compromises were reached among the various conflicting political forces represented within the legislative arena.[12]

Yet, in spite of high leadership discontinuity in a single office, some degree of overall leadership continuity evolved. In some instances the executive wanted to keep some of its loyal supporters in some type of leadership position as a reward for their services. Also, some ambitious political leaders found ways of building coalitions and developing power bases. The solution was the rotation from one leadership position to another, thus avoiding the legal restrictions against reelection. As an illustration, consider Senators Petrônio Portella, Filinto Müller, Nilo Coelho, and Jarbas Passarinho, all of whom occupied party leadership and institutional leadership positions.

In the Senate, where a smaller number of members exists (only sixty-nine in 1984), all of whom enjoy a term of eight years, considerable circulation occurs among the different types of leadership positions. Table 2.5 displays the index of continuity across different types of leadership. In the Chamber, the indexes of continuity for party and institutional leaders, party and committee leaders, and institutional and committee leaders were all low (1.22, 1.20, and 1.23, respectively). In the Senate, party and institutional leadership combined enjoyed an index of continuity of 1.83. Party and committee leadership combined enjoyed an index of continuity of 3.32. Institutional and committee leadership combined enjoyed an index of continuity of 3.31. Party, institutional, and committee leadership combined enjoyed an index of continuity of 3.41.

In the Chamber, a lower degree of continuity occurred across different types of leadership, if compared to the Senate (see Table 2.5). This was expected since membership in the Chamber was larger (479 members in 1984), and the deputies also enjoyed a shorter term of four years. Party and institutional leadership combined enjoyed an index of continuity of 1.22. Party and committee leadership combined enjoyed an index of continuity of 1.20. Institutional and committee leadership combined enjoyed an index of continuity of 1.23. Party, institutional, and committee leadership combined enjoyed an index of continuity of 1.45. Therefore, at best, the continuity of leadership in the Chamber reached 1.54, and that was the case of party leaders and vice-leaders.[13]

Table 2.6 illustrates the frequency distribution of continuity across different types of leadership. In the Senate, the maximum number of leadership terms (across types of leadership) enjoyed by any one member was nine terms. The majority of the senators that achieved leadership position occupied between two and five terms. The average leader occupied any one type of leadership for 3.41 terms, or nearly seven years.

Table 2.5

Index of Continuity Across Different Types of Leadership
in the National Congress of Brazil

Leadership:	Positions:	Occupants:	Continuity:
Chamber 1970-1984			
Party and Institutional	71	58	1.22
Party and Committee	125	104	1.20
Institutional and Committee	152	124	1.23
All Types	605	418	1.45
Senate 1970-1986			
Party and Institutional	169	92	1.83
Party and Committee	359	108	3.32
Institutional and Committee	308	93	3.31
All Types	419	123	3.41

Table 2.6

Frequency Distribution of Continuity Across Different Types of Leadership
in the National Congress of Brazil

Frequency	Chamber: 1970-1984	Senate: 1970-1986
9	-	1
8	-	-
7	-	6
6	3	5
5	4	18
4	19	21
3	35	23
2	74	31
1	283	18

In the Chamber, notwithstanding the high degree of instability, some deputies managed to occupy leadership positions for several terms. The maximum number of leadership terms (across types of leadership) enjoyed by any one deputy was six terms. However, the majority of the deputies that achieved leadership position occupied them for a single term only. The average leader occupied any one type of leadership for 1.45 terms, or nearly three years.

Although seniority was not supposed to be the criteria for leadership appointment, seniority was normally associated with the attainment of those positions. In the Senate, during the period between 1970 and 1986, the average seniority across different types of leadership was thirteen years. For the presidency and chairmanships, it was higher, fifteen years. On average, a senator need be reelected only once in order to aspire to the presidency of the Senate.

In the Chamber, the situation was similar. During the period between 1970 and 1984, the average seniority across different types of leadership was eight years. For the presidency it was twelve years, and for the chairmanships it was ten years. On average, a deputy need be reelected twice in order to aspire to the presidency of the Chamber.

Although the military regime succeeded in weakening leadership in the Congress by keeping the Congress in constant rotation through the manipulation of internal rules, the military did not entirely succeed in eliminating it. Rather than stressing specialization and careerism, members chose to circulate from one position to the other in order to conform to the rules.

Even within the constraints of the rules, a number of legislators were able to specialize in particular policy areas, such as education, labor, economics, finances, and foreign affairs. Indeed, even under the military regime, some members were invited to assume executive positions, such as minister of justice, of education, and others. Between 1985 and 1990, the various cabinets of President José Sarney included a significant number of ministers who received their training either as senators or as deputies.

The rotation of leadership had a negative impact on the ability of the Congress to participate in the policy process or to perform its many other constitutional responsibilities. Members who were constantly moving from one position to another saw no incentive in working hard or specializing in order to build a career. Leadership positions, especially within the Mesa, afforded many a one-time opportunity to indulge themselves and reward their supporters and cronies. Mismanagement of staff, services, privileges, and other material resources was rampant. Effective use of the permanent congressional bureaucracy was minimal. Neither the elected member nor the permanent staff had any incentive to engage in hard and innovative work. For the congressional member, it was more rewarding to do little, please supporters, and exploit whatever could be exploited without creating many enemies. For the staff member, the best strategy was to find a patron to work with and duck any initiative or innovative work that might create some sensitivity among the members or the staff. A good staff became the one that was rarely seen or heard. Staff with a developmental agenda were likely to face trouble, especially once their patrons had completed their two-year terms. Although this situation was tolerable under a two-party system, with a majority party in control during the military regime, it deteriorated into a state of anarchy with the return to the multiparty system and the decline of the power of the government party in the early 1980s. The bureaucratic infighting, which is examined in later chapters, increased. The absence of a majority party aggravated the bureaucratic conflict within the Congress.

The rotation of leaders reduced the ability of the Congress to negotiate agreements among its members. New and untested leaders were unable to persuade their colleagues to pursue agreed-upon policies. The difficulties the National Constituent Assembly (NCA) faced in reaching agreements, in spite of the dedication and personal qualifications of those who led the negotiations, was attributed to the absence of a strong permanent leadership. Agreements that were supposed to have been already concluded were being constantly renegotiated until the vote in the plenary session.

Without effective leadership, the power of the Congress to influence, change, or formulate public policy diminished. In a presidential system of government, the Congress was transformed into a debating society, where oratory and eloquence in delivering a speech counted more than the content of the speech. Even after 1985, although the Congress had regained much of its power, the business of legislation was still being conducted through executive decrees or provisional measures. The initiatives continued to be exercised by an executive whose competence, sincerity, and legitimacy was continuously being questioned by leading members of the Congress, even within his own party.

One important function of a legislature in a presidential system of government is to control the executive through the exercise of oversight. Yet a constantly rotating leadership was unable to discharge this function. The 1988 work of the CPI of the Senate in examining the flagrant corruption in the executive illustrated those difficulties. The investigatory committee faced problems in finding appropriate staff; its members faced constant intimidation; and its chairman, Senator Carlos Chiarelli (PFL/Rio Grande do Sul), was removed from his party leadership role under pressure from President Sarney.

Finally, the instability of leadership in the Congress had a profound negative impact on the consolidation of political parties. Enough has been written on the state of affairs of political parties in Brazil. Scholars have observed that parties in Brazil have been unstable and in constant flux. There have been many suggestions of how to fortify political parties and make them more stable. Some of these suggestions, such as changes in electoral laws, party fidelity, and other legal and political manipulation, have been tried during the military regime and have been rejected as failures. Less attention has been paid to how leadership in Congress could work as a mechanism to strengthen party leadership and consequently parties. Most solutions have envisioned a radical transformation of society as a condition for the emergence of strong and coherent political parties. Since such a radical transformation is not likely to occur in the near future, other mechanisms are needed. If the strengthening and consolidation of parties is a desired goal, perhaps the strengthening of congressional leadership could serve as a means of achieving that goal. The U.S. experience is a case in point. In spite of the weaknesses of the American political parties, the U.S. Congress assumes a leadership role in all areas of public policy. Congressmen attain their political agenda by working diligently as members of their parties in congressional committees. Congressional leaders and party leaders are coterminous. The role of those leaders is crucial in what the Congress is able to do.

However, whether a strong party system can make the presidential system of government work is doubtful. A strengthened political party system, through strengthened congressional leadership, would undoubtedly enable the Congress to play a more assertive role in the formulation of public policy. An assertive Congress, however, will exacerbate the tension between the executive and the legislature in a presidential system of government, a malaise that has plagued presidential systems of government in Latin America and that has produced many political instabilities.

There are many ways to strengthen the democratic institutions in Brazil. Organizing the legislature and providing it with the resources to discharge its constitutionally prescribed functions could serve to strengthen democratic institutions. In spite of its importance, very few political leaders have given the legislature the importance it has demanded. Indeed, the Constitution of 1988 stipulated that presidents of the Chamber of Deputies and the Federal Senate cannot be reelected for two consecutive terms, and it perpetuated the myth that the running of a political body such as the legislature was a neutral operation. A shift to a parliamentary system of government was another option that received serious attention but failed to materialize. It could surface once again.

NOTES

1. For the importance of leadership in the work of the U.S. legislature, see Wayne Francis, "Leadership, Party Caucuses, and Committees," *Legislative Studies Quarterly*, 10, no. 2 (May 1985), pp. 243-58; Barbara Sinclair, *Majority Leadership in the U.S. House* (Baltimore, Md.: Johns Hopkins University Press, 1983); John Pitney, Jr., "Leaders and Rules in the New York Senate," *Legislative Studies Quarterly*, 7, no. 4 (November 1982), pp. 491-506; Joseph Cooper and David W. Brady, "Institutional Context and Leadership Style: The House from Cannon to Rayburn," *American Political Science Review*, no. 75 (June 1981), pp. 411-25; and Robert L. Peabody, *Leadership in Congress* (Boston: Little, Brown & Co., 1976).

2. The classic work on the committee system in the U.S. Congress is Richard F. Fenno, Jr., *Congressmen in Committees* (Boston: Little, Brown & Co., 1973). See also Steven Smith, "The Central Concepts in Fenno's Committee Studies," *Legislative Studies Quarterly*, 11, no. 1 (February 1986), pp. 5-18; and Steven Smith and Christopher J. Deering, *Committees in Congress* (Washington: Congressional Quarterly Press, 1984).

3. The data on leadership in the Congress of Brazil were obtained from the annual reports of the presidents of the Federal Senate and the Chamber of Deputies, respectively. The biographic data were obtained from the data bases of Prodasen.

4. See *Regimento Interno* (Brasília: Câmara dos Deputados, 1986), and *Regimento Interno* (Brasília: Senado Federal, 1986).

5. See Petrônio Portella, *Tempo de Congresso, II* (Brasília: Senado Federal, 1980).

6. Regarding the importance of continuity to institutionalization, see Nelson W. Polsby, The Institutionalization of the U.S. House of Representatives," *American Political Science Review*, no. 62 (1968), pp. 144-168.

7. With the return to the multiparty system, two contesting groups that had previously belonged to Getúlio Vargas's PTB were struggling over the right to use this acronym. At first, Leonel Brizola's faction, of which Deputy Alceu Colares was a part of, won this right. However, a later court decision handed the use of the acronym to Ivete Vargas's faction. The latter, also a deputy, was a blood relative of Getúlio Vargas—her grandfather was Getúlio Vargas's brother. Brizola's group then opted for calling their party *Partido Democrático Trabalhista (PDT)*, or Democratic Labor Party.

8. Senator Portella was also able to occupy the position of leader of ARENA for two terms. His career culminated with his appointment as Minister of Justice in March 1979, a very important position under the military regime. He died in January 1980.

9. See Richard F. Fenno, Jr., *The Power of the Purse: Appropriation Politics in Congress* (Boston: Little, Brown & Co., 1966).

10. Rank-and-file representation in the Senate and Chamber also favored the Northeastern region. In the Senate, since each state was allowed three senators irrespective of the state's population, the Northeastern region, composed of nine of twenty-three Brazilian states (in 1984), enjoyed a representation of 39.2 percent. In the Chamber, because of the imposed ceiling on the number of representatives from a single state, the greatly populated states of the Southeastern region (only region affected) were undermined. As a result, the Northeastern region enjoyed a representation of 31.1 percent (also in 1984). For the distribution of congressional seats in relationship to number of population by ration see David Fleischer "O Regionalismo na Política Brasileira: As Bancadas Nordestinas na Câmara Federal (1983)," Nohlen (ed.), *Wahlen und Whalpolitik in Latinamerika* (Heidelberg: Esprint-Verlag, 1984), pp. 189-214; "The Constituent Assembly and the Transformation Strategy: Attempts to Shift Political Power from the Presidency to Congress," Graham and Wilson (eds.), *Contemporary Issues in Brazilian Public Policy* (Austin: University of Texas Press, 1990).

11. Tânia Bacelar, Secretary of Treasury of the state of Pernambuco, reacting to a first draft of this chapter at a conference in Recife, the state's capital. The conference was sponsored by the Joaquim Nabuco Foundation in May 1988.

12. See the speech of Senator Fernando Henrique Cardoso at the conference sponsored by the União Parlamentar Interestadual (UPI, Interstate Parliamentary Union—the Brazilian NCSL) and Associação Nacional para o Desenvolvimento das Atividades Legislativas (ANDAL, National Association for the Development of Legislative Activities—a national association for legislative staff), in Brasília, in April 1988. The conference is published in UPI and ANDAL, *A Nova Constituição e as Constituições Estaduais: Seminário* (Brasília: Senado Federal, 1988). In spite of his recognition of the importance of a strong leadership, Senator Cardoso did not support a strong legislative leadership. The 1988 Constitution maintained the same pattern of leadership as before.

13. It is ironic that a large institution such as the Chamber of Deputies, which requires strong leadership to manage its affairs, had the most unstable leadership. It was no accident that this political leadership vacuum in the Chamber was filled by the secretary-general of the Chamber, who for all practical purposes emerged as de facto leader. Since 1964, the office of the secretary-general, under the leadership of Paulo Affonso Martins de Oliveira, provided a needed continuity and imposed some semblance of rationality and order on both the staff and the elected members. Even until recently, the work of the Chamber was under the able leadership of Paulo Affonso, who also functioned as secretary-general of the NCA. Paulo Affonso managed to maintain his position even when the leadership of the Chamber changed from Flávio Marcílio, of the conservative PDS, to Ulysses Guimarães, of the progressive PMDB.

Chapter 3

Congressional Staff: Evolution and Structure

The main determinants of congressional behavior in Brazil between 1964 and 1985 were the authoritarian regime and the various policies and actions it pursued and implemented and the type of presidentialism under which it operated. Yet the structure of the Congress had an important influence on the way it conducted its business and the role it came to play.

As can be seen from the examination in Chapter 2 of congressional leadership, it has been observed that the structure of the Congressional leadership and the functions of the elected members contributed to (1) leadership instability; (2) the weakening of the control and coordination of Congress's own operations; and (3) the undermining of the development of the necessary expertise and power base to bargain with the executive. This chapter investigates the evolution and structure of the congressional staff and the role they came to play in managing the institution and helping it in its various functions. To avoid duplication, these agencies are discussed from the Federal Senate's perspective only. The Chamber of Deputies developed a similar structure, and its units perform similar functions, with few exceptions.

During the past quarter of a century, the study of legislative staffing in the United States at the federal and state levels became a legitimate activity for congressional and legislative scholars.[1] At present there is an almost general recognition of the central role played by legislative staff in the legislative process. Some decry this development as being detrimental to the democratic system of government and to the proper role of the legislative institution. Others see it as a necessary and welcome development, since it allows the legislature to be kept informed about the complexity of contemporary public policy issues that it considers.

For those who view the development and expansion of legislative staff with apprehension, their main emphasis is on the experience of the U.S. Congress. According to this group, the expansion of staffing at the congressional level, in both committee and personal staffing, has created a legislative bureaucracy unknown to and uncontrolled by the electorate. This bureaucracy plays an important role in the determination of public policy by filtering the information that a member receives from his constituencies or about any public policy issue under discussion. To justify its existence, this bureaucracy is inundating congressmen with information, leading them to undertake public policy initiatives just for the sake of building the congressmen's legislative resumes, and forcing them to be involved in minute administrative and implemental details that are better left to the executive bureaucracy. The activities of these "unelected representatives" have transformed the Congress from an arena for the debate of general public policy to an institution bogged down in technical details of legislation.[2]

Taken together with the politicizing of the federal bureaucracy in recent years, the relationship between the executive and the Congress has been strained, and in many instances a political impasse with regard to foreign policy, budgeting, and other policy areas has developed. According to this group, a leaner congressional staff that would restore to the elected member his role as a legislator, advocate, and integrator of public policy would be the proper approach to follow.

On the other hand, those who view the development of legislative staff more positively see the phenomena as a necessary mechanism to correct the imbalance that has developed between the powers of the President and those of the Congress.[3] The advances in science and technology and the need to act in a timely and appropriate manner to societal problems requires Congress to strengthen its informational capabilities. This increased information supplied by a loyal professional staff, enables the Congress to respond to presidential initiatives, to participate on equal footing with the executive in the initiation of public policy, to escape the hold of specialized interest groups, and to respond to constituency concerns. Without the staff, it is argued, the Congress has no ability to exercise its oversight function over an executive bureaucracy that has been continuously expanding its activities and areas of concern since the New Deal era.

Regardless of the merits of the arguments presented by each side, the fact remains that legislative staff, at least in the United States, are an empirical phenomena that has attracted scholarly concern, and whose positive and negative impact have been subjected to scholarly analysis. The central issues in this debate are not whether or not to have legislative staff, but rather how much? What type of staff? How should it be structured and kept under the proper political control of the elected member?[4] The issue of political control, partisanship, and staff neutrality is of special importance because the manner in which these concerns are resolved determines the extent to and the manner in which the staff plays its role in the legislative process.

Although congressional staff in Brazil are also an empirical phenomena, with significant implications as to the way the Congress has been able to exercise its various powers under the constitutional order of the authoritarian regime, they have attracted no scholarly attention.[5] With the adoption of a new Constitution in 1988, bestowing on the Congress a central role in the policy process, the likely organization, orientation, and role of the legislative staff has become even more central to our understanding of the role of the Congress and how it has discharged or is likely to discharge its role.

BRAZILIAN CONGRESSIONAL STAFF IN A HISTORICAL PERSPECTIVE

In the National Congress of Brazil, legislative staff development can be divided into four distinct stages: the Competitive period, from 1946 to 1960; the Welfare period, from 1960 to 1970; the Institutional period, from 1970 to 1985; and the Political period, from 1985 to 1988.

The Competitive Period (1946-1960)

During the Imperial and Old Republic periods, congressional needs for legislative staff were minimum. The principal work was the recording of the minutes of the sessions and for that purpose the legislature made use of a handful of part-time executive employees.

After 1946, a stable legislative staff began to develop. The creation of a separate staff to serve the legislature came about as a result of two important developments: the establishment of a separate and strong Congress and the general civil service reforms initiated by President Getúlio Vargas in 1938. The Constitution of 1946 established a presidential system of government, with a Congress that was separate and independent from the executive and that exercised important legislative and budgetary functions. Vargas's civil service reform called for the creation of a merit career bureaucracy to lead the economic development of the country. Both of these developments provided the legislature with the need and the justification to begin developing its own staff.

From the beginning, legislative staff development in Brazil followed the pattern established for the executive bureaucracy, with hierarchical organization and staff permanency. The two most important offices that were created in both houses were the General Secretariat of the Mesa, and the General Directorate. The secretary-general, head of the General Secretariat, was responsible for all legislative activities, such as providing secretarial support for the Mesa, recording the minutes of the sessions, and organizing the daily agenda of the president and members of the Mesa. The director-general, head of the General Directorate, was responsible for all administrative matters, such as personnel and finances. The director-general, like his counterpart in the executive ministries, headed a bureaucracy that included departments for personnel, budgeting, finances, accounting, housekeeping, security, and so on.[6]

During this phase, the Federal Senate and the Chamber of Deputies, together, had only a few hundred employees, most of them clerical or custodial staff. Although some were recruited through examinations, most were appointed to their jobs as a result of their political connections and networks of friendship or as a reward for their political support. Since most of the staff worked in secretarial, clerical, and custodial services, working for the legislature was not a sought-after occupation. In the culturally rich and resort-type environment of Rio de Janeiro, ambitious people sought employment in the private or public sector, or decided to run family-owned farms or businesses.

By the time Congress moved from Rio de Janeiro to the new capital, Brasília, in 1960, legislative staff assistance with any direct relationship to the legislative work of the Congress was limited to the individual and institutional support that the office of secretary-general provided and to a small core of reference, legal, and library clerks. Most of the work was done by the members themselves, many of whom had legal and professional backgrounds. A legislator depended on his own efforts and those of his friends and associates and on advice and instruction from his political party in order to conduct his work. Professional staff with any policy input, as understood in the present U.S. context, was yet to be developed.

The Welfare Period (1960-1970)

Brasília was built in the wilderness of the Centralwest region of Brazil. It had few amenities and none of the infrastructure that the members of Congress were accustomed to in Rio de Janeiro, Brazil's, and perhaps South America's, cultural capital. Housing, hospitals, transportation, schools, social clubs, and restaurants were all scarce or nonexistent. Brasília offered little to those who were accustomed to living near the rich cultural and social environments of Copacabana and Ipanema beaches.

With the move of the Congress to the new capital in 1960, a new staffing pattern developed. Few members were willing to relocate to Brasília. Indeed, for several years, many of the congressmen lived in Rio de Janeiro and commuted to Brasília only to conduct business. If the members were to relocate, they had to be given a strong incentive to do so. The incentives came in the form of a set of services and benefits that made it attractive and profitable to relocate. All of these services and benefits required hiring additional legislative staff.

During this period, in addition to the general incentives for development offered at the time, such as land sold at symbolic prices, Congress began providing its members and its staff what amounted to a welfare package. Housing accommodations in furnished apartment complexes owned by the Senate and Chamber were provided to senators and deputies, respectively. Even the holders of key staff positions lived in some of these apartments. To compensate for the lack of appropriate medical facilities, the Congress established its own medical services to give assistance free of charge to the members, the staff and their families as well. The inappropriate and deficient city transportation system was compensated for by the creation of a central motor pool in each congressional house, to serve not only the members and the staff, but in time, their families as well. Special clubs and facilities were built and run by the Congress to provide members and staff with recreation and other services.

For every service to be provided, a corresponding staff unit was created to run it directly or to supervise those who were contracted to provide the services. For example, an engineering unit was established to provide maintenance for the existing building and grounds facilities and to supervise new construction.

Within a decade, the number of employees directly hired by the Congress jumped from the hundreds to the thousands. Ironically, the newly hired employees had nothing to do with the legislative and political activities of the Congress. Instead, most of them were low-level bureaucrats working in the maintenance, domestic, housekeeping, and technical areas.

The more staff that was hired to provide for these services, the greater the size of the legislative community, and therefore, the greater the need for additional staff to serve the additional people. A vicious cycle was created that could only be satisfied by the continuous expansion of the legislative bureaucracy. This vicious cycle continued until the leadership in the Congress shifted to the PMDB after 1985.

The Institutional Period (1970-1985)

This is the most significant period in terms of its impact on legislative staff development in Brazil. During this period, the Congress began a systematic and ambitious program of equipping itself with permanent and centrally organized professional staff units to attend to its institutional needs. It also initiated a human resources policy to train its staff in various areas of management and legislative work, both in Brazil and in the United States.

The orientation and direction of the new legislative agencies were shaped to a large extent by the executive vision, and by the principles of the new political system the authoritarian regime was establishing.[7] By 1967, the executive had completely overhauled the executive bureaucracy, adopting a new personnel system and systematizing labor laws that governed permanent and temporary employees in the public sector. In theory at least, the new legislation reaffirmed the principle that all appointments to government jobs were to be in accordance with the merit system. The purpose of this administrative reform plan was to create a capable, professional, and merit-oriented techno-bureaucracy to lead and implement the economic development efforts of the country. The new rational order that the authoritarian regime sought to establish claimed that politics, especially partisan and clientele politics, had no place. Although the Congress was allowed to continue functioning, it could do so only if it subscribed to this rationalistic, antipolitical ideology of the regime. As we have seen earlier, when the Congress confronted the executive, it was either suspended, or further restrictions were imposed upon it.

The thrust of the legislative staffing reforms introduced during this period was to equip the legislature with the institutional capabilities to process the information received from the executive. Various administrative offices in existence were strengthened and new important units were created. The General Secretariat of the Mesa was strengthened and given access to important resources. Undersecretariats were created to deal with specific aspects of the legislative process, such as the monitoring and coordinating of proposed legislation. The library units in both houses were expanded and their reference, research, and information staff were strengthened. Units providing services to the members and staff were also strengthened. Several new units were added to improve the image of the whole institution and to provide it with capabilities to generate, store, and retrieve information relevant to the Congress.

The strengthening of the institutional staff and information capabilities of the Congress provided congressional leaders and their senior staff with tremendous opportunities to provide employment to their family members, relatives, and supporters—a practice that became so widespread in the 1980s that it elicited criticism and ridicule from the public and the press.

According to the internal rules of the Senate, its administrative structure is divided as follows (see Figure 3.1):

I. *Comissão Diretora*, often referred to as the *Mesa*
II. Higher Advisory Units
   - General Secretariat of the Mesa
   - *Assessoria* or Advisory Office
   - Public Communications Secretariat
   - *Consultoria Geral* or General Counsel Office
   - *Auditoria* or Audit Office
III. Supervised Units
   - Prodasen, the Center for Data Processing
   - *Centro Gráfico* (Cegraf), the Printing Shop
IV. Special Unit
   - Senate Office in Rio de Janeiro City
V. Higher Planning and Control Unit
   - Administrative Council
VI. Central Unit for Coordination and Implementation
   - General Directorate, which is composed of:
       — Administrative Secretariat
       — Legislative Secretariat
       — Documentation and Information Secretariat
       — Special Services Secretariat

One of the most important innovations was the creation of Prodasen. Prodasen and Cegraf have no equivalent in the Chamber. Although these two agencies are funded and supervised by the Senate, they perform a great deal of services for the Chamber as well.

Figure 3.1

The Administrative Structure of the Federal Senate

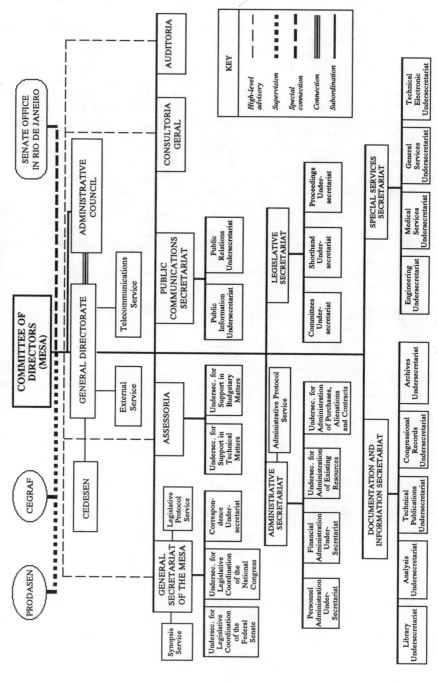

General Secretariat of the Mesa

The General Secretariat has two services, three undersecretariats, and the secretary-general's office. It is responsible for the coordination and execution of all floor activities. These responsibilities include keeping track of all legislation that is being voted on, the schedule for voting and correct procedures, informing legislators on the status of bills that have been voted or will be voted on, issuing the daily agenda, assisting members of the Mesa in the proper   procedures and agenda to be followed during sessions, undertaking follow-up measures regarding the legislation that has been acted on (sending it to the President of the Republic for ratification or to the Chamber for review), and the recording of roll calls.

Assessoria—Advisory Office

The *Assessoria* is a central unit composed of highly specialized advisors who can be used by individual senators, committees, and the administration. On administrative matters it reports to the director-general. Substantively, it works in close cooperation with the Mesa and the secretary-general. In 1988, there were more than 110 advisors in the Senate and approximately forty-five in the Chamber.

The *Assessoria* is headed by a director who is appointed by the Mesa from among the permanent advisors. The advisors are recruited on a competitive basis through open written examinations and are highly remunerated. Advisors are grouped informally by areas of specialization, such as economic analysis, social problems, and education. Formally, two undersecretariats exist:

- Undersecretariat for Support in Technical Matters
- Undersecretariat for Support in Budgetary Matters

The former does research upon technical and legal matters, while the latter is responsible for research related to budgetary matters. Since the early 1980s, the Undersecretariat for Support in Budgetary Matters has developed considerable autonomy. It has undertaken a number of initiatives to build its own specialized staff and to expand its role in the evaluation of the budget.

In consultation with the director of the *Assessoria*, advisors are assigned to work with individual senators, party leaders, and committee chairmen. As tenured staff members, the advisors are expected to give objective advice and analysis only when requested. Informally, however, they help members write their speeches and   prepare draft legislation for members they personally support.

During the authoritarian regime, the formal role of the advisors was limited to writing summaries of proposed legislation, with little analysis or recommendation. However, since 1985, and, more recently, since 1988, the functions of the *Assessoria* were expanded, and its budget and other resources were quadrupled. Chairmen of committees can now request their advisors from among the *Assessoria*, and they are beginning to rely on them for substantive advice in public policy areas. In accordance with Senate resolution 210/1988, the *Assessoria* was given the resources to contract for services from the outside and to issue bulletins for the press, radio, and television on the substance of legislation under consideration. The role of the Undersecretariat for Support in Budgetary Matters was expanded to enable the Congress to discharge its new role in the budget process.

The same resolution, however, reconfirmed its corporate orientation by requiring that only the permanent advisors themselves can serve as directors of the *Assessoria* or of its undersecretariats. The relationship between the advisors and the elected members is tenuous, and measures encouraging trust and confidence are yet to develop. Nevertheless, the *Assessoria* is the "brain" of the Senate and has the potential of providing congressmen with important assistance and valuable information.

In the Chamber of Deputies, given the small size of its *Assessoria*,[8] and the relatively large number and political diversity of deputies to be served, the role of the *Assessoria* has been less pervasive. Only the leaders have access to the services of the advisors. Many deputies have developed their own expertise and discharge their legislative role without much assistance from the advisors. After the adoption of the Constitution of 1988, the role of the advisors began to be seriously debated and reevaluated. There is a new recognition of their potential contribution to the legislative process. A move to increase their number and to decentralize the Chamber's *Assessoria*, and attach them to the permanent committees, was underway in 1989.

Public Communication Secretariat

The responsibilities of the Public Communications Secretariat are to plan, manage, and control the public information on Senate activities. Its responsibilities are divided among two undersecretariats:

- Public Information Undersecretariat
- Public Relations Undersecretariat

The main role of the Public Information Undersecretariat is to prepare the Senate's part of the *Hora do Brasil*, a nationwide, legally mandated radio broadcast about the activities of the government. The Senate and the Chamber have fifteen-minute periods in which to discuss their activities. During the authoritarian regime, the secretariat was in charge of improving the public image of the Congress by preparing press and radio releases.

The Public Relations Undersecretariat is in charge of programs of official visits to the Senate by outside authorities. It organizes and services special events, receptions, and parties. It prepares letters of congratulations and condolences on behalf of the president of the Senate and runs Senate tours.

Consultoria Geral—General Counsel Office

The *Consultoria Geral* is comprised of the general-counselor and a handful of advisors, all of whom are lawyers. Under the general-counselor's guide, the *Consultoria Geral* assists and advises the administration in legal matters. It examines propositions and requests in regard to administrative reforms and projects as well as contracts with other parties and gives its legal position. It advises the administration on lawsuits against the Senate and ensures that its actions conform with the law. In reality, the work of the *Consultoria*, which operates closely with the director-general, is to provide the Senate with legal advice on employee rights and interpretation of labor legislation affecting employees.

Auditoria—Audit Office

The *Auditoria* is a relatively small office, composed of the auditor and his clerical staff. It is responsible for auditing the execution of the Senate budget. It analyzes the financial procedures involving Senate funds and expenses, looking closely at the services that are contracted out and at the administrative procedures regarding Senate assets.

The *Auditoria* is responsible for internal auditing. Under the authoritarian regime, the *Auditoria* superficially discharged its responsibilities in reviewing the accounts. It rubber-stamped the final accounts without any critical analysis. After 1988, the *Auditoria* began to critically evaluate the accounts and to conduct management evaluation and organizational development studies.

Centro Gráfico (Cegraf)—The Printing Shop

The *Centro Gráfico do Senado Federal* (Cegraf) enjoys an administrative status similar to that of Prodasen. It is also supervised by the Senate's Supervising Council, whose president and vice-president are also the first-secretary and director-general of the Senate.

Cegraf is responsible for printing and publishing legislative journals, documents, books, periodicals, and other materials. Some of its most important pieces are the *Diário do Congresso Nacional*, or Congressional Record, and the *Revista de Informação Legislativa*, or Legislative Information Journal. Although Cegraf is supervised by the Senate, and operates within the Senate's budget, it serves the needs of the Chamber as well. Cegraf's activities are implemented and coordinated by its executive director.

Senate Office in Rio de Janeiro City

Although the National Congress moved to Brasília in the early 1960s, the Senate still maintains a representation office in Rio de Janeiro. The official justification for its existence relies on historical factors and on Rio de Janeiro's cultural and economic importance. For one thing, almost all international flights arrive and leave the country through *Galeão*, Rio de Janeiro's international airport. Most of the Senate office's activities involve the reception and departure of congressmen, congressional staff, and visiting international guests. Furthermore, many, if not all, international guests include Rio de Janeiro in their visiting program. However, a great deal of controversy exists over the necessity of this office and whether official justifications, or rather unofficial motivations, such as the personal interests of those who work there and those who use it (specially the senators from that state), keep it from being abolished.

Administrative Council

The Administrative Council is presided over by the director-general, with the participation of the secretary-general of *Assessoria* and the directors of the following entities: Public Communications Secretariat, Administrative Secretariat, Legislative Secretariat, Documentation and Information Secretariat, and Special Services Secretariat. This council is used for deliberative and advisory purposes regarding administrative matters. The director-general prepares the agenda and calls the meetings.

General Directorate

The director-general, the head of the General Directorate, is at the top of the administrative hierarchy. He is responsible for the coordination of all administrative services. As has been pointed out, he acts as vice-president of the supervising councils of Prodasen and Cegraf. He also serves as a link between the Mesa and the various administrative units and ensures that the Senate staff is working in accordance with the direction of the elected members.

The director-general coordinates a huge bureaucracy that discharges various responsibilities. In order to perform all the administrative activities involved, from personnel administration to medical assistance, the director-general is assisted by two services—a center for staff development and four secretariats (each of the secretariats contains three to five undersecretariats).

Administrative Secretariat

The Administrative Secretariat is in charge of planning, executing, and supervising the administration of personnel, finances, assets, and inventories. It is composed of the following:

- Administrative Protocol Service
  - Personnel Administration Undersecretariat
  - Financial Administration Undersecretariat
  - Undersecretariat for the Administration of Existing Resources
  - Undersecretariat for the Administration of Purchases, Alienations, and Contracts

Legislative Secretariat

The Legislative Secretariat provides technical assistance to the Senate floor and committee meetings. It works in close association with the secretary-general and complements the services provided by the General Secretariat. It is composed of the following:

- Committees Undersecretariat
- Shorthand Undersecretariat
- Proceedings Undersecretariat

The Committees Undersecretariat attends to the needs of the committees by scheduling the meetings, ensuring that space is available, recording committee meetings, and performing other "housekeeping" tasks for the committees.

The Shorthand Undersecretariat records all floor meetings of the Senate, the joint sessions of the Congress, and, upon request, committee meetings, seminars, conventions, and other events. The shorthand notes are word processed and made available to the Proceedings Undersecretariat which revises them and prepares the final drafts of session meetings. The Proceedings Undersecretariat is also in charge of preparing the daily agenda and of reviewing the published *Diário do Congresso Nacional*.

Documentation and Information Secretariat

The Documentation and Information Secretariat is in charge of coordinating and operating the Senate information systems. It is composed of five undersecretariats, which are responsible for different aspects of the information system:

- Library Undersecretariat
- Analysis Undersecretariat
- Technical Publications Undersecretariat
- Congressional Records Undersecretariat
- Archives Undersecretariat

Special Services Secretariat

This administrative unit is responsible for planning, executing, and supervising engineering, medical, security, transportation, cleaning, and electronics services. It is divided into four undersecretariats:

- Engineering Undersecretariat
- Medical Services Undersecretariat
- General Services Undersecretariat
- Technical Electronic Undersecretariat

Prodasen—The Center for Data Processing

The *Centro de Informática e Processamento de Dados do Senado Federal* (Prodasen) is supervised by the Senate's Supervising Council. Prodasen is responsible for the planning, elaboration, and implementation of information systems necessary to fulfill the legislative and administrative needs of the Senate. The Supervising Council establishes the priorities, but the execution of the tasks and the general maintenance of the hardware, software, and services are carried out by Prodasen's executive director.

The Political Period (1985-1988)

As mentioned previously, with the maturing of the *abertura*, and with the return to full-party politics, the institutional leadership of both the Federal Senate and the Chamber of Deputies went to the opposition party, PMDB. Indeed, as early as 1982, PMDB began to occupy more of the Mesa positions and to exert some influence on staffing decisions.

The return to open-party politics spurred the call for new staffing patterns so as to serve the interests of the party or the individual legislators. Since all legislative staffs were centrally organized and enjoyed job security, the question arose as to who would control these centrally organized units. The personnel system adopted by the Congress gave the political leadership some flexibility in appointing their senior advisors and chief administrative officers on a political basis, rather than on a strict merit system. During the 1970s, when the Congress was under the absolute control of the ARENA and its successor, the PDS, the political needs of each new leadership were accommodated by appointing more and more people to the legislative bureaucracy. With the return to open-party politics, beginning in the mid-1980s, conflict among the various political blocs was translated into conflict over the control of the central staff.

Another manifestation of the political orientation of this period was the demand of senators and deputies to have control over the hiring and firing of their personal staff. In the Senate, although the senators had long enjoyed the support of personal staff (e.g., administrative assistants, secretaries, drivers), they had to choose their staff from among the Senate's permanent staff. Since 1986, senators have been allowed to appoint up to three assistants from outside the permanent staff, if they chose to do so. However, since the existing system encourages the use of the permanent staff, many still resort to choosing from among their numbers. Permanent staff are more experienced and well integrated within the staff network of the legislature, and, therefore, are more useful to the congressmen.

Resorting to permanent staff has the additional advantage of costing the member no additional money, while ensuring the service of additional staff. Yet, some senators have found it more profitable to hire people from their state to look after the interests of their constituency.

In the Chamber, the personal staff allocation is very meager—a secretary and a driver only. Therefore, few members are able to hire a professional staff to help them. Abuses associated with the allocation of the member's personal staff budget have occurred. For example, some deputies have resorted to unethical maneuvering, such as hiring one person officially, but having his or her salary split into two or three different no-show employees. This is an area of potential embarrassment for some members.

Finally, one significant political manifestation of this phase is the increased attention being given to the staff and information needs of the committees. Specialized staff within the *Assessoria* began to emerge in the early 1980s to serve the needs of the Committee of Constitution and Justice and the Joint Budget Committee. Since 1985, the professional staff of the Joint Budget Committee has been strengthened and has been given autonomy from the *Assessoria*.[9]

INFORMATION SYSTEMS AND STAFFING IN THE NATIONAL CONGRESS

The centerpiece of the efforts of the National Congress to build its staff and information capabilities was the establishment in 1970 of the *Centro de Informática e Processamento de Dados do Senado Federal* (Prodasen), or Center for Data Processing of the Federal Senate. Prodasen was to spearhead the reform movement of the Senate's administrative operations to provide the Congress with up-to-date, timely, and relevant information that would enable the members to exercise their constitutional function.[10]

Prodasen's evolution can be divided into four distinct phases: the Technological phase (1970-1975), the Integrative phase (1975-1982), the Consolidation phase (1982-1985), and the Political phase (1985-present).

The Technological Phase (1970-1975)

The mission of Prodasen was to acquire the necessary resources and technologies to collect, process, store, and retrieve information relevant to the improvement of the efficiency and effectiveness of the legislative process. [11]

Prodasen's broad-ranging mission was not intended to meet the immediate needs of the Congress (for all practical purposes, the Congress during those years was excluded from any meaningful participation in public policy or in overseeing the executive); instead, it was given a broad mandate to create the necessary conditions for congressional participation in public policy, executive oversight, and modernization of the legislative process and of the internal administration of the legislature itself. Prodasen's services during this phase were extended and made available not only to the Congress and its members and staff, but also to the federal executive, the courts, state governments, private organizations, and individuals. In effect, though it was under the supervision of the Senate, Prodasen was to function as a national data base.

In his first memo to the president of the Senate, the executive director of Prodasen convincingly argued for Prodasen's autonomy from the administration of the Senate.[12] He pointed out that to attract skilled people to staff Prodasen, a special salary scale needed to be devised. Furthermore, he said he believed that since the activities of Prodasen were distinguishable from those performed by the regular legislative staff, it should be run more like a public corporation rather than be subjected to rules and regulations under which the regular bureaucracy of the Congress operated. The innovative role it was supposed to play, and the unchartered path it was supposed to navigate, necessitated maximum managerial and financial autonomy to contract for services, decide on priorities, and promote the development of the new technology. Resolution No. 58/72, of the Committee of Directors of the Federal Senate, which was approved by the full Senate, granted Prodasen all that its executive director had requested.

Prodasen was to operate outside the normal structure of the Federal Senate and to be supervised by a Supervising Council appointed by the Senate's Mesa. The members of this council could come from within the Senate or from the outside. As of 1980, two of the four council members were supposed to represent the Chamber of Deputies. In fact, the Chamber never sent representatives, since it objected to the location of Prodasen within the Senate rather than as a truly joint unit. The Supervising Council was therefore actually dominated by the first-secretary of the Senate, who was the council's president, or his designee. Since this council served for only a two-year nonrenewable term, its supervisory role was at the general policy level only. For its day-to-day operations, Prodasen operated autonomously under its executive director. The Supervising Council was utilized at the discretion of the executive director and usually during the budget season to help secure necessary funds.

Resolution No. 58/72, which established Prodasen, also established the Documentation and Information Secretariat within the Senate so as to link Prodasen to the legislative process. This unit was charged with planning, supervising, and coordinating all the information needs of the Senate, including the Senate library. The Documentation and Information Secretariat, however, had no formal direct method to coordinate its work with Prodasen, since administratively it was subordinated to the General Directorate of the Senate. Indeed, Prodasen and the Information Secretariat functioned as parallel organizations, with minimal functional coordination.[13]

This phase of Prodasen realized several important technological achievements. Either through contract with IBM or other consultants, or through internal resources of the Senate or Prodasen, several data bases were developed from scratch. They can be divided into two areas: the *Sistema de Informações do Congresso* (SICON), or Congressional Information System, and *Sistema Administrativo Integrado* (SAI), or Integrated Administrative System.[14]

During its technological phase, Prodasen was able to institutionalize itself as a viable and permanent staff unit within the Senate. It also initiated and developed important basic data bases relevant to the Congress and its administration.

Prodasen was able to recruit a professional staff and create interrelationships among various governmental and private agencies for the purpose of creating essential data bases. Legislatures in the United States were able to recruit professional staff, already in abundance, from the private sector and to use data bases developed by commercial outfits. The National Congress of Brazil, however, had to create both the staff and the data bases. The autonomy that Prodasen enjoyed during this phase and the weakness of the Congress worked to provide it with the needed resources and time to work on long-range projects, with little immediate benefit to the Congress. The weakness of the Congress enabled the specialists to undertake long-range planning and to acquire and institutionalize the necessary technology. By 1975, Prodasen had installed seventeen terminals in the Congress, fifteen terminals in the federal executive branch, and twelve terminals in various public and trade organizations throughout the states.[15]

The Integrative Phase (1975-1982)

The Integrative phase was indeed an expansionist period. From the beginning, it attempted to capture those functions of Prodasen that were neglected during the Technological phase and to expand on those initiatives already started. However, it was integrative in the sense that its leadership came from the legislative staff and its system development emphasized legislative priorities.

In 1975, under the leadership of Eduardo Jorge Caldas Pereira, Prodasen began to acquire new functions and new directions.[16] In a series of memos to the president of the Senate, the new executive director of Prodasen outlined the priorities that Prodasen should address (all of these priorities were eventually formalized by the Committee of Directors and the full Senate, through Resolution No. 57/76).

The new priorities included a redefinition of goals and priorities, with an emphasis on staff recruitment and training, and the development of new systems to meet legislative needs and priorities.[17]

In addition to fundamental revisions and updating of the existing data bases, Prodasen's Integrative phase saw the development of several new data bases within SICON and SAI. The data bases that were added to SICON during this phase include the following: The *Sistema de Disseminação de Informações* (SDI), or Information Dissemination System, used by the various data bases in SICON to select pertinent information contained in bills and to distribute the relevant information to individual legislators in accordance with previously established profiles of the members. The *Sistema de Endereçamento Parlamentar* (SEP) was developed to assist legislators in keeping track of their mail, especially their constituency mail. The *Sistema de Orçamento* were budget systems which included figures of the budget as presented by the executive and passed by the Congress since 1980. The *Biografia dos Senadores* (BSEN) system contained important biographic information on those who served in the Federal Senate since Brazil's Imperial period. The *Sistema de Composição de Texto do Cegraf,* Cegraf's word processing system, transmitted information for printing from Prodasen to Cegraf.

During this phase, Prodasen also developed several systems that were intended to improve and modernize the administrative services of the Congress. Programs under SAI computerized many administrative activities in the Congress, such as personnel records, payroll, accounts, inventory, retirement, and other benefits.[18]

In addition to the systems developed internally, Prodasen hooked up with a number of data bases collected by other government agencies.

Undoubtedly, this phase marked the golden era of Prodasen in terms of programs it developed for both the members and the Senate administration. This phase also represents the high point of human and technical resources available in the institution. Competent staff were recruited and trained. New equipment was purchased, and Prodasen's physical capabilities were expanded to accommodate its staff, which was more than 200 people by the end of this phase. Computer terminal purchases increased to seventy-nine in the Senate, six in the Chamber, twenty-two throughout the federal agencies located in the capital, and nine in other states.

The Consolidation Phase (1982-1985)

Prodasen's success during the Integrative phase, namely, the expansion of its services, the building and strengthening of its human, physical, and technological capabilities, and its reorientation of priorities to address the needs of the Congress, particularly those of the Senate gave it unprecedented visibility in the country as a whole, and within the Senate in particular. Its services touched and affected both congressmen and senior legislative staff. Soon, its autonomy, the resources it commanded, and the high status its staff and directors enjoyed were objects of envy among elected members and staff of the Congress.

In August 1982, the executive director of Prodasen lost his position after an acrimonious fight that left the staff of Prodasen divided and demoralized. A new executive director, Rui Janiques, who had recently concluded graduate studies with a specialization in information technologies, and who had been with Prodasen for only a short period, assumed the leadership of Prodasen.

The period between 1982 and 1985 could best be described as Prodasen's Consolidation phase. The rapid expansion in programs, characteristic of the Integrative phase, was halted, though the technical capability (hardware) increased tenfold. The technical energy of the staff was spent in fine-tuning existing programs and making them available to members and staff. PROTEUS, a new system intended to serve the political, legislative, and administrative needs of individual legislators and their personal staff, was consolidated and put to use.

During this phase, there was a massive increase in the number of terminals available to Prodasen users. Each of the seventy-six senators received a terminal. An additional forty-seven terminals were in use by various administrative units within the Senate, while Cegraf alone had thirty-four terminals. Prodasen itself was using sixty-four terminals. The Chamber of Deputies had eleven; forty-one terminals were being used outside the Congress in the nation's capital; and twenty-six in other states. By 1985, more than 299 terminals were hooked up to Prodasen.[19]

The Political Phase (1985-1988)

The Political phase began in 1985, and in 1988 was still continuing. It was characterized by the Senate's attempt to politicize Prodasen and by Prodasen's attempt to redefine its role and adapt to the new political reality.

By 1985, the dismissal and appointment of an executive director for Prodasen had become a political issue. The dismissal of the executive director was no longer based on performance or personality conflict. Rather, the dismissal came about because certain influential senators demanded it. The appointment of a new director was no longer based on his qualifications or any other objective associated with Prodasen, but on the fact that he had political support and was therefore acceptable. Indeed, the new executive director, Waldwyn Bueno Neto, appointed in 1985, was neither a computer specialist nor a legislative staff. He was a compromise candidate acceptable to the main two protagonists who supported different candidates.

Another manifestation of the politicizing of Prodasen was the appointment of additional staff who were not requested nor needed by Prodasen. Both of these actions signaled the end of the autonomy that Prodasen had long enjoyed. While few would take issue with the need for political control, many would find the manner in which this political control was exercised as inappropriate and unfortunate.

The autonomy that Prodasen had enjoyed enabled it to escape the malaise that infested the whole legislative staff structure and operations. Prodasen had developed a highly competent staff that undertook pioneering work. The manner in which the Senate began to exercise its political control over Prodasen could only weaken that institution and undermine its credibility and capabilities. Since its creation, Prodasen has earned the respect of the professional community in Brazil for the quality of its work and has been a pacesetter in the programs it developed. The constant change in its leadership since 1982 has begun to affect the morale of its staff and has driven some of them to seek employment elsewhere.

The other problem that Prodasen began facing during this phase was the question of identity and mission. When the Congress was weak, Prodasen had the luxury to invest resources and spend years in developing its systems without having to worry about the immediate utility of its programs. With a reinvigorated Congress, Prodasen was under pressure to prove its worth.[20]

Prodasen tried to prove itself through the development of the Constitutional Project, which had three components. The first component involved the computer inputting of more than thirty-five constitutions from Brazil and other countries for comparison and reference. The second component involved a campaign for popular participation in drafting the new constitution. Suggestions were collected through a questionnaire developed by Prodasen and distributed throughout the country with support from the media. Thousands of citizens' suggestions were input into the computer system and they could be researched in different manners, but primarily by subject matter. The third component was designed to aid the National Constituent Assembly in its drafting functions during constitutional deliberations of 1987 and 1988.

Advocates of this project argued that these initiatives would also help the incumbent senators in the election of 1986, by improving the Senate's image. Moreover, the project would help orient the Senate to the real concerns of the people. Finally, the project would provide the NCA with a good source of reference on existing and past constitutions of Brazil and other countries, and therefore aid in speeding the drafting procedures.

Part of the Constitutional Project proved essential to the work of the NCA in drafting the new constitution as we shall see in Chapter 8. However, regardless of the merits or demerits of the Constitutional Project, the fact remains that since 1985 Prodasen has entered a new chapter in its relations and relevance to the Senate. The way it defines its mission and its relationship will be crucial to its viability and creditability. The crisis of leadership however continues without a solution in sight.[21]

There is general agreement among Brazilian legislative staff strategists that the National Congress of Brazil needs both information and staffing support. In Brazil, with the presidential system of government, the Congress is expected to play an active role in the policy-making process. Brazil is a large and diverse country, the size of the continental United States. Unlike in the United States, however, geographic mobility in Brazil is low, and regional differences are striking. A Congress deliberating public policy in the isolation of Brasília needs all the assistance it can get in understanding the public issues facing a rapidly changing industrial society and how these changes affect the various parts of the country and the various segments of the increasingly differentiated Brazilian society.

The need for an independent source of information for the Congress is crucial. The information provided by the various executive departments is aggregated on a vertical basis, while the Congress needs horizontal information regarding distribution by regions and groups. Furthermore, executive bureaucrats present information that supports their perceived priorities, corporate interests, and ideological biases.[22]

Although the need for information is generally recognized, serious doubt remains as to whether the staffing patterns that the Congress developed and the type of staff it attracted can meet those needs. With the exception of the 1970 reforms, the growth of congressional staff has been haphazard and lacks a clear institutional justification. Beginning in the late 1970s, during their two-years mandate, successive Mesa members round it in their interest to bring in as many temporary employees as they possibly could. Since they could not be reelected to their office, their last act before surrendering their leadership to their successors was to bestow on those temporary appointed staff the final bliss of a permanent appointment. Brazilians, with their acute sense of political humor, dubbed this process as the *trem da alegria*, or the "happiness train."

Surveys conducted by the author in 1981 and 1986 illustrate the magnitude of this problem (see Table 3.1). In 1981, of the 162 people in the sample, 45 percent had been hired between 1971 and 1980, as a result of the 1970 reforms. In 1986, of the 168 people in the sample, 33.9 percent had been hired between 1976 and 1985, as a result of the *trem da alegria*. The fifteen years preceding each survey were responsible for the attachment of 63.5 percent (1981 survey) and 68.5 percent (1986 survey) of the employees of the Federal Senate.

The personnel practices instituted under the *trem da alegria* approach had a greater impact on the composition of the Senate staff than did the 1970 reforms. In 1986, only 13.1 percent of the Senate employees had joined the service of the Senate during or before 1970.

Table 3.1

Question: When did you start working in the Congress?

Category	1981 No.	%	1986 No.	%
Before 1951	6	3.7	2	1.2
Between 1951-1955	4	2.5	0	0.0
Between 1956-1960	11	6.8	4	2.4
Between 1961-1965	37	22.8	16	9.5
Between 1966-1970	30	18.5	31	18.5
Between 1971-1975	54	33.3	51	30.4
Between 1976-1985 (1981)	19	11.7	57	33.9
After 1985	-	-	7	4.2
No response	1	0.6	0	0.0
Total	162	100.0	168	100.0

Source: Data collected by the author in 1981 and 1986.

Since the 1970 reforms, both the Federal Senate and the Chamber of Deputies undertook a number of initiatives to build up and develop professional staff capabilities. Initially both the Senate and the Chamber showed equal interest in upgrading their staff. However, in 1976, with the appointment of the then-director-general of the Chamber, Luciano Brandão Alves de Souza, to the TCU, authority in the Chamber was centralized under the leadership of the Secretary-General Paulo Affonso who placed less importance on staff development and paid more attention to political considerations.

The large number of deputies serving in the Chamber and the continuous leadership changes made this centralization inevitable, if any semblance of order and continuity was to be maintained. Paulo Affonso's top priorities were (1) the orchestration of the political game within the Chamber, (2) the building of coalitions to support the institutional leadership of the Chamber, and (3) seeing that the needs of the various deputies, states, and regional blocs and parties were properly met within the constraints imposed on the legislature. Affonso's emphasis on the political agenda placed on hold the administrative reforms and human resource development. Two exceptions were the attempt to institutionalize an internship program for university students in the late 1970s, and an attempt to structure the Chamber library and create a documentation and research center to provide the *Assessoria* and the deputies with information and research support.

With its small size, the Senate developed a highly decentralized staff structure. The secretary-general of the Senate, Sarah Abrão, developed her own power base and controlled those resources essential for the performance of her work. The director of the *Assessoria*, Pedro Cavalcanti, had his autonomy in controlling the *Assessoria*. The executive directors of Prodasen and Cegraf also enjoyed a high degree of autonomy. The role of the director-general covered all other staff units, although many of the directors of the secretariats and undersecretariats under his control had direct access to the Mesa, and therefore managed to maintain some autonomy in their own operations.

The decentralized structure gave the Senate the opportunity and autonomy to pursue various staff development strategies. In 1971, Sarah Abrão and Pedro Cavalcanti of the Senate initiated a staff and legislative development agreement with the Comparative Development Studies Center (CDSC) of the University at Albany, State University of New York (the center's name has since been changed to Center for Legislative Development, CLD). Under the terms of this open-ended agreement, which was elaborated on by Eduardo Jorge Caldas Pereira and Lourival Zagonel dos Santos and ratified in 1979, approximately twenty Senate staff members received graduate education in public administration at the University at Albany, with concentrations in legislative administration and/or information systems. Moreover, several hundred senior staff received short-term training in the United States, or attended seminars in Brazil that were organized by University at Albany faculty on such legislative technology topics as budget analysis, legislative environment and information systems, fiscal analysis and public policy analysis. Prodasen, under Eduardo Pereira, a University at Albany alumnus, took the lead in initiating many of the staff and information development reforms.

In 1979, the first-secretary, Senator Alexandre Costa (ARENA-PDS/Maranhão), and the vice-president, Senator Lourival Baptista (ARENA-PDS/Sergipe), took an active interest in staff development under the terms of the agreement. Between 1985 and 1987, the director-general, Lourival Zagonel dos Santos, another alumnus, attempted a major organizational and personnel reform. The structuring, recruitment, classification, and staff development of the Senate staff became once again a top priority for the administrative and political leadership of the Senate. However, with the election of 1986, and the change of the Mesa, political support for these reforms eroded. Zagonel, and many of the top administrative leaders, were replaced with individuals less committed to staff development.

Three important features of the new reforms instituted during this period survived though with different emphasis. First, under the leadership of Zagonel, the Senate became more centralized under the General Directorate. Second, a significant pay raise and reclassification was given to the advisory staff working in the *Assessoria* and to the personal advisors of individual senators. Third, training and human resources development became an organized and continuous activity under Cedesen, a special unit within the Senate established to meet human resource development needs.

In the case of Brazil, it seems that Prodasen succeeded in establishing a technological-ly viable institution because of the autonomy it enjoyed from political intervention. Had there been strong political intervention, the short-term needs of the legislators would have taken precedence over the long-term needs of building the institution.

Perhaps one should distinguish between the development of the technology, which is time consuming, and its use. The American legislatures did not have to develop this type of technology; it was developed by private institutions. Furthermore, experts in this area were also available and could be recruited if necessary. In Brazil, on the other hand, neither the technology nor the expertise was available. Such long-range planning would not have been permissible had the Brazilian Congress been involved in the day-to-day operations of Prodasen.

Legislative scholars need also to distinguish between political oversight, which legitimate legislatures can properly exercise, and political meddling, which weak ille-gitimate legislatures are likely to engage in. The Brazilian Congress under the military regime was incapable of exercising legitimate political oversight. When it recently got the opportunity to flex its muscle, it used Prodasen for political patronage. Even when Prodasen was passing through an identity crisis, few of the elected members were involved in the discussions aimed at clarifying the priorities of the institution. This task was left in the hands of the staff. Yet political meddling and rotation of leadership continued unabated.

For students of legislative studies, the Brazilian case provides an excellent illustration of the importance of stable political leadership for the working of representative institu-tions. Under the guise of democratizing the legislature, Brazil succeeded in bureaucratiz-ing Prodasen and prevented the emergence of stable, strong leadership. With the return to competitive politics, the difficulties in managing an institution without a stable and strong leadership were accentuated. With the constant turnover of institutional, party, and committee leadership, the staff is likely to continue to be poorly motivated and the mem-bers will continue to misuse their staff and the resources that the Congress has provided them. Unless democratic institutions are properly managed, at least in developing countries, it is difficult to build their legitimacy vis-à-vis other competing institutions.

Finally, the Brazilian experience may shed some light on the controversy over when to supply legislatures with staff and information. It has been argued that a weak legislature either does not need staff and information, or that such staff and information could be counterproductive in the sense that a weak legislature could become a prisoner of its staff.[23] The Prodasen experience shows that, in some cases at least, it is appropriate to begin the development of legislative support systems when the legislature is still weak. Had the Brazilians waited until the Congress became stronger before building their electronic data processing (EDP) capabilities, it would have been too late. The day-to-day work would have consumed all the energies of a strong legislature. The National Constituent Assembly, when it convened in 1987, had under its command a sophisticated information system that made the task of drafting a new constitution technologically feasible.

NOTES

1. For an example of this literature, see Abdo I. Baaklini and James J. Heaphey (eds.), *Comparative Legislative Reforms and Innovations* (Albany: State University of New York, 1977); Harrison W. Fox, Jr., and Susan Webb Hammond, *Congressional Staffs: The Invisible Force in American Lawmaking* (New York: The Free Press, 1977); John Worthley, *Public Administration and Legislatures* (New York: Nelson Hall, 1976); Abdo I. Baaklini, "Legislative Staffing Patterns in Developing Countries: Problems and Prospects," James J. Heaphey and Alan P. Balutis (eds.), *Legislative Staffing: A Comparative Perspective* (New York: Sage Publishing, 1975); Eric Redman, *The Dance of Legislation* (New York: Simon & Schuster, 1973); and Kenneth Kofmehl, *Professional Staff of the Congress* (West Lafayette, Ind.: Purdue University Press, 1962).

2. See Michael J. Malbin, *Unelected Representatives: Congressional Staff and the Future of Representative Government* (New York: Basic Books, 1979).

3. See James J. Heaphey (ed.), "A Symposium: Public Administration and Legislatures," *Public Administration Review*, 35, no. 5 (September/October 1975).

4. See Abdo I. Baaklini, "Legislative Reform or the Bureaucratization of the Legislature?" *Administration* (Dublin, Ireland), 24, no. 2 (Summer 1976), pp. 138-58.

5. See Abdo I. Baaklini, "Legislative Reforms in the Brazilian Chamber of Deputies," Baaklini and Heaphey (eds.), *Comparative Legislative Reforms and Innovations*, op. cit. (1977); Abdo I. Baaklini and James J. Heaphey, *Legislative Institution Building in Brazil, Costa Rica, and Lebanon* (Beverly Hills: Sage Publications, 1976); *Organização Administrativa da Câmara dos Deputados: Resolução No. 20/71* (Brasília: Câmara dos Deputados, 1976); and Milton Campos and Nelson Carneiro, "Organização dos Parlamentos Modernos," *Revista Brasileira de Estudos Políticos*, 25, no. 6 (July 1968/January 1969), pp. 139-63.

6. See *Relatório da Primeira Secretaria do Senado Federal* (Brasília: Senado Federal, 1987, 1986, and 1985); *Resoluções da Câmara dos Deputados, 47ª Legislatura: 1983-1986*, vol. 10 (Brasília: Câmara dos Deputados, 1987); *Legislação Interna da Câmara dos Deputados* (Brasília: Câmara dos Deputados, 1987); and *Regulamento Administrativo do Senado Federal* (Brasília: Senado Federal, 1983).

7. See *Anais do Seminário sobre Modernização Legislativa e Desenvolvimento Político: 7 a 11 de junho de 1976* (Brasília: Senado Federal, 1976).

8. In 1989-1990 a new competitive examination was held to hire advisors for the chamber. On February 15, 1991, eighty additional advisors were hired.

9. With the adoption of the new Constitution in 1988, and the strengthening of the committee system in the Congress, there is now a strong sentiment among some congressional leadership to provide each of the committees with its own professional permanent staff. Whether the committee staffs would be hired directly by the committees or be allocated through the *Assessoria* has not yet been determined.

10. The importance of information, and the use of modern information technology in the legislative process, both at the federal and state levels in the United States, has long been a topic of academic inquiry. For examples, see Stephen E. Frantzich, "Computerized Information Technology in the U.S. House of Representatives," *Legislative Studies Quarterly*, 4 (May 1979), pp. 255-79; Robert Zeler, "The Search for Information: Specialists and Nonspecialists in the U.S. House of Representatives," *Legislative Studies Quarterly*, 4 (February 1979), pp. 31-42; Robert Lee Chartrand, "Congressional Management and the Use of Information Technology," *Journal of System Management* (August 1978), pp. 10-15; John A. Worthley (ed.), *Comparative Legislative Information Systems* (Washington: National Science Foundation, 1976); and Richard Bolling, "The Management of Congress," *Public Administration Review* (September/October 1975), pp. 49-55.

11. See Act No. 58/72 of the Committee of Directors of the Federal Senate.

12. The need for autonomy was argued by the executive director of Prodasen in memorandum DE-14/71, addressed to the president of the Federal Senate.

13. See Yamil e Souza Dutra, "Automação e Formação de uma Rede de Informações Jurídico-Legislativa: Experiência no Senado Federal," in *Informática Jurídica* (Fundação Petrônio Portella—Ministério da Justiça), no. 3 (1985), pp. 47-68.

14. See Prodasen's annual report of 1975.

15. See Prodasen's annual report of 1980.

16. Eduardo Jorge Caldas Pereira is a graduate of the University at Albany, State University of New York. He was executive director of Prodasen from 1975 until 1982. During this period, he undertook a number of basic changes that reoriented the mission of Prodasen to make it more compatible and in line with its original mission, which was to serve legislative needs.

17. See memoranda EMDE-14/76 and 16/76, from the executive director of Prodasen to the president of its Supervising Council; and memorandums DE-391/76 and 393/76, from the executive director of Prodasen to the president of the Federal Senate.

18. See Prodasen's annual report of 1986.

19. See Prodasen's annual report of 1986.

20. In July 1986, during an interview in Brasília, Sinval Senra Martins Jr. (acting executive director of Prodasen) suggested that, fortunately for Prodasen, it seems that this group has gained the ascendancy. To guard against the vagaries of political intervention associated with the rotation of the Mesa every two years, this group has successfully developed and convinced the Supervising Council of Prodasen to adopt a long-range planning document in which the priorities of Prodasen are well elaborated.

21. At present, Prodasen is facing a crisis of leadership. The appointment of an alternate executive director only delayed the hour of reckoning. The executive director lasted only a few months on the job. An acting executive director was appointed when the executive director was involved in a car accident that required him to be hospitalized for a long period. In July 1986, Rui Janiques, the former executive director, who was forced to resign under political pressure, was reappointed as the permanent executive director. After the election of November 1986, and the election of a new Mesa in March of 1987, the executive director was forced to resign and a new executive director was appointed. The new executive director was a former Prodasen staff member who resigned in 1983 to protest the removal of the then-executive director. In 1989, a new Mesa assumed power, and immediately proceeded to appoint a new executive director. How long this will last and how effective it will be remains to be seen. What is already clear is that this rotation of leadership underscores the political nature of this new phase in the life of Prodasen. One can only hope that Prodasen has by now developed the kind of competent and sophisticated staff that will enable it to cope in the rough times ahead.

22. Martha Dolabelo de Lima, "Fluxo de Informação na Câmara dos Deputados." Master of Arts thesis in library sciences, University of Brasilia, Federal District, 1990.

23. See Samuel Patterson, "The Professional Staff on Congressional Committees," *Administrative Science Quarterly*, no. 15 (March 1970).

Chapter 4

Legislative Staffing and Congressional Performance

Starting in the early 1970s, legislative staff development centered on equipping the National Congress with the institutional staff and information resources necessary to discharge its constitutional functions in an orderly, timely, and objective fashion. Yet the staffing patterns adopted and the personnel policies and practices enforced during this period contributed to the bureaucratization of the Congress and, in some ways, complemented the authoritarian regime's attempts to weaken the institution.

Staff organization and personnel practices followed the pattern set by the executive to reform the bureaucracy (as discussed in Chapters 1 and 2). The bureaucratization of the Congressional staff accentuated the weakness of the political parties and undermined the power of Congressional leaders, and it helped transform the Congress into a ratifying institution for the policies formulated by the executive. American Congressional staff patterns, with their emphasis on leadership staff, committee staff, and personal staff, had little appeal to an institution where congressional leaders were supposed to be administrators and managers rather than politicians. Committees were expected to be transient expediters of legislation presented by the executive, rather than centers for evaluating, shaping, and formulating public policy. Members of the Congress were expected to follow the lead of the executive-dominated party leadership, rather than become advocates for their own constituencies.

Although the Congressional staffing patterns developed during this authoritarian period seemed to fit the strategic needs of the executive in weakening the Congress and in rationalizing the legislative process, Congressional leaders acquiesced for reasons of their own. This chapter analyzes the consequences of the personnel policies and staffing patterns on the kind of people who came to work for the Congress, their orientation to their work and to the legislative institution, their relationship with the elected members and to legislative politics in general, and finally, on their contributions to the work of the Congress.[1]

RECRUITMENT AND PERSONNEL POLICIES

Given the political, constitutional, and organizational limitations under which the National Congress operated during the Brazilian authoritarian regime, the recruitment and personnel policies it adopted to build its institutional capabilities seemed appropriate. The system was expected to attract an academically and professionally qualified staff to work for the legislature and serve its needs. Recruitment was to be in accordance with merit, as measured by a national competitive examination, to fill various positions whose job titles and position descriptions had already been identified in accordance with a comprehensive position classification plan. Temporary employment was to be allowed in special cases, and those positions were to be governed in accordance with the existing labor laws (the CLT).

The top management positions were to be filled by merit-recruited employees and were to be known as DAS (*funções de direção e assessoramento superiores*). Those hired were to serve the Mesa members of each house. DAS employees were supposed to be nonpartisan and politically neutral, as the Mesa which appointed them. Appointments were supposed to recognize the individual professional contributions to the Congress. With the exception of the CLT employees, congressional employees were to enjoy job security and be career oriented. Their loyalty was supposed to be to the institution as a whole rather to political parties, individuals, or groups within the Congress.

Our staff survey showed that some of those expectations were realized, while others failed to materialize. The political nature of the institution reasserted itself and determined recruitment and personnel policies, notwithstanding the formal rules and regulations governing recruitment, promotion, transfer, and tenure. The superimposition of bureaucratic over political rationality seemed to have produced conditions that were bureaucratically unjustifiable and politically undesirable. The expected benefits of a bureaucratic structure, such as impersonality, objectivity, tight control, neutrality, and efficiency, were partially realized. However, political responsiveness and information relevant to public policy were in scarce supply.

As illustrated in Table 4.1, in the 1981 sample, the survey data showed that 40.1 percent of those hired were recruited in accordance with a competitive examination; 22.8 percent were promoted internally without a competitive examination; and 24.7 percent were selected on a personal or political basis; and the rest were employed temporarily or on another basis. In the 1986 survey, those who were recruited on the basis of a competitive examination dropped to 6.5 percent, while those recruited on the basis of political recommendations rose to 52.4 percent. And 22.6 percent obtained their present position through internal promotion.

Table 4.1

How were you selected for your present job?

	1981		1986	
By means of a competitive exam	65	40.1%	11	6.5%
By means of a promotion exam	37	22.8%	38	22.6%
By means of a personal interview	11	6.8%	14	8.3%
By means of a temporary contract	8	4.9%	13	7.7%
By means of a recommendation	40	24.7%	88	52.4%
Other	1	0.6%	2	1.2%
No response	0	0.0%	2	1.2%
Total	162	100.0%	168	100.0%

The bureaucratic structures adopted by the Congress as a result of the reforms in the early 1970s imposed on the members of Congress guidelines and policies that were difficult to sustain. Beginning with the *abertura,* the political nature of the institution began to assert itself. This political assertion took place within the restrictions imposed by the 1970 and 1972 reforms. Thus, staff appointed as CLT staff or on the basis of personal or political recommendations, in time, managed to acquire permanent status. New entrants and their political or staff mentors learned that all it took to acquire all the privileges and job tenure of the merit-appointed staff was merely to get the initial appointment, regardless of the conditions. Once hired, a staff career future depended on his family and friends' network, such as influential politicians and senior staff.

The Senate had three categories of positions.[2] The first was the DAS classification, which had a range from a low of grade 1 to a high of grade 6. With the exception of the director general and secretary-general, who occupied DAS-6, most of the DAS jobs were grades 3 or 4. All the advisors (members of the *Assessoria*) were classified as DAS-3, regardless of their seniority or duties.

The second category of jobs called *nível superior* (NS), or superior level staff, consisted of twenty five grades. To be classified as a superior level staff, an employee needed a college degree. Few titles were classified below NS-14. The overwhelming majority were at the highest end of the scale in NS-25.

The third category was that of *nível médio* (NM), or middle level staff, and consisted of thirty five grades. In this level, few jobs were classified under grade 28. The overwhelming majority of the employees in this category occupied positions in grade NM-35. A high school diploma is needed for entry to this level.

The 1988 employee roster of the Senate showed that working for the Congress was a privilege and that the staff made the best use of it under the pretense of bureaucratic efficiency, regardless of their actual contributions to the institution. Monetary and other privileges were bestowed upon whoever succeeded in becoming a staff member of the legislature, regardless of how they got the job. Senate employees were overwhelmingly at the top echelon of each job category, regardless of their seniority, how they were recruited, or their qualifications, performance, or political connections. All eighty-eight advisors were classified as DAS-3. Legislative technicians, for example, could be classified from NS-14 to NS-25. Of the 421 NS-employees, 379 were NS-25; only twenty-eight were between NS-22 and NS-24, and fifteen were between NS-16 and NS-21. NS-14 and NS-15 were completely vacant. In the Stenography Undersecretariat of the Senate, all forty-six shorthand employees were NS-25. NS-14 to NS-24 were vacant.

Yet, in spite of this informal network that the congressional staff used to get in and to rise to the top of their job titles, few of them felt indebted to the elected members for their career, as shown by the results in Table 4.2. When asked what type of relationship they had with the legislators before they were appointed, the 1981 survey showed that 20.4 percent of the employees mentioned some sort of friendship, 8.6 percent had a family relation, only 3.7 percent mentioned a political party connection, and 15.4 percent were casual acquaintances of the elected members. Half of the respondents had no relationship with the elected members, and presumably were recruited through their contacts with other congressional staff.

The 1986 survey showed a slight change in favor of family relations, rising from 8.6 percent in 1981 to 16.7 percent in 1986. Party affiliation also showed some slight increase from 3.7 percent to 4.8. The rest of those surveyed indicated that they either had occasional encounters or no encounters at all with the legislators before they were appointed.

Table 4.2

What was your relationship with the congressman you work for before you started working in the Congress?

	1981		1986	
Friendship	33	20.4%	7	4.2%
Relatives	14	8.6%	28	16.7%
Members of the same political party	6	3.7%	8	4.8%
Casual acquaintances	25	15.4%	55	32.7%
No relation	82	50.6%	7	4.2%
No response	2	1.2%	63	37.5%
Total	162	100.0%	168	100.0%

For those who had casual acquaintances with the legislators before being hired, more than 60 percent of the appointees had met them in Brasília, not in their state or municipal districts, as one might expect (see Table 4.3). This shows that the government's move to Brasília created special circumstances for recruitment to government jobs, especially for the Congress. Isolated from the rest of the country, Brasília became a government town where politicians and bureaucrats engaged in intensive social interactions, during which networks of friendships developed with significant implications for obtaining a job in the Congress.

Table 4.3

Where did you develop your relationship with the congressman you work with?

	1981		1986	
At the municipal level	13	8.0%	9	5.4%
At the state level	13	8.0%	20	11.9%
At the federal level	50	30.9%	65	38.7%
Others	9	5.6%	5	3.0%
No response*	77	47.5%	69	41.1%
Total	162	100.0%	168	100.0%

* No prior relationship with their congressman.

As illustrated in Table 4.4, the 1981 survey showed that 42.5 percent of those who worked for the Congress were from the private sector, 14.3 percent were from the state and municipal levels of government, 32 percent were from the federal government, and

11 percent were self-employed. The 1986 survey showed an increase to 48.8 percent for those from the private sector, and a decline to 14.9 percent for those from the federal level. Staff with state and municipal government experience also declined to 7.7 percent. The self-employed category rose to 20.2 percent.

Table 4.4

What was your job experience before working in the Congress?

	1981		1986	
In the private sector	77	42.5%	82	48.8%
In the municipal service	8	4.4%	2	1.2%
In the state service	18	9.9%	11	6.5%
In the federal service	58	32.0%	25	14.9%
As an autonomous professional	20	11.0%	14	8.3%
No response	0	0.0%	34	20.2%
Total*	181	100.0%	168	100.0%

* In 1981, some listed more than one variable.

Employment opportunities in the Congress expanded and began to attract professionals and individuals from the private sector who had no government experience. The increase of those who were recruited from the private or professional sectors reflected the staffing needs of Prodasen, Cegraf, the *Assessoria,* and the medical, engineering, public relations, and other professional units. The increase of those without government experience also reflected the needs of senators, deputies, and senior staff, who needed to find employment opportunities in the Congress to ensure that their families and friends were gainfully employed and conveniently located in Brasília. Although the percentage of staff reporting special relationships or acquaintances with legislators before their appointment to the staff was low compared with legislative staff recruitment in the United States, in a country where the law and the norms supposedly emphasized merit and competitive examinations, nonmerit family and personal considerations were often the determining factors in appointments of congressional staff. Corruption, nepotism, and clientelism in congressional staffing became favorite topics of the Brazilian press.

The decline of congressional staff with experience in the public sector, especially at the state and local levels, affected their approach to their work, to politics, and to the legislative institution. Legislative staff, with no political experience and lacking local roots and connections, were poorly prepared to understand the nature of legislative politics, the various roles that a legislator has to play—especially in his relationship with his constituencies—and the special demands of running and winning elections. Thus, the isolation of the member, as a result of being in Brasília and his dependency on information provided by the executive, was compounded by a staff that had little experience in the public sector at the state and local levels. For those with experience, such experience was gained at the federal level, in the private sector or as self-employed. Some were recruited right from high school or college without any experience.

The academic qualifications of the staff continued to improve over the years, reflecting the improved educational opportunities in Brasília. Many of the congressional staff benefitted from those opportunities, since the demands of their work were such that they were able to pursue full academic programs while employed at the Congress as full-time employees. Furthermore, many of the relatives of the members and permanent staff upon graduation from college found employment with the Congress convenient, since it paid well and allowed them to continue living near their parents and families.

As illustrated in Table 4.5, in 1981, 19.8 percent of the staff had completed primary education, 34.6 percent had high school education, 38.9 percent had undergraduate degrees, and 6.8 percent had graduate degrees. In the 1986 survey, only 13.1 percent had primary educations, those with secondary educations rose to 39.3 percent, and those with college degrees rose to 41.7 percent. Of the total work force, those with a graduate degree declined to 4.6 percent. Those with elementary or secondary educations constituted more than 50 percent of the population.

Table 4.5

What is your educational background?

	1981		1986	
Primary school	32	19.8%	22	13.1%
High school	56	34.6%	66	39.3%
College	63	38.9%	70	41.7%
Master's degree	6	3.7%	6	3.6%
Doctorate degree	4	2.5%	1	0.6%
Postdoctorate	1	0.6%	2	1.2%
No response	0	0.0%	1	0.6%
Total	162	100.0%	168	100.0%

In the 1981 survey the highest percentage of academic specialization was law (17.9 percent), followed by business administration (9.3 percent), as shown in Table 4.6. Economics, library science, and other fields of study followed. In 1986, law was replaced by business administration as the most frequent academic specialization (14.9 percent); law fell to 8.9 percent. Economics and communication followed with 5.4 and 2.4 percent, respectively.

Staff Orientation Toward Work

The survey data confirmed the assumption that the recruitment policies and practices, the structure of the staff, and the structure of congressional leadership were not conducive to the development of a responsive, politically sophisticated legislative staff that could provide the kind of assistance the Congress needed. The policies and practices of the authoritarian regime, it was suggested, were principal factors in the policies adopted and the structures developed by the Congress. The survey instrument administered in 1981 and 1986 sought to assess the orientation of the staff to their jobs, to the legislative environment, and to the type of support the elected member had from the staff.

As illustrated in Table 4.7, in 1981, when asked what they liked best about their congressional jobs, 37.2 percent of the staff listed job security. Meeting important people followed with 19.1 percent. Salary was highly valued at 15.9 percent. Job prestige ranked forth with 13.7 percent. The competitive nature of the job ranked low in the minds of the respondents with 6.9 percent.

Table 4.6

What is your area of specialization?

	1981		1986	
Business Administration	15	9.3%	25	14.9%
Library science	5	3.1%	-	-
Communication	2	1.2%	4	2.4%
Psychology	1	0.6%	1	0.6%
Law	29	17.9%	15	8.9%
Economics	10	6.2%	9	5.4%
Engineering	2	1.2%	2	1.2%
Mathematics	1	0.6%	2	1.2%
Literature	2	1.2%	3	1.8%
Medicine	2	1.2%	1	0.6%
Others	8	4.9%	9	5.4%
No degree	85	52.5%	97	57.7%
Total	162	100.0%	168	100.0%

Table 4.7

What do you like best about your job?

	1981		1986	
Meeting important people	53	19.1%	76	45.2%
Its competitive nature	19	6.9%	26	15.5%
Its security	103	37.2%	31	18.5%
Its prestige	38	13.7%	7	4.2%
Salary	44	15.9%	2	1.2%
No response	0	0.0%	1	0.6%
Other	20	7.2%	25	14.9%
Total	277	100.0%	168	100.0%

The politics of *abertura* and the improved image of the Congress elicited a different response in 1986. According to this group, the political environment and the excitement of meeting people with political power ranked first, with 45.2 percent. Job security is the preferred second option with 18.5 percent. The competitive nature of the job showed a preference of 15.5 percent. Only 4.2 percent said prestige was the best feature of the job. Other responses included assertions that the job had a noncompetitive nature, was not prestigious, and lacked security. On a whole, the responses showed a high degree of ambiguity regarding staff feelings toward their jobs. Although the image of the Congress has shown improvement over time, neither the competitive nature of the job nor its prestige showed significant improvement. Job security as an attraction declined over time and began to be taken for granted by the staff.

The respondents were also asked to classify their job responsibilities into one of four categories: managerial, technical, political, or operational. As shown in Table 4.8, in 1981, 36.4 percent of the congressional staff worked in operational categories, 34 percent were in technical jobs, and 13.6 percent were in management. Only 1.9 percent of the respondents said they performed any functions that could be classified as political.

Table 4.8

How do you classify your actual job responsibility?

	1981		1986	
Managerial	22	13.6%	41	24.4%
Technical	55	34.0%	64	38.1%
Political	3	1.9%	7	4.2%
Operational	59	36.4%	51	30.4%
Others	15	9.3%	5	3.0%
No response	8	4.9%	0	0.0%
Total	162	100.0%	168	100.0%

The 1986 sample showed that those with technical jobs were at the top with 38.1 percent, followed by operational jobs with 30.4 percent, and management jobs with 24.4 percent. The politically related jobs remained at the bottom with 4.2 percent.

The majority of the staff had little appreciation for the political environment of the Congress and the role of the member as illustrated in Table 4.9. Thus, in 1981, when asked to name the role of the legislative staff, 33.3 percent in 1981 said the job of the staff was the most important in the legislative process; 22.2 percent said their contributions were more objective than the legislators'; and 9.3 percent said their jobs were more important than the legislators'. Only 20.4 said the job of the staff member should be anonymous, and 8 percent felt that their job was to defend the interests of the legislator. In 1986, the data show that even a smaller percentage believed the job of the staff member should be anonymous (7.1 percent), or that their job was to defend the interests of the legislator (3 percent). Moreover, a greater percentage believed that their jobs were more important than that of the members' (15.5 percent). Another question probed the attitude of the staff on the same variable, but in a different manner. Once again the majority of the staff showed little appreciation for the political environment and the role of the member, as shown in Table 4.10. In 1981, 34.6 percent said they did not think the work of the staff should be anonymous; 21.6 percent disagreed with the statement that their job should be to defend the legislators. In 1986, the results were even more dramatic. More staff affirmed that their work should not be anonymous (42.3 percent). These results show the importance that these staff were attaching to their contribution to the Congress and a corresponding disregard to the contribution of the elected member.

Table 4.9

With which of the following statements do you agree most?

	1981		1986	
Legislative staff work should be anonymous.	33	20.4%	12	7.1%
Legislative staffs are better qualified than elected members; therefore, they should be the ones to decide on public policy.	54	33.3%	56	33.3%
Legislative staffs should defend the legislators, even when they do not agree with their legislators' decisions.	13	8.0%	5	3.0%
Legislative staffs are more important in the legislative process than the legislators.	15	9.3%	26	15.5%
Legislative staffs are more objective in their decisions than the legislators.	36	22.2%	39	23.2%
No response	11	6.8%	30	17.9%
Total	162	100.0%	168	100.0%

Finally, when asked to identify the criteria upon which they base decisions at work, most staff indicated that they did what they thought was right or what they thought would be in the national interest (see Table 4.11). Few respondents identified the member, the party, or the committee as having any significance in their work.

These answers were not surprising. Few of the respondents worked directly with members, committees, or parties. If they had to consult someone, it usually was their administrative supervisor, and not the elected member. This bureaucratic orientation became even more evident when we asked the respondents to identify the channels of communication that they would follow to discuss new ideas. As shown in Table 4.12, nearly half said they would go through their supervisors.

Table 4.10

With which of the following statements do you disagree most?

	1981		1986	
Legislative staff work should be anonymous.	56	34.6%	71	42.3%
Legislative staffs are better qualified than elected members; therefore, they should be the ones to decide on public policy.	17	10.5%	14	33.3%
Legislative staffs should defend the legislators, even when they do not agree with their legislators' decisions.	35	21.6%	35	20.8%
Legislative staffs are more important in the legislative process than the legislators.	24	14.8%	9	5.4%
Legislative staffs are more objective in their decisions than the legislators.	10	6.2%	5	3.0%
No response	20	12.3%	34	20.2%
Total	162	100.0%	168	100.0%

Table 4.11

Which of the following statements best suits your conduct at work?

	1981		1986	
I do what I think is right.	44	27.2%	40	23.8%
I do what my superior thinks is right.	22	13.6%	18	10.7%
I look after the interests of my legislators.	13	8.0%	17	10.1%
I serve the legislators of my state.	0	0.0%	0	0.0%
I serve the interest of the executive.	0	0.0%	3	1.8%
I serve the party whose program I agree with.	0	0.0%	1	0.6%
I serve the political party I am assigned to.	0	0.0%	0	0.0%
I serve the National Congress as I see fit.	9	5.6%	9	5.4%
I serve the nation, as I see fit.	45	27.8%	38	22.6%
I serve the congressman I am assigned to.	9	5.6%	8	4.8%
I serve the committee I am assigned to.	1	0.6%	9	5.4%
No response	19	11.7%	25	14.9%
Total	162	100.0%	168	100.0%

Table 4.12

What would you do if you had a good idea to reform the legislature?

	1981		1986	
I would transmit my idea to those in power.	48	29.6%	52	31.0%
I would transmit my idea to my immediate supervisor.	78	48.1%	99	58.9%
I would do nothing about it; there's no use in trying.	32	19.8%	11	6.5%
No response	4	2.5%	6	3.6%
Total	162	100.0%	168	100.0%

In the 1981 survey, 48.1 percent said they would discuss their new ideas with the supervisor, 29.6 percent said they would go directly to those in power, and 19.8 percent said they would forget the whole thing and do nothing. In 1986, 58.9 percent of the respondents said they would transmit their ideas to their immediate supervisors, and 31 percent said they would go directly to those in power. Only 6.5 percent said they would do nothing about their new ideas. Perhaps the centralization efforts within the Senate during 1985 and 1986 accounted for the added emphasis on the immediate supervisor as the best channel for communicating new ideas or complaints.   When asked to whom they would report a mistake or problems at work, the surveyed staff responded in a similar fashion, as shown in Table 4.13.

Table 4.13

If you found a mistake at work, who would you report it to?

	1981		1986	
I would report it to those in power.	51	31.5%	59	35.1%
I would report it to my immediate supervisor.	91	56.2%	100	59.5%
I would do nothing about it; there's no use in trying.	14	8.6%	5	3.0%
No response	6	3.7%	4	2.4%
Total	162	100.0%	168	100.0%

According to the surveys, the typical congressional staff member came from the private sector or was recruited directly from high school or college. Few had any public work experience before joining the congressional staff. Those who had some experience in the public sector worked mostly at the federal level and therefore had no local roots in the districts of the elected members. Although recruitment was supposed to be based on merit through a competitive examination, most of the respondents occupied their present position through nonmerit and noncompetitive methods and criteria. Although some of them said they were somehow acquainted with the elected members before they were appointed, most had no relationship or only a casual relationship with the members. The majority of the staff had a high school or university degree. Those with degrees came from the business administration, law, or economics fields. Other professions, such as medical or engineering, were also represented.

Once appointed, congressional staff developed their own network of protectors and guardians from among the legislators and the senior staff, using in the process family connections and a willingness to render special services and favors to the protector or guardian. The fact that most of those working as staff members were promoted to the highest grade of their category suggested that almost every congressional staff found a protector or a guardian. Merit and performance evaluations to determine promotions or salaries were not given serious consideration. Promotions and privileges were acquired on a collective basis, rather than as rewards for performance.

Since their job security and well-being were guaranteed by law and by institutional norms, and since many lacked sensitivity toward politics or local issues, most congressional staff developed a negative attitude toward politics and to the ability of a legislator to reach good independent decisions. Instead, staff members emphasized their autonomy and objectivity as the best criteria for reaching decisions. They had an exaggerated sense of their importance and their contribution to the legislative process.

In accordance with the bureaucratic structure under which they functioned, their attitude toward work and their duties and responsibilities was colored largely by bureaucratic norms. The overwhelming majority defined their job as technical, operational, or managerial. Few considered themselves working in a political environment. Their jobs' strongest attractions were security and salary, though in recent years with the revival of the Congress a feeling of belonging to a powerful elite had begun to look attractive to some. Few listed the challenge of the job as a factor in joining the congressional staff. Finally, the majority seemed content to follow the bureaucratic lines of communication to report innovative ideas or register complaints.

Orientation Toward Congress

Although the respondents were negatively predisposed to politics and to politicians, they displayed an institutional loyalty to and support of the congressmen, as illustrated in Table 4.14. In 1981, when asked which branch of government should have more power, 58 percent of the respondents said the three branches of government should have equal power, 27.2 percent said Congress should have more power, and 12.3 percent said the President should have more power. This trend in support for an equal and stronger role for Congress was reinforced in the 1986 survey, where 50.6 percent indicated a preference for equal powers among the three institutions, and 36.9 percent were in favor of a Congress stronger than the President. Only 9.5 percent of the respondents indicated a preference toward a stronger President. In both surveys, few indicated a preference for a judiciary stronger than the two other branches of government.

Table 4.14

Which of the following statements do you agree with most?

	1981		1986	
The three branches of government have equal power.	94	58.0%	85	50.6%
The executive should have more power.	20	12.3%	16	9.5%
The legislature should have more power.	44	27.2%	62	36.9%
The judiciary should have more power.	2	1.2%	1	0.6%
No response	2	1.2%	4	2.4%
Total	162	100.0%	168	100.0%

This loyalty to the institution in which they worked also manifested itself when the respondents were asked if they trusted the congressmen (see Table 4.15). In 1981 and 1986, as many as 79 and 81 percent, respectively, answered positively. Only 16 and 11.3 percent, respectively, gave a negative response.

Table 4.15

Do you trust the congressmen?

	1981		1986	
Yes	128	79.0%	136	81.0%
No	26	16.0%	19	11.3%
No response	8	4.9%	13	7.7%
Total	162	100.0%	168	100.0%

Finally, although more than half of the respondents said they would consider changing jobs, few showed a preference for working for the executive branch of government. Most of those who would consider quitting their jobs with the Congress would do so either to start their own business or to work in the private sector. The staff of Congress seemed to be satisfied with their own jobs and only a better salary would entice them to leave.

IMPLICATIONS OF STAFF STRUCTURE AND ATTITUDES TOWARD THE
FUNCTIONING OF A REJUVENATED CONGRESS

Although the orientation of the staff changed very little between 1981 and 1986 regarding the important dimensions that the surveys sought to explore, some movement was evident. More important for our purpose here is that 61.3 percent of those surveyed felt that there was some improvement, such as minor improvement in the congressional staff's understanding of the political nature of the institution and its importance in the political system. The staff remained convinced, however, that their work was more important or as important as the elected members, and, as such, they were satisfied with their jobs. Respondents' reasons for increased job satisfaction varied:

1.   14.9 percent said the new political openness contributed to a better work environment;
2.   11.3 percent attributed it to the new style of administrative leadership;
3.   11.9 percent cited a better appreciation of legislative staff by those in power;
4.   9.5 percent said it was due to the increased power of the Congress; and
5.   others cited the increased training efforts (8.3 percent) and better communication (5.4 percent).

The augmented power of Congress under the 1988 Constitution could ultimately worsen its structural problems. According to our analysis, a tension existed between the attributes of the Congress as a political institution and as an efficient organization as perceived by the staff. By imposing a bureaucratic structure on the Congress as regards its leadership and staff, the political attributes of the institution were compromised. Furthermore, its bureaucratic efficiency was destroyed.

The most desirable function of a legislature as a political institution according to our analysis is that of a forum where members are able to reach agreements. Leadership and staff roles need to reflect this political priority. Staff objectivity and accuracy may be politically relevant to the extent that they contribute to the formulation of policies that can be agreed upon. The destabilization of political leadership under the guise of equality and democracy would only hamper such agreements. Congressional leadership under the rules of the Congress (unfortunately, reaffirmed and ratified in the new Constitution), prohibited those leaders from developing the necessary expertise and, more important, the necessary power base to facilitate the reaching of agreements within the Congress and between the Congress and the President.

From the elected member's point of view, power within the Congress did not provide a sufficient deterrent to influence his behavior and his voting regarding proposed legislation. To serve his electoral interests, a member found it politically acceptable to defy his party and his congressional committee and vote in favor of legislation opposed by the congressional leaders. Executive agencies were a source of many favors and perks that the member needed in order to serve his constituents.

Even Congressional leaders were always aware of the transient nature of their position in the Congress. Decisions that might upset their colleagues or staff (who have permanent appointment status) were usually avoided. It was the political expediency of the moment that shaped the decisions of the leaders and the staff. A congressman holding an institutional leadership position (member of the Mesa) or a staff person holding the directorship of a secretariat avoided making unpleasant decisions and opted instead to create as many favors as possible, hoping to cash in on those favors once out of their positions. Since Mesa members were not rewarded for hard and responsible work, they chose to make the best of their one-time, two-year term by using and abusing the resources of the institution. Consequently, staff holding administrative leadership positions suffered from the same instability, because they were chosen by the Mesa members.

During the authoritarian regime this state of affairs was tolerated, if not welcomed. The Congress was expected to ratify executive initiatives. When it disagreed, as it often did, typical responses were in the form of speeches denouncing the proposed policy, or proposing a bill outlining a different policy. Although all legislatures value oratory and eloquence, the Brazilian Congress placed special importance on those skills.

Such a role can be considered appropriate for a legislature operating under a parliamentary system, where the role of the opposition is to denounce the policies of the government, and the role of the government-sponsored party is to defend the government policies. Defiant speeches and the introduction of bills, even when they had no chance of being adopted, could be conceived of as important political acts.

Indeed, the Congress under the authoritarian regime mastered these instruments, either to embarrass the executive or to set an alternate agenda regardless of how unfeasible that agenda was. Under these conditions, the role of the legislator was not to propose legislation that was acceptable and workable, but to outbid the executive and appeal to the crowd. Reasonable solutions and agreements under the authoritarian regime only benefitted the executive and compromised the legislator.

Under the new competitive party system, electoral imperatives demanded a defiant member, one who proposes and enunciates general principles and is not willing to compromise with others to arrive at clearly specified policies. The opposition and small parties had no incentive to seek an agreement with the government-sponsored party, because that would only benefit the executive and the government-sponsored party. To engage in bargaining would undermine the purity of the opposition member or party and consequently lead to a loss in electorate support. Even the government party had problems identifying with the executive position, since it would pay a political price during an election year.

While these negative responses were considered politically significant in a legislature stripped of its power under an authoritarian regime, they posed serious problems to a constitutionally strong Congress. Unfortunately, the structure of the leadership and the staff could only produce defiant speeches and enunciation of positions of principle, when what was needed were agreements that required attention to details and, most important, a willingness to compromise within the Congress and between the Congress and the President. A strong Congress and a strong President, as the new Constitution stipulated, may not simply be a reestablishment of a necessary balance as some have argued, but rather a recipe for instability and the reemergence of impasses between the executive and the Congress.

The structure of the congressional leadership and the staff posed as much of a problem for the staff as it did for the elected members. In spite of the presence of a high percentage of academically qualified and motivated staff members, few had the opportunity or the necessary political backing either to conduct politically relevant research or to manage the institution according to bureaucratic norms of efficiency and economy.

The legislative staff, even the few that were theoretically involved in providing information and research, such as the Prodasen, and the *Assessoria* and information and documentation units of each house, were not in a position to do so. Centrally organized and wedded to the norm of objectivity, they were located outside the loop of public policy-making. Even members of the staff who were politically sensitive and astute (both houses had a number of them) found it either difficult or inadvisable to take an openly political or partisan role, because the leadership of the institution was in constant change.

The staff member did not have the opportunity to acquaint himself with the priorities and needs of the leader. It was inadvisable because an openly political or partisan role may bring the hostility of another elected member, or the immediate supervisor. Although the job security of the staff person was not at stake, his opportunity to be appointed to the sought-after DAS jobs would have been jeopardized.

Legislative staff in the United States derive a lot of satisfaction from their ability to influence the shaping of public policy, even when the credit goes to the elected member. There is a vicarious feeling of satisfaction and a real sense of professional accomplishment. Legislative staff are usually rewarded with better salaries or promotional opportunities, both while in service and after leaving to assume a position in the private sector. In Brazil, however, this incentive was absent, because the purpose of the legislature under the authoritarian regime was not to arrive at policies, but rather to ratify executive policies or refute, denounce, and protest against them in the form of speeches.

For the Brazilian legislative staff, hard work and clear identification with certain policies were unfruitful and dangerous. An ambitious staff member was advised to play it safe, not to rock the boat, and to develop amicable connections with all factions of the political spectrum via individual services and patronage, rather than through identification with a public policy issue. His interest was in promoting his career within the bureaucracy of the Congress and having access—for himself and his family and friends—to the benefits and privileges of the institution, rather than seeking jobs in other branches of government or the private sector. The strategy of those who sought better financial rewards was to do as little as possible and to pursue an independent career in the private sector as a side job. An overly enthusiastic staff member reduced his opportunity to advance internally and to find second job opportunities outside the Congress.

In spite of these negative incentives and the absence of positive incentives, a number of staff members informally and secretly associated themselves with politically outspoken elected members. The reorganization and reclassification introduced in 1986 gave the members of the *Assessoria* and the administrative assistant of each senator an automatic grade of DAS-3 and increased the salary and the prestige of advisors and personal staff in the Senate. This was a partial attempt to address the imbalances between the salaries and benefits of the administrative staff and those of the advisory, information, and research staff. Coupled with a stronger and more assertive Congress and committee system, these measures could induce some of the staff to become more politically informed and relevant. For this potential to be realized, however, some basic structural changes need to be introduced.

The Congressional staff operations were neither efficient nor economic. In exercising their administrative functions the staff managed to get the job done, but at a high price and inefficiently. It has been reported that the Senate employed approximately 7,000 employees and the Chamber approximately 6,000 in 1988. However, what is known in Brazil as *funcionários fantasmas,* or no show employees—who receive salaries without showing up for work—makes an accurate count of the staff very difficult.[3]

Regardless of the actual number, a legislative bureaucracy representing an inverse pyramid, where almost all the employees are at the top of their job grade and salary scale, could hardly be characterized as efficient or economical. Staff tended to rise to the top of their job grade and salary scale regardless of the type of work they were doing, their qualifications, their job performance, or their contributions to the institution. Neither the political leadership nor the administrative leadership had an interest in effecting change or the power to do so. As interim leaders, congressmen gained more by expanding the employment pie and increasing salaries rather than implementing measures intended to promote efficiency and economy. An expanding employment pie offered them a good opportunity to employ their supporters, friends, relatives, and family members. High salaries for the existing staff benefitted them, since the life of the member and his family in Brasília depended on the good will of the staff. The staff provided them with housing facilities, transportation, communication and travel opportunities, printing services, medical services, and other benefits. Pleasing the staff was a strategic investment, especially when the member was no longer in a leadership position.

Finally, the congressmen had no incentive or interest in using staff or services offered by the Congress in an efficient and economic manner, since they were free resources offered to the members in general. To economize in the use of these resources was not in the legislator's best interest. Furthermore, austerity could produce staff hostility and enable other more prodigal members to overindulge their insatiable appetites. The proclivity of political leaders was to embark on an expansionist staff policy, the success of which was measured by the amount of additional resources and expanded services they were able to generate for themselves and their colleagues during their term in office. Since DAS positions were in constant rotation to coincide with the leadership rotation within the Congress, administrative leaders tried to expand employment opportunities and staff benefits and privileges. Neither the political nor the administrative leadership had the interest or the incentive to see a lean, efficient, and economic congressional staff bureaucracy.

Ironically, congressional bureaucracy during the authoritarian regime served some important functions. It offered congressmen employment opportunities; sustained the institution when it was suspended; attended to its management needs; preserved essential services; maintained the institutional memory; recruited, developed, and updated skills and technologies relevant to the legislature; and served as a symbol for congressional presence.

NOTES

1. The data in this analysis were collected in two separate but identical surveys conducted in 1981 and 1986 on the staffs of the Federal Senate and of the Chamber of Deputies. In each survey 500 questionnaires were sent to a random sample of the staff of both houses. A total of 162 and 168 completed questionnaires were received in 1981 and 1986, respectively. Extensive interviews over the past eight years were also conducted with various congressional staff to explore various points raised by the results of the surveys.

2. See *Boletim de Pessoal* (Brasília: Senado Federal), for the years of 1987, 1988, and 1989.

3. These figures were cited as estimates by the general directors of each house in an interview with the author.

Chapter 5

Congress at Work

Academic interest in the study of legislatures in developing countries is of recent vintage.[1] The literature generated in the past two decades has postulated a number of propositions on the role of legislatures in societies. Many of these propositions are insightful and challenging; however, little empirical research has been conducted to support the proposed generalizations. With few exceptions, most of the empirical research uses a macro-system approach, and to the extent that legislatures are discussed, they are dealt with as a residual or dependent variable. Emphasis is normally placed on such generic societal variables such as the economy, political parties and elections, societal stratification, and executive-bureaucratic politics. Given the minimal role that many legislatures play in the setting of public policy, dealing with legislatures as residual categories is understandable.

In their analyses, Latin American scholars in general, and Brazilian scholars in particular, predominantly under the influence of the Marxist sociological logic, eschew not only the legislative institution, but all kinds of political institutions.[2] Their scholarly emphasis has been on the "State" and its relationship with "civil society" domestically and with the world economic system internationally. Even among those Brazilian scholars who have recently been moving away from the Marxist mode of analysis toward a social sciences approach, legislatures as institutions have not yet attracted their attention.[3]

In this chapter we explore the legislative role of the National Congress of Brazil under the authoritarian regime between 1964 and 1985. First, we focus on the activities that the Congress actually performed, the importance of those activities, and the contribution those activities made to the transition to an open and competitive political system. Thus, we emphasize not only the roles that the Congress played, but also how it played those roles. Furthermore, studying the role of the Congress in Brazil during the past quarter of a century allows us to examine the extent to which the authoritarian regime was able to resolve the problems associated with the presidential system of government discussed in Chapter 1.[4]

MANIFESTATIONS OF CONGRESSIONAL BEHAVIOR

In reviewing the records of the Congress and observing its behavior during the past two decades,[5] one is struck by the many activities it undertook, many of which were clearly not related to public policy, yet were important to the viability of the Congress in its role during the democratic transition. Congressional activities could be classified into seven categories, not necessarily in order of importance.

Constitutional Amendments

Every year, the Congress considered a number of constitutional amendments. In countries such as Brazil, where constitutions are also detailed statements of public policies, there is often a need to amend the constitution when public policy imperatives change.

In the case of Brazil, when the military came to power, the resort to constitutional amendments, especially between 1964 and 1969, was necessitated by the desire of the regime to have the constitution reflect the decrees, institutional acts, and complementary laws that were promulgated by the President, which in many cases contradicted provisions of the constitution that was in force.

After 1969, members of Congress tried to undo the restrictions imposed by the President by presenting their own constitutional amendments. Thus, constitutional amendments can provide us with an indication of the tension between the President and the Congress. The stronger the Congress, the more constitutional amendments it would propose. From the President's perspective, in Brazil's case, constitutional amendments represented a means of expanding his power while maintaining the facade of rule of law. Table 5.1 shows the number of constitutional amendments presented in selected years.

Table 5.1

Constitutional Amendments Presented in Selected Years

Type of Legislation:	Presented by:	1962	1964	1968	1972	1976	1980	1984
Constitution Amendments	**Legislative**							
	Senators						14	9
	Deputies	4	12				83	75
	Congress			4	0	29		
	Executive		6		1	1	2	1
	Total	4	18	4	1	30	99	85

Source: *Annual Reports of the President of the Chamber of Deputies.*

Until 1976, the regime was able to rule in accordance with the Constitution of 1969, with minimum challenge from the Congress. Beginning in 1976, however, the Congress began to challenge the legitimacy of the Constitution. In 1976, the number of constitutional amendments proposed jumped to thirty. In 1980, the number increased to ninety-nine, and in 1984, eighty-five constitutional amendments were proposed.

Proposed Bills

A significant activity of the Congress during the authoritarian regime was introduction of bills either proposing new laws or amending existing ones. In the Brazilian legislative context, bills could be sponsored in each house by either the members, the committees, and the Mesa, or by the executive, the judiciary, and states' governors.

The 1967 to 1969 constitutional provisions stipulated that the President could present his bills under an urgency provision. Bills presented through the urgency method were dealt with by the Congress within thirty days.[6] The budget was presented under a special process to be discussed in Chapter 6, while financial and economic bills were normally presented through the urgency method. Unless the bills were acted upon within the prescribed period, the President was entitled to promulgate such bills as laws through the provision of *decurso de prazo*, or time limitation.

If the Congress behaved as the regime expected, we would expect that most bills introduced by the President would be either approved or rejected within the allocated time. We would also expect that the more control the President enjoyed over the legislature, the more he could control their agenda. Thus bills introduced by the President would be ratified by the legislature on time, making it unnecessary for the President to promulgate those bills as decree laws. There would be no need for the President to resort to the issuance of decree laws, or to use the time-limitation provision. The resort to the use of decree laws or the time-limitation provision might indicate a reluctance on the part of the Congress to accommodate the presidential agenda. An increase in the number of laws issued as decree laws or through the time limitation provision could therefore be construed as an indicator that the President's control over the Congress was weakening, or that the Congress was exercising its powers in a more assertive manner. By forcing the President to resort to these exceptional measures, the Congress would, in effect, be denying the President political legitimacy that might have been granted if the Congress had approved the measures as the President had hoped.

During the authoritarian regime, Brazilian presidents also enjoyed both partial and full veto powers. We stipulate that, the weaker the Congress, the less likely it would be to pass legislation that did not enjoy presidential support, and therefore the less the President would need to use his partial or total veto power. On the other hand, the more assertive the Congress, the more likely it would be to pass legislation not supported by the President, and the more likely that the President would be forced to resort to the use of veto power.

As to bills presented by the members, we expect that, the weaker the Congress, the fewer bills it would propose. In a weak Congress, we would also expect a small percentage of those bills presented by members to be approved or even considered by the whole body. On the other hand, the stronger the Congress, the greater the number of bills it would introduce and the greater the number of bills it would approve, at least in the house where they were introduced. With the weakening of state and local governments in Brazil after 1967, we would expect few bills to be introduced by states' governors, since most local and state affairs fell under the control of the executive.

The proposal and approval rates of bills, both at committee level and floor level, will be closely examined in future sections of this chapter.

Legislative Decrees

These are measures that could affect public policy; they fall within the prerogative of both houses of the legislature. Decrees represent residual powers that the Congress maintained, such as ratification of treaties and other international matters.

The number of decrees passed each year does not show a pattern that allows meaningful generalizations. With the exception of 1964, when the Congress passed 102 legislative decrees, the number stabilized between thirty-five and forty-eight legislative decrees each year.

Complementary Laws

Constitutional provisions, or institutional acts issued by the President with the force of constitutional provisions, were elaborated by the Congress through the instrument of complementary laws.

In accordance with the logic of the authoritarian regime, we would expect the executive to elaborate its own laws and provide its own guidelines and ask the Congress to only ratify those laws. The regime would not be predisposed to requesting that the Congress ask for guidelines. The Congress, on the other hand, in trying to regain its power, would be expected to attempt to present and pass its own version of complementary laws in order to impose on the executive some guidelines it considered appropriate. The more assertive the Congress became, the more it would try to propose complementary laws or amend those laws presented by the executive. Table 5.2 shows the number of complementary laws proposed in selective years.

Table 5.2

Complementary Laws Presented in the Chamber of Deputies in Selected Years

Type of Legislation:	Presented by:	1962	1964	1968	1972	1976	1980	1984
Complementary Legislative Laws	Senators						3	3
	Deputies			17			82	115
	Chamber Commissions							
	Executive			4			3	3
	(Total)				7	65		
	Total	0	0	22	7	65	88	121

Source: *Annual Reports of the President of the Chamber of Deputies.*

We notice a continuous increase in the number of complementary laws proposed by the Congress over the years. In 1976, while the executive proposed sixty-five complementary laws, the Congress proposed none. In 1980, however, we find that the executive proposed only three out of eighty-eight complementary laws, and in 1984, it proposed three out of 121. The Congress proposed the rest.

Resolutions

Resolutions are actions taken by each house to regulate and manage its own internal affairs. Resolutions may also refer to the exclusive competence of one house, such as the Senate's power to grant authority to allow local and state governments to borrow money and to issue bonds. Resolutions dealing with legislative management and process were important because they regulated the behavior of the individual members and the thousands of staff that worked for them.

Resolutions could impose restrictions on the individual member's ability to travel, hold hearings, or use financial and human resources to undertake his legislative activities. With regard to the legislative staff, resolutions were important because they affected who was hired, what salaries they received, and what type of work they undertook. The building of the institutional capabilities of the Congress (see Chapters 3, 4, and 5) was regulated through resolutions.

Table 5.3 shows the number of resolutions passed by the Congress in selected years. They ranged from eight in 1962 to 305 in 1980. As the Congress regained its autonomy and increased in complexity, the number of resolutions it passed to administer and regulate itself showed a similar increase.

Table 5.3

Resolutions Presented in Selected Years

Type of Legislation:	Presented in:	1962	1964	1968	1972	1976	1980	1984
Resolutions	Chamber of Deputies	8	48	36	29	45	96	131
	Senate			72	68	122	206	138
	Congress	*	*	2	2		3	2
	Total	8	48	110	99	167	305	271

* Data not available

Source: *Annual Reports of the President of the Chamber of Deputies* and *Annual Reports of the President of the Federal Senate*.

Reports

Legislatures in presidential systems of government resort to standing committees to scrutinize and analyze proposed legislation. Research on the U.S. Congress, for example, revealed that the fate of legislation is largely sealed within the committee, before it reaches the floor.

Although the committee system within the Brazilian context was weakened through a series of measures (see Chapters 1 and 2), committees continued to function in spite of their institutional weaknesses. One of the main products of committee work within the Brazilian Congress was the reports they produced on proposed legislation. These reports, called *parecer(es)*, were often prepared by a member of the committee with the assistance of legislative staff. The *parecer* normally contained a summary of the proposed legislation and occasionally a recommendation for action. Such reports were submitted for approval, first in the committee, then in the whole body.

Whether these reports contributed to the formation of public policy is not clear. They were, however, important in providing the individual members with legislative training and exposure to various policy alternatives. During the authoritarian regime, members utilized the *pareceres*, first to familiarize themselves with the proposed policy, then later to propose legislation themselves.

The figures shown in Table 5.4 indicate a gradual but steady increase in the number of reports written by senators. Statistics on the reports written by the Chamber of Deputies were not available.

Table 5.4

Reports Presented in Selected Years

Type of Legislation:	Presented by:	1962	1964	1968	1972	1976	1980	1984
Reports	Deputies	*	*	*	*	*	*	*
	Senators	*	*	1062	*	1163	1496	1225
	Total	*	*	1062	*	1163	1496	1225

* Data not available.

Source: *Annual Reports of the President of the Federal Senate.* Table 5.4. Reports Presented in Selected Years.

Requests for Information

When denied a meaningful role in the formation of public policy, the congressmen resorted to the practice of asking the executive to furnish information regarding the workings of the bureaucracy and various aspects of public policy. Many times, they asked that the person responsible appear and present a report on the workings of his department.

Many of these requests for information were not merely to solicit information, but to draw the attention of the executive to critical policy considerations or to embarrass the executive for its failures. *Comissões Parlamentares de Inquérito* (CPIs), or Parliamentary Inquiry Committees, were sometimes formulated to explore critical policy areas or to highlight policy failures.

The record shows that until 1968 the Congress requested information from the executive on a frequent basis, as illustrated in Table 5.5. Thus, in 1968, the Congress requested information from the executive 2,812 times. The Constitution of 1969 imposed restrictions on the use of this instrument. Consequently, the number of requests for information declined drastically, to six in 1972 and forty-two in 1976. Only after the election of 1982 did the requests begin to increase again. Thus, in 1984 there were 134 requests for information, and most were made by deputies.

Table 5.5

Requests for Information Presented in Selected Years

Type of Legislation:	Presented by:	1962	1964	1968	1972	1976	1980	1984
Requests for	Deputies	483	1437	2666	6	34	14	117
Information	Senators	*	*	146	0	8		17
	Total	483	1437	2812	6	42	14	134

* Data not available.

Source: *Annual Reports of the President of the Chamber of Deputies.*

(The rest of this chapter analyzes the work of the committees and the Congress in terms of the bills considered and the disposition of those bills. Particular attention will be paid to the evolutionary nature of that work during the authoritarian regime and the contribution of the Congress to the final phase of political opening in 1986.)

COMMITTEES IN CONGRESS

Analyzing the role that committees have played within the Congress of Brazil poses a special problem. There is no written material in either English or Portuguese on their role.[7] As we mentioned in Chapter 2, committees were in a constant state of flux. Committees were reformulated every two years. Both committee leadership and membership were constantly changing. Although committee meetings were not secret, there was little publicity or press coverage of their work. There is, however, a detailed statistical account of their work prepared by the committee undersecretariats of each house and published in the annual report of each house.[8]

Importance of Committees

Committees within the Congress of Brazil have varied in importance, work load, and relevance to different regions of the country. The permanent committees could be classified into three groups, in accordance with importance and national visibility: those with national orientation, the executive-security-oriented committees, and the distributive committees.

Membership in the Committees of Constitution and Justice, Foreign Affairs, Budgeting, and Economy may bring a certain national visibility and could carry some rewards. The Committee of Constitution and Justice, the busiest of all the committees, was in charge of reviewing all legislation to see that it conformed to the constitution and the laws already in effect. This Committee was usually composed of distinguished lawyers and jurists and had the power to kill proposed legislation by declaring it unconstitutional, in violation of existing laws, or technically deficient. Over the years, it had diligently exercised this function, and, in doing so, it acted as a filtering mechanism.

The Senate's Committee on Foreign Affairs was a prestigious committee, since it considered the confirmation of ambassadors and received foreign delegations. Its members often traveled to foreign countries, attended international conferences at the United Nations, the Inter-Parliamentary Union, and other forums.

The Committee on the Economy (later named Industry and Commerce) provided its members with an opportunity to deal with economic and fiscal policies that had national implications. During the authoritarian regimes those functions were predominantly dominated by the executive, but a review of their work shows that they received a large number of bills generated by the members. Since many of the bills were presented by members who were attempting to legislate in an area that the executive perceived as its preserve, supporters of the government in those committees managed to reject many of the private members' bills. Table 5.6 shows the work of those committees in selected years.

As expected, the Committee of Constitution and Justice received the largest number of bills, followed by the Committee on the Economy (Industry, and Commerce). The Committee on Budgeting had few bills, since the budget had to be presented to the Congress as a whole, rather than to each house separately.

Constituency service-oriented members of the Congress were likely to seek appointment to a number of distributive committees, such as Health, Labor and Social Legislation, Public Service, Education and Culture, Agricultural and Rural Affairs, and Communication. These ministries controlled huge resources and provided extensive employment opportunities. Even though distributive committees during the authoritarian regime were in no position to challenge the executive, familiarity with the projects being proposed by the government and the working relationship they developed with the bureaucrats who administered those programs gave committee members access to information and influence that they were able to use in channeling some of those resources to their regions and supporters. Table 5.7 shows the work of those committees in selected years.

Table 5.6

Work Load and Action of Selected
Nationally Visible Chamber Committees in Selected Years

Committees:	Status of Bills:	1962	1964	1968*	1972	1976	1980	1984
Constitution	Approved	280	677		212	724	1068	1633
and Justice	Rejected	92	176		139	274	213	296
	Others	148	274		385	1181	1170	1171
	Total	520	1127	0	736	2179	2451	3100
Budgeting**	Approved		115		2			
	Rejected		45		0			
	Others		376		3			
	Total	0	536	0	5	0	0	0
Economy,	Approved	55	107		24	114	124	82
Industry and	Rejected	27	18		21	204	44	94
Commerce***	Others	50	49		81	120	121	314
	Total	132	174	0	126	438	289	490
Foreign	Approved	4	33		24	32	48	48
Affairs	Rejected	0	1		1	0	4	3
	Others	8	13		6	8	18	15
	Total	12	47	0	31	40	70	66
Total	Approved	666	1619		513	1385	2356	3147
All Chamber	Rejected	201	413		308	604	506	578
Committees	Others	546	1079		752	2454	2153	3219
	Total	1413	3111	0	1573	4443	5015	6944

Others: archived, canceled, postponed, etc.

* Data not available
** Committee on Budgeting and Accounting in the years 1962 and 1964.
*** Committee on the Economy in the years 1962, 1964, 1968 and 1972.

Table 5.7

Work Load and Action of Selected
Distributive Chamber Committees in Selected Years

Committees:	Status of Bills:	1962	1964	1968*	1972	1976	1980	1984
Labor and	Approved	19	60		6	99	263	130
Social	Rejected	1	7		28	22	72	29
Legislation**	Others	27	32		115	368	383	756
	Total	47	99	0	149	489	718	915
Education and	Approved	29	45		25	51	90	106
Culture	Rejected	6	20		25	62	55	49
	Others	41	25		31	82	70	118
	Total	76	90	0	81	195	215	273
Health	Approved	14	7		7	20	37	16
	Rejected	5	13		1	11	17	11
	Others	5	37		13	32	39	88
	Total	24	57	0	21	63	93	115
Public	Approved	15	31		23	22	41	78
Service	Rejected	2	15		16	1	6	3
	Others	5	15		6	11	7	6
	Total	22	61	0	45	34	54	87
Total	Approved	666	1619		513	1385	2356	3147
All Chamber	Rejected	201	413		308	604	506	578
Committees	Others	546	1079		752	2454	2153	3219
	Total	1413	3111	0	1573	4443	5015	6944

Others: archived, canceled, postponed, etc.

* Data not available
** Committee on Social Legislation in the years of 1962, 1964, 1968, and 1972.

A majority of the bills presented to distributive committees were either approved or simply not acted upon. Only a few of the bills presented by the members were rejected outright. This may indicate that deputies supported each other—logrolling—by approving each other's pet bills. Distributive committees had a higher percentage of their bills generated by individual members seeking special favors for their regions and states. Distributive committees, therefore, normally received a large number of bills that needed to be screened before they were reported to the floor. Thus a high percentage of the bills presented to these committees were either rejected or postponed.

Executive-security-oriented committees considered legislation of concern to the executive, such as national security matters or the harnessing of nuclear energy. In doing so, those committees did not attract the interest of individual members, either because they were considered the exclusive prerogative of the executive (National Security), required special knowledge not easily available to the members (Science and Technology), or they were not distributive in nature and therefore did not offer the opportunity for constituency services.

As Table 5.8 illustrates, committees that dealt with legislation generated mainly by the executive had a smaller volume of work, (since the executive presented general authorization bills and left all the details to be elaborated by the bureaucracy). Executive-dominated committees approved most of the bills they received. This was the case of the Committees on Science and Technology, on Mines and Energy, and on National Security.

Committees' Work Load

The volume of work performed by committees varied from year to year in accordance with the saliency of the issues the country was facing. There were some observable patterns, however. The work of the committees showed a sharp decline during election years. Every four years, the whole Chamber of Deputies, and, alternatively, one- or two-thirds of the Senate, were busy running election campaigns, and, therefore, were not in Brasília pushing for new legislation. Immediately after an election, each house spent most of the first legislative session (March to June) trying to reorganize itself and compose its leadership and committees. New members spent their time familiarizing themselves with the workings of the Congress and the policy issues facing each committee. Thus, while the number of committee meetings showed some increase, there was no corresponding increase in the number of bills introduced. In accordance with the internal rules of the Congress, the bills presented to either house, unless acted upon, remained in effect for a period of four years. So, in the first year after an election, bills that had been rejected or sent to the archives by the committees or the whole house, often were resurrected by their original sponsor or members of the same party. The bulk of the legislative work of the committees took place during the second and the third years after the election. During those two years, committees received and acted upon a higher number of bills.

The volume of work and the action that committees undertook varied from one period to the other, reflecting the political climate. Between 1960 and 1964, the committees' work was interrupted twice: in 1961, during the resignation of President Jânio Quadros, and in 1963, after the adoption of the parliamentary system of government, to prevent Vice-President João Goulart from assuming full presidential powers. In 1964 the work of committees increased, with the return to the presidential system of government. That year committees held more than 504 sessions, approved a record 2,231 bills, rejected 413 bills, and postponed consideration on 1,079 bills.

Table 5.8

Work Load and Action of Selected
Executive-Security-Oriented Chamber Committees in Selected Years

Committees:	Status of Bills:	1962	1964	1968*	1972	1976	1980	1984
National	Approved	13	27		6	6	15	54
Security	Rejected	7	17		3	4	8	3
	Others	11	17		4	8	2	18
	Total	31	61	0	13	18	25	75
Mines and	Approved		25		4	3	16	19
Energy	Rejected		1		0	1	3	14
	Others		12		1	13	10	42
	Total	0	38	0	5	17	29	75
Science	Approved					11	12	29
and Technology	Rejected					3	0	4
	Others					10	8	16
	Total	0	0	0	0	24	20	49
Total	Approved	666	1619		513	1385	2356	3147
All Chamber	Rejected	201	413		308	604	506	578
Committees	Others	546	1079		752	2454	2153	3219
	Total	1413	3111	0	1573	4443	5015	6944

Others: archived, canceled, postponed, etc.

*   Data not available

The work of the committees showed a significant decrease between 1965 and 1970. Indeed, during this period, the *Annual Reports of the President of the Chamber of Deputies* failed to mention the work of the committees. In 1967, a passing reference in the report stated that committees considered 106 bills. The President, using his emergency prerogatives, froze the regular work of the Congress and ruled for the most part by executive decrees and institutional acts. Committees did not meet during 1968, since the Congress was suspended.

Activities of the committees increased in 1971. In the Chamber of Deputies, committees held 613 meetings, approved 728 bills, rejected 440 bills, and amended 90 bills. Between 1972 and 1985, the work of the committees picked up. Table 5.9 shows a progressive increase in the work of committees.

Table 5.9

All Committee Work in the Chamber during the Years 1972-1985

YEAR	72	73	74	75	76	77	78	79	80
Bills Approved	513	1431	1285	1434	1385	1635	2162	1801	2355
Bills Rejected	308	516	367	343	604	706	1531	490	506
Others	84	134	72	49	611	419	1119	64	75
Bills Postponed	668	736	881	1199	1838	2021	2379	1443	1719
Total Bills Rec	1016	2304	1794	2998	3243	2945	5153	3983	3572

YEAR	81	82	83	84	85
Bills Approved	1906	1289	2456	3147	2904
Bills Rejected	498	340	237	578	656
Others	60	97	109	104	165
Bills Postponed	2092	2607	2053	3615	3687
Total Bills Rec	3251	2320	5114	4723	4524

The committees approved more than 50 percent of the bills they received. Their approval rate ranged between a high of 71 percent in 1974 to a low of 41 percent in 1978. The approval rate was lower immediately after an election year (1975, 1979, and 1983) and increased as the legislative session progressed. The percentage of bills rejected varied between 30 percent in 1972 to a mere 4 percent in 1983. The rejection rate averaged 15 percent. We also noticed a progressive decline in the percentage of bills rejected. This trend was particularly evident after the elections of 1978 and 1982: the opposition parties scored significant gains in the Chamber of Deputies and the government-controlled party continued its decline.

Each year, significant numbers of bills were not considered. Some of those bills were returned to the authors or withdrawn by them, others were sent to the archives, while still others were tabled to be considered at a later date.

Benefits Derived from Committee Work

Committees in the National Congress of Brazil served a number of useful purposes.

Germination of Ideas and Shaping of Legislation

Committees appear to have served a useful function in shaping legislation that the executive introduced. On occasions, as a result of committee deliberations, the executive was persuaded to withdraw its own proposed bills and reintroduce them in an amended form. In some cases, the executive used the various bills introduced by members and committees as trial balloons to test the political climate. Often the executive co-opted popular themes and programs considered by committees and introduced them as executive bills. Thus, committee work may have provided the executive with a series of mini-laboratories that enabled the executive to see how new ideas and policies were popularly received. Committees may have provided the executive with a controlled and secure test tube for the germination of new policies and programs in tackling societal problems. As a result of the amendments that the executive introduced on its own bills, committees may have saved the executive from some political embarrassment and costly mistakes.

Screening Legislation

Committees seem to have performed a very useful function in screening legislation. Although committees approved more than 50 percent of the legislation that was presented to them, the other 50 percent was either rejected, amended, or postponed. This process gave more opportunity for the whole body to concentrate its efforts on fewer bills that had already benefitted from some committee expertise.

Training Members in Subject Matter of Policies and the Skills of Political Bargaining

Perhaps the most important function of committee work in Brazil was the training it provided the political elite during two decades of authoritarian rule. The instability of leadership, the frequent changes of committee members, and the lack of committee resources forced many members to become generalists on a wide range of public policies. Committee rooms became classrooms for educating members in policy affairs, and committee activities offered committee members the opportunity to work with individuals from various states and with different political perspectives. Members of the parties of the government and the opposition learned to work together and trust each other. The committees provided the working arena for the evolution of a pragmatic, problem-solving political culture that provided the military with a secure bridge to gradually exit from politics without risking a violent breakdown of the system. The committees were the cells within which the bond of familiarity and trust developed between the government and its opponents. Such familiarity and trust were necessary factors that contributed to the special characteristics of the Brazilian transition to democracy.

ACTION IN THE PLENARY SESSIONS

Under the authoritarian regime, the importance of committee work was de-emphasized in favor of action on the floor. Committees were not expected to act independently and prevent the whole body from expressing its views on proposed legislation. Although this norm was justified as enhancing democracy and the constitutional equality of all members of the legislature, it nonetheless played into the hands of the regime by weakening the work of the committee and expediting legislation deemed important to the executive. It enabled the President to have his legislative agenda expediently approved without serious and informed discussions at the committee level.

Notwithstanding the important work that the committees did in terms of screening legislation, the most significant public and open role that the Congress played in determining public policy was undertaken at the plenary sessions. As we have seen, more than 50 percent of the bills considered by the committees were reported to the plenary sessions for final action. Committees did not feel that they had the authority, the expertise, or the political power to determine the fate of a bill that had some significant support. Unless a bill was overwhelmingly rejected at the committee level or of no significance to the executive or a group of legislators, it was likely to find its way to the floor for final determination.

The various restrictions imposed on the Congress during the authoritarian regime reduced its power in determining public policy, but apparently did not diminish its role in debating it. Although constitutionally operating under a presidential system of government, with separate but not equal power to determine public policy, the Congress, during the authoritarian regime, was behaving more like a legislature within a parliamentary system of government. Under the imposed two-party system, the role of the government party was to support the government's legislative agenda, and that of the opposition party to oppose it. However, the contradictions between the constitutional provisions of the presidential system of government and the expectation of the military that the government party act as a parliamentary block provided a hybrid behavior on the part of the Congress, which was characteristic of neither a presidential nor a parliamentary system of government. Of course, on many occasions the government party and, to some extent, the opposition party supported most of the bills proposed by the executive. Yet we noticed that the Congress retained its constitutional prerogative to propose its own bills and, occasionally, even approve them outside the executive legislative agenda.

This propensity to propose legislation, debate it, and even approve it was shared by legislators from both parties. Legislators from the government party found themselves competing with legislators from the opposition party in sponsoring legislation that did not have the approval of the executive. Although many of the members' sponsored bills had little chance of being approved by the house as a whole or by both houses, sponsoring those bills was important for electoral purposes. Both parties felt the need to establish a legislative record to enhance their standing during electoral campaigns. In many cases, members of the government party pleaded with the executive for certain legislation to help them in their electoral campaigns. On occasions they sponsored legislation in direct opposition to the executive, something a parliamentary party would not do. Furthermore, even among the most ardent supporters of the executive within the legislature, there was widespread hostility toward the executive for the harsh measures taken against the Congress and its members.[9]

This feeling of confrontation between the legislature and the executive led many members of all political persuasions to adopt a defiant attitude toward the executive. Although it was not politically feasible or, according to some, advisable to defeat bills sponsored by the President, or even to significantly modify them, the defiant attitude of the legislators manifested itself in sponsoring scores of bills expressing points of principles and general policy directions in contradiction to the policies and practices of the executive. It was through such symbolic activities of defiance, and not the actual impact on public policy, that the Congress, during the authoritarian regime, redeemed itself and began to symbolize the aspiration of what has been referred to as the civil society.[10]

Another important symbolic activity dominating congressional work during the authoritarian regime was the animated debates that became the hallmark of the plenary sessions. Indeed, debates and oratory at the sessions were among the most distinguished attributes of political leadership in Brazil. Deliberations of the Congress were public, relatively free, and widely publicized, even during the height of the authoritarian regime. Each house had its internal press and public relations department to package and publicize the work of the Congress to the press and to the concerned public. The Senate printing shop published not only the verbatim debates, but a host of other publications dealing with public policy issues and controversies. Each house had its own corps of accredited journalists and reporters representing the major news media in the country.[11]

Plenary sessions were presided over by the president and vice-presidents of each house or their representatives in accordance with the internal rules of each house. The legislative battle, however, was orchestrated and managed by the party leaders and vice-leaders. In spite of the attempts of the government party to control debates, major battles erupted and highly politically charged speeches were made. On occasion, the conflict was so intense that the executive either had to suspend the Congress or impose additional restrictions on it. The more the Congress found itself powerless in determining public policy, the more it resorted to floor debates to register its dissatisfaction. Legislators of the opposition parties, on occasion, were joined by members of the government party to exercise the residual power left to them: that of discussion, educating the public, and setting the future political agenda.

Any study of the role of Congress during this period that excludes those great debates and the failed attempts of the Congress to initiate and influence public policy will necessarily miss an important phase of the political opening in Brazil and the issues and the individuals who helped shape and direct that process. The seeds of the gradual return to a civilian rule that culminated in the election of Tancredo Neves to the presidency in 1985 were sown in the wombs of those debates and proposed legislation.

Evolution of Congressional Power

Although the preceding discussion characterizes the legislature's behavior during the authoritarian regime as a whole, the way it actually performed its legislative function varied from one period to the other, in accordance with changes in the country's political and economic climate. Periodic elections brought different individuals to the legislative process and changed the composition and strength of the political parties within the Congress. Although strictly manipulated by the executive, elections sent a message to both the government and the opposition and, therefore, influenced the legislative agenda and the behavior of the Congress vis-à-vis the executive. Both the level of legislative activities and their directions varied from one congressional election to another and from one president to another. The continuity of policy and behavior that was provided by the military establishment was offset by changes and adjustments forced by the contradiction within the military bureaucratic coalition and the political and economic development within the country. The most significant of those adjustments were the various measures associated with the politics of *abertura* (see Chapter 1).

To gain an inside view of the legislative work of the Congress, we examined the role of the Congress between 1970 and 1986.[12] The legislative role was divided into four periods: 1970 to 1974, 1975 to 1978, 1979 to 1982, and 1983 to 1986. However, before we turn our attention to the work of the Congress during these four periods, it is important to discuss the conditions in the country during the early 1960s that precipitated the coup of 1964.

In July 1961, President Quadros resigned. Goulart, his Vice-President, was allowed to assume the presidency in September of 1961, but only after the Constitution was amended to create the office of the prime-minister, to share the executive power with the President. Between September 1961 and January 1963, President Goulart and his supporters were mobilizing their forces for a plebiscite to amend the constitution in order to regain presidential power and eliminate the office of the prime-minister. In January 1963, the Constitution was amended and the office of the prime-minister was eliminated. In March 1964, against the background of mass demonstrations and high inflation, the military removed Goulart from power and declared that a revolution had taken place. In 1966, all political parties were dissolved and in their place two government-sanctioned parties were created: ARENA, the pro-government party, and MDB, the purged opposition party.[13]

This period saw the demise of the democratic Constitution of 1946, the overthrow of a duly elected civilian government, radical changes in the nature of political parties, and the imposition of a new Constitution which embodied the vision of the bureaucratic authoritarian regime and a new political and economic order.

The work of the Chamber of Deputies reflected the vicissitudes of this period. Table 5.10 details the work of the Chamber of Deputies during this period.

Table 5.10

Legislative Work of the Chamber of Deputies between 1960 and 1966

YEAR	1960	1963	1964	1965	1966	TOTAL
Ordinary Executive Bills	208	142				350
Urgency Executive Bills			188	233	220	641
Legislative Bills	728	1244	666	593	159	3390
Total Bills Received	936	1386	854	826	379	4381
Bills Approved	203	179	360	365	150	1257
Bills Rejected	6	7	44	4	28	89
Bills Changed	73	23	1	14	9	120
% Bills Approved	22%	13%	44%	40%	29%	29%
% Bills Rejected	1%	1%	5%	0%	7%	2%

The year 1960 is perhaps the last year of normalcy that the Congress experienced before the April 1964 coup d'état. During that year the Chamber of Deputies received a total of 936 bills, 208 of which were presented by the executive and the remaining 738 by the Congress. The Chamber approved 22 percent of those bills, rejected 1 percent, and changed 8 percent. Reliable statistics were not available for the years 1961 and 1962.

In 1963, the work of the Chamber was similar to its work in 1960. The main difference was the increased confrontation between the legislature and the President, which led to a higher number of bills presented by the legislature and a decline in the percentage of bills approved, from 22 percent in 1960 to 13 percent in 1963. The conflict between President Goulart and the Congress reached its height in 1964. In that year, which was dominated by the new military regime, the Chamber was able to approve 44 percent of the bills it received.

Another important difference was the new regime's resort to urgency measures. In 1964, the executive introduced all its legislative programs under the urgency provision. This became the norm for 1965 and 1966. In 1965, in spite of the military coup and the harsh measures adopted against the Congress, many in the country believed that these measures were temporary in nature and, as soon as law and order were restored, the congressional prerogatives would be reinstated. Many still believed that the military acted to preserve the Constitution against the presumed threat of Goulart and the Left. The actions of the Chamber reflected those beliefs. The executive presented 233 urgency bills, and the Congress presented 593 bills. The Chamber of Deputies approved 40 percent of those bills. This meant that, in addition to the bills sponsored by the executive, the Chamber approved 132 of its own sponsored bills.

Tension between the Congress and the executive increased in 1966 and led to the suspension of the Congress from October to November. The civilian opposition in the country coalesced to formulate a grand front known as *Frente Ampla*, against the permanency of the military in power. In response to the intensification of the civilian resistance to usurpation of power by the military, the *linha dura*, or hard-line group, within the military emerged, determined to change the political structure of the country once and for all. The actions of the hard-liners, including the restrictions they imposed on political activities and the work of the Congress, were to become apparent in the years to come. In 1966, the Chamber presented only 159 bills as compared to 1,244 in 1963, the year before the coup. It approved 150, all of which were presented by the executive under the urgency provision. The Congress began to lose its prerogative as a policy initiator. In accordance with the military vision of legislative politics, the role of the Congress was reduced to ratifying executive initiatives.

The work of the Chamber between 1967 and 1970 reflected the harsh political environment within which it operated.[14] After the 1966 election the hard-liners within the military were in the ascendant. In 1967, the various amendments and decrees passed by the military government under institutional and complementary acts were incorporated into a new constitutional document, which, with its major amendments in 1969 and other minor amendments in subsequent years, remained the active constitution of Brazil until October 1988.

The valiant attempts of the Congress to introduce amendments to the proposed Constitution that the military had drafted led to a one-week suspension of Congress in 1966. All the amendments the Congress had introduced were item-vetoed by the executive. The 1967 Constitution was born, embodying all the changes that the military had undertaken through its emergency powers.

In 1968, popular resistance under the leadership of the *Frente Ampla* was intensifying. In response to agitation by students and faculties, the generally strong support students received from the Congress, and the defiant stand that some members took against the military authorities, a series of institutional acts was passed by the military, including the infamous Institutional Act No. 5 of 1968. The latter gave the executive wide-ranging powers to limit political and press freedoms, denied opponents of the government their political and civil rights, and gave the executive the power to close the Congress. Using these emergency powers, the executive suspended Congress indefinitely, and many opponents of the regime were jailed, exiled, or banished. Some went underground and initiated armed resistance against the regime, thus providing the military with a justification for imposing additional restrictions and resorting to the use of wide-scale coercion and torture.

Toward the end of 1969, the Congress was reconvened to elect a successor to Costa e Silva after his unexpected death. During that same year a major constitutional amendment embodying all the institutional acts passed since 1967 was promulgated by the military. After the ranks within the Congress that opposed the military were banished or intimidated, the Congress had no power and acceded to all the military's requests, accepting the 1969 amendments and electing Médici as successor to Costa e Silva. This period represented the efforts of the military to consolidate its power by imposing harsh restrictions on the Congress and all other political activities that it considered threatening. These restrictions and repressive measures are reflected in the work of the Chamber, as Table 5.11 shows.

Bills introduced by the executive were ratified with little debate. The Chamber had no political power to mount any meaningful resistance. During the four-year period, only two bills proposed by the executive were rejected, to be approved later. In 1969, the activities of the Chamber ceased, since it was suspended and the country was ruled by executive decrees and acts. Only the legislative bureaucracy continued functioning.

Bills presented to the Congress as a whole were also overwhelmingly approved.[15] Out of a total of sixty-two bills introduced in the Congress during this period, fifty bills (81 percent) were approved. The remaining bills were approved at the beginning of the next legislative session. None of the bills were rejected. We also noticed that, after the purges of 1969, the Congress started ratifying executive bills without even the delaying tactics it had resorted to earlier.

Bills introduced by the judiciary were not as lucky as executive-sponsored bills because the judiciary, as a separate branch of government, was authorized under specific conditions to present its own bills directly to the Congress. Out of a total of forty bills submitted by the judiciary during this period, eighteen or 45 percent were approved, and the remaining were not considered by the Chamber. None of the bills submitted by the judiciary, however, were rejected outright by the Chamber.[16]

Bills presented by congressional committees fared well during this period. Normally those bills were compromise bills forged between the executive and the legislature and presented by committees for ratification by the whole body. During the five-year period, thirteen bills were presented and ten were approved. None were rejected.

Bills approved and introduced by the Senate had a better chance of being approved than those introduced by the Chamber. The Senate, with fewer members, introduced fewer bills than its larger counterpart, the Chamber. Furthermore, it was easier for the military to control a smaller body like the Senate through its leadership and other electoral manipulations in the Northeast, such as the representative predominance of the smaller states, even when the opposition party dominated most of the larger states of the country. Senators from the smaller rural states always tipped the balance in favor of the government. Because of the electoral laws, it was easier for members of opposition parties to be elected to the Chamber rather than to the Senate. The Chamber therefore emerged as the workhorse of the Congress in terms of the number of bills it presented and considered each year.

Of the eighty-six bills approved by the Senate and sent to the Chamber, thirty-two bills or 37 percent were approved, two were rejected, and the rest were tabled. On the other hand, 2,003 bills were presented by the Chamber. Only 174 bills, or 9 percent, were approved, and 283 bills, or 14 percent, were rejected. The rest were either tabled, withdrawn, archived, or not even considered.

Table 5.11

Legislative Work of the Chamber of Deputies between 1967 and 1970

Bills Presented:	1967 No.	1967 %	1968 No.	1968 %	1969 No.	1969 %	1970 No.	1970 %	TOTAL No.	TOTAL %
Executive	72		111		5		49		237	
Approved	73	101*	102	92	4	80	45	92	224	95
Rejected	2	3	2	2			1	2	5	2
Congress	17		38				7		62	
Approved	14	82	30	79			6	86	50	81
Rejected	0	0	0	0			0	0	0	0
Chamber	773		969		36		225		2003	
Approved	36	5	95	10	17	47	26	12	174	9
Rejected	10	1	25	3	2	6	248	110	283	14
Senate	23		51		1		11		86	
Approved	6		12	24	8	800	6	55	32	37
Rejected	0		2	4	1	100	0	0	2	2
Committees	7		4		0		2		13	
Approved	7	100	3	75	0	0	0	0	10	77
Rejected	0	0	0	0	0	0	0	0	0	0
Judiciary	6		27		0		7		40	
Approved	3	50	12	44	3	0	0	18	45	
Rejected	0	0	0	0	0	0	0	0	0	0
Total Presented	898		1200		42		295		2435	
Total Approved	139	15	254	21	32	76	83	28	508	21
Total Rejected	12	1	29	2	3	7	249	84	290	12

* The percentage is above 100 because of bills approved that were referred from previous session.

After 1969 the independent initiatives of both the Senate and the Chamber were significantly curtailed. In 1967 and 1968, the Chamber introduced 773 and 969 bills, respectively. In 1970, the Chamber introduced only 225 bills, while the Senate introduced eleven bills, as compared to twenty-three and fifty-one in 1967 and 1968, respectively. Undoubtedly, the harsh measures adopted by the hard-liners imposed severe restrictions on the Congress and forced it to curtail its legislative activities.

Yet two significant patterns of behavior of the Brazilian military in power became apparent. First, the military was determined to institutionalize the succession to power among its members and prevent the emergence of a single military dictatorship. Rotation of leadership was to become the pattern. The second important pattern was the resort to elections as a means of obtaining political legitimacy. Having decided to remain in power longer than their civilian friends had expected, the military decided to seek political legitimacy through election and the legislative process. Notwithstanding their proclamation, on the eve of the coup, that the new regime obtained its legitimacy through the success of its revolution, rather than through the Congress, we find that throughout their stay in power, the military sought legitimacy from a Congress and an electoral process.

Having claimed to be defenders of the constitutional order, the military was unable to totally break with the past constitutional order. Its attempt to create and structure a new political order had to be worked out through the despised civilian politicians, purged, restricted, and purified as they may have been. In time, the dynamics of this involuntary relationship were to provide the necessary conditions and, at the same time, opportunity to gradually and peacefully exit from power.

It was ironic that the same institutions—the political parties, electoral processes, and the Congress—which they molded to provide them with legitimacy were the same institutions that de-legitimized them and compelled them, albeit peacefully and gradually, to exit from power.

The Médici Period (1970-1974)

This may appropriately be called the Médici period. Although elected to the presidency in 1969, after the sudden death of President Artur da Costa e Silva, General Emílio Garrastazú Médici had to operate until the end of 1970 with a Congress elected in 1966. With the promulgation of the Constitution of 1969 and the election of 1970, President Médici stabilized his regime and institutionalized the political vision of the hard-liners.[17] The predominance of the executive during this period was at its zenith. Using the newly enacted constitution and the threat of internal armed resistance, Médici imposed his iron will on the Congress. The election of 1970, under the restrictions imposed and the political purges undertaken by the military, provided the government with a comfortable majority within the Congress. The political power of the Congress reached its lowest, as can be seen by its legislative record (see Table 5.12).

Bills introduced by the executive were assured a 100 percent approval rate as compared to 13 percent for bills introduced by the Senate, and 10 percent for bills introduced by the Chamber. Judiciary bills fared a little better, with a 15 percent rate of approval. The remaining bills introduced by the Senate and the Chamber were either rejected or not considered at all. ARENA leadership in the Congress made sure that many of those bills were not even brought to the attention of the committees. During this period, Congress rejected 32 percent of Senate bills and 13 percent of Chamber bills.

Table 5.12

Legislative Work of the Congress between 1970 and 1974

Bills Presented:	1971 No.	%	1972 No.	%	1973 No.	%	1974 No.	%	TOTAL No.	%
Executive	91		145		228		307		771	
Approved	92	101*	150	103*	220	96	306	100	768	100
Rejected	0	0	1	1	0	0	0	0	1	0
Senate/ Committees	19		97		184		190		490	
Approved	0	0	19	20	25	14	19	10	63	13
Rejected	0	0	49	51	56	30	54	28	159	32
Chamber/ Committees	461		576		658		663		2358	
Approved	0	0	76	13	90	14	73	11	239	10
Rejected	241	52	94	16	85	13	113	17	533	23
Judiciary	20		0		0		4		33	
Approved	0	0	1*		0		4	100	5	15
Rejected	0	0	0		0		1	25	1	3
Total Presented	600		818		1070		1164		3652	
Total Approved	92	15	246	30	335	31	402	35	1075	29
Total Rejected	241	40	144	18	141	13	168	14	694	19
Executive Veto	0		1		13		8		22	
% Veto Approved		0		0		4		2		2
Passed/Time Limit	0		0		0		2		2	
% Time Limit/ Approved		0		0		0		0		0

* Because of bills referred from previous sessions.

Although the Congress during this period continued to introduce its own bills and, occasionally, to approve some of them, the legislative agenda was dominated by the executive. The power of the executive was so pervasive that the President used his veto power only twenty-two times and the time-limitation provision twice. This shows that the executive not only had the power to pass its legislation intact, but also that the political support it controlled within the Congress ensured that no embarrassing legislation introduced by the members was approved or even debated. Only benign bills introduced by the majority party and approved by the executive were approved or debated. Executive hegemony was pervasive. The only symbolic resistance the Congress was able to mount was the introduction of bills, even though their chance of approval or debate was limited. The number of bills introduced by the Senate and by the Chamber continued to climb, in the case of the Senate from nineteen in 1971 to 190 in 1974. The number of bills introduced by the Chamber rose from 461 in 1971 to 663 in 1974.

The Legislative Period (1975-1978)

Three factors shaped congressional legislative work during this period. The election of 1974, though returning a 56 percent majority of ARENA members to the Chamber, produced a big surprise in the Senate. Of the twenty-two Senate seats that were contested during that year, MDB won sixteen seats, including the most populous states of São Paulo, Rio de Janeiro, Minas Gerais, and Rio Grande do Sul. Since the other two-thirds of the Senate seats were not up for election that year, the ARENA party maintained its majority within the Senate, but lost whatever electoral legitimacy it may have had.

This surprisingly strong showing by the MDB coincided with the diminishing of the Brazilian economic miracle. During the Médici period, Brazil had enjoyed its highest economic boom, averaging annual increases of 9 percent in its GNP. The 1973 oil embargo forced the military to heavily borrow in the international market to finance development plans and to offset the increase in the cost of energy. The resulting world recession and Brazil's difficulties in increasing its exports to finance its mounting debts had a negative impact on the performance of the Brazilian economy. Whatever legitimacy the military had derived from a strong economic performance began to disappear.

Finally, the elevation to the presidency of General Ernesto Geisel in 1974 set in motion a series of liberalization measures meant to release the mounting political tensions in the country. All of these changes affected the work of the Congress and were reflected in its legislative work (Table 5.13 details the legislative output of the Congress between 1975 and 1978).[18]

The total number of bills introduced by the executive declined from 771 in the previous four-year period to 518 during this period. By contrast, the number of bills introduced by the Congress jumped significantly. Bills introduced by the Senate jumped from 490 during the previous period to 1,398 during this period. Similarly, bills introduced by the Chamber increased from 2,358 during the past four years to 6,557 bills during this period. Undoubtedly, members of Congress, encouraged by the good political showing of MDB in the 1974 election, and prompted by the worsening economic crisis, were willing to undertake more independent initiatives by proposing new legislation.

Another significant development was the fate of bills introduced by the executive. Although the Congress continued to approve the overwhelming majority of those bills and to reject none, it took more time in granting approval. Thus, 91 percent of the bills were approved on time, while the remaining 9 percent were postponed or delayed, forcing the executive to issue eleven of those bills as decrees.

Table 5.13

Legislative Work of the Congress between 1975 and 1978

Bills Presented:	1975 No.	%	1976 No.	%	1977 No.	%	1978 No.	%	TOTAL No.	%
Executive	120		120		137		141		518	
Approved	114	95	104	87	144	105	111	79	473	91
Rejected		0		0	1	1		0	1	0
Senate/ Committees	313		355		347		383		1398	
Approved	35	11	28	8	19	5	11	3	93	7
Rejected	90	29	146	41	153	44	99	26	488	35
Chamber/ Committees	1898		1795		1528		1336		6557	
Approved	92	5	98	5	100	7	80	6	370	6
Rejected	136	7	223	12	300	20	221	17	880	13
Judiciary	0		2		7		3		12	
Approved	0		3	150*	2	29	4	133*	9	75
Rejected	0		0	0	0	0	0	0	0	0
Total Presented	2331		2272		2019		1863		8485	
Total Approved	241	10	233	10	265	13	206	11	945	11
Total Rejected	221	10	369	16	454	22	320	17	1369	16
Executive Veto	26		8		8		7		49	
% Veto Approved		11		3		3		3		5
Passed/Time Limit	0		6		1		4		11	
% Time Limit/ Approved		0		3		0		2		1

* Because of bills referred from previous sessions.

With regard to bills introduced by members, the Congress approved a higher number of bills introduced by the Senate (ninety-three as compared to sixty-three in the previous period) and the Chamber (370 as compared to 329 in the previous period). The percentage of bills approved, however, declined to 7 percent for bills introduced by the Senate and 6 percent for bills introduced by the Chamber.[19]

Another significant development was the number of bills vetoed by the President. During this period, the number of bills that received partial or total presidential veto increased from twenty-two during the previous period to forty-five. This represented 5 percent of the bills approved. This increase in the use of the presidential veto power underlined two significant developments. First, the Congress was beginning to pass legislation that did not meet the approval of the executive, and second, the Congress was amending some of the bills introduced by the executive.

During this period, the Congress discussed and rejected 488 bills introduced by the Senate and 880 bills introduced by the Chamber. The year before the Congress discussed and rejected 159 of the bills introduced by the Senate and 533 introduced by the Chamber. Within the context of the authoritarian regime, to be able to introduce controversial legislation and discuss it, even when it was eventually defeated, represented a significant challenge to the authority of the executive. The Congress began developing its agenda. At the same time the military began taking notice of the demands of the civil society. Bills introduced and rejected became the basis for bills that were introduced by the executive in future sessions.

Few bills were introduced by the judiciary. Of the twelve bills introduced, nine were approved and the rest were postponed.

The Figueiredo Period (1979-1982)

The work of Congress during this period reflected the intensification of the process of *abertura* that was started under President Geisel and was to be accelerated under his successor, General João Figueiredo, and his Chief of Staff, General Golbery do Couto e Silva, who was credited as being the true mastermind behind the strategies and processes of the opening process.[20]

Beginning in 1976, Geisel introduced the "April 1977 Package," which changed the electoral laws, among other things, and called for the state legislators in 1978 to indirectly elect one-third of the Senate and all the governors. This was an attempt by the government to maintain its majority control of the Congress after the defeat it suffered in the Senate race in 1974. After the election of 1978, the much-hated Institutional Act No. 5 was abolished. In 1979, political prisoners and exiles were granted amnesty and permitted to return to the country. Also, in 1979, a law was passed permitting a return to a multiparty system, though under strict regulation.

Furthermore, during this period, the union movement, especially in the industrial region of São Paulo under the leadership of Luis Inácio "Lula" da Silva, began to challenge the authority of the government by staging a number of illegal strikes. Indeed, this was a period when the civilian politicians were emboldened to stage serious challenges to the military authorities, sensing that it was only a matter of time before the military departed from power. The legislative actions of the Congress demonstrated this new resurgence.

Table 5.14

Legislative Work of the Congress between 1979 and 1982

Bills Presented:	1979 No.	%	1980 No.	%	1981 No.	%	1982 No.	%	TOTAL No.	%
Executive	119		150		116		100		485	
Approved	100	84	132	88	98	84	122	122*	452	93
Rejected	0	0	0	0	0	0	0	0	0	0
Senate/ Committees	462		445		429		263		1599	
Approved	40	9	48	11	20	5	14	5	122	8
Rejected	112	24	100	22	64	15	29	11	305	19
Chamber/ Committees	2793		1910		1882		1204		7789	
Approved	164	6	127	7	129	7	144	12	564	7
Rejected	355	13	96	5	232	12	248	21	931	12
Judiciary	3		6		7		11		27	
Approved	6	200*	6	100	2	29	12	109	26	96
Rejected	0	0	0	0	0	0	0	0	0	
Total Presented	3377		2511		2434		1578		9900	
Total Approved	310	9	313	12	249	10	292	19	1164	12
Total Rejected	467	14	196	8	296	12	277	18	1236	12
Executive Veto	30		28		7		39		104	
% Veto Approved		10		9		3		13		9
Passed/Time Limit	3		10		20		2		35	
% Time Limit/ Approved		1		3		8		1		3

* Because of bills referred from previous sessions.

Despite the gradual political liberalization, the authoritarian regime, through electoral manipulation, maintained a slim majority in the Chamber and a comfortable one in the Senate. This ensured that none of the bills proposed by the executive were rejected. Of the 485 bills presented, 452 were approved and the remaining were promulgated into law through the time-limitation provision. Yet the Congress began to display certain vigor. In 1981, during the illness of Figueiredo, which necessitated his being outside the country, his civilian Vice-President Aureliano Chaves was allowed to assume the presidency. The number of bills proposed and adopted by the Congress showed significant increase. The number of instances that the President had to resort to either a veto to prevent the enactment of legislation it did not approve, or the use of the time limitation to pass legislation it failed to have the Congress approve on time also increased.

The Senate, despite having one-third of its members as bionic senators, showed renewed vigor, as evidenced by the number of bills it introduced and approved. Of the 1,599 bills it introduced, it approved 122, or 8 percent, a 1 percent increase from the previous period. It rejected 305, or 19 percent, a sharp decrease from the previous period. Some of the bionic senators were able to tie up the legislative process and thus prevent the Senate from considering much of its legislative agenda. Debate and speeches on the Senate floor became extensive. Government supporters succeeded in slowing down the legislative process.

Bills proposed by the Chamber also jumped from 6,557 in the previous four years to 7,789 during this period. Of the bills proposed, 564 were approved and 931 were rejected. A heightened legislative activity within the Chamber became apparent, in terms of the number of bills introduced, approved, or rejected.

An analysis of the sources of bills introduced during this period also revealed an interesting trend. While the number of bills introduced by the executive was stabilized or began to decline in absolute numbers, bills introduced by the legislators continuously increase. Furthermore, the percentage of those bills approved was either declining or stabilizing for the executive-sponsored bills and increasing for the legislative-sponsored bills.

Another indication of the vigor of the new Congress was the number of cases in which the President was forced to resort to the use of the veto power or the time-limitation provision. During this period, the President used his veto power 194 times as compared to only forty-nine times in the previous period. This represented a jump from 5 percent of the bills approved in the previous period to 9 percent during this period. During this period the President's resort to the veto method increased from eleven cases under Geisel to thirty-five cases during this period, a jump from 1 percent to 3 percent of the bills approved.[21]

The Transition to Civilian Government Period (1983-1986)

During this period, the work of the Congress was influenced by the culmination of the process of the political opening. In the election of 1982, five political parties (the Communist parties were excluded) were permitted to participate. In spite of advantages afforded the government party by the restriction of electoral laws regulating campaigning and electoral alliances, list formation, and other electoral procedures, the opposition scored significant gains, especially in the Chamber of Deputies. Also in 1982, the election for the state legislatures were combined with the election for the National Congress. State governors were directly elected for the first time since 1965.

Some of the most important states elected governors who belonged to the opposition parties. Rio de Janeiro, for example, elected Leonel Brizola, a long-time opponent of the military regime and the leader of PDT; São Paulo, Franco Montoro; and Minas Gerais, Tancredo Neves of the PMDB. Several state legislatures fell under the domination of opposition parties, including São Paulo, Rio de Janeiro, Paraná, and Rio Grande do Sul. In addition to PMDB, other left-of-center parties such as PDT and PT gained representation at the federal, state, and local levels. In 1985, cities that had been classified as security zones under the military were permitted to have direct election of mayors. Several big cities elected mayors from PMDB, PDT, PT, and PFL.

PDS, ARENA's successor as the government-supported party, maintained its majority in the Senate but lost it in the Chamber. Furthermore, PDS maintained its majority in the Electoral College that was expected to elect a civilian successor to President Figueiredo. However, fighting within PDS split the party and led to the creation of PFL, under the leadership of Senator Marco Maciel and Vice-President Aureliano Chaves. The combined forces of the National Front (PMDB and other opposition parties) and PFL elected Tancredo Neves as President and Sarney as Vice-President of Brazil. The terminal illness of Tancredo, announced only a few hours before he was to assume office in March of 1985, and his death thirty-seven days later, elevated Vice-President Sarney to the presidency.

Although acting as the leader of the Democratic Alliance, Sarney did not have the total support of the National Front members that were in control of the Congress after 1984. Although the Constitution of 1969 remained in force until October 1988, the office of the presidency was politically weakened and the Congress became the hub of legislative activities. The conflict between the Congress and the executive as evidenced by action on the floor, increased in spite of the fact that the President belonged to the same coalition that controlled the Congress. The work of the Congress during this period showed this transformation (see Table 5.15).

Executive bills were no longer assured automatic passage. Indeed, in 1985, President Sarney's first year in office, only 68 percent of the bills introduced by the executive were approved. Even in 1983 and 1984, under President Figueiredo, the Congress approved 85 and 83 percent of bills introduced by the executive. Later, during 1986, the Congress approved 93 percent of the bills introduced by President Sarney, reflecting the partnership that the President was able to forge between the executive and the Congress, under the leadership of Deputy Ulysses Guimarães, the national president of PMDB and the president of the Chamber of Deputies. Deputy Guimarães in the Chamber of Deputies, and Senator Fernando Henrique Cardoso in the Senate, working as shadow prime-ministers to the President, ensured that his legislation was approved by the Congress.[22]

Although the Congress did not reject any executive bills during this period, it introduced major amendments and passed different versions from what the executive had intended, including several bills intended to open up the political system and ensure wider political participation by the people.

In 1983, the President used the veto provision thirty-nine times (9 percent of the bills approved) and the time-limitation provision forty-two times (9 percent). This use of the veto power continued to rise to 10 percent in 1984, 21 percent in 1985, and 18 percent in 1986. Similarly, in 1984, President Figueiredo used the time-limitation provision forty-two times (8 percent of the bills approved), and in 1985 and 1986, respectively, Sarney used it on 10 percent of the bills.

Table 5.15

Legislative Work of the Congress between 1983 and 1986

Bills Presented:	1983 No.	%	1984 No.	%	1985 No.	%	1986 No.	%	TOTAL No.	%
Executive	145		149		251		165		710	
Approved	123	85	124	83	170	68	154	93	571	80
Rejected	0	0	0	0	0	0	0	0	0	0
Senate/										
Committees	339		314		475		396		1524	
Approved	32	9	45	14	97	20	136	34	310	20
Rejected	12	4	19	6	30	6	85	21	146	10
Chamber/										
Committees	3517		2428		2441		1551		9937	
Approved	293	8	336	14	271	11	212	14	1112	11
Rejected	223	6	172	7	116	5	44	3	555	6
Judiciary	10		9		29		23		71	
Approved	8	80	8	89	22	76	13	57	51	72
Rejected	0	0	0	0	0	0	0	0	0	0
Total										
Presented	4011		2900		3196		2135		12242	
Total										
Approved	456	11	513	18	560	18	515	24	2044	17
Total										
Rejected	235	6	191	7	146	5	129	6	701	6
Executive										
Veto	39		49		117		94		299	
% Veto										
Approved		9		10		21		18		15
Passed/Time										
Limit	42		42		58		49		191	
% Time Limit/										
Approved		9		8		10		10		9

In the Senate, the number of bills introduced during this period fell slightly short of the previous period (from 1,599 bills to 1,524 bills). However, the number of bills approved increased from 122 bills to 310 bills, or 20 percent of the bills introduced. The work of the Chamber showed a similar increase. The total number of bills introduced during this period jumped from 7,789 bills to 9,937 bills. The number of bills approved also increased from 564, or 7 percent of the total, to 1,112 bills, or 11 percent of the total. In both the Senate and the Chamber, the number and percentage of bills introduced by the legislatures and rejected showed significant declines. In the Senate, the number of bills rejected fell from 305, or 19 percent of the bills proposed in the previous period, to 146, or 10 percent during this period. In the Chamber, the decline of bills rejected was as dramatic. It fell from 931, or 12 percent in the previous period, to 555, or 6 percent during this period.

The statistics regarding the work of the Congress during this period showed the gradual unfolding of the measures associated with the political opening and the transition to democracy in Brazil and the effect this had on the legislative work of the Congress. Although the Constitution of 1969 remained in effect, the assertiveness of the Congress in discharging its limited power became evident.

NOTES

1. The only systematic effort to study the role of legislatures in developing countries was the work of the consortium of four universities: Duke, Hawaii, Iowa, and SUNY at Albany. The product of this work was published in Durham, N.C., by the Duke University Press, in the 1970s: John D. Lees and Malcolm Shaw (eds.), *Committees in Legislatures: A Comparative Approach* (1979); Michael L. Mezey, *Comparative Legislatures* (1979); Joel Smith and Lloyd D. Musolf (eds.), *Legislatures in Development: Dynamics of Change in New and Old States* (1979); Albert Eldridge (ed.), *Legislatures in Plural Societies* (1977); Abdo I. Baaklini, *Legislative and Political Development: Lebanon, 1842-1972* (1976); and G. R. Boynton and Chong Lim Kim (eds.), *Legislative Systems in Developing Countries* (1975). Two books published by Duke University Press preceded this series: Alan Kornberg (ed.), *Legislatures in Comparative Perspective*, op. cit. (1973); and Alan Kornberg and Lloyd D. Musolf (eds.), *Legislatures in Developmental Perspective*, op. cit. (1970). The only book available on legislatures in Latin America is by Weston Agor (ed.), *Latin American Legislatures: Their Role and Influence* (New York: Praeger, 1971). In all of these books, only one chapter was devoted to the Congress of Brazil; it was Robert A. Packenham's "Legislatures and Political Development," Kornberg and Musolf (eds.), *Legislatures in Developmental Perspective*, op. cit. (1970). With few exceptions, the research reported does not deal with legislatures in developing countries in an empirical and detailed manner. Recently, a number of Ph.D. dissertations have been written at the University at Albany, State University of New York, dealing with this topic; see Henry Akwo Elonge, "A Political and Administrative History of the Cameroon National Assembly, 1946-1986" (1989); Jassim M. Khalof, "The Kuwait National Assembly: A Study of its Structure and Function" (1984); and Abdullal al Khatib, "The Jordanian Legislature in Political Developmental Perspective," (1975).

2. See Robert A. Packenham, "The Changing Political Discourse in Brazil, 1964-1985," Selcher (ed.), *Political Liberalization*, op. cit. (1986), pp. 135-73.

3. The literature in Portuguese on the Congress of Brazil has been written from a legal, advocacy, historical, or personal memories perspective. See Auro Soares de Moura Andrade, *Um Congresso Contra o Arbítrio: Diários e Memórias, 1961-1967* (Rio de Janeiro: Nova Fronteira, 1985); José Honório Rodrigues, *O Parlamento e a Consolidação do Império, 1840-1861* (Brasília: Câmara dos Deputados, 1982); Octaciano Nogueira, "Poder Legislativo no Brasil," *O Poder Legislativo*, vol. 1 (Brasília: Departamento de Imprensa Nacional, 1981); Nelson Saldanha,

"Separação de Poderes," *O Poder Legislativo*, vol. 2, ibid.; *Poder Legislativo: Prerrogativas* (Brasília: Câmara dos Deputados, 1980); Flávio Portela Marcílio, "Conjuntura Política Nacional" (Brasília: Câmara dos Deputados, 1979); Waldemar de Almeida Barbosa, *A Câmara dos Deputados como Fator de Unidade Nacional* (Rio de Janeiro: J. Olympio, 1977); Waldemar de Almeida Barbosa, *A Câmara dos Deputados e o Sistema Parlamentar de Governo no Brasil* (Brasília: Câmara dos Deputados, 1977); Nelson de Sousa Sampaio, "O Poder Legislativo no Brasil," *Política*, no. 5 (July/September 1977), pp. 39-88; Afonso Arinos de Mello Franco, *A Câmara dos Deputados: Síntese Histórica* (Brasília: Câmara dos Deputados, 1976); Carlos A. Astiz, "O Papel Atual do Congresso Brasileiro," Cândido de Almeida Mendes (ed.), *O Legislativo e a Tecnocracia* (Rio de Janeiro: Imago, 1975); Clóvis Brigagão, "Poder Legislativo no Brasil: Análise Política da Produção Legal de 1959 a 1966" (Master's thesis presented to the Instituto Universitário de Pesquisas do Rio de Janeiro—IUPERJ, 1971); and Barão de Javary, *Câmara dos Deputados: Organizações e Programas Ministeriais desde 1822 a 1889* (Rio de Janeiro: Imprensa Nacional, 1889). For some empirical work, see Gláucio Ary Dillon Soares, "La Cancelación de los Mandatos de Parlamentarios en Brasil," *Revista Mexicana de Sociologia*, 42, no. 1 (January/March 1980), pp. 267-86; Luiz H. Bahia, Olavo B. Lima, Jr., and Cesar Guimarães, "Perfil Social e Político da Nona Legislatura," *Jornal do Brasil* (March 22, 23, and 24, 1979); Gláucio Ary Dillon Soares, "Military Authoritarianism and Executive Absolutism in Brasil," *Studies in Comparative International Development*, 14, nos. 3/4 (Fall/Winter 1979), pp. 104-26; Maria Isabel Valladão de Carvalho, "A Colaboração do Legislativo para o Desenvolvimento do Executivo durante o Governo JK" (Master's thesis presented at the Instituto Universitário de Pesquisas do Rio de Janeiro—IUPERJ, 1977); Rosinethe Monteiro Soares and Abdo I. Baaklini, *O Poder Legislativo no Brasil* (Brasília: Câmara dos Deputados, 1975); Sérgio Henrique Hudson de Abranches, "O Processo Legislativo: Conflito e Conciliação na Política Brasileira" (Master's thesis presented at the University of Brasília, 1973); and Sérgio Henrique Hudson de Abranches and Gláucio Ary Dillon Soares, "As Funções do Legislativo," *Revista de Administração Pública*, vol. 7, no. 1 (1973).

4. According to the military, Brazil could not afford the constant squabbling between the executive and the legislature. The executive supremacy in foreign affairs, national security, and economic development should be reasserted. The Congress, according to the Doctrine of National Security and Development espoused by the military, was expected to ratify and endorse executive initiatives.

5. The statistics contained in this chapter have been collected from the annual reports of the presidents of the Federal Senate and Chamber of Deputies issued between 1972 and 1986. Figures on the work of the Congress between 1972 and 1986 are based on the data bases of Prodasen and were researched under the supervision of the author by the research staff of Prodasen. Furthermore, the author, in his capacity as the director of the Comparative Development Studies Center of the University at Albany, State University of New York, has been directing a cooperative program between the University at Albany and the Congress of Brazil. This program includes training, technical assistance, and research components. As such, the author had several opportunities to visit and interact with both the political and staff leadership of the Congress of Brazil between 1972 and the present.

6. This provision was later expanded to forty-five, and, then, to sixty days.

7. The only exception is an internal publication by the Chamber of Deputies about the work of investigative committees between 1946 and 1982: *Comissões Parlamentares de Inquérito, 1946-1982* (Brasília: Câmara dos Deputados, 1983).

8. The analysis of the work of the committees is based on the *Report of the President of the Chamber of Deputies*, published between 1960 and 1986. The data were supplemented by interviews with committee members and staff.

9. In 1988, in an interview with the author, Flávio Portela Marcílio (three times the president of the Chamber of Deputies under the authoritarian regime) underscored that his most important contribution to the democratic process in Brazil was the fight he led for several years against the military to reassert the prerogatives of the Congress and the security guarantees of its members against arbitrary arrest and harassment by the executive. See also, Marco Maciel, *Liberalismo e Justiça Social* (Brasília: Senado Federal, 1987); Flávio Portela Marcílio, *Atividades*

Parlamentares: Presidência da Câmara dos Deputados (Brasília: Câmara dos Deputados, 1985), and *Atividades Parlamentares: Discursos, 1963-1982* (Brasília: Câmara dos Deputados, 1984); Marco Maciel, *Vocação e Compromisso* (Rio de Janeiro: José Olympio, 1982); Lourival Baptista, *Atuação Parlamentar: Atividades no Senado Federal* (Brasília: Senado Federal, 1980); Hugo Abreu, *O Outro Lado do Poder* (Rio de Janeiro: Nova Fronteira, 1979); Milton Cabral, *Ação Parlamentar* (Brasília: Senado Federal, 1976); and Marcos Freire, *Oposição no Brasil, Hoje* (Rio de Janeiro: Paz e Terra, 1974). The above list includes congressmen of all political persuasions represented in Congress.

10. See Maria Helena Moreira Alves, *State and Opposition*, op. cit. (1985), which has an excellent discussion of the apparatus of the authoritarian regime and the institutions of the civil society, such as the church, labor unions, professional associations, and neighborhood organizations.

11. Even during the height of the authoritarian regime, press censorship did not apply to floor speeches made by the senators and deputies. It was not uncommon, for example, for a journalist or a reporter to leak a sensitive story to a sympathetic legislator so that it could be mentioned in the press without censorship liabilities to the journalist or to the newspaper.

12. After 1972, Prodasen began to collect systematic data on the work of the Congress in both its houses. Data on the work of the Congress before 1972 had to be extracted from the report of the president for each house. To simplify matters we decided to examine the work of the Chamber of Deputies for the years 1960 to 1970 for purposes of illustration and concentrate on the work of the Congress for the years 1970 to 1986.

13. This period encompasses the rule of President Castelo Branco. For a review of his presidency, see John W. F. Dulles, *President Castelo Branco: Brazilian Reformer* (College Station: Texas A&M University Press, 1980); Eurico de Lima Figueiredo, *Os Militares e a Democracia: Análise Estrutural da Ideologia do Presidente Castelo Branco* (Rio de Janeiro: Graal, 1980); John W. F. Dulles, *Castelo Branco: The Making of a Brazilian President* (College Station: Texas A&M University Press, 1978); Carlos Castelo Branco, *Os Militares no Poder* (Rio de Janeiro: Nova Fronteira, 1976); Luiz Viana Filho, *O Governo Castelo Branco* (Rio de Janeiro: José Olympio, 1975); and Luisa Maria Gaspar Gomes, "Cronologia do Governo Castelo Branco," *Dados*, nos. 2/3 (1967), pp. 112-32.

14. The presidency of Costa e Silva is discussed by Carlos Chagas, *113 Dias de Angústia: Impedimento e Morte de um Presidente* (Porto Alegre: L&PM, 1979); Jayme Portella de Mello, *A Revolução e o Governo Costa e Silva* (Rio de Janeiro: Guavira Editores, 1979); Irene Maria Magalhães et al., "Segundo e Terceiro Ano do Governo Costa e Silva," *Dados*, no. 8 (1971), pp. 152-233; and Lúcia Maria Gaspar Gomes, "Cronologia do 1º Ano do Governo Costa e Silva," *Dados*, no. 4 (1968), pp. 199-220. For a pre-presidency biography, written by a journalist with the purpose of improving the then-war minister's image, see Nelson Dimas Filho, *Costa e Silva: O Homem e o Líder* (Rio de Janeiro: Edições O Cruzeiro, 1966).

15. Bills presented to the Congress sitting in a joint session are always executive bills dealing with budgetary matters, national security, or constitutional issues. They require the approval of the whole Congress in a joint session. The resort to joint Congressional sessions was one of the innovations the military introduced, and they used it quite frequently during their rule to force the Congress to ratify measures introduced by the executive that were considered urgent. Their intention was to bypass the scrutiny of the two-chamber legislative process.

16. This is another one of the strategies the military developed, perfected, and used frequently in their dealings with the Congress. If the executive felt that the bills on the agenda of the Congress were likely to generate intensive public debate, even by a minority of the members, the executive used the leadership of the Congress and the government party to bypass that legislation, either by not including it on the agenda, or, if included, by ensuring that no quorum was present. Consequently, the session would be canceled. This strategy effectively killed any legislation presented by members of the Congress, without even the benefit of public debates. Bills the executive presented, but did not want debated for fear of publicity and press coverage, were similarly removed from the legislative agenda, only to be later promulgated as laws under the urgent provision.

17. The presidency of Médici is discussed by Hélio Silva and Maria Cecília Ribas Carneiro, *Emílio de Médici: O Combate às Guerrilhas, 1969-1974* (São Paulo: Grupo de Comunicação Três, 1983); Margaret J. Sarles, "Maintaining Political Control through Parties: The Brazilian Strategy," *Comparative Politics*, 15, no. 1 (October 1982), pp. 41-72; Youssef Cohen, *Popular Support for Authoritarian Regimes: Brazil under Médici* (Ann Arbor: University of Michigan Press, 1979); and Emílio Garrastazú Médici, *O Jogo da Verdade* (Brasília: Secretaria de Imprensa da Presidência da República, 1971).

18. For a discussion of the electoral results during this period, see David V. Fleischer, "Renovação Política—Brasil 1978: Eleições Parlamentares sob a Égide do 'Pacote de Abril,'" *Revista de Ciência Política*, no. 32 (1982), pp. 57-82; Luis Navarro de Britto, "As Eleições Legislativas de 1978," *Revista Brasileira de Estudos Políticos* (July 1980), pp. 7-99; Bolivar Lamounier (org.), *Voto de Desconfiança, Eleições e Mudança Política: 1970-1979* (Petrópolis: Vozes, 1980); Orlando de Carvalho, "Os Partidos Políticos e a Legitimação do Processo Político Brasileiro," *Revista de Informação Legislativa*, no. 16 (October/December 1979), pp. 57-66; Fábio Wanderley Reis, *Os Partidos e o Regime: A Lógica do Processo Eleitoral Brasileiro* (São Paulo: Símbolo, 1978); and Fernando Henrique Cardoso, "Partidos e Deputados em São Paulo: O Voto e a Representação Política," Cardoso and Lamounier (eds.), *Partidos e Eleições no Brasil* (Rio de Janeiro: Paz e Terra, 1975).

19. This low percentage was due to the higher number of bills introduced by each house.

20. See the following regarding the *abertura*: David V. Fleischer, "The Brazilian Congress: From 'Abertura' to 'New Republic'", Selcher (ed.), *Political Liberalization*, op. cit. (1986), pp. 97-133; Luciano Martins, "The 'Liberalization' of Authoritarian Rule in Brazil," O'Donnell, Schmitter, and Whitehead (eds.), *Transitions from Authoritarian Rule*, op. cit. (1986), pp. 72-94; Luiz Gonzaga de Souza Lima, "A Transição no Brasil: Comentários e Reflexões," *Contexto Internacional*, 1, no. 1 (January/June 1985), pp. 27-59; Blanca P. Muñoz, "Brazilian Elections 1982: The Ambivalent Legacy of Vargism," *Electoral Studies*, no. 2 (December 1983), pp. 207-27; Peter McDonough, "Repression and Representation in Brazil," *Comparative Politics*, 15, no. 1 (October 1982); Robert Henry Srour, *A Política dos Anos 70 no Brasil: A Lição de Florianópolis* (São Paulo: Econômica, 1982); and Murillo Macêdo, *Trabalho na Democracia: A Nova Fisionomia do Processo Político Brasileiro* (Brasília: Ministério do Trabalho, 1981).

21. The delay in considering legislation within the time prescribed by the constitution could be caused by several factors. Fearing an adverse action by the legislature, the executive could call upon its supporters to boycott the session and therefore prevent a quorum, thus delaying consideration of the proposed bill. It could ask its supporters to engage in delaying tactics, thereby preventing the Congress from dealing with the proposed legislation on time. Finally, opponents of the bill within the Congress could use delaying tactics that would prevent the Congress from approving the proposed bill, thus forcing the executive to resort to the time-limitation provision. This tactic allows the opponents of bills to achieve two objectives. One, by not approving the legislation, they deny the executive the political legitimacy it seeks from the Congress. If the bill is not popular, that is, if many of the elected members of both parties do not wish to be identified with it, promulgating it into law through the time-limitation provision ensures them a good political "out." Second, the resort to the veto power and the time-limitation provision are good barometers of the executive-legislative relationship within a presidential authoritarian system. It measures the extent to which the executive is in full control of the legislature.

22. Since Sarney's relations with the Congress began to sour during the drafting of the Constitution, from 1987 to 1988, the resort to the so-called *medidas provisórias*—provisional measures—whereby the executive legislates provisional laws as decree laws and asks the Congress to approve or reject them, has increased significantly.

Chapter 6

The Congress as an Advocate and Educator

In the preceding chapter we detailed Congress's volume of legislative work, the source of its legislative agenda, the mechanisms it used to dispose of its work, and the final disposition of the legislation presented to it. We postulated that although the Congress was in no position to defeat or seriously alter legislation presented by the executive, it continued to present and advocate its own legislation, though with limited success. We concluded that the failed attempts by the Congress to advocate its version of public policy was important, because it helped to create a general vision and sentiment of what needs to be done and to mobilize public support for those visions and sentiments.

This chapter explores the extent to which the legislation presented by the Congress actually represented alternate visions and sentiments. We seek to evaluate the significance of the proposed bills presented by the Congress. Were those bills presented to the Congress by its members and committees of general importance, or were they simply, as some have contended, private bills advocating particularistic benefits?[1]

The answers to these questions pose serious methodological problems. How do we decide what was significant and what was not? How can one differentiate between a particularistic bill and a bill with a universalistic scope? Rather than adopt an arbitrary measure and impose it on our data, we decided to follow the definition of what the political leaders of the Congress considered to be important, as represented by the constitutional document that the Congress adopted in 1988. We posited that the constitutional assembly elected in 1986 to draft the new Constitution was the proper authority to determine what was important public policy and what was not. Their collective decisions were embodied in the constitutional document they adopted. Therefore, using the Constitution of 1988 as an expression of what the Brazilian political leaders conceived as their priorities seemed to be justified. The Constitution of 1988 is a detailed document of 245 permanent articles and seventy provisional articles, detailing the priorities of the Brazilian society in every aspect of public policy. This then is our questions: To what extent did the legislation between 1970 and 1988 actually address the priorities that were eventually embodied in the Constitution?

Based on data provided by the synopsis unit of the Chamber of Deputies, a total of 6,526 pending bills presented by the Congress and 144 bills presented by the President were found to be addressing issues and principles that had been adopted by the Constitution of 1988.[2] In accordance with the categories used in the Constitution, we classified the bills (see Table 6.1) into ten categories:

1. individual rights and consumer protection;
2. labor legislation;

3. social security;
4. family, children, elders, and Indian affairs;
5. political rights and the electoral system;
6. social order and the media;
7. government organization;
8. economic order;
9. protection of the environment; and
10. fiscal system and budgeting.

Table 6.1

Distribution of Bills Proposed to the Chamber of Deputies, 1970-1988

Title:	Source of the Proposal:	
	Legislature	Executive
Individual rights	442	6
Labor legislation	994	10
Social security	3,690	63
Family, children, elders, and Indians	106	3
Political rights and electoral system	133	2
Social order and media	366	9
Government organization	272	26
Economic order	305	13
Protection of the environment	85	6
Fiscal system and budgeting	133	6
Total	6,526	144

INDIVIDUAL RIGHTS AND CONSUMER PROTECTION

The authoritarian regime, in its attempt to build a new political and economic system, voided many of the rights and protections that the Constitution of 1946 had guaranteed Brazilian citizens. Those rights and protections that were not suspended through executive decrees were violated by executive actions and bureaucratic arrogance. From the beginning, the Congress found itself in a constant battle to reinstate those rights to the citizens and to define new rights and protections that emerged as a result of new economic and legal developments. When the Constitution of 1988 was completed, the Chamber of Deputies found in its archives and active agenda a total of 442 bills proposed by legislators and six bills proposed by the executive, all dealing with important issues that were embodied in the Constitution. These issues included privacy rights and freedom of information, such as eliminating secrecy on information collected by police officials during investigations; the right of citizens to know what the government was collecting on them; defining the type of information the government could and could not collect about its citizens; and controlling the activities of credit bureaus.

Another category of rights dealt with artistic and intellectual freedoms, rights that the authoritarian regime had suspended through its censorship policies. Proposed legislation in this category included the protection of the rights of artists and intellectuals to express themselves in writing, movies, television, and theater; the protection of their copyrights and the encouragement of artistic and intellectual production by providing economic incentives, removing government restrictive regulations, and protecting the national market against foreign competition.

A large number of bills in this category addressed the need for consumer protection against fraud by both producers and the incompetence of government regulations. Bills were introduced to regulate the production and sales of pharmaceutical drugs, the regulation of the food industry, to ease credit and installments for the poor, and many other issues of concern to the consumer, such as controlling and regulating the price of utilities and ensuring that the poor have access to electricity, gas, and water.

A number of bills in this category sought to define and simplify bureaucratic procedures that affected the citizens' access to certain government services and benefits, such as birth certificates, identification cards, legal aid, rights of prisoners and criminal proceedings, and the defense of constitutional guarantees, especially in declared emergencies.

The policies advocated in this category of legislation were substantially incorporated in Articles 5, 22, 23, 48, 173, 174, 177, 192, and 238 of the new Constitution. The defense of individual and human rights and the protection of artistic and intellectual freedoms were contentious attempts by the Congress to embarrass the executive and to expose the violation of those rights. For those attempts many Congressmen were stripped of their political rights, and the Congress itself was either suspended or placed under additional restrictions. The restoration of those rights became one of the first priorities of the framers of the new Constitution.

Labor Legislation

The regime that overthrew President João Goulart displayed intense hostilities toward labor and their organizations and accused them of being an instrument of the international Left.[3] Union activities were prohibited, leftist sympathizers were banished, and the government grip on the official labor movement was tightened. Collective bargaining was restricted, and labor management affairs were to be decided in accordance with labor laws as interpreted by labor courts. In addition to these legal restrictions, the economic development strategy adopted by the new regime emphasized capital accumulation and led to the weakening of the purchasing power of labor.[4] Labor was to pay the political and economic price of the policies of the new regime.

Over the years Congress became more sympathetic to labor demands. Some opposition members tried unsuccessfully to redress some of the blatant abuses of labor rights. Between 1970 and 1988, congressional members dealing with labor issues proposed 994 bills to the Chamber of Deputies, labor issues that the new Constitution eventually embodied in its provisions.

Proposed legislation in this category was wide-ranging. Some of the bills dealt with such basic issues as determining policy for hiring, dismissals, training compensation, and retirement. Bills were presented to outlaw arbitrary dismissals of employees in the public and the private sectors, to stop discrimination against the handicapped and women in hiring and salaries, to ensure that women in the labor force had additional rights such as paid maternity leave, to regulate women's work during night shifts, and to protect pregnant women against dismissal. Other proposed legislation called for the establishment of a special savings fund to help workers and protect their earnings, to ensure that labor salaries and wages were properly indexed against inflation, and to provide some financial relief to indebted workers who were unemployed or had low salaries. Legislation was also proposed to protect workers against the onslaught of automation, to provide funds to ease the impact of automation on labor, and giving workers some voice in the process of adopting new technologies and the rate of its introduced into the workplace.

With the rampant inflation that became the hallmark of the Brazilian economy in the early 1980s, the Congress introduced a number of bills intended to protect employees against delays in receiving their paychecks, a practice that had become attractive to employers who preferred to pay in inflated money. Bills were proposed to prevent and limit such practices and to impose monetary penalties against perpetrators of such acts and provide compensation for those adversely affected.

One of the most serious problems that plagued Brazilian workers was the question of retirement benefits and how to keep them indexed with inflation. More than 154 bills were presented to regulate the adjustment of retirement benefits to the inflation rate. Conditions under which retirement would become effective were also proposed in order to help the handicapped and the disabled. Various schemes were proposed to encourage the participation of labor in the ownership of the companies in which they worked and to share in the realized profits.

With the rapid industrialization of the country, the need to protect the health of workers against job-related hazards and unsafe health conditions became paramount. Several hundred bills were proposed to force employers to conform to safe work environment standards, to punish violators, and to compensate affected workers. Other proposed bills attempted to define the union-management relationship and to establish workers' rights to collective bargaining and their right to strike in the pursuit of their demands. The proposed bills sought to define and regulate the practice of the various professions so as to protect the workers and the consumers. Proposals were made to extend rights earned in the private sector to the public sector, to establish and implement the merit system in the public area, and to extend the benefits for the unemployed and the handicapped. Finally, legislation was proposed to limit the wages of executives in government-owned corporations and companies in an attempt to limit the corruption and nepotism that prevailed in those publicly owned entities.

These labor policies were eventually embodied in Articles 7, 8, 9, 21, 22, 37, 143, 187, 197, 206, 213, and 239 of the new Constitution.

Social Security

In the welfare society that Brazil became in the 1970s, proposed legislation to define and regulate the benefits and entitlements due to the citizens from the state became the primary preoccupation of the Congress. A total of 3,690 bills proposed by the Congress were found to be relevant to the provisions of the new Constitution. The protection of citizens' rights against the arbitrariness of the bureaucracy and the uncertainties caused by uncontrolled inflation dominated the list of proposed legislation in this area.

One of the areas in which the executive allowed free debate and active congressional participation was social security. Electoral considerations and campaign strategies necessitated close attention to this area of concern. Both government supporters and opponents were active in proposing legislation that would expand the social security benefits of the workers. Proposed legislation dealt with the system of benefits and the fiscal soundness of the social security system, dependents' rights and benefits, work-related accident benefits, victims of catastrophic accidents, exemption of payments to the systems under specified situations, retirement benefits by type of employment and time on the job, special provisions for the handicapped and the disabled, rural workers' benefits, unemployment insurance, alcoholism and mental disabilities on the job, and benefits for the elderly and other categories of employees.

As in other legislatures, the Brazilian Congress played a leading role in the distributive policies of the state. Indeed, during the authoritarian regime, where many areas of public policies were arrogated as the prerogatives of the executive either for national security or economic reasons, involvement in the promotion and definitions of social security benefits for all types of groups and individuals in society became a favorite activity of the Congress. As in the other policy areas, although the congressional agenda in this regard was not fully accepted by the executive, many of the positions advocated were eventually adopted and included in the new Constitution. Articles 197, 201, 226, and 231 established guidelines for the social security system and benefits for the new civilian regime.

Family, Children, Elders, and Indian Affairs

In a country where the overwhelming majority of the population is Catholic, where until the late 1970s divorce was illegal, where the rights of husbands over their wives were almost absolute, where over half of the population was 20 years old or younger, and where more than 13 million homeless children were roaming the streets of the big cities, laws defining and regulating family affairs were contentious political issues. During this period 106 bills were found to address issues that were incorporated into the new Constitution. Some of these bills attempted to regulate marriages, for example, to limit the husband's authority within the family, to define and regulate instances in which divorce would be permitted, and the rights of each spouse, along with children's rights and custody procedures.

The plight of homeless children in Brazil was one of the most pressing social and economic issues facing Brazilian policymakers. Various legislation was presented to ease their plight. Proposals included regulating the conditions of work for the employment of minors, establishing funds to take care of deserted children, giving support to mothers without incomes, regulating the process of adoption, protecting unmarried mothers, and proposing special institutions to exclusively deal with the welfare of minors. Similar proposals were presented to deal with the problems of the elderly. Other proposals dealt with Indian rights, the protection of the national forests that support Indian survival, and the protection of the mineral resources on Indian territories and reservations. Most of these proposals were eventually adopted in Articles 197, 201, 226, and 231 of the new Constitution.

Political Rights and the Electoral System

One of the principal instruments the authoritarian regime used to maintain political power and control was the constant manipulation of the electoral laws. Other instruments of control included the restriction of citizens' political rights and the arbitrary recognition, dissolution, and restructuring of political parties (see Chapter 1).

Congressional legislative initiatives that were eventually embodied in the new Constitution numbered 133 proposed bills. The general direction of these bills was to put some limitation on the arbitrary power of the executive to impose the death penalty for political crimes, the regulation of nuclear plants for military purposes, the definition of the term of office of the President, and the need for political consultation before local government entities could be created or abolished. Several of the bills attempted to introduce changes in the electoral system to ensure a fairer distribution of seats between the Northeast and the South in accordance with population and to install electoral systems that would be more representative of the views of the electorate.

A number of the proposed bills sought to define and expand the eligibility of citizens to run for public office, define residency and educational requirements, and define the crimes that would disqualify individuals from running for office. These same bills tried to define the instances under which individuals could be denied the right to vote. Others attempted to define the conditions under which political parties could be created and officially registered, the code they needed to follow in their internal operations, and the ways they could contest elections. Some of the bills addressed the issues of campaign financing and access to the media before and during electoral campaigns. Finally, legislation was introduced to reinforce the immunity of the congressmen from prosecution under the various emergency powers that the executive normally employed to silence its political critics within the Congress.

Challenging the executive in these sensitive areas required a lot of courage and involved great political risk. Articles 14, 16, 17, 18, and 45 of the Constitution incorporated some of the principles advocated in these proposed bills.

Social Order and the Media

During the authoritarian regime, the state became the principal economic and social actor. Through the arbitrary power it arrogated to itself, it controlled the media and decided what the people could and should know. Through its expanded extractive capabilities and the hegemonic role it played in the economy, it was able to have a near-monopolistic role regarding the provisions of housing, health services, education, and other essential services. The records of the Chamber of Deputies revealed a total of 366 proposed bills that raised public policy issues relevant to the provisions of the new Constitution. These bills involved definitions of various crimes and the appropriate punishment.

Legislators sought to limit the arbitrary use of police powers against suspected criminals, to differentiate between the jurisdictions of the military and civilian courts, and to clarify the definitions of crimes set forth under the national security legislation. Legislation was proposed to define cases exempted from the military draft and the applicability of the draft to women and men occupying religious posts. In all of these cases, the proposed legislation sought to provide the citizen with recourse to due process and to limit the arbitrariness of the military or civilian bureaucracy.

Regarding provisions for social services, proposed legislation sought to encourage the ownership of homes through the provision of easy credit. It advocated public housing for the poor and the rural workers, some form of basic health services, *Sistema Único de Saúde*, throughout the country, regulation of the blood supply, and the prevention of blood exploitation for profit making. It sought to regulate organ transplants and to prevent the exploitation of the poor who might be induced to sell their organs for a profit.

Other proposed legislation sought to expand educational opportunities and to define rules for the selection of scholarship recipients. Finally, legislation was proposed to end censorship on movies, theater, radio, and television production and to protect citizens against misleading advertisements.

The main provisions of these bills were embodied in Articles 5, 14, 18, 21, 23, 49, 89, 143, 173, 187, 199, 200, 201, 203, 213, 214, 215, 220, and 225 of the new Constitution.

Government Organization

The thrust of the government organization category of proposed legislation was to place some restrictions on the discretion of the federal and state executives in the exercise of their functions and to expand the power of the Congress in exercising its policy and oversight functions over the executive. A series of proposals were presented to limit government expenditures to what was stipulated in the budget, to define administrative procedures for checking the abuse of government economic power, to mandate a merit-career bureaucracy so as to limit nepotism in hiring, to eliminate wage discrimination in similar job titles, to eliminate abuse in government bidding and public tenders, and to regulate the use of public property and its distribution.[5]

To stem the centralization tendency of the federal government, the proposed legislation sought to strengthen the state and municipal governments and to restrain abuse of power by those in charge. Thus, proposed legislation sought to define the appropriate procedures to be followed during the creation, abolishment, or consolidation of municipalities; the municipalities' rights in exploration of mineral resources within their jurisdictions; the limit of INCRA's power to tax rural property;[6] and the means to prevent local officials from incurring debts toward the end of their term of office. Similar legislation was introduced with regard to the states and territories. For example, legislation was introduced to allow the states to regain control over their military police after they had lost control to the federal government, mandating an automatic transfer of federal funds to states and localities in accordance with a prescribed formula rather than the discretion of the federal government, a power often used by the federal government to reward its supporters and punish its opponents. Other proposed legislation attempted to restructure the federal executive and create new departments and to strengthen the power of the Congress to exercise its control over the bureaucracy. Similar legislation was introduced to restructure the judiciary and redefine its jurisdictions, especially with regard to labor matters.

A total of 272 proposed bills were found in this category, leaving a bearing on what the new Constitution eventually adopted. Articles 5, 18, 20, 21, 22, 24, 29, 33, 37, 48, 52, 59, 73, 74, 91, 93, 102, 113, 144, 145, 146, 153, 158, 160, 163, 169, 173, 188, 213, and 236 of the new Constitution addressed many of the concerns raised by these bills.

Economic Order

The centerpiece of the authoritarian regime was the economic order it adopted to achieve rapid industrialization and diversification.[7] Using a new classical economic approach, the regime sought to realize capital accumulation needed for investment through a tripartite partnership of the government, the multinationals, and the national private capital. The state was to play the leading role in this relationship. To improve the chances of success, the regime adopted a centralized, long-range development planning strategy where all economic fiscal and monetary decisions became the exclusive prerogative of the executive. To finance foreign capital borrowing and to pay for the needed technology, the economic model placed heavy emphasis on sectors with an export potential to the detriment of small producers, the agriculture sector, and the domestic consumers. The Congress was excluded from playing a significant role in charting the economic plans and priorities of the country.

When the regime's economic model began to show strains in the late 1970s, as a result of the first and second oil crises and the worldwide recession that ensued in the early 1980s, dissenters against the economic policies of the government became vocal within the Congress. Beginning in the late 1970s, a series of bills challenging various facets of the economic policy of the government were introduced and debated in the Congress. The challenge raised by the Congress involved every aspect of the economic model. Floor debates were heated. Between 1970 and 1988, a total of 305 bills proposed new policy directions that were eventually incorporated within the new Constitution.

Those bills detailed policies with regard to computers and data processing, pharmaceutical and other chemical products, regulating and protecting the domestic market against premature external hegemony, extending government credits and tax advantages to small agricultural enterprises, heavy government investment in irrigation, and rural electrification.

Other proposed legislation called for the establishment of free enterprise zones, encouragement of tourism and scientific and cultural exchanges, investment in alternate sources of energy such as the alcohol fuel program, redefinition of Brazil's industrial policy, protection of mineral exploration and reserving those rights to the federal government, handling of Brazilian international debt, improving the transportation network, calling for a daring agrarian reform and land distribution, soil preservation and rationalization of public enterprises, and bringing those enterprises under congressional scrutiny. Finally, a series of laws were proposed to protect national enterprises and place restrictions on foreign enterprises. Many of the new economic policy initiatives were embodied in the articles of the Constitution that dealt with the economic order (Articles 170-192). One of the most important aspects of the economic policy was the acquisition of science and technology and the protection of the domestic market from external competition (see the last section of this chapter).

Protection of the Environment

One of the casualties of the economic development model practiced by the authoritarian regime was the disregard for environmental concerns. Local and international critics of the environmental protection policies of the regime have often pointed out not only the health hazards that the petrochemical industries in the São Paulo area posed for the people living there, but also the destruction and expropriation of Indian lands, and, most important, the irreversible damage caused by farmers and other corporate developers to the rain forest of the Amazon region.

More than eighty-five proposed bills raised policy concerns that were eventually adopted by the new Constitution. These concerns ranged from the need for a general environmental impact statement before any proposed development was to be approved to more specific measures, such as the creation of a special standing committee within the Congress to monitor measures that might affect the environment. Proposed legislation recommended safeguards to protect the environment and the citizens against toxic and radioactive material, defined the maximum levels of pollutants allowed in the air, recommended the preservation of natural forests, rivers, and coasts, and the preservation of natural wildlife and microorganisms. These goals were emphatically incorporated into Articles 22, 173, 187, and 225 of the new Constitution.

Fiscal System and Budgeting

When the authoritarian regime assumed power in 1964, it centralized the budget-making process within the executive and stripped the Congress and the state government of any significant budgetary authority. During this period the Congress fought many battles to regain part of its budgetary and fiscal authority, but to no avail. Some of the 133 proposed bills in this category sought to strengthen the auditing and controlling arm of the Congress (the *Tribunal de Contas da União*, TCU) to give the Congress a stronger role in the adoption of the budget, to limit government spending practices so as to comply with existing budgetary authority, and to rationalize and simplify the government accounting procedures.

Several attempts were made to revamp the tax system and to make it more equitable and to define cases where tax exemptions were to be applied to benefit various groups of people and economic activities. Articles 145, 146, 153, 155, 156, 160, 163, and 169 of the new Constitution incorporated many of the main points advocated in these proposals.

CONGRESS AND THE BUDGET

Congressional scholars have convincingly argued that perhaps the most important manifestation of the power of the Congress is its role in the budget process. Producing the budget is perhaps the single most important legislative act. Relinquishing the power of the purse is tantamount to relinquishing many other powers, such as program authorization, control of the executive, and bureaucratic oversight.

The role of the Brazilian National Congress in the budgetary process during the authoritarian regime is illustrative of a legislature playing a minimal role. It should be remembered that beginning in the late 1960s economic planning and budgetary decisions were reserved exclusively for the executive branch in accordance with the Doctrine of National Security and Development espoused by the military.

Among scholars, two conflicting conceptions on budgets prevail: one, budgets are political documents balancing incrementally the various needs in society, or two, budgets are economic documents meant to achieve the monetary and fiscal policies of the government.

Aaron Wildavsky has persuasively argued that the process of determining national priorities identified in the budget is essentially a political process and should remain so; however, others, following the Keynesian conception of the budget, have tended to emphasize the economic rationality of the budget over its political nature. In the United States since World War II, various budgetary reforms have been advanced to facilitate either the political or the economic functions of the budget. For example, the budget as a planning and economic document led to the transfer of the budget office from the

Department of Treasury to the presidency as early as 1939. The preeminence of the executive in the budget area was reemphasized under Presidents John F. Kennedy, Lyndon B. Johnson, and Richard M. Nixon. The administrations of Presidents Kennedy and Johnson emphasized the planning and programming functions of budgeting, while Nixon's administration emphasized the management function of the budget.

As far as the U.S. Congress is concerned, the budget remains—with some changes—a political document that outlines the distribution of burdens and benefits. Until the passing of the Budget and Impoundment Act of 1974 and the establishment of the Congressional Budget Office (CBO), the Congress dealt with the budget in a disjointed and piecemeal fashion. Program authorization was the function of the various, almost autonomous, substantive committees of the House of Representatives and of the Senate—that is, the Ways and Means Committee of the House and the Finance Committee of the Senate dealt with budget revenues and taxes, while the expenditure committees of the House and Senate handled budget expenditures. Since the budget was rarely considered in one single document, it had limited use as an instrument of fiscal and monetary policy. Furthermore, the independent role that states and localities enjoy in raising taxes under the U.S. federal system undermines whatever fiscal or monetary policy the federal budget might attempt to pursue.

With the passage of the Budget and Impoundment Act of 1974, and the creation of the CBO, some weaknesses in the congressional review of the budget have been partially corrected. The CBO and the House and Senate budget committees can now view the budget more comprehensively and can impose some general guidelines on the substantive and fiscal committees of both houses.

Despite these developments and attempts by both the executive and the legislature to relate planning and programming to budgeting, the budget has remained essentially a political document, the preparation of which Richard Fenno and Wildavsky have so aptly described, analyzed, and rationalized. While economic development rationalities continue to play an important role in budgeting, the dominant political rationality of the budget remains. The 1985 passing of the Gramm-Rudman Act, calling for a balanced budget in 1991, cuts across the board to achieve such a goal.

The ability of Congress and the President to agree on priorities was another indicator of the political nature of the budgeting and the budget process in a political democracy. The dominance of political rationality and its acceptance as legitimate by most of the American public, especially the significant and influential groups in society, has enabled the Congress to use the budgetary process to control government programs, to oversee the bureaucracy's implementation of approved programs, and recently, to evaluate the effectiveness of these programs.

The Competitive Period (1946-1964)

The role the National Congress of Brazil played in the budget process during the Competitive Period was determined by constitutional provisions, structural characteristics of the legislature, and the nature of the party system, including its strength in the legislature and its power base in the states.

During this period, the Congress played a strong role in the budgetary process. The Constitution of 1946 granted it the power of the purse. The executive budget was reviewed by the budget committees of each chamber, and usually underwent significant changes as a result of congressional intervention. Amendments to the budget were considered both within the budget committees and even on the floor of each chamber. The Congress also had the power to decide on the structure and size of the civil service.

Although the Constitution bestowed on the Congress a strong role in the budget process, the actual exercise of these constitutional powers varied from one administration to another and was shaped by the nature of the political parties within the Congress and how the Congress actually discharged its role.

Perhaps the most important political consideration was the nature of the political parties represented in the Congress and their regional power base. During the Competitive period, three major political parties dominated the Congress: the PSD, Social Democratic Party; the PTB, Brazilian Labor Party; and the UDN, National Democratic Union. PSD and PTB had their origin in Getúlio Vargas's *Estado Novo*, during the 1930s and early 1940s. The PSD represented the conservative elements in the society, using the state machines that Vargas created to spread its influence throughout the country, particularly in the Northeast and the poorer regions of the country. The PTB had its strength in the urban labor movement, which was also generated and harnessed by Vargas. Its power base was, with the exception of São Paulo, in the industrialized South and Southeast. The UDN, the major opposition party, was composed of diverse elements within the society, such as liberals opposed to the dictatorship of Vargas and middle-class urban dwellers who felt ill at ease with the populism of PTB and the conservatism of PSD.

In the election of 1950, PSD lost its absolute majority in the Congress, with no other party taking its place. Presidents Getúlio Vargas (1951-54), Juscelino Kubitschek (1956-61), and João Goulart (l961-64) were forced to govern with a coalition of PSD and PTB, though Kubitschek had an easier time passing his legislation compared to the other two. Decisions in the Congress could only be reached through hard bargaining and the building of coalitions of parties with irreconcilable differences. The weakening of the major political parties after 1954 and the emergence of smaller political parties accelerated the disintegration of the decision-making capacity of the Congress. This disintegration was reflected in the way the Congress dealt with the budget.

Critics characterized the budgetary process as being partisan, parochial, and regional in its outlook, lacking comprehensiveness and long-range planning, and being incremental and antidevelopmental in nature. The critics argued that to satisfy demagogic interests among the voters (basically in the agriculture and industrial labor sectors), the budget became excessively inflationary in nature. Through its system of subsidies, the budget distorted the economy and set the country on the road to bankruptcy and continuous underdevelopment.[8] According to one critic,

> The Constitution of 1946 had been so liberal that it allowed many distortions in the budgetary process. The process was distorted in the sense that it permitted an unlimited number of interventions by the legislators during the budgetary process. Being a member of the Budget Committees of the Senate or of the Chamber meant a high political status. It would allow the member enormous power to decide on the allocation of federal funds. Such funds were always available to satisfy parochial and political interests of legislators. Between 1948 and 1963, such interventions became scandalous as more than 20,000 amendments to the budget were introduced each year.[9]

In 1961, former Deputy Oswaldo Trigueiro, who was later to become minister of the STF, complained about some of the abuses of the Congress in the budgetary process, citing as an example the introduction of more than 20,000 amendments, most of them concerning very specific programs, that benefitted certain areas in detriment to other more deserving areas in order to satisfy the political interests of the legislators. In a recent interview, the director of the Undersecretariat for Support in Budgetary Matters of the Federal Senate recalled those years, stressing what he clearly identified as congressional abuses of the budgetary process. "Deputies and senators knew in advance that their amendments would not be approved (almost all amendments were concerned with pork barrel projects), but they would introduce and fight for them anyway, so that their constituents would know about it."[10]

Another observer criticized the budget process during the Competitive period and the role the Congress played in that process by highlighting its nondevelopmental and parochial characteristics. "Laws, such as the budget," he said, "in order to be approved by the legislature, would depend upon exchange of interests and upon bargaining among the legislators, making impossible the formation of any global and effective policy-making for the nation."[11] Whether these practices are indeed an aberration of the congressional process in Brazil, or whether they are the norm of congressional politics, is a controversial issue, that we shall not attempt to resolve here.[12] What concerns us here is the extent of the role the Congress in Brazil actually played in the budgetary process during this period.

An examination of the budgets between 1960 and 1964 reveals that many of the points raised by the critics were indeed correct. For example, in 1960, more than 13,825 amendments were presented by the Congress and 9,302 of these amendment were approved. The net effect was that the budget increased by 17.62 percent, from the base presented by the executive. Furthermore, when it was implemented, the budget increased by 55.11 percent from the total approved, with a deficit 29.41 percent higher than the revenues raised during that year. These patterns persisted until 1964 when the coup took place. In 1964, for example, more than 33,348 amendments were presented, of which 10,531 were approved. The approved totals were 52.1 percent more than those proposed by the executive. The total value of the programs implemented increased by 31.3 percent of the approved budget, with the final deficit being 37.8 percent higher than the revenues raised during that year.

Dissatisfied political leaders, particularly those from the UDN, found it in their interest to ally themselves with the bureaucratic-military elements of society so as to push for a new political order and a new budgetary process. This new coalition blamed the Congress for the worsening economic conditions that Brazil found itself in on the eve of the 1964 military coup.

The Authoritarian Period (1964-1985)

In addition to the constitutional, political, and structural changes introduced by the regime after 1964 to weaken the Congress (see Chapters 1 and 2), specific constitutional provisions were enacted to weaken the legislative role in the budget process. In accordance with the Constitution of 1967 and its 1969 amendments, Congress was stripped of its right to undertake any alteration in the budget that might add or decrease public expenditures. All public expenditures were to be in accordance with a multiyear development plan. Such a plan once approved could not be altered by subsequent legislative action without executive initiative. No project could be approved or funded unless it was specifically included in the plan. The preparation of this comprehensive plan, and the yearly or multiyear budget (many projects were financed on a multiyear basis), were entrusted to a super ministry, the Ministry of Planning.

In 1969, the Joint Budget Committee was established to review the budget. This committee was composed of forty-five deputies and fifteen senators selected annually by each house. The chairman of the committee was elected on an annual basis, and the chairmanship alternated between the Senate and the Chamber. Although the committee met as a whole to consider the budget, voting was calculated for each house separately.

The Joint Budget Committee was given a total of ninety days to get the budget approved by the Congress. If by the end of November the budget was not approved, the executive could promulgate the budget through an executive decree. Once the budget was referred to the plenary session of each house, it was voted on as a whole, and amendments could not be accepted unless one-third of the members of the Chamber or the Senate requested them. During its budget deliberations, the Joint Budget Committee was assisted by fewer than five staff members, and their work was limited to the clerical preparations of the various items of expenditures to be approved by the committee. The Congress was required to pass a balanced budget but was not authorized to introduce measures with the purpose of raising revenues or creating new expenditures. Since the only projects entitled to funding were those contained in the multiyear development plan that was already approved, the yearly consideration of the budget by the Congress amounted to a simple act of ratification of an executive document. With this ironclad system, the executive sought to control congressional politics and eliminate "inflationary and distortive" acts that the Congress was accused of committing under the Competitive period, which was ruled by the Constitution of 1946. To what extent was congressional behavior in conformity with the constitutional provisions and the executive directives? This we tried to answer through a detailed examination of the budget that was presented between 1965 and 1986.

Between 1965 and 1970—just before the drastic curtailment of the Congress's power in the budgetary area—the Congress continued to manifest the same kind of behavior as far as amendments were concerned. Thus in 1965, the Congress introduced 37,011 amendments and approved 28,579 of them. In 1967, the number of amendments introduced climbed to 44,485, and the amendments approved reached 39,248. Even in 1969 when the Congress was suspended for part of the year, the number of amendments introduced reached 9,398, and the number of amendments approved 5,259. One thing was different, however. Although these amendments affected slightly the distribution of the amounts allocated among the various items of expenditures, they did not result in any net addition to the total amount presented by the executive. Furthermore, the budget when implemented was closer to the total approved. The increase ranged between 4 and 17 percent of the amount originally approved. Even deficit spending was curtailed. The budgetary deficit was reduced from 22.8 percent above the revenues in 1965 to 2.1 percent in 1968, and 5.2 percent in 1969. From a budgetary point of view, at least, the budget seemed to have been brought under the control of the executive. Although the Congress continued to introduce amendments, these amendments did not affect the totals approved. Only internal distribution within a particular department or ministry may have been affected.

As far as the implementation of the budget was concerned, the executive held the line on total expenditures, but the distribution among the various ministries and departments varied. Some ministries lost while others gained, depending on how the executive assessed their needs.

Because the budget was brought under control, the drastic measures introduced after 1969 were not justified from a budgetary point of view. In 1970, the budget was approved through an executive decree, since the Congress was suspended for most of 1969. Furthermore, beginning in that year, the budget format was changed. In addition to the traditional ministries, which constituted the main items of expenditures as far as the executive was concerned, the budget began to reflect general budget categories outside the ministries. The main expenditure items were allocated under the following general funds:

- National Development Fund
- National Urban Development and Support Fund
- General Obligations of the Federal Government
- General Support Grant to States and Localities (revenue sharing)
- Categorical Grants to States and Localities
- Federal Social Security Payments
- Contingency Reserve Fund

Between 1970 and 1986, more than 52 percent of the budget was put into these general funds.

The number of amendments introduced and approved began to decline drastically. Thus, in 1971, of the 16,345 amendments introduced, only 117 were approved, none with any financial implications on the totals or the distribution among the various categories of expenditures. In 1973, of the 4,110 amendments introduced, only seventeen were approved, with no implications on the amounts allocated. The Congress soon came to realize that debating the budget was not earning it any points. Fewer and fewer amendments were introduced, and yet fewer amendments were approved. The amendments introduced ranged from a few hundred a year to as low as thirty-eight, and those approved ranged from a low of two to a high of seventeen. Notwithstanding these amendments, the budget was approved in the form the executive had presented.

Yet the manner in which the budget was implemented continued to vary significantly from that requested by the executive and ratified by the Congress. Indeed the planning function, which the executive sought to maximize by eliminating what it considered political meddling, seemed to have deteriorated. Except for the years of the Brazilian economic miracles between 1971 and 1978, the difference between the budget as requested and as implemented ranged from a low of 4 percent to a high of 47 percent. Worse still, to maintain some control over the total amount spent, the executive used its arbitrary powers to move funds from one category of expenditure to another, irrespective of what it had submitted to the Congress. Some expenditures categories increased in one year several hundred percent from what was originally requested, while others were reduced to a fraction of what was originally authorized. Not a single department, ministry, or program was left untouched. What was introduced and labeled as planning became simple arbitrariness on the part of the executive to get its political needs and economic exigencies of the moment met.

CONGRESS AND THE DEVELOPMENT OF COMPUTER INDUSTRY POLICY IN BRAZIL

Because of the centrality of the informatics policy to the military regime, a more elaborate examination of the role of the Congress is illuminating. Such an examination will show how the Congress gradually expanded its influence in another area of public policy long considered the prerogative of the executive.[13]

Brazil's National Informatics Policy was developed and elaborated by a small group of technocrats within the executive aptly called by Emanuel Adler the "pragmatic anti-dependency guerrillas" who "used their scientific, technological, and managerial knowledge, as well as their access to political power, to mobilize not only the *know-how* and *know-what* but also the *know-where-to* regarding computers."[14] Given the supremacy of the executive in setting public policy during the authoritarian regime in Brazil, congressional participation was gradual and contingent upon the degree of conflict within the executive and the opening and relaxation of the political climate within the country. [15]

Informatics Policy: Executive Initiative and Congressional Reaction

In the military's development ideology, the computer policy occupied a prominent position.[16] The regime was committed to a development policy that would encourage the rapid transfer of technology and capital to Brazil from the advanced Western countries. The regime was also committed to an economic policy that would encourage local capital to develop industries, not only for import substitution, but also to compete internationally. The main issue was what type of technology should be allowed to be imported from overseas, or manufactured in Brazil by subsidiaries of foreign multinationals, and what should be reserved for Brazilian manufacturers?

Adler identified two groups within the Brazilian intelligence with distinct ideologies that sought to define the economic model and Brazil's relationship with the international economic order. The "structural dependency" group, in classical Marxist logic, argued for an end to the dependency on multinational corporations (MNCs) as the only road to achieve autonomy in the economic and technological arena. But this call for autonomy was judged to be beyond Brazil's reach because the solution required global structural changes. The solution, therefore, required concerted action among all developing countries to change the international economic system. Brazil's elites were either unable or uninterested in following such a path, because their existence in power depended on the support of the same forces that they needed to change.

The second group, while accepting the theoretical logic of the dependency theorists, believed that it was possible to end this structural dependency by following a pragmatic approach, emphasizing a mixture of state intervention, national capital, and the cooperation of the MNCs. It was this group of pragmatic antidependency theorists under the leadership of men like José Pelúcio, Ricardo Saur, and others that eventually succeeded in defining and implementing the informatics policy of Brazil.[17]

In addition to the economic logic, the informatics policy occupied a special position in the priorities of the authoritarian regime. The regime saw a close connection between computers, data bases, and intelligence gathering. The regime saw in computers an excellent instrument for spying on and controlling its opponents. The Congress raised questions about the technology's affect on privacy, on the regime's ability to suppress opposition, and on the labor market. Concerns were expressed regarding the appropriate structures, participation in, and control and accountability of the institutions in charge of developing and managing the informatics policy.

As early as 1971, Brazil recognized the need for developing a policy in the area of informatics. Between 1971 and 1985, an intense debate raged, first within the executive and later within the Congress, over the appropriate policy the country should follow. During that period, the role of Congress in setting the informatics policy ranged from the marginal to the pivotal. For purposes of understanding the issues raised and the role that the Congress played, three periods can be distinguished: 1971-1978, 1979-1981, and 1981-1986.

The Formative Period (1971-1978)

The first official act in addressing the informatics policy occurred in 1971,[18] when the government created a special working group composed of naval officers and some bureaucrats from the Ministry of Planning, working under the auspices of the navy.[19] This working group had the task of planning the development and manufacturing of an electronic computer prototype for naval operations. The immediate goal was to equip a number of navy frigates being purchased from British and Brazilian suppliers with such computers as needed.

From this military beginning, the need for an industrial policy for the manufacturing and operations of data processing equipment (hardware), programs (software), and human resources began to emerge. Both the National Development Plan of 1972-1974 and the Basic Science and Technology Development Plan of 1973-1974 mentioned the needs required to develop a minicomputer industry and to establish a computer technology.[20]

To address those needs, a presidential decree in 1972 established the Coordinating Commission for Electronic Processing Activities (CAPRE), an executive agency under the Ministry of Planning (then Planning Secretariat, SEPLAN).[21]

CAPRE established a market-reserve policy for mini- and microcomputers, which meant they were to be built in Brazil by Brazilian companies. The computers could neither be imported nor manufactured in Brazil by foreign corporations. The rationale for such a policy was that, although multinational corporations operated in Brazil building mainframes, Brazilian companies should have a monopoly on the minicomputer market, since the technology was available and the necessary capital investment was relatively small. Before the policy could be implemented, however, Brazilian companies that would produce those computers had to be established.

CAPRE's authority to examine and set up various aspects of the informatics policy was augmented both in 1975 and 1976. In 1975, with the deepening foreign exchange crisis, Brazil's National Council for Foreign Commerce Council (CONCEX), in an effort to cut down on computer imports, empowered CAPRE to examine all aspects of data processing imports.[22] In 1976, another presidential decree created a special plenary council to oversee CAPRE's work and, at the same time, to give CAPRE broad power to propose goals for a national informatics policy and to present it to the new plenary council, which represented various civilian and military departments. Although CAPRE was to have the executive power to set up the policy and implement it, the council would set policy guidelines and hear administrative appeals in cases of disagreement among the various administrative units affected by the policy.[23]

That year CAPRE selected in a bidding process four private companies and a new public corporation, Computadores e Sistemas Brasileiros (COBRA, or Brazilian Computers and Systems), to build the first new minicomputers, and authorized them to use specific foreign technology, if necessary, in their production.

In the meantime, international pressure against Brazil's market-reserve policy was mounting, especially by American multinational corporations. IBM lobbied strongly against the market-reserve policy, because it affected the production of its minicomputer line. In 1977, IBM presented five new equipment projects to be produced in Brazil, in apparent violation of the market-reserve policy. Nevertheless, the largest two of the five projects were approved, against fierce opposition, within the plenary council of CAPRE.[24]

The decision to allow IBM to produce two products in Brazil split CAPRE's council and brought into the open the conflict within the executive over the informatics policy. The press, the national companies, the users, and the Congress criticized the decision to allow IBM to produce certain kinds of computers in Brazil; they viewed it as a sellout to the interests of the multinationals and as a serious violation of the market-reserve policy.

Stripped of its most important powers and placed under severe constitutional and political limitations, the Congress was in no position to initiate or affect meaningfully public policy during this period. Individual members of the Congress, however, continued their practice of proposing new legislation to draw the attention of the executive to important areas of the policy.

During this period, the role of the Congress in setting up the informatics policy was limited to requests for information and to sensitizing the executive to areas of privacy, labor implications, the need for market reserve and some areas of possible uses. Congressional activity did not involve policy making or the review and control of whatever policy was formulated by the government. Informatics policy was an executive domain, debated and promulgated by CAPRE under the domination of the military and bureaucrats. In fact, informatics policy emerged in, and continued to be controlled by, the bureaucratic and intelligence organizations of the military regime. As long as there was agreement within the executive regarding this policy, even when that policy was ambiguous and in flux, the Congress had neither the power nor the means to influence it. It could only wage "individual guerrilla acts," to embarrass the government or to draw public attention to some facet of the policy.

The Limited Engagement Period (1979-1981)

During the second phase, the Limited Engagement period, new institutions became involved in making the informatics policy. In response to the mounting criticism against CAPRE, the newly installed administration of President João Figueiredo called for a comprehensive study of the informatics policy and the institutions in charge of setting that policy. Having openly committed himself to the policies aimed at the opening of the political system, he appointed a commission on April 19, 1979, composed of members of the National Information Service (SNI), National Security Council (CSN), Ministries of Planning, Foreign Affairs, and the General Staff of the Armed Forces (EMFA, the armed forces military school), to examine the structure and status of all data processing industries, and to propose a new structure that would oversee all informatics policy. The commission was given 120 days to present its recommendations. Ambassador Paulo Cotrim, whose only achievement in the field of informatics came from having been the chief of a division in the Ministry of Foreign Affairs in charge of administrative application of computers within the ministry, was appointed head of the commission. Cotrim's appointment was widely criticized by the press and by data processing professionals because was not a known informatics policy specialist. His appointment raised the suspicion of "window dressing," to give civilian legitimacy to a commission that was clearly dominated by the military.

The commission report presented in September 1979 was critical of CAPRE's work and policies.[25] It called for the dismantling of the CAPRE council and the creation of a Special Informatics Secretariat (SEI) that would operate under the secretary of the CSN, which was headed by General Danilo Venturini. The commission recommended that an increase in the market reserve include medium-sized computers in addition to the minicomputers, which meant a strengthening of "national enterprises" and a freeze on new public corporations in the computer sector.[26]

Notwithstanding the negative reaction against the commission's recommendations, a presidential decree accepted those recommendations and established SEI in October 1979.[27] The reaction against the establishment of SEI was swift. On October 25 in a university meeting in Porto Alegre, the data processing community adopted a resolution condemning the "authoritarian process of creating SEI, a process that does not take into consideration the views of technical and scientific personnel, in total contradiction with the process of political liberalization."[28]

CAPRE's demise, according to Adler, signaled the erosion of the political base of the "pragmatist anti-dependency guerrillas" and their "egalitarian nationalism" economic policies. From the beginning, CAPRE policies met with intense resistance from many diverse quarters. SEPLAN, under Minister Antonio Delfim Neto in 1979, was not very hospitable to the market-reserve policies. Since he could not eliminate the policies established under his predecessors, Delfim tried to weaken the interpretation of those policies.

CAPRE, in spite of its valiant attempt to mobilize all the government sectors behind its quest for technological autonomy, was unsuccessful. Several ministries and state enterprises maintained their autonomy and on several occasions adopted policies and purchasing practices favoring foreign producers. Small national enterprises opposed certain aspects of the policy, such as the National Institute for Industrial Property (INPI) which supported the absorption of technology by the national enterprises. Disagreement among the scientific community became apparent as the policy progressed. Those in academia who were engaged in pure scientific research felt that the policy discriminated against them in favor of applied science and economic development. Finally, the various government entities who were engaged in one aspect or the other of the informatics and science policies failed to adequately coordinate among themselves, which led not only to conflicts over turf, but to bottlenecks, overlapping, and contradictions.[29]

SEI, under its Secretary Octávio Gennari, was a true reflection of the predominantly military influence that brought it into existence. Although Gennari was a civilian electronic engineer, the policies of SEI fell under the sway of the military elements who occupied senior positions within the organization, and to whom SEI reported. The establishment of SEI under the CSN was intended to consolidate all informatics policy under one agency and to end bureaucratic squabbles about the direction of that policy. Consolidation was achieved, but not the ending of confusion and bureaucratic conflict between those in favor of a market reserve and those who, under international pressure, favored a relaxation or even the total elimination of the market-reserve policy.

In May 1980, SEI reaffirmed the market-reserve policy and rejected a proposal by IBM to build two medium-sized computers (Models /38 and 4331) in Brazil.[30] SEI argued that such a request violated the established market-reserve policy. In August, however, SEI reversed itself and allowed IBM and Burroughs to build medium-sized computers and Hewlett-Packard to manufacture microcomputers for scientific applications. The IBM proposal was identical—except for a slight increase in computer memory—to the one rejected in May earlier that year.

SEI's informatics policy was once again confused. Conflict between the proponents of a market reserve and those of a free market broke out again, this time with each trying to mobilize public opinion and congressional support. On the one side were the users and the electronic trade associations who supported the new policy. On the other side were the computer manufacturers and trade associations who were against the relaxation of the market-reserve policy. A lobbying group called Alliance for the Defense of National Technology was formed to support market reserve. It consisted of associations of professionals and manufacturers. The controversy was joined by new groups of university professors, government employee organizations, and the Brazilian Society for Scientific Advancement.

In spite of the mounting criticism from both within Brazil and the international computer manufacturers, the power and jurisdiction of SEI continued to expand. In March 1981, for example, the government issued a decree expanding the mandate of SEI. Now SEI was to "plan, supervise, and control research and development and industrial policy of semi-conductors and micro-electronic components."[31] It was branching out into other industrial areas where electronic chips were being increasingly used, for example, in communication equipment, toys, and appliances. This increase in the power and jurisdiction of SEI went hand-in-hand with increased policy ambiguity and internal conflict as to the course to follow. The more the internal conflict, the more SEI found itself in need of external support and legitimization, especially from the Congress.

In 1982, when Gennari departed as secretary-general of SEI for "personal reasons,"[32] his deputy, an army colonel, Joubert Brizida, was made secretary, and Edson Dytz, another colonel, was made executive-secretary, thus completing the "militarization" of the organization under the overall supervision of General Danilo Venturini, the head of the CSN. This militarization of SEI did not help much in eliminating the conflict over the policy that would ultimately be adopted. In October of 1982, for example, Venturini stated that the "future entrance of foreign enterprises in the reserved market would depend on further government studies." This announcement worried the pro-reserve lobby, since it raised the possibility of another policy shift and added another uncertainty to the market.

During this period, the role of Congress increased in both boldness and sophistication. The creation of SEI and its placement under military control outraged politicians from both the Right and the Left. Free traders, such as Senator Roberto Campos (PDS/Mato Grosso), objected to the market-reserve policy adopted by SEI and argued for its liberalization in favor of an open-trade policy. The nationalists were outraged because of the control the military and security organisms had over the informatics policy. They feared that such a monopoly over the informatics policy and the use of data processing technology would undoubtedly strengthen the repressive institutions of the regime, which could lead to further abuses and violations of individual rights, and corruption and profiteering among those involved in the implementation of the policy. They also feared that those within the military who were advocating free-trade policies would soon give in to international pressure and abandon the market-reserve policy.

During this period, the Congress initiated nineteen bills and requests for information related to informatics policy.

For the first time, Congress attempted, though unsuccessfully, to propose public policy and devise mechanisms to control the actions and policies of the executive. What began in the Competitive period as uncoordinated, individual "guerrilla skirmishes" with the government developed in the second period into limited engagements, where Congress, though cognizant that it could not have its way against the government policy, ventured to suggest policy, control the executive, and mobilize the concerned public.

The Third Period (1981-1986)

During this period the role of the Congress began to change dramatically. Two favorable developments accounted for this change. The first development was the political reforms introduced by the policy of *abertura* and initiated by Figueiredo in 1979, and the second was the intensified conflict within the executive branch over the future direction of the informatics policy and the institutions that should be put in charge of shaping and implementing such a policy.[33]

Furthermore, with the second oil shock in the late 1970s, the economic policy of the government was facing its severest challenge in the form of mounting inflation, a recession, and an extremely high foreign debt. The political relaxation and the worsening economic climate accentuated the bureaucratic conflict over the informatics policy.

Thus, in 1983, while Colonel Joubert Brizida was reconfirming SEI's market-reserve policy to a group of U.S. businessmen, Mário Garneiro, president of the Brazilinvest Finance Corporation and a supporter of a strong foreign role in Brazilian industry, gave a lecture at the Ministry of Communication in which he said the government was studying the unification of communication and computer industrial policy, implying the acceptance of joint ventures to build computers. Brizida, on the other hand, began lobbying opposition members in the Congress in favor of his pro-market reserve policy.

In 1984, Brizida left SEI to take the position of military attaché to the Brazilian Embassy in London, leaving Colonel Dytz in charge of SEI. At the same time, SEI announced the results of a bid by Brazilian enterprises that qualified them to build a new type of computer called the super-minicomputer. Eight companies were chosen, all owned entirely by Brazilians, but five of them needed to acquire the technology abroad before they could build the computers. This was considered a deviation of the market-reserve policy, since SEI had maintained from the beginning that the upper portion of the market would be filled by Brazilian minicomputer manufacturers, who would upgrade the technology in their research facilities, rather than importing it. The super-minicomputer was one size larger than the minicomputers that were being built in Brazil and therefore should have been manufactured by upgraded technology developed internally.

Those shifts in the reinterpretation of existing policy gave additional fuel to critics who saw the bureaucracy as an inappropriate instrument for setting public policy. SEI, representing the intelligence community, was supported, oddly enough, by the opposition parties and was committed to a market-reserve policy. The government's top economic team, headed by Minister of Planning Delfim Neto, was skeptical of the whole policy and argued that it would undermine the ongoing negotiations over the Brazilian foreign debt. Two other important ministers in Figueiredo's cabinet—Minister of Communication Haroldo Mattos and Minister of Industry and Commerce Camilo Penna—were also opposed to the market-reserve policy on the grounds that it ruled out joint ventures, which were permitted in the communication industry.[34]

Congress suddenly became the object of intense lobbying by the various feuding factions within the government. The stage was set for a strong congressional role in the determination of the informatics policy and the structure for its management, implementation, and control. Congress also became the place for sorting out the conflict among senior administrative officials. The Chamber of Deputies, where the opposition party was better represented, emerged as the champion of a market-reserve policy under the control of civilian institutions. The opposition parties wanted SEI to be controlled by civilians and to declare itself unequivocally in favor of a strict market-reserve policy. The pro-government party while opposed to the pro-market-reserve policy of SEI nonetheless voted in favor. It called for a stronger role for ministries with free-market orientation, such as the Ministries of Planning, of Communication, or of Industry and Commerce.

The heavy-handed way in which the government first set up the Cotrim Commission and later established SEI and placed it under the control of the intelligence community seemed to have galvanized the opposition within and outside the Congress. SEI's policies and actions, unlike CAPRE, were watched by a number of computer-related organizations that had come into existence mainly in the 1970s, such as the Association of Data Processing Service Enterprises in 1976, the Brazilian Association for Computer and Peripheral Equipment, the APPD, the National Laboratory of Computer Networks, and the Brazilian Society for Computer Affairs (SBC), all in 1978.[35] These groups supported a pragmatic market-reserve policy and resisted any move on the part of SEI or the other government institutions that were promoting a more open policy toward the MNCs. Indeed, in 1980, a coordinating committee representing all of these entities was organized to lobby the legislature, the executive, and the judiciary, and to use all available legal means to prevent the reversal of the informatics policy.

Between 1983 and 1984, the Congress gave the informatics policy serious consideration. Twenty-six bills were introduced. Hearings and seminars were conducted and speeches were also delivered, all dealing with informatics policy.

Of the twenty-six bills introduced in Congress, two in the Chamber of Deputies and two in the Federal Senate were of special importance. The two bills introduced in the Chamber by Deputies Cerqueira and Cristina Tavares originated in the opposition party (PMDB), while the two bills introduced in the Senate by Senators Roberto Campos and Carlos Chiarelli originated in the pro-government party (PDS).

The Cerqueira bill was intended to regulate data processing services furnished to government agencies, stipulating that the contracts for such services would only be given to Brazilian companies.[36] The bill introduced by Tavares was a broad-ranging bill, calling for the regulation of the entire computer industrial policy through laws enacted in Congress rather than through administrative acts, directives, or by fiat.[37] As the author mentioned in the bill's justification, the bill aims at "giving a legal foundation to the national policy for the production of data processing equipment, a policy that up until now has been regulated by administrative fiat of the SEI of the Presidency of the Republic, an organization with technical expertise, but that is not the proper forum for discussions about and implementations of an industrial policy of the highest importance for the country." Tavares' bill called for the imposition of an import restriction by an act of Congress rather than an administrative act. It also called for a complete embargo on foreign capital in Brazilian companies manufacturing computers.

In the Senate, the bill introduced by Senator Campos called for the deregulation of the computer industry, and contrary to SEI's policy, advocated a return to a free-trade policy.[38] Senator Chiarelli's bill, on the other hand, tried to strike a balance between the Tavares and the Campos bill by calling for a mild government reserve as advocated by SEI, with increased congressional oversight over informatics policy.[39]

Other bills dealt with measures to prevent abuses and arbitrariness by SEI and with the application of the new technology to the electoral process and its effects on privacy, consumer credit, and related concerns.

In addition to the introduction of bills, the Congress tried to shape the informatics policy by sponsoring a series of seminars and speeches dealing with the various dimensions of informatics policy. In 1981, for example, the Chamber's Committee on Science and Technology held a five-day seminar on national informatics policy under the leadership of Deputy Tavares. During the seminar, the committee was able to hear presentations by Gennari (then SEI's secretary-general), by Saur (former CAPRE's executive-secretary), computer industry trade leaders, presidents of government computer companies, and several university professors. As a result of this seminar, the final report of the committee concluded that the country needed a coherent and consistent policy and that Congress, not SEI, was the appropriate forum to formulate such a policy.

During 1983 and 1984, as the national debate over informatics policy intensified, many speeches about the policy were made on the floor of the Congress. Senate majority leader Aloysio Chaves (ARENA-PDS/Pará) and Senators Roberto Campos, Fernando Henrique Cardoso, Marco Maciel, Fábio Lucena, Henrique Santillo (MDB/Goiás), Jutahy Magalhães (PDS/Bahia), Nelson Carneiro (MDB-PMDB/Rio de Janeiro), and others representing diverse policy orientations gave frequent speeches about informatics policy before the Senate.[40]

In June 1983, the Senate held a seminar on informatics dealing with the government policy, the question of the "informatization" of society, the national computer industry, and informatics and national sovereignty. Among the participants were SEI's Secretary Brizida, the secretary-general of the Ministry of Communication Rômulo Furtado, as well as representatives of trade associations (manufacturers, users, and service bureaus), academics, and politicians of various political orientations.[41]

In 1984, for the first time, the Senate's Committee on the Economy, chaired by Campos, an influential and outspoken critic of the market-reserve policy, held a well-publicized hearing. Campos gave extensive coverage to his own bill, which called for the deregulation of the computer industry and a return to free trade. The committee undertook a wide-ranging debate on the whole industrial policy of the government, especially in the high technology area. High government officials (Venturini, Mattos, and Penna), industrialists, politicians, and even the two presidential candidates (Tancredo Neves and Paulo Maluf) were called to testify.[42]

All of these activities served the purpose of educating the Congress and the public on the controversies surrounding the informatics policy. The openness of the discussion and the opportunities that these activities provided for the various protagonists were in sharp contrast to the way SEI undertook its deliberations or aired its policy differences. For the first time in twenty years, Brazil was able to develop its public policy through free and open congressional deliberations.

The gestation period came to its climax when on July 30, 1984, the President sent to Congress a bill detailing his informatics policy.[43] Instead of resolving the ongoing controversy, the executive bill seemed to have refueled it. An editorial in the *Jornal do Brasil* called it an "Orwellian nightmare," through which the intelligence community was "fostering the dream of transforming the authoritarian state into a totalitarian state, that is to say, the very opposite of all we intended to achieve with the political liberalization process and our endeavor to create institutions that would guarantee democracy." The newspaper called upon the Congress "to give priority to the question of informatics policy." The Congress, it added, "cannot absent itself and permit the approval of such a totalitarian measure, since it contradicts the liberalization process."[44]

The government bill called for the continuation of the market-reserve policy. It also kept SEI under the supervision of the CSN. A new council drawn exclusively from senior government officials was to oversee the Secretariat. According to the provisions of the bill, SEI was to be given a free hand in deciding the informatics policy and in supervising its implementation, only this time (if the bill passed the Congress as presented) with the full blessing and legitimacy of the Congress.

The government tried to argue that all concerned parties had been consulted before the bill was presented, but according to one of the participants in those so-called consultations the presidential palace merely called them in to inform them of what had already been decided, rather than to consult with them. None of their suggestions was taken into consideration. The military could not or did not realize that the political landscape in Brazil was changing rapidly.

In August 1984, a congressional joint committee was created to study the bill. The pro-government party, PDS, was represented in the committee by eleven senators and deputies. Nine senators and deputies represented the major opposition party, PMDB, while one deputy represented another opposition party, PDT. Although PDS had a one-vote majority in the joint committee, the voting pattern in the committee was not along party lines, since many of the PDS members were against the government's market-reserve policy.[45] During the committee's deliberations on the bill, more than 261 amendments were presented, and seventy-two of those amendments were finally approved by the committee. The hearings conducted by the committee involved eighteen people, including Minister of Industry and Commerce Badaró, Minister of Communication Mattos, CSN Secretary Venturini, and SEI Secretary Colonel Dytz.

The committee also heard the testimony of the two presidential candidates, trade association representatives, and industrialists. Brazil's divergent elements were on hand for the first time to legitimize for both domestic and international opinion whatever policy the Congress might choose to enact.

While the government bill was still in the committee, Senator Virgílio Távora (ARENA-PDS/Ceará) proposed a substitute bill that eventually was adopted by the Congress instead of the government bill.[46] Although it maintained many of the points of the government bill, Távora's substitute bill increased the scope of the market reserve, established enforceable goals for the companies benefiting from the market reserve, created export districts in the North and Northeast with special tax incentives, set up an annual informatics plan to be submitted by the executive to Congress (thus sharply limiting SEI's autonomy), and established a National Council on Informatics and Automation (CONIN), to operate directly under the presidency, rather than under CSN.

CONIN's composition was expanded to include, in addition to representatives from the executive, people who would represent professional, scientific, trade, manufacturing, and citizens' organizations. The main function of CONIN was to oversee the work of SEI, which was removed from under CSN and placed under the direct authority of the President. Later, after the new civilian regime was installed in March 1985, SEI was placed under a newly established Ministry of Science and Technology.[47]

Two amendments to Távora's substitute bill that were introduced by the PT in the Chamber were rejected by the committee but approved by the plenary session of the Congress. The two amendments dealt with the protection of individual privacy and called for assistance for workers who had lost their jobs as a result of automation. Both of these amendments were later item-vetoed by the President.

NOTES

1. In 1988, in a personal interview with Paulo Affonso, secretary general of the Chamber of Deputies, he expressed skepticism as to the importance of the legislative agenda of the Congress by pointing out that most of the bills presented by the members were of a private nature.

2. In July of 1988, after the draft of the Constitution was completed, the president of the NCA asked the secretary general of the Chamber to review all pending bills presented between 1972 and 1988 that had immediate relevance to the articles of the new Constitution. A total of 6,526 bills were summarized as being relevant. With the assistance of Oswaldo Sanches, an adviser in the Senate, the author and his assistants classified those bills in accordance with the main sections of the Constitution. Since we were working from the bill summaries rather than the full text, some errors in the classification could have occurred because of the ambiguity of some bills. The ambiguous cases, however, were too few to affect our conclusion.

3. For state intervention in the affairs of unions, see Angelina Maria Cheibub Figueiredo, "Política Governamental e Funções Sindicais" (Master's thesis presented at the Department of Social Sciences of the Universidade de São Paulo, October 1975).

4. For competing perspectives on the authoritarian regime's economic policies and their impact on the income distribution, see Werner Baer, *The Brazilian Economy: Growth and Development* (New York: Praeger, 1983); José Serra, "Three Mistaken Theses Regarding the Connection between Industrialism and Authoritarian Regimes," Collier (ed.), *The New Authoritarianism*, op. cit. (1979), pp. 99-163; and Edmar Bacha, *Os Mitos de uma Década: Ensaios de Economia Brasileira* (Rio de Janeiro: Paz e Terra, 1976).

5. For a lucid discussion of the government corruption that prevailed during the military regime, see José Carlos de Assis, *A Chave do Tesouro: Anatomia dos Escândalos Financeiros, Brasil 1974-1983* (Rio de Janeiro: Paz e Terra, 1983).

6. INCRA stands for Instituto Nacional de Colonização e Reforma Agrária, or National Institute for Colonization and Agrarian Reform. Among its prerogatives is the collection of tax revenues from owners of rural properties.

7. For a critical evaluation of the economic model followed by the authoritarian regime, see Antonio Barros de Castro and Francisco Eduardo Pires de Souza, *A Economia Brasileira em Marcha Forçada* (Rio de Janeiro: Paz e Terra, 1985); Celso Furtado, *O Mito do Desenvolvimento Econômico* (Rio de Janeiro: Paz e Terra, 1974); Donald E. Syvrud, *Foundations of Brazilian Economic Growth* (Stanford, Calif.: Hoover Institution Press, 1974); Celso Furtado, *Análise do 'Modelo' Brasileiro* (Rio de Janeiro: Civilização Brasileira, 1972); Roberto Campos, *Reflections on Latin American Development* (Austin: University of Texas Press, 1968); Celso Furtado, *Um Projeto para o Brasil* (Rio de Janeiro: Saga, 1968); and Cíbilis da Rocha Viana, *Estratégia do Desenvolvimento Brasileiro: Uma Política Nacionalista para Vencer a Atual Crise Econômica* (Rio de Janeiro: Zahar Editores, 1966).

8. One outspoken critic of the budget process under the Competitive period was Deputy Roberto Campos, an economist and former minister and senator. Campos argued that democratic systems have no ability to undertake basic economic reform and stabilization policies; see Roberto Campos, *Temas e Sistemas* (Rio de Janeiro: Apec, 1969). For a refutation of this thesis, see Barry Ames, *Political Survival: Politicians and Public Policy in Latin America* (Berkeley and Los Angeles: University of California Press, 1987), and "The Congressional Connection, the Structure of Politics, and the Distribution of Public Expenditures in Brazil's Competitive Period," *Comparative Politics*, no. 19 (1987), pp. 147-71; Karen Remmer, "The Politics of Economic Stabilization: IMF Standby Programs in Latin America, 1954-1985," *Comparative Politics*, 19, no. 1 (October 1986), pp. 1-24; and Barry Ames, "Rhetoric and Reality in a Military Regime: Brazil since 1964," *Sage Professional Paper in Comparative Politics*, op. cit. (1973).

9. Getúlio Carvalho, "Processo Decisório: A Fronteira Política e os Limites Econômicos," *Revista de Administração Pública*, 7, no. 1 (January-March 1973), pp. 10-11.

10. Oswaldo Trigueiro, "A Federação na Nova Constituição do Brasil," *Revista Brasileira de Estudos Políticos*, no. 60/61 (January/July 1985), pp. 147-75.

11. Afonso Arinos de Mello Franco, "Ato Institucional No. 1: Considerações sobre os Artigos 3 e 4," *Revista de Informação Legislativa*, 1, no. 2 (April/June 1964) pp. 13-17.

12. Students of the U.S. congressional role in the budget process have often reported similar findings. Many justified, even praised, the role that the Congress played in the budget process as being more attuned to local needs. Indeed, such a role is at the base of the representative nature of the Congress.

13. This section is based on an article written by Abdo Baaklini and Antonio Carlos Pojo do Rego, "Congress and the Development of a Computer Industry Policy in Brazil," in David M. Olsen and Michael L. Mezey (eds.), *Legislatures in the Policy Process: the Dilemmas of Economic Policy*, Cambridge University Press, 1991.

14. Emanuel Adler, "Ideological Guerrillas and the Quest for Technological Autonomy: Development of a Domestic Computer Industry in Brazil," in *International Organization*, 40, no. 3 (1985).

15. The role of legislatures in different political systems has been analyzed in a series of books published by Duke University Press. Among these books, see Mezey, *Comparative Legislatures*, op. cit. (1979); and Smith and Musolf (eds.), *Legislatures in Development*, op. cit. (1979).

16. Brazil's informatics policy has been the subject of many scholarly works. For a review of how the policy was formulated, an evaluation of the problems it has faced, and the success it has achieved, see Emanuel Adler, *The Power of Ideology: The Quest for Technological Autonomy in Argentina and Brazil* (Berkeley and Los Angeles: University of California Press, 1987); SEI, *Transborder Data Flows and Brazil: Brazilian Case Study* (New York: United Nations Center on Transnational Corporations, 1983); and Peter Evans, "State, Capital, and the Transformation of Dependence: The Brazilian Computer Case," *World Development*, 14, no. 7 (1986). The Portuguese written sources include Abdo I. Baaklini and Antonio Carlos Pojo do Rego, "O

Congresso e a Política Nacional de Informática," *Revista de Administração Pública*, 22, no. 2 (1988), pp. 87-105; Gilberto Paim, *Computador Faz Política* (Rio de Janeiro: Apec, 1985); Benakouche Rabah (ed.), *A Questão da Informática no Brasil* (São Paulo: Brasiliense, 1985); *A Informática e a Nova República* (São Paulo: Hucitec, 1985); Silvia Helena, "A Indústria de Computadores: Evolução das Decisões Governamentais," in *Revista de Administração Pública*, 14, no. 4 (1980); and Luciano Martins, *Industrialização, Burguesia Nacional e Desenvolvimento* (Rio de Janeiro: Saga, 1968). For the theoretical elaboration and critique of dependent development, see Fernando Henrique Cardoso, "Associate-Dependent Development in Democratic Theory," Alfred Stepan (ed.), *Democratizing Brazil: Problems of Transition and Consolidation* (New York: Oxford University Press, 1988); Maria da Conceição Tavares and J. Carlos de Assis, *O Grande Salto para o Caos: A Economia Política e a Política Econômica do Regime Autoritário* (Rio de Janeiro: Zahar, 1985); Fernando Henrique Cardoso and Enzo Faletto, *Dependency and Development in Latin America* (Berkeley and Los Angeles: University of California Press, 1979); Peter Evans, *Dependent Development* (Princeton, N.J.: Princeton University Press, 1979); Eli Diniz and Renato Boschi, *Empresariado Nacional e Estado no Brasil* (Rio de Janeiro: Forense, 1978); Fernando Henrique Cardoso, "Hegemonia Burguesa e Independência Econômica: Raízes Estruturais da Crise Política Brasileira," *Revista Civilização Brasileira*, no. 17 (January/February 1968); and Fernando Gasparian, *Em Defesa da Economia Nacional* (Rio de Janeiro: Saga, 1986). In defense of an open market policy, see Roberto Campos, *Além do Cotidiano*, 2d ed. (Rio de Janeiro: Record, 1985), and "Senator Roberto Campos' Address to the Federal Senate on June 8, 1983" (Brasília: Senado Federal, 1983).

17. See Adler, *The Power of Ideology*, op. cit. (1987).

18. Ibid. Adler states that the roots of the policy go as far back as the 1968 Strategic Development Plan.

19. See Paulo B. Tigre, *Technology and Competition in the Brazilian Computer Industry* (New York: St. Martin's Press, 1983).

20. The First National Development Plan (1972-74) mentioned the importance of technology transfer as a precondition for economic development "associated with a strong internal technology development." Quoted by F. Biato and M. A. Figueiredo, *Transferência de Tecnologia no Brasil* (Brasília: Ipea, Série Estudos para o Planejamento, no. 4, 1973), p. 2.

21. See *Decreto No. 70370*, published in the *Diário Oficial* (April 5, 1972), p. 11.

22. See Tigre, *Technology and Competition*, op. cit. (1983), p. 42.

23. The council was composed of representatives of SEPLAN, the National Council of Scientific and Technological Development (CNPq), the Armed Forces General Staff (EMFA), and of the Ministries of Communications, Education and Culture, Finance, and Industry and Commerce.

24. In his recorded vote, one of CAPRE's plenary members stated that this was a "policy retreat that meant the loss of an important market share to MNCs, diminishing the market for Brazilian computer manufacturers, which is crucial to our autonomy." Quoted by Cristina Tavares and Milton Seligman, *Informática, A Batalha do Século XXI* (Rio de Janeiro: Paz e Terra, 1984), p. 67.

25. Cotrim himself was openly critical of CAPRE's policy role, as shown in an interview with *O Globo* (May 12, 1979). He charged that "there is no informatics policy, as there is no organization that is charged with policy making and policy implementation."

26. Tavares and Seligman, *Informática, A Batalha do Século XXI*, op. cit. (1984), p. 69., provided evidence of the various negative reactions by the public and the professional community against the Cotrim's report.

27. See *Decreto No. 84067*, published in the *Diário Oficial* (October 8, 1979), p. 23.

28. Tavares and Seligman, *Informática, A Batalha do Século XXI*, op. cit. (1984), p. 69.

29. See Adler, *The Power of Ideology*, op. cit. (1987), pp. 214-15.

30. See Tavares and Seligman, *Informática, A Batalha do Século XXI*, op. cit. (1984), p. 73.

31. *Diário Oficial* (March 6, 1981).

32. Gennari was the first executive director of Prodasen, before he occupied the directorship of SEI.

33. Adler, *The Power of Ideology*, op. cit. (1987), p. 217.

34. See *Jornal da Tarde* (March 15, 1984), and *Gazeta Mercantil* (March 17, 1984).

35. See Adler, *The Power of Ideology*, op. cit. (1987), pp. 266-70.

36. See *Projeto de Lei No. 406*, published in the *Diário do Congresso Nacional*, Seção 1 (April 13, 1983), p. 1573.

37. See *Projeto de Lei No. 1384*, published in the *Diário do Congresso Nacional*, Seção 1 (June 21, 1983), p. 5538.

38. See *Projeto de Lei No. 48*, published in the *Diário do Congresso Nacional*, Seção 2 (April 5, 1984), p. 485.

39. See *Projeto de Lei No. 93*, published in the *Diário do Congresso Nacional*, Seção 2 (June 8, 1984), p. 1832.

40. See *Diário do Congresso Nacional*, Seção 2 (March 23, 1983), pp. 506-8; (May 20, 1983), p. 1861; (June 16, 1983), p. 2464; (June 18, 1983), p. 2548; (August 5, 1983), p. 3156; (August 6, 1983), p. 3196; (March 22, 1984), p. 243; (April 10, 1984), p. 620; and (August 11, 1983), p. 3308.

41. The seminar was held on June 14 to 16, 1983. A 352-page volume contains the verbatim conferences and debates. It was published by the Cegraf (Senate's printing office) in that same year: *Seminário de Informática do Senado Federal* (Brasília: Senado Federal, 1983).

42. The depositions and debates were published verbatim in the *Diário do Congresso Nacional*, Seção 2, from May until September 1984. The first deposition was given on April 4, by National Security Council secretary, General Danilo Venturini. It was published on May 9, 1984, p. 1,100.

43. This bill, *Projeto de Lei No. 10/84*, was sent to Congress through *Mensagem No. 77/84*, published in the *Diário Oficial* (August 27, 1984). It finally became law on October 29, 1984. See *Lei No 7232*, published in the *Diário Oficial* (October 29, 1984), p. 15842.

44. See *Jornal do Brasil* (May 29, 1984).

45. The committee's report-writer, Senator Virgílio Távora, has since published a two-volume, 1,422-page book, on the informatics bill; see Távora, *Política Nacional de Informática* (Brasília: Senado Federal, 1985). The book covers all the legislative life of *Lei No. 7232*, from the initial executive message to the final text. It also contains all the shorthand records of the hearings conducted by his committee.

46. See Senator Távora's substitute bill and report in the *Diário do Congresso Nacional* (September 29, 1984), p. 2287.

47. The Ministry of Science and Technology (MCT) was created by *Decreto No. 91146*, published in the *Diário Oficial* (March 15, 1985), p. 4708. Article 2 put under the authority of the Ministry of Science and Technology, CONIN, SEI, the Technology Center for Informatics (CTI), the Informatics Export Districts, and the Special Fund for Informatics and Automation, both instruments that were also created by *Lei No. 7232*. The other major government organization included in MCT's jurisdiction was CNPq, the National Council for Scientific and Technological Development, which was already in operation under the Secretary of Planning. A former Federal Deputy from the State of Maranhão, Renato Archer, was chosen by Tancredo Neves as the first Science and Technology minister.

Chapter 7

To Write a Constitution

Legislatures are not often called upon to write a new constitution. Yet that was the mission of the National Congress of Brazil elected in 1986. The newly elected Congress was called upon to act as a National Constitutional Assembly (NCA) and to draw up a new constitution. The new Constitution was to be the final stage of a long struggle toward returning Brazil to civilian democratic rule, a struggle that started as soon as the military took power in 1964, then intensified in 1974, and finally became the main preoccupation of the Congress by 1978 with the election of the last military President, General João Figueiredo.

Drafting a new Constitution or amending a Constitution is a risky endeavor even in the most stable of democracies. The mere thought of a constitutional convention to amend the U.S. Constitution creates tension and concern among significant segments of the population for fear of what may or may not occur. In developing countries few legislatures are ever called upon to draft a new constitution. When new constitutions are written, they are usually the gift of a retreating colonial power, a triumphant executive, a coup d'état, or a small committee of jurists. The legislature, if it has a role at all, is usually only asked to ratify an executive-prepared document. Quite frequently the legislature is totally bypassed and the document is presented for a referendum, where the population is asked to ratify the constitutional document. Opposition forces are often left out of the whole process, kept under control, or denied any meaningful role in the drafting or ratification of the document.[1]

The Brazilian experience in drafting the Constitution of 1988 may be a pacesetter in this regard.[2] This chapter discusses the political climate within which the National Constitutional Assembly (NCA) was called upon to draft the constitution, the external challenges it faced, the internal composition of the NCA, how it organized itself, the procedures it adopted to conduct its business, the strategies it used to arrive at agreements, and the approaches used by the main political parties to mobilize their internal and external resources.

THE NATURE OF THE BRAZILIAN TRANSITION TO DEMOCRACY

Authoritarian regimes exit from power in a number of ways. According to Donald Share and Scott Mainwaring, there are three ways in which this transition to democracy is normally achieved. Transition through "regime breakdown or collapse" is the most common way. Under this form, the collapsing regime has little control over the direction of events under the new regime. The authoritarian regime in this type of transition is discredited and delegitimized, either as a result of a coup, a revolution, or some internal or external crisis or defeat. The authors cited as examples of this transition Germany, Italy, and Japan after World War II; Greece and Portugal in 1974; and Argentina from 1982 to 83.[3]

The second type of transition to democracy is through "extrication." In this case, "the authoritarian elites set limits regarding the form and timing of political change but are less capable of controlling the transition beyond the moment of the first election."[4] They simply manage to retain some control over the transition. The examples cited include Peru (1980), Bolivia (1979-1980), and Uruguay (1982-1985).[5]

The least common type of transition is through "transaction," in which the authoritarian regimes initially control most aspects of the transition, and over time the degree of control over the process of transition begins to decline. In the opinion of Share and Mainwaring, between 1974 and 1982 Brazil was solidly within this third type, and only after 1983 did it begin to manifest some of the characteristics of transition through extrication. Under the third type of transition, the authoritarian elites control the timing of the transition, they insist on excluding some actors from the transition, and they try to control policy output and insist on ruling out punitive measures against the leaders of the authoritarian regime. A close examination of the drafting of the Constitution shows that the transition to democracy in Brazil was through transaction, all the way, and that the regime did not extricate itself from power but was willing to share it in accordance with new rules that it had negotiated. This chapter elaborates on how the authoritarian elites tried to control the drafting of the new Constitution and what their principal demands were. Finally, it reflects on the extent to which they were able to achieve their demands.

The behavior of the authoritarian elites in Brazil, before and during the writing of the Constitution, approximates the transaction model of transition. Although the regime's legitimacy began to erode after 1984, its ranks remained intact, and it was able to quickly adapt and successfully compete in the election of 1986. The grave illness of Tancredo Neves and his untimely death on April 21 1985, thirty seven days after he was to assume power, elevated José Sarney to the presidency. Sarney's assumption of power gave the authoritarian elites sympathetic support at the top echelons of power. Not only was Sarney a close ally of the authoritarian regime as the president of the pro-government party (PDS), but he continued to be considered an outsider by many of the important members of the Democratic Alliance that brought him to power. Just prior to the election of 1986, Sarney's popularity reached its height as a result of his proposed economic measures, which became known as *Plano Cruzado*. President Sarney mobilized enough support for his party (the PFL) and indirectly through his ability to forge alliances between defectors of PDS and ARENA, and the moderate elements of the PMDB, the party that led this process of transition. The Congress that was elected in 1986, while dominated by the PMDB, included many moderate members who in the 1960s and 1970s were collaborators of the authoritarian regime and therefore had no interest in taking positions in the NCA that might put the interest over the former elites in jeopardy. Indeed, the first handicap that the NCA was to face in drafting a new Constitution (which sets the Brazilian experience apart from many other experiences) was that it was called upon to create a new order while many of the pillars of power of the military order were still comfortably in place.

The retreating order maintained significant support both outside and inside the NCA. Throughout the deliberations over the new Constitution in 1987 and 1988, the retreating authoritarian elites were able to mount many successful campaigns to defend their vital interests. This fact was always present in the minds of the new civilian leadership and shaped their strategies and actions and consequently the outcome of the new Constitution.

Before the convocation of the constitutional assembly, the retreating elites negotiated a number of assurances with the newly created Democratic Alliance under the leadership of Tancredo Neves regarding the way the new Constitution would be written. They won on some points and lost on others.[6]

Their first victory was in blocking all efforts by the opposition, which, during January to April of 1984, was able to organize mass rallies in support of amending the Constitution and electing the President in a direct election. The various maneuvers to amend the Constitution failed, and Tancredo Neves, the leader of the Alliance, agreed to be elected through the Electoral College, which was engineered by the authoritarian elites to elect their own candidate. Although the split within PDS denied Paulo Maluf (the PDS candidate) the victory, the authoritarian elites in exchange for supporting and allowing Neves to be elected managed to negotiate with him and the Alliance a number of points that they considered vital to a smooth transition, without retribution and *revanchismo*, or revenge.

The authoritarian elites resisted the convening of an exclusive constitutional assembly, for fear that such an assembly would be dominated by liberal and leftist elements.[7] They insisted, therefore, that the election of 1986 be a regular congressional election under the existing electoral rules drafted by the elites themselves. This meant that the call for an election was for a normal Congress exercising its normal prerogatives, as defined by the Constitution of 1967/69. Two-thirds of the Senate seats (forty-eight) and all 487 deputies were up for election. One-third of the senators were elected in 1982 and continued to serve as full voting members in the 1986 NCA. The amending of the existing constitution, or drafting of a new constitution, was only one task of the new Congress.

The insistence that the Congress elected in 1986 should serve the dual function of legislative power and constitutional assembly gave the regime several advantages.[8] In the first place, electing a Congress ensured that many of the political elites who had been cooperating with the military regime would run and win in the election. The election, as with all other elections, was waged on local, family, and constituency-related services, rather than on the candidate's position on the proposed constitution. Second, the debate on the proposed Constitution was muted during the electoral campaign, because the election was for both a congress and governors, which overshadowed the election of a constituent assembly. The fear that a debate limited to the new Constitution would provide newcomers and radicals an advantage over the old guards was thus avoided. Third, a newly elected Congress was more likely to convene and operate under its time-honored structures, procedures, and leaders, rather than devising completely new structures and procedures, as a newly elected constitutional assembly might do. Existing structures and procedures favored the elites, since they were more stable and predictable. Finally, by insisting the new Congress perform its various roles specified by the Constitution of 1967/69, it would be left with little time to spend on drafting a new constitution. This, it was felt, would make it easier for the executive to draft the new Constitution and have it ratified by the Congress in a few joint sessions.[9] This last expectation did not materialize because of the format the new Congress decided to adopt.

Another expectation of the authoritarian regime was that the new Constitution would be drafted by a committee representing both houses acting on a constitutional document already prepared by the executive, as was the case in 1946. To ensure that leftist elements were barred from the election, the regime insisted that the existing provisions in the Constitution of 1967/1969 and the electoral laws of 1979 be adhered to. This meant, in effect, that parties with Communist labels or confessed Communists could not compete in the election. The 1979 electoral laws also made it difficult for new parties to be created, since they needed to win a certain minimum percentage of votes in a minimum number of states before they were recognized as national parties. These electoral laws also required that parties contesting elections field a complete list of candidates to all the contested seats, thus eliminating the possibility of forming electoral coalitions among different parties. This, in the estimation of the elites, was supposed to favor the government party, since it enjoyed the support of the state apparatus and therefore could field candidates in all the electoral districts. Opposition parties were expected to suffer from this requirement, because many who were unable to use the federal apparatus had only regional, state, or local power bases.

One year before the congressional term was to expire (during the honeymoon period between Sarney and the Democratic Alliance formed by PMDB and PFL), the Congress passed Constitutional Amendment No. 26, on May 27, 1985. This amendment opened the way for new political parties to compete in the elections, including the Communist and leftist political parties. The electoral laws were also relaxed, eliminating many of the 1979 restrictions. Political parties were no longer required to present a complete list covering all the contested seats. Through political agreements negotiated in the Congress in 1986, the campaign and political propaganda laws were also changed, giving small and new parties free access to radio and television time.[10]

ECONOMIC CONSTRAINTS

Another limiting factor that shaped the writing of the new Constitution was the mounting economic crisis that Brazil was facing, especially in 1987 and 1988.[11] The initial success of the first *Plano Cruzado*, which froze wages and prices, and devalued the currency and created a new monetary unit called the *Cruzado*, came to an end immediately after the 1986 election. Producers in the manufacturing sectors and the agricultural industry openly defied the government pricing policies. Many consumer goods disappeared from the market, while others were in short supply. Black market prices became prevalent. Some manufactures, using loopholes in the regulations, resorted to the introduction of new products or packaged existing products under different names or in different covers to bypass the pricing freeze. Productivity of essential consumer goods, especially meat, was seriously curtailed.

When the government eased its controls, it put in motion an inflationary cycle reaching more than 600 percent per year. Subsequent economic measures to deal with the spiraling inflation only accentuated the crisis and put Brazil on a dangerous course toward an internal explosion. Riots and acts of violence broke out in Brasília, Rio de Janeiro, São Paulo, and many other major cities. The threat of a military takeover as a final solution became a topic that was openly debated on the front pages of the major newspapers and was discussed in the halls and conference rooms of the Congress.

This worsening economic crisis forced the government to undertake urgent negotiations with the World Bank on needed economic restructuring before the government could receive any additional help on servicing its $140 billion debt. Policies recommended by the World Bank to restructure the economy and the investment policies of the government included the rationalizing of the public sector by freezing if not reducing the number of public employees, privatization of many of the state-owned companies and public enterprises, reducing if not eliminating many of the subsidies on basic foods, and scaling down many domestic social programs. In the summer of 1987, the conflicting economic demands, both from the domestic and the international communities, forced Brazil to declare a unilateral moratorium on payments of principal and interest until questions concerning debt rescheduling, interest rate reductions, and new loans were settled.

It was in this highly tense environment that the NCA convened to draft the constitution. The economic crisis raised the specter of a violent and bloody clash between the poor and the rich. The poor, representing more than 75 percent of the population, saw in the return to democracy an overdue opportunity to redress the many economic inequalities that the military regime had perpetrated. Unions that were suppressed during the authoritarian regime became vocal in demanding better wages and benefits to their members. Agricultural workers and landless peasants demanded a fair return for their labor and pressed for land distribution. The progressive elements of the Catholic church mobilized their supporters, and some even encouraged them to takeover land by force.

Landlords and leaders of the industries saw their vital interests being threatened and began organizing to prevent this from happening, by legal means if possible, and through force if necessary. During the general electoral campaign of 1986, it was rumored that the manufacturers from São Paulo and other industrial states raised a war chest of more than $50 million, which was to be spent on the electoral campaigns of candidates who were likely to look favorably on their economic needs. In the rural areas, landlords began arming their supporters and paid henchmen to evict by force land squatters and to prevent others from overtaking their land.

The deepening economic crisis was hardly the appropriate atmosphere within which a new constitution, embodying a minimum degree of consensus and consequently of legitimacy, could be written. Indeed, the specter of a military takeover and the frequent intervention of military spokesmen on many of the issues under discussion by the NCA was a permanent feature of the economic and political environment within which the NCA had to work. The authoritarian elite, while not in full control, was represented throughout the new order negotiations that ended in the adoption of the new Constitution on October 5, 1988.

THE ELECTION OF 1986 AND THE COMPOSITION OF THE NCA

The retreating authoritarian elites did all they could to ensure a smooth and orderly transition to democracy, thereby hoping to share power without retribution or threat. They also made sure that they had enough influence in the Congress elected in 1986 so that they could shape the new constitution. Although there were more than thirty-four parties that competed in the election, only eleven parties managed to be represented in the Congress. Table 7.1 illustrates the party and regional representation of the Congress elected in 1986.[12]

The 1986 election did not bring many surprises to the departing elites. The left, as represented by the two Communist parties (PCB, Brazilian Communist Party, and PC do B, the Communist Party of Brazil), the Socialist Party (PSB), and the Workers Party (PT), was able to elect only twenty-seven members out of 559. Even if one adds the twenty-six members elected under the Democratic Labor Party (PDT) of Brizola, the traditional enemy of the 1964 authoritarian elites, the whole leftist element occupied less than 10 percent of the NCA. Furthermore, the Left showed strength in only a few selected places in the country. Most of its members came from the Southeast and the South. They were unable to secure representation in many of the states. The lion's share went to PMDB with 298 seats and PFL with 133, the same Democratic Alliance with which the elites had negotiated their departure.[13]

Table 7.1

Party and Regional Representation of the Congress Elected in 1986

Party	North	Northeast	Southeast	South	Centralwest	Total
PMDB	35	84	91	55	33	298
PFL	16	69	26	12	10	133
PDS	5	14	8	9	2	38
PDT	2	1	16	6	1	26
PTB	2	2	14	-	1	19
PT	-	-	14	2	-	16
PL	-	-	7	-	-	7
PDC	-	-	2	-	4	6
PSB	1	-	1	-	-	2
PCB	-	4	-	2	1	7
PC do B	-	4	2	-	1	7
Total	61	178	181	86	53	559

Source: David Fleischer, "Um Perfil Sócioeconômico, Político e Ideológico da Assembléia Constituinte de 1987," a paper presented at the 11th annual meeting of ANPOCS, Águas de São Pedro, 1987.

Note: These figures represent a preliminary assessment of party affiliation. As the work of the assembly proceeded, some members changed their party affiliation. The major split, however, occurred in June 1988, when more than 54 members, mainly from PMDB, left the party and created a new party known as PSDB.

The departing elites were also heartened by the relatively low turnover of members in the Congress. After twenty-two years of authoritarian rule many feared that the country would elevate to power a whole new generation of politicians to replace those who supported or cooperated with the military. Yet, upon close analysis, we find that 49 percent of those elected had no prior experience at the federal level,[14] while 51 percent had some experience.[15]

At first glance, the victory of PMDB was impressive. It won 298 seats, almost seventeen seats above the absolute majority needed in the NCA. It also won twenty-two out of the twenty-three governorships, losing only in Sergipe to its ally, the PFL. With such a majority, one would have expected the PMDB to have its will uncontested within the NCA. However, the fragility of PMDB, and for that matter all the other centrist parties, started to show as soon as the NCA began its work.

An ideological and socioeconomic analysis of party affiliation showed a low degree of party homogeneity. As in most Brazilian elections, a number of electoral coalitions of convenience were made for the purpose of winning the election. As soon as the elections were over, the coalitions disintegrated. David Fleischer found that of the 298

PMDB members seventy-two had been members of ARENA in 1979, fourteen had been members of other parties, and twenty-eight were new politicians. Indeed, of the total 559 members of the NCA, Fleischer found that 217 members were ARENA affiliates at one time or another.

A socioeconomic analysis of the NCA showed a high degree of heterogeneity. Those who were affiliated with the business sector represented 27 percent; professionals, 24.5 percent; agriculture, 16.3 percent; public employees, 12.9 percent; the media, 9.1 percent; and the military, only 0.9 percent. Forty percent of the members received their incomes principally from capital investments, and 60 percent from salaries. Only 12 percent of the NCA members openly stated that they represented the interests of the urban and labor classes.

Ideologically, the NCA had 9.3 percent as left, 22.5 percent as center-left, 32.4 percent as center, 23.5 percent as center-right, and 12.3 percent as right.[16]

The election of 1986 brought a full spectrum of Brazilian society to power. The Brazilian transition included representatives from all political shades of society, rather than a dominant political ideology or a new power elite. This pluralism, and the fragile nature of political parties in general and PMDB in particular, made the transition to democracy gradual and hesitant. The task facing the NCA was complicated. With a new majority party that was divided, a retreating elite that was well represented in the state institutions as well as in the NCA, and a small but very vocal, and perhaps very popular, progressive group advocating radical changes, negotiating new agreements regarding the provisions of the new Constitution posed a tough challenge to the creativity and perseverance of the new leaders. The Congress, supposedly a marginal institution, was called upon to undertake one of the toughest tasks that any legislature can face: the restructuring of the basic political, economic, and social fabric of a society. How did the Brazilian Congress, acting as a national constitutional assembly, meet this challenge?

THE STRUCTURING OF THE NCA

For the executive, interested in transition through continuity, the writing of the Constitution was supposed to be a peripheral activity to the regular work of the Congress. President Sarney had hoped that the Congress, in accordance with its internal rules, would elect its Mesa and committees and then set up a joint congressional committee to review and adopt a draft Constitution prepared by the executive. Sarney also expected the Constitution of 1967/69 to be fully observed—just as it had been negotiated between Tancredo and the military—until the new Constitution was completed. This meant that the NCA would not deal with the mandate of the President during his term.[17]

Indeed, on July 18 of 1985, President Sarney had already nominated a blue-ribbon commission under the chairmanship of a distinguished jurist and respected politician and public figure, Afonso Arinos, to draft a Constitution for presentation to the Congress for discussion and adoption. The forty-nine member Arinos Commission issued its report on September 26, 1986. It recommended, among other things, that Brazil adopt the parliamentary system of government as a way out of its institutional instability and the impasses that had developed between the executive and the legislature. In spite of the draft's many positive features, it was never presented to the NCA for consideration. President Sarney and his supporters disagreed with many of the provisions in the constitutional document, especially its recommendation of a parliamentary system of government. Although the recommendation came from an official commission the

President had appointed, was published by the official journal of the Congress, and enjoyed the support of the leadership of PMDB and other progressive parties, Sarney decided to ignore the commission's report. The NCA was faced with drafting a Constitution with no official document from the executive.[18]

In addition to the proposed Arinos constitutional document, several other groups and individuals circulated their own version of a new constitution. As early as 1986, the Senate, in an attempt to create a favorable image of itself and its leaders, instructed Prodasen (see Chapter 3) to launch a major initiative known as the Constitutional Project. The Constitutional Project of the Senate had three parts: First, to collect and compare all the previous Brazilian constitutions, as well as state constitutions. This part also included the collection and translation of the constitutions of more than thirty-six countries, including those of Portugal, Spain, West Germany, Italy, Japan, and the United States. The purpose of the collection was to make the constitutions available to the NCA for easy reference. The second part involved sending thousands of questionnaires to citizens and groups throughout the country to solicit their suggestions on what they thought the new Constitution should contain. The responses were coded and fed into a computer; they were to provide members of the NCA with information on the popular sentiments regarding the new Constitution. The third component of this initiative involved the setting in motion of a computer capability to provide the NCA with appropriate information and, most important, to assist them in drafting, processing, sorting, and printing their daily work.[19]

In 1984, a major initiative under the direction of Afonso Arinos was undertaken by the prestigious Getúlio Vargas Foundation to outline the major provisions of a new constitution. The results were published in December 1984, in a special issue of the *Revista de Ciência Política*, under the title "Por uma Nova Constituição: As Aspirações Nacionais." Other university research centers, professional associations and syndicates, publishing houses, individuals, and groups also published their own versions of what they thought the new Constitution should contain. All of these efforts and activities were in anticipation of the work to be done by the NCA. They were intended to mobilize public opinion in favor of certain proposals, thereby influencing the work of the NCA.[20]

The NCA was seated on February 1, 1987, by the president of the Supreme Federal Court (STF), Minister José Carlos Moreira Alves. On February 2, 1987, the NCA elected Deputy Ulysses Guimarães as its president and began deliberations on its internal rules and structures. Three important areas were to be clarified: First, the relationship between the Congress and the NCA; second, the jurisdiction of the NCA; and third, the structure and procedures that the NCA needed to follow in its deliberations. All of these areas were hotly contested among two competing camps.

The first camp represented the departing elites and coalesced around President Sarney. It was supported within the NCA by such political parties as the PFL, PTB, PDS, and many PMDB members previously associated with ARENA or PDS. In the other camp were newly elected members of PMDB, other parties known as the "little angels" (*anjinhos*), the progressive elements within PMDB known as the *xiitas*, and several others from the minor leftist parties, such as PDT, PT, PSB, PC, and PC do B, who were pushing for radical changes and a total break with the past.

The Relationship Between the NCA and the Congress

By the time the NCA convened, its relationship with the Congress had already been determined. Under the leadership of PMDB, the Senate on January 30 elected its Mesa and its party leadership. The Chamber followed on January 31. The decision was made to have two completely separate leadership structures. The Senate and the Chamber were to follow their normal work in accordance with their internal rules, with only minimal adjustment to ensure coordination with the work of the NCA. This meant that both the Senate and the Chamber each had its separate Mesas and committee chairs. To facilitate the work of the NCA, no permanent committees were formed in either house, as stipulated by the internal rules. The Senate and the Chamber also resolved to discharge their constitutional functions in plenary sessions, to be held only in the mornings. In the interest of attending only to important governmental matters, each house decided to dispense with private members' initiated bills and restricted its legislative activities to bills introduced by the executive. A joint budget committee was reactivated to deal with the budget and other matters. Each house reserved the right to create special committees as needed. The Senate Parliamentary Inquiry Committee (*CPI*)—created in 1988 to investigate financial wrongdoing and allegations of corruption by the President and his former minister of planning and other public officials—became the core of the work of the Senate.

The presidency of the Chamber went to Deputy Guimarães, who, in addition to being the president of the NCA, served as the national president of PMDB. As the president of the chamber, he also served as acting President in the absence of the President of the Republic. The prominent leadership role that Guimarães came to play represented the triumph of the moderate wing within the PMDB. Guimarães's election to the presidency of the Chamber, which some argued was contrary to the internal rules prohibiting the reelection of the president for a second term, prevented Deputy Fernando Lyra (PMDB/Pernambuco), the progressive candidate, from being elected. It also meant that the Chamber and NCA had a joint leadership structure, making it difficult for the Chamber to pursue its constitutional function as a legislative body. Its energies were instead concentrated on drafting the constitution. Finally, the concentration of the three presidencies, in the person of the moderate Guimarães, provided him with an opportunity to play the role of an arbitrator among the various conflicting forces in his party, among the various factions within the NCA, and between the NCA and the executive.

During the drafting of the constitution, the legislative role of the Congress was reduced to a few general sessions, where speeches were made and verbal battles were fought regarding the way the government was handling the economy and what many termed as crises of legitimacy and governability. With the exception of the well-publicized work of the Senate CPI on corruption, the executive continued to take the initiative in proposing new laws and when necessary issuing decree laws, including the promulgation of a multi-billion dollar supplementary budget in June of 1988 against an outraged Congress.

The Jurisdiction of the NCA

Under the leadership of Senator Fernando Henrique Cardoso, (PMDB/São Paulo) who served as the relator of the Internal Rules of the NCA, the progressive forces within PMDB and the other leftist parties tried to give the NCA sweeping power to deal with all issues left hanging during this protracted period of transition. This included what the departing elites feared most: the amendment of the Constitution of 1967/69 through a series of legislative acts requiring only an absolute majority of the NCA members. These legislative acts targeted a series of authoritarian measures adopted by the military that were still in force, such as the emergency laws, various national security laws that defined the conditions and the manner under which the military could interfere to protect the national security, press freedom, the right of labor unions, the right to strike, immunities and prerogatives of legislators, the right of the executive to issue decree laws, and a series of acts intended to absolve the legislature of many of its prerogatives (see Chapter 1). This progressive group tried to have these measures immediately abolished through constitutional amendments, even before the new Constitution was promulgated.

The attempt to define widely the jurisdiction of the NCA met with stiff resistance from the Sarney forces, who argued that such an attempt to amend the Constitution through an absolute majority of the NCA, rather than the two-thirds majority of the Congress as specified by the constitution, would be unconstitutional, and therefore would set a bad precedent for a body that was to reinstate the rule of law against the arbitrariness of the departing authoritarian regime. By late March the basic internal rules defining the jurisdiction, structure, and processes of the NCA, as drafted by Senator Cardoso, were renegotiated and a compromise was agreed upon. The NCA was given a free hand to deal with all issues pertaining to the provisions of the new Constitution by an absolute majority of its members. The NCA through strong military pressures and the threat of coups was prevented from amending the existing Constitution through legislative acts. The NCA was also authorized to promulgate a series of transitory provisions specifying the term of office of President Sarney.[21] It also gave the NCA the authority to decide how the new Constitution was to be promulgated; should it be promulgated under the signature of the President and members of the NCA, or through general plebiscite?

The Structure of the NCA

The structure and procedures adopted by the NCA were shaped by tradition, the familiar and the emerging political forces within the NCA. Prior to the election of 1986, the Senate, under the leadership of its director-general, Lourival Zagonel dos Santos, took the lead in organizing a working group of staff advisors to prepare for the work that lay ahead. The Chamber of Deputies sent staff representatives to the working group. The group debated several alternatives for organizing itself, especially the advisory staff, Prodasen and Cegraf, to be prepared to assist in the NCA work. With the election of Guimarães to the presidency of the Chamber and the presidency of the NCA, the task for working out the basic structure and the parliamentary procedures fell to a group of veteran legislative staff [22] who worked closely with Senator Fernando Henrique Cardoso from São Paulo and Deputy Nelson Jobim from Rio Grande do Sul, both from the leadership of PMDB.

The NCA adopted a structure and parliamentary procedures familiar to the Congress. The NCA was to have a Mesa composed of a president, three vice-presidents, and five secretaries. Their power was defined in language similar to that of the members of the Mesa in the Chamber. In its deliberations, the NCA was to use the same parliamentary procedures as the Congress. Members were given ample opportunity to speak and debate issues. All of these provisions were embodied in Resolution No. 2 of the NCA.

The second important factor that shaped the structure and procedures of the NCA was the political forces active within it. Two major political trends emerged. On the one hand, the progressive political forces within PMDB and the other small leftist parties were pushing for as open a process as possible, not only for the elected members, but, more important, for the social and political forces outside the NCA. They adopted this strategy for several reasons. First, they wanted to transform the occasion of drafting a Constitution into a symbolic political act, to show the public how a civilian democratic regime transacted its most important business as compared to the authoritarian regime. They wanted the process of drafting a Constitution to be as public and transparent as possible, in contrast to the secret and private manner in which the previous regime conducted its business. Second, they were concerned that a closed process would give the retreating authoritarian elites the opportunity to pressure many of the maverick members of the NCA who were elected under the banner of a progressive party such as the PMDB. Hence, they wanted the debate and voting to be readily and instantly available to the public. Third, this group felt the need to keep up public pressure on the members of the NCA. As stated earlier, the election of 1986 was not waged exclusively for the election of an NCA.

Few members had been elected on the basis of their standing regarding the proposed constitution. The progressive political forces felt that the public should be informed and should have the opportunity to make its position known to the elected members regarding the various provisions of the constitution. This was to be done through organized efforts to communicate with the members, through rallies and demonstrations, and even through the presentation of proposals and amendments to those involved in drafting the constitution.

Finally, since many of the progressive members were newcomers, elected for the first time, they did not have much confidence in the established leadership, much of which was formed during the 1970s and 1980s under the authoritarian regime. In accordance with the political ethos of the moment, they wanted direct participation. Indeed, some of them were in favor of an immediate referendum on any constitutional document drafted by the NCA, as the only guarantee that the NCA would not compromise the general interest in favor of the special interests of the economic and political elites that were feared to be still powerful, both within the institutions of the state and the private sector.

The progressive elites wanted to be in control of the internal process of drafting the constitution. If they could not, they wanted as much pressure from the progressive public as possible. These forces, under the leadership of Senators Cardoso, Mário Covas (PMDB/São Paulo), and Deputy Nelson Jobim (PMDB/RS), were to a large extent responsible for drafting and adopting Resolution No. 2 of the NCA, regarding the internal rules of the NCA.

Initially, the conservative forces within the NCA were scattered and disorganized. President Sarney was still enjoying his brief honeymoon as the leader of the Democratic Alliance of PMDB and PFL. The conservative forces needed a cause and a leader to rally around.

The rift between Sarney and the progressive forces within PMDB was getting wider. Capitalizing on the parliamentary experience they had gained during the past two decades of working within the Congress, the conservative forces adopted a wait-and-see policy. They recognized that the euphoria of the election would soon pass and that the hard reality of reaching agreements over concrete proposals would not only expose the fragility of the alliance between Sarney and the Democratic Alliance, but would also break the Democratic Alliance itself. Even the progressive forces within the Democratic Alliance were to experience serious tension between those represented by small parties to the left and the progressive elements with PMDB. Thus, rather than adopting a rigid ideological position, the conservative forces opted for a flexible but dynamic strategy. They decided to wage a series of tactical battles over specific issues, hoping that the cumulative effect of these maneuvers would give them enough support to win the issues that were important to them, such as the form of government, the length of the President's term in office, the economy, land reform, and the role of the armed forces.

The first opportunity for this group to assert itself was in January 1988, when it succeeded in amending the internal rules specified under Resolution No. 2 and adopting

Resolution No. 3, which specified new rules on how the Constitution was to be voted upon in the plenary session. This procedural victory had tremendous impact not only on the way the Constitution was adopted and who the principal participants were in the process of elaborating the constitution, but also on what eventually was adopted. Let us see how this struggle between the progressive forces, as represented by Resolution No. 2, and the conservative forces, as represented by Resolution No. 3, unfolded, then turn our attention to the impact of those changes.

Resolution No. 2 elaborated the internal rules of the NCA, particularly the procedures governing debate and the prerogatives of the Mesa. For the elaboration of the Constitution, this resolution established nine committees. Eight of them were called thematic committees, and each was divided into three subcommittees. Each of these committees dealt with a specific topic of the constitution. The ninth committee chaired by Afonso Arinos was called the Systematization Committee. Its function was to put together, in one document, the final reports submitted to it by the thematic committees. Table 7.2 shows the committees and subcommittees and their jurisdictions.

Each subcommittee dealt with a specific area within the proposed constitution. Subcommittees received suggestions and proposals not only from their own members, but also from other members of the NCA and the public. The proposals approved by each subcommittee were later forwarded to the parent committee and then to the Systematization Committee. The Systematization Committee would use these drafts to produce the first draft of the constitutional document, and which would then be submitted to the whole NCA for approval, article by article.

Each committee and subcommittee was headed by a president, two vice-presidents, and a rapporteur. Members of the NCA were distributed among the committees and subcommittees in proportion to their party representation in the NCA. Members of the Mesa of the Senate, the Chamber, or the NCA were excluded from occupying leadership positions in these committees or subcommittees. A member was limited to one leadership position, at the committee or subcommittee level, to allow as many members as possible to participate. Within this idealistic and logical scheme, the most important role was given to the rapporteur, because he was responsible for integrating the hundreds of conflicting, overlapping, and repetitive proposals into a single text. Table 7.3 shows how the leadership of the committees and subcommittees was distributed among the various parties represented in the NCA.

The progressive forces within PMDB managed to control the rapporteurs of the committees and subcommittees in order to control the drafting of the Constitution and its eventual approval. The rapporteurs of the nine committees were monopolized by the historical forces of the PMDB, such as Senators Paulo Bisol, José Richa, Severo Gomes, and Almir Gabriel; and Deputies Egídio Ferreira Lima, José Serra, Artur da Távola, and Bernardo Cabral. Cabral, a former president of the bar association, was the rapporteur of the Committee of Systematization and played the leading role in producing the first draft of the constitution. PFL, as part of the Democratic Alliance, got eight of the nine committee presidencies and PDS got one. To further its grip on the committees, PMDB got six out of the nine first vice-presidents, and the remaining were distributed among the medium-sized parties. The smaller parties to the left and to the right were not represented in the leadership of the nine parent committees.

Party representation in the twenty-four subcommittees was more diverse. The smaller parties were represented with at least one member or more. Yet PMDB ensured its dominance by appointing either the president or the rapporteur of these subcommittees from among its members. Table 7.4 shows the distribution of the leadership of the subcommittees among the political parties.

Table 7.2

Committees and Subcommittees of the NCA, 1987

Committee:	Subcommittee:	
1. Committee on Sovereignty, Rights of Men and Women	a)	Subcommittee on Nationality, Sovereignty and International Relations
	b)	Subcommittee on Political Rights, Collective Rights, and Guarantees
	c)	Subcommittee on Individual Rights and Guarantees
2. Committee on State Organization	a)	Subcommittee on the Union, Federal District and Territories
	b)	Subcommittee on the States
	c)	Subcommittee on the Municipalities and Regions
3. Committee on the Organization of the Powers and the System of Government	a)	Subcommittee on the Legislative Power
	b)	Subcommittee on the Executive Power
	c)	Subcommittee on the Judicial Power and the Public Ministries
4. Committee on Electoral System, Parties, and Institutional Guarantees	a)	Subcommittee on the Electoral System and Political Parties
	b)	Subcommittee on the Defense of the State Society and its Security
	c)	Subcommittee on the Safeguard of the Constitution its Reforms and Amendments
5. Committee on Revenues, Budget, and Finance	a)	Subcommittee on Revenues, Participation, and Distribution of Receipts
	b)	Subcommittee on Budget and Fiscal Oversight
	c)	Subcommittee on Financial Systems
6. Committee on Economic Order	a)	Subcommittee on General Principles, Intervention of the State, Ownership of Underground Resources, and Economic Activities
	b)	Subcommittee on Urbanization and Transport
	c)	Subcommittee on Agricultural Policy, Rural Policy and Agrarian Reform

Table 7.2 (continued)

Committee:		Subcommittee:
7. Committee on Social Order	a)	Subcommittee on the Rights of Workers and Public Servants
	b)	Subcommittee on Health, Security, and Environment
	c)	Subcommittee on Blacks, Indigenous Population, Handicapped, and Minorities
8. Committee on the Family, Education, Culture and Sports, Science and Technology and Communication	a)	Subcommittee on Education, Culture and Sports
	b)	Subcommittee on Science and Technology and Communication
	c)	Subcommittee on the Family, Minors and Elderly
9. Committee of Systematization		

Table 7.3

Distribution of Leadership of Committees of NCA, by Political Party

Party:	President	1st Vice-President	2nd Vice-President	Rapporteur	Total
PMDB	0	7	6	9	22
PFL	8	0	1	0	9
PDS	1	0	1	0	2
PDT	0	1	1	0	2
PTB	0	1	0	0	1
TOTAL	9	9	9	9	36

Source: Computed by the author from the records of the NCA.

Table 7.4

Leadership of Subcommittees by Political Parties in the NCA

Party:	President	1st Vice-President	2nd Vice-President	Rapporteur	Total
PMDB	15	11	13	13	52
PFL	5	9	4	5	23
PDS	1	2	1	2	6
PDT	2	0	1	1	4
PTB	1	1	1	1	4
PDC	0	0	1	1	2
PL	0	1	1	0	2
PT	0	0	0	1	1
PCB	0	0	1	0	1
PC do B	0	0	0	0	1
Total	24	24	24	24	96

Either the presidency or the position of rapporteur of every subcommittee went to PMDB. In some cases, both positions went to PMDB members. Of the ninety-six available leadership positions at the subcommittee level, PMDB controlled fifty-three, PFL controlled twenty-three, and the remaining twenty went to all of the other parties, from the left and right. PMDB used what it considered as an overwhelming electoral victory and a mandate from the people to ensure that the new Constitution reflected its priorities and vision of the new Brazil. To counterbalance the openness of the process, it concentrated the responsibility of drafting the text in the hands of its party members.

To execute this political formula, PMDB needed extensive staff support. Some were needed as advisors, administrators, and communicators. Others were needed to ensure that the work of NCA was adequately and accurately covered in the various news media. The professional staff and technical and informational capabilities that were developed and groomed by the Congress during the past two decades proved invaluable.

With almost half of the members of the NCA elected for the first time and therefore completely inexperienced with Brasília and the Congress and its information and research capabilities, the task facing the administrative, information, and research staff was gigantic. The new members needed to be oriented to their new environment and instructed in the intricacies of the legislative process. Their offices needed to be managed, and the flood of mail they were receiving needed to be answered. For those who occupied leadership positions, whether in the Senate, the Chamber, or the NCA, their needs included special information and research on the various responsibilities they were to handle, including dealing with other members and leaders, and party needs and tasks.

In addition to the needs of the elected members, the staff had to deal with numerous individuals, groups, and organizations, all demanding information and all trying to influence the provisions of the new Constitution. Suddenly, the tranquility and docility of the life of a legislative staff was permanently shattered. Working in the office of an influential Senator or Deputy, assisting a committee or subcommittee, or being attached to a political party became a prized appointment, if not a historical opportunity. For the first time, many of those top- qualified professionals who had been hibernating for years tasted the sweetness of accomplishment. Working an eighteen-hour day for seven days a week became the norm for many of them. For those who were directly involved in the most sensitive political negotiations and compromises, providing a piece of needed information, or sorting, coordinating, and reporting the NCA activities; or completing a draft proposal or amendment in the wee hours of the morning all provided them with an exhilaration rarely felt in the halls of the Congress before.

Prodasen and Cegraf also worked around the clock to make sure the thousands of proposals and amendments were processed and sorted out, the duplications and contradictions were identified, and similarities were fused together. With more than 60,000 proposals, suggestions, and amendments at various stages of the drafting of the constitution, the capabilities that were groomed within Prodasen and Cegraf were appropriately utilized. The daily work was inputted, cleaned, and printed for distribution the next day. Without this capability, drafting the Constitution in accordance with the open approach adopted by the NCA would have been technically impossible within the limited time available. The process would have come to a halt. An impasse might have developed.

Finally, the staff—many of them with journalistic backgrounds—organized a press, radio, and television communication center to ensure that the work of the NCA was summarized, written, and produced for distribution either directly or through the regular news media throughout the country. Through this mechanism, the NCA was assured that its actions and resolutions would be widely reported and explained. Indeed, the work of this unit became an authoritative source of information for those interested in following the work of the NCA.[23]

Between April 7 of 1987 and June 15 of 1988, when the various committees and subcommittees submitted their reports to the Systematization Committee, 182 public hearings were held and seventy-four constitutional bills were prepared, with 14,920 amendments. The Committee also received 9,653 suggestions from private citizens and 2,347 suggestions from groups and organizations.

As to the work of the Systematization Committee, which presented its first draft on June 17, 1988—in a period of 224 days, it held 125 meetings, prepared five different draft constitutions, and entertained 35,111 amendments proposed within the plenary session and 122 submitted by outside groups. The Constitution was voted on in two turns. In the first turn, the NCA held 119 sessions and undertook 732 votes for a total of 476 hours and 32 minutes. It considered 2,045 amendments and 2,277 motions for specific voting on minor amendments. In its second turn of voting on the constitution, the NCA held thirty-eight sessions and considered 1,834 amendments and 1,744 specific votes on minor amendments.

As to the work of the media section, it produced 716 TV programs, recorded 3,000 hours of video, and undertook 4,871 interviews with NCA members and 300 with nonmembers. The radio section produced 700 programs covering sixty hours. The press section produced sixty-four editions of its weekly journal, *Jornal da Constituinte*, which was distributed to more than 70,000 local government and state officials, universities, and research institutions.[24]

These statistics covered only the formal work of the NCA. As in all legislative institutions, the formal work represented only the tip of the iceberg. Formal sessions were occasions to ratify agreements reached. Most of those agreements took place somewhere else, usually in small groups and gatherings. The work of the NCA in drafting the Constitution was not an exception. Formally and informally, the legislative staff proved essential in getting the job done.

CENTRÃO AND ITS ROLE IN THE CONSTITUTIONAL PROCESS

By the time the Systematization Committee was about to report its first draft of the constitutional document, forces within the center and to the right of the center of the political spectrum had loosely coalesced to form a parliamentary front known as the *Centrão*. This was a broad coalition of NCA members that cut across party lines, united by what they felt was the excessive dominance of the progressive and leftist forces in the drafting of the constitution, as reflected by the draft document prepared by the Systematization Committee.[25] President Sarney and his supporters, through the distribution of presidential largess, such as radio and television concessions, public work contracts, appointments to public offices and others, were able to forge a temporary alliance among dissatisfied groups from PMDB, PFL, PDS, PTB, and other small, conservative parties which felt that some of their vital interests were being threatened. Some of the issues that brought this coalition together included the form of government (parliamentary or presidential), length of President Sarney's term in office (four or five years), agrarian reform (a broad definition of the land to be subject to distribution, or a narrow definition), the economy, and law and order issues.

The Systematization Committee had recommended a parliamentary system of government; a four-year term for Sarney, with a presidential election set for November 1988; a broad definition of agrarian reform with land earmarked for distribution to peasants and farmers, productive as well as nonproductive land, plus state-owned land. The land issue provided the rallying point for *Centrão*, and soon members of this newly organized coalition had positions on most of the provisions of the draft constitutional document. Although a loose alliance among various groups with divergent interests and goals, *Centrão* managed to hold itself together to score a number of impressive victories on issues of paramount concern to the departing elites. Its first impressive victory came in December 1987, when it succeeded in amending the process by which the draft document was to be considered within the NCA plenary session.

In accordance with Resolution No. 2, the draft prepared by the Systematization Committee was supposed to be the only document that the NCA plenary session was to consider. The draft could be amended only if approved by a majority. Such amendment would take precedence over the draft version of the Systematization Committee. The work of the Systematization Committee was to be based on the reports presented by the eight thematic committees. What the Systematization Committee actually received, however, was twenty-four uncoordinated drafts produced by the twenty-four subcommittees, plus thousands of suggestions and amendments presented by NCA members, citizens groups, and organizations. In its June 17 draft, the Systematization Committee tried to synthesize the various parts presented to it. This was not an easy task. It was no surprise, therefore, that the committee's first draft met with dissatisfaction from many of the conservative elements who felt that they were shut off from drafting the new constitution.

As the work of the NCA unfolded, several parliamentary groups were formed, cutting across party lines. By mid-February of 1988, according to one account, twelve overlapping factions could be identified within the NCA. In addition to the *Centrão*, these factions included the historic founders of PMDB; the Movement for the Unity of the Progressives (MUP); the *Centrinho*, or small center; the *anjinhos* (newly elected PMDB members); the evangelicals, a group of Protestant ministers in favor of strict moral standards in society; the Democratic movement; the Democratic center; the modernists; the Consensus group; the Group of Thirty-Two; and the Northeasterners (*Nordestinos*). Some of these groups were ideologically homogeneous and waged a concerted campaign regarding the issues facing the NCA; others were temporary alliances of diverse individuals with little in common except for issues relating to the constitution. A member could belong to one or more of these groups depending on the issues he or she advocated.

Within this flux, late in 1987, the political experience and sophistication of *Centrão* succeeded in convincing enough NCA members to adopt Resolution No. 3 of the NCA, defining how the Constitution was to be adopted. Instead of having the draft of the Systematization Committee as the only document to be debated in the plenary session of the NCA, Resolution No. 3 outlined a new process, which in effect sent the drafting process back to the drawing board. Rather than representing the collective will of the NCA, the report of the Systematization Committee was viewed by *Centrão* as representing a minority progressive group within the NCA, and therefore, as the only version, the report had no credibility during the NCA plenary debate.

Resolution No. 3 authorized NCA members to propose up to four proposals or amendments to the draft document of the Systematization Committee. It also specified that proposals or amendments proposed under the signature of an absolute majority of the NCA members (280 signatures) would be presented for action to the NCA before those proposals presented by the Systematization Committee. Systematization Committee proposals would be considered only if the proposals presented by the absolute majority failed to get the 280 votes needed for passage after a cooling period of three days. If the Systematization Committee proposals also failed to get the minimum 280 votes needed for passage, then the whole article fell into what was jokingly called *buraco negro*, or "black hole". This meant that a deadlock had been reached.

Having won this procedural battle, *Centrão* produced a draft document that proposed modifications and amendments to most of the articles of the draft document presented by the Systematization Committee. While many of the proposals included minor amendments, several of them presented changes totally at variance with those proposed by the Systematization Committee. The ability of *Centrão* to challenge the work of the Systematization Committee—by having the majority of NCA adopt Resolution No. 3, and later by presenting its draft constitutional proposals under the signature of more than 280 NCA members—gave the conservative forces a political victory and a new feeling of self-confidence that they were able to rely upon as the work of the NCA plenary session progressed. The progressive forces within PMDB and the other small parties suddenly realized that their electoral victory was a mere mirage. What was already known to PMDB became clear: that the unity of the party could not be sustained on the controversial provisions of the constitution.

The encouragement and support of a significant number of PMDB members enabled *Centrão* to win its procedural and substantive battles. Disgruntled members of PMDB shifted either to the left or to the right, as was predicted. Others decided to take a wait-and-see attitude while calling for a total break with President Sarney, who until then was supposed to be heading a cabinet representing the Democratic Alliance of PMDB and PFL.

Perhaps the most significant outcome of this procedural victory of the *Centrão* was that it forced the NCA to adopt the provisions of the Constitution by complex informal methods of political negotiation and compromise among the leaders of the progressive and conservative forces, rather than the idealistic, rationalistic process that Resolution No. 2 envisioned. With the injection of the *Centrão* proposals, the leadership of PMDB and the Systematization Committee found that the only way it could approve a proposed article was to ensure that the main objections of *Centrão* were satisfactorily answered. Typically, this compromise involved the NCA's formal adoption, in principle, of the amendment presented by *Centrão*, and then through a series of informal meetings among the various political leaders—called the Leadership Meeting—the hammering out of compromise versions that integrated the *Centrão* and the Systematization Committee versions.

Final voting was on this integrated version. Since this version represented a political compromise of the largest groups within the NCA, it normally was approved by an overwhelming majority. Only in a few cases, where compromises were not possible, was the NCA called upon to vote on two divergent proposals, and the victory went to those who got more than 280 votes. Some of these contested votes were won by *Centrão*, others by supporters of the Systematization Committee.

The presence and work of *Centrão*, however, forced the NCA to adopt most of the provisions of the Constitution by what may approach a process of consensus. It introduced an element of moderation in some areas and curbed some exaggerated tendencies on the part of some members from both sides. It created an atmosphere of "no vanquished and no victors"—the mark of the Brazilian transition to democracy. The supporters of the new order were able to embody in the new Constitution many of their priorities, especially in the realm of both individual and group social, economic, and political rights. Defenders of the retreating order were ensured that their vital interests were protected.

NOTES

1. In many countries, the executive has the exclusive prerogative in drafting a new constitution, with as little popular participation as possible, so that each new executive finds it necessary to enact his own constitution upon assuming power. The Egyptian system, where each new president since Nasser has drafted his own constitutional document and submitted it unopposed to a public referendum, is a typical way to draft constitutions in many developing countries.

2. Recent developments in the Eastern bloc countries of Hungary, Poland, and the USSR show the increasing prominent role of legislative bodies in amending existing constitutions. The process and obstacles encountered by the NCA in Brazil may shed some light on similar experiences in the Eastern bloc countries.

3. See Donald Share and Scott Mainwaring, "Transitions through Transaction: Democratization in Brazil and Spain," Selcher (ed.), *Political Liberalization*, op. cit. (1986), pp. 175-215.

4. Ibid., p. 178.

5. See Scott Mainwaring, "The Transition to Democracy in Brazil," *Journal of Inter-American Studies and World Affairs*, 28, no. 1 (Spring 1986), pp. 149-79.

6. See David V. Fleischer, "Eleições e Democracia no Brasil: Transição ou Transformismo," *Humanidades*, no. 3 (August/October 1986), pp. 84-92; and Gilberto Dimenstein, et al., *O Complô que Elegeu Tancredo* (Rio de Janeiro: JB, 1985).

7. See Eliézer Rizzo de Oliveira (ed.), *Militares: Pensamento e Ação Política* (Campinas: Papirus, 1987); Flávio Flores da Cunha Bierrenbach, *Quem Tem Medo da Constituinte?* (Rio de Janeiro: Paz e Terra, 1986); Alfred Stepan, *Os Militares: Da Abertura à Nova República* (Rio de Janeiro: Paz e Terra, 1986); and José Eduardo Faria, "Constituinte: Seus Riscos e Seus Muitos Desafios," *Jornal da Tarde* (January 5, 12, and 19, 1985).

8. Ulysses Guimarães tried to change this in a bill approved by the Chamber of Deputies in November 1986; however, the bill was defeated in the Senate by those elected in 1982 and lame-duck biônicos. See David Fleischer, "The Constituent Assembly and the Transformation Strategy: Attempts to Shift Political Power from the Presidency to Congress", in ibid.

9. See Centro de Estudos e Acompanhamento da Constituinte (CEAC), *O Anteprojeto Constitucional e o Dia-a-Dia do Cidadão* (Brasília: Departamento de Imprensa Nacional, 1986).

10. See Flávio Koutzii (ed.), *Nova República: Um Balanço* (Porto Alegre: L&PM, 1986); and Gláucio Ary Dillon Soares, *Colégio Eleitoral, Convenções Partidárias e Eleições Diretas* (Petrópolis: Vozes, 1984).

11. For the economic conditions facing the new republic, see Julian M. Cachel, Pamela S. Falk, and David V. Fleischer, *Brazil's Economic and Political Future* (Boulder, Colo.: Westview Press, 1988); John D. Wirth, Edson Oliveira Nunes, and Thomas E. Bogenschild (eds.), *State and Society in Brazil* (Boulder, Colo.: Westview Press, 1987); O'Donnell, Schmitter, and Whitehead (eds.), *Transitions from Authoritarian Rule,* op. cit. (1986); Peter T. Knight, *Economic Policy and Planning* (Boston: Northeastern University 1985); and Kenneth Meyers and F. Desmond McCarthy, *Brazil: Medium-Term Policy Analysis* (Washington: World Bank, 1985).

12. For the composition and orientation of the NCA, see Leôncio Martins Rodrigues, *Quem é Quem na Constituinte* (São Paulo: Oesp-Maltese, 1987); and *Repertório Biográfico dos Membros da Assembléia Nacional Constituinte de 1987* (Brasília: Câmara dos Deputados, 1987).

13. For information regarding the progress of the two main political parties, PMDB and PFL, see Marco Maciel, "Constituição para o Futuro" (Brasília: Senado Federal, 1987); Luiz Carlos Bresser Pereira, *O PMDB e as Eleições de 1986* (São Paulo: Fundação Pedroso Horta, 1987); Partido da Frente Liberal, *Carta Compromisso: Projeto* (Brasília: PFL, 1986), and *Manifesto, Programa e Estatuto* (Brasília: PFL, 1985). For information regarding the small political parties, see José Arthur Rios, "As Eleições de 1982 e os Pequenos Partidos," *Revista Brasileira de Estudos Políticos* (July 1983), pp. 187-216. Regarding PT, see Haroldo Lima and Aldo Arantes, *História de Ação Popular da JUC ao PC do B* (São Paulo: Alfa-Omega, 1984); Mário Morel, *Lula, O Metalúrgico* (Rio de Janeiro: Nova Fronteira, 1981); and Mário Pedrosa, *Sobre o PT* (São Paulo: Ched, 1980).

14. Taking into account those former senators who in 1986 ran for seats as deputies, or deputies who ran for Senate seats, as well as those alternate congressman in previous periods who were elected as principals in 1986, and finally, those senators and deputies who served before 1982, we find that 49 percent of the NCA were new members. This represents a normal degree of turnover under normal elections. But the election of 1986 was supposed to be a departure and a break with the past. Therefore it is considered to be a low turnover.

15. More than 51 percent of the members of the NCA have had some previous experience. The NCA has a high degree of continuity. Many of those elected have had dealings with the military in one form or another. Indeed, this is the whole mark of the Brazilian transition to democracy. The authoritarian elites have negotiated their departure and have counted on dealing with a well-tried elite. To a large extent, they got what they expected. This is by no means to suggest that all of those who have had previous electoral experience at the national level supported the military, nor to suggest that all of the newcomers can be counted as opponents of the military. Indeed, some of the principal opponents of the regime were among those with prior experience who survived the purges of the military. Nevertheless, 49 percent of the newcomers will pose a formidable problem; they will need to be socialized to and integrated into the work of the NCA. Having been elected for the first time, with no prior experience in a parliamentary setting, they will make the task of the leaders of the political parties and the NCA difficult.

16. All of these figures are based on David V. Fleischer's analysis in "Um Perfil Sócioeconômico, Político e Ideológico da Assembléia Nacional Constituinte de 1987" (a paper presented at the annual meeting of ANPOCS in Águas de São Pedro, in 1987).

17. See José Sarney, "Brazil: A President's Story," *Foreign Affairs,* no. 1 (Fall 1986), pp. 105-6.

18. There are many theories as to why Sarney decided to ignore the Arinos report. One, he disagreed with the parliamentary system of government. Two, the composition of the NCA and Sarney's high popularity immediately after the election may have convinced him to go directly to the NCA. Three, the composition of the NCA was less radical than he expected. Four, it was expected that the NCA would reach an impasse and request that the President propose a constitution. Indeed, as the work of the NCA proceeded, it faced several impasses. The executive tried its best to create doubts and accused the NCA of endangering the stability and security of the

country by its inability to finish its task on time.

19. As a result of the work of Prodasen, two volumes were published to assist the work of NCA. See *Constituição da República Federativa do Brasil: Quadro Comparativo*, 5th ed. (Brasília: Senado Federal, 1986); and *Constituições do Brasil*, 2 vols. (Brasília: Senado Federal, 1986). The information about the constitutional project and its justification was provided by the director-general of the Senate, Dr. Lourival Zagonel dos Santos. The last phase of the constitutional project was completed by Dr. Sérgio de Otero Ribeiro, the then-executive director of Prodasen.

20. See Osny Duarte Pereira, *Constituinte: Anteprojeto da Comissão Afonso Arinos* (Brasília: Universidade de Brasília, 1987); Centro de Estudos e Acompanhamento da Constituinte (CEAC), *Constituinte: Temas em Análise*, Caderno CEAC/UnB, ano 1, no. 1 (Brasília: Gráfica Ipiranga Ltda, 1987); and Luís Flávio Rainho and Osvaldo Martines Bargas, *As Lutas Operárias e Sindicais dos Metalúrgicos em São Bernardo: 1977-1979* (São Bernardo: EG, 1983). For a PT perspective on the need of a democratic order, see Francisco C. Weffort, *Por que Democracia?* (São Paulo: Brasiliense, 1984).

21. The options were six years, as the Constitution of 1969 provided; five years, as Sarney and his supporters demanded; or four years, as the majority of the progressive forces, who were in favor of direct election, wanted.

22. Three leading staff members from the Senate participated in this process, Eduardo Jorge Pereira, Guido Carvalho, and Sarah Figueiredo. From the Chamber's side, the main actors were Paulo Affonso, Antonio Pojo do Rego, and Rosinethe Soares. Pereira, Carvalho, Pojo, and Soares have all received graduate degrees from University at Albany, State University of New York. Figueiredo and Affonso have attended short seminars at the University at Albany.

23. The best authoritative source for studying the work of the NCA is the *Diário do Congresso Nacional*—the official journal of the Congress, and a special journal, published by NCA staff, called *Jornal da Constituinte*. Of the latter, a total of fifty-five weekly journals were published, elaborating on the work of the NCA and the views of its prominent members on the issues debated.

24. All of these statistics were collected and furnished by the secretariat of the NCA and were based on information provided by Prodasen and Cegraf.

25. The emergence of the *Centrão* as a political front provides another clear illustration of the fragility of political parties in Brazil, and the important role that the departing authoritarian elites were still able to exercise in the shaping of the new regime.

Chapter 8

The New Constitutional Order

The Constitution of 1988 contains 245 articles. In addition, it contains another seventy transitory articles. Like many modern constitutions, it deals not only with the foundation of the government and how future public decisions are to be reached, but also with a whole array of public policy areas. As the titles of the twenty-four subcommittees suggest (see Chapter 7), the new Constitution is a detailed document of goals and priorities touching every aspect of Brazil's political, economic, social, and cultural life. As a statement of principles and priorities, the Constitution therefore represents a peace treaty among the various competing elites trying to shape Brazil's future. Its promulgation on October 5, 1988, was the juridical culmination of the transition to democracy.

In this chapter, we examine the principal features of the Constitution and how the various contending forces influenced its outcome, with specific emphasis on the behavior of the political parties. Since in Chapters 6 and 7 we discussed the various legislative activities of the Congress under the authoritarian regime, in this chapter we will examine the extent to which those "futile" battles which characterized the legislative process have influenced the various policy options that were embedded in the Constitution. Our contention has been that bills introduced by the Congress under the authoritarian regime, even when they failed to win approval, were important because they shaped the future legislative agenda of the executive and educated the public on the issues. With the reemergence of the Congress as the center of public policy, those futile attempts at influencing public policy became the bases for the new policies.

POLITICAL PARTIES AND THE NEW CONSTITUTION

Like all democratically drafted constitutions, the Brazilian Constitution was a compromise among the significant political forces within the country pursuing different and conflicting goals. For research purposes we have identified two different types of forces. Broadly speaking, the members of the NCA were divided into two camps: those who were associated with the authoritarian elites and those who were pushing toward a new political order, with as complete a break with the past as possible. The same forces could also be categorized in accordance with the political parties they identified with.

In the discussion that follows we use both classifications. We use the broad classification to examine the victories, the losses, and the ties that each of the two main contending camps scored, as reflected in the final Constitutional document. This approach highlights the final terms of the agreement that the retreating elites were able to secure for their exit.

The party classification was used to study the voting behavior of these parties in regard to the most controversial provisions of the Constitution. This approach highlights the level of party cohesion, the ideological orientation of the various parties, and the agenda upon which those parties were likely to wage future election campaigns.

For discussion purposes, we decided to concentrate on twenty-seven controversial articles within the Constitution that have broad implications for the whole country. This emphasis by no means suggests that the other constitutional provisions were not important or were noncontroversial. The issues we selected have occupied the attention of the NCA, the press, the media, and the public and generated the most intensive lobbying by organized groups. Most important, these issues were vigorously contested by the two main camps—the authoritarian regime, and its critics.

The twenty-seven constitutional issues studied were grouped into two major agendas. The first includes those issues that were a priority to the authoritarian elites; the second includes those issues that were a priority to the emerging elites. In discussing these issues, we pointed out when the victory or defeat was total and when a compromise was reached and how the political parties voted regarding those issues.

AGENDA OF THE AUTHORITARIAN ELITES

The departing elite, given their initial numerical weakness within the NCA, concentrated their efforts on a few issues. Of those, we have selected five that were of utmost significance: the longevity of President Sarney's term in office; the form of government (presidential or parliamentary); the role of the armed forces; land reform; and job security in the private sector. Table 8.1 illustrates the voting behavior by party on these constitutional issues. On the first two issues, the elite adopted a confrontation strategy, because over these issues there could be only one winner.

President Sarney's Term in Office

Since the NCA allocated to itself the right to decide on the term of the President already in office, the debate revolved around whether Sarney should be given a four- or five-year term.[1] Those who had supported direct election for the President in 1984 proposed a four-year term. They argued that the deteriorating economic situation in the country required a strong President with popular legitimacy, which could only be acquired through popular election. President Sarney, they suggested, lacked political legitimacy, since he was selected only as a Vice-President to the popular Tancredo Neves. He belonged to the party that was associated with the military regime. For the transition to democracy to be completed, it was suggested, Sarney should have stepped down and allowed for a popular election as soon as the Constitution was completed, thereby leaving at the end of his fourth year.

Sarney's supporters, on the other hand, argued that the term of the President should be defined as five years[2], and that the NCA should not undertake retroactive decisions. They emphasized the need for political stability and continuity in order to deal with the worsening economic problems and to facilitate the smooth transition to democracy. A premature presidential election, it was suggested, would send the wrong signal to foreign investors and creditors and would plunge the country into political chaos, with unpredictable consequences to the economy and the process of transition. Sarney's supporters defended the five-year term proposal. On June 2, 1988, the NCA voted to approve the five-year term, by a vote of 328-223, with 3 abstentions.

Table 8.1

Centrão's Agenda

Issues:	PCDOB	PCB	PDC	PDS	PDT	PFL	PJ	PL	PMB	PMDB	PSB	PSDB	PT	PTB	PTR	W/P	TOTAL
Sarney's 5-year Term																	
Y	0	0	4	24	0	110	-	3	0	168	0	-	0	16	1	2	328
N	5	3	2	10	25	17	-	4	1	123	5	-	16	9	0	3	223
A	0	0	0	0	0	0	-	1	0	2	0	-	0	0	0	0	3
T	5	3	6	34	25	127	0	8	1	293	5	0	16	25	1	5	554
Presidential System																	
Y	0	0	3	21	25	113	-	5	1	145	0	-	15	16	0	0	344
N	5	3	3	15	2	17	-	2	0	148	5	-	0	9	1	2	212
A	0	0	0	0	0	0	-	0	0	2	0	-	1	0	0	0	3
T	5	3	6	36	27	130	0	7	1	295	5	0	16	25	1	2	559
Restrictive Role of the Armed Forces																	
Y	5	3	2	3	17	1	0	0	0	28	3	24	15	0	0	1	102
N	0	0	6	24	3	83	1	4	1	157	0	22	0	22	1	2	326
A	0	0	0	1	1	0	0	0	3	0	0	0	0	0	0	0	5
T	5	3	8	28	21	84	1	4	4	185	3	46	15	22	1	3	433
Distribution of Land																	
Y	5	3	0	3	17	5	-	0	1	85	5	41	16	3	0	2	186
N	0	0	6	25	2	92	-	5	0	83	0	1	0	18	1	0	233
A	0	0	0	0	0	1	-	0	0	8	0	1	0	1	0	0	11
T	5	3	6	28	19	98	0	5	1	176	5	43	16	22	1	2	430
Absolute Job Security In Private Sector																	
Y	5	3	-	2	20	8	-	2	0	82	3	-	15	5	1	1	147
N	0	0	-	21	3	61	-	2	1	114	0	-	0	6	0	1	209
A	0	0	-	0	0	0	-	0	0	4	0	-	0	0	0	0	4
T	5	3	0	23	23	69	0	4	1	200	3	0	15	11	1	2	360

Source: Prodasen's data base.

Form of Government

The most controversial issue discussed prior to and during the constitutional debate was the form of government Brazil should have. The authoritarian elites and many fellow travelers favored a presidential system. The progressive forces within PMDB and other parties favored a parliamentary system. The left was divided. Those parties with a prominent presidential candidate, such as Brizola of PDT and Lula of PT, voted for presidentialism. The two Communist parties and the Socialists voted for parliamentarism. The main centrist parties split their votes. On March 22, 1988, presidentialism won with 344 in favor, 212 against, and 3 abstentions. Since the form of government has long been in contention in the Brazilian political discourse, as we discussed in the Introduction and in Chapter 1, the arguments presented in favor of presidentialism deserve special emphasis.[3]

The Cultural Imperative

NCA proponents of a presidential system of government argued that Brazil since its inception as a Republic had always been ruled under a presidential system of government. Although during the Empire period, the role of the Emperor was more akin to a head of state with a prime-minister in charge of the day-to-day affairs of the state, supporters of the presidential form of government equated the Emperor's role with that of a modern partisan President. It was neither advisable nor feasible, they argued, to simply cast off this heritage and experiment with a system of government alien to the Brazilian political tradition.

The Federal Nature of Brazil

Changing to a parliamentary system of government at the federal level, it was argued, entailed corresponding changes at the state and municipal levels. Parliamentary forms of government at those lower levels would cause disturbances in the way the federal government dealt with the state and municipal governments. The unity of Brazil might be threatened by centrifugal forces in control of the states and municipalities. So governors and those aspiring to be governors opposed parliamentarism.

The Political Party Logic

Advocates of presidentialism argued that, for parliamentarism to work, it was necessary to have coherent, stable, and national political parties that could command working majorities to form a cabinet. Given the fractured and unstable nature of the Brazilian political parties, with their parochial orientations, the country would suffer from continuous cabinet crises. Not only would the legislature be paralyzed, but the government as well.

The Bureaucratic Logic

Advocates of presidentialism argued that under a parliamentary system of government the cabinet in power was likely to politicize the bureaucracy to the advantage of its supporters. There were more than 100,000 discretionary jobs in the bureaucracy and state-run companies and boards; cabinet instability would de-professionalize and demoralize this bureaucracy. Within the Brazilian context, even political appointees have usually kept their jobs after their sponsors have departed. It was argued that the parliamentary form of government would bring an end to the merit bureaucracy and would lead to a spiraling increase in the number of bureaucrats. For parliamentarism to work, a stable, professional, and competent bureaucracy was needed.

The Development Logic

As a rapidly developing country, Brazil needed proper planning and timely action. A cabinet that had to worry about the day-to-day survival of its majority in the legislature was not likely to be concerned about the long-range needs of the country. Only a President not burdened by a vote of confidence, mobilizing professionals and specialists, could bring the necessary economic and administrative rationality to the development of Brazil. Politicians, it was argued, especially parliamentary politicians, would not have the long-range vision and economic rationality needed to lead the country.

The Geographic Logic

Politicians from the Northeast of the country feared that a parliamentary system would sooner or later create an electoral system of "one man, one vote." Under the present presidential system, states in the North and Northeast with small populations were allocated more Deputies per capita than the highly populated states of the Southeast (São Paulo, Rio de Janeiro, and Minas Gerais). For example, during the meeting of the NCA, the state of São Paulo was represented in the Chamber of Deputies by sixty deputies, out of a total of 487. If the principle of one man, one vote was adopted, the state of São Paulo alone would have 113 deputies.[4]

The Institutional Logic

The normally subservient role of the Senate in a parliamentary system of government was another factor criticized by the presidentialists. According to the existing presidential system in Brazil, the Senate was the upper house. The senators were elected for an eight-year term and enjoyed higher political status than their counterparts in the Chamber of Deputies. A number of legislative functions were the exclusive prerogative of the Senate, as occurs in the United States. Since all states, regardless of size, were represented by three senators, once again, the smaller but numerous states of the North and Northeast had an overwhelming advantage over the larger but few states of the South and Southeast. It was no accident, therefore, that the fight for parliamentarism was led by politicians from the populous states of the South and the Southeast, while presidentialism was advocated by politicians from the smaller states. Within the Senate, the fight for parliamentarism was led by senators from São Paulo, Paraná, Rio de Janeiro, and Rio Grande do Sul.[5] Needless to say, the shift to a parliamentary system of government threatened also the institutional interests of the senators. Accordingly, the majority of the senators voted for the maintenance of the presidential system.

The Self-Interest Logic

A number of influential groups in society advocated presidentialism because of their perceived self-interests.

The military was divided. The hard-liners advocated presidentialism because they felt it was easier to deal with, control, and, if necessary, depose a President than a whole cabinet and Congress. As the commander-in-chief of the armed forces, the President came to identify and appreciate the military point of view. Once elected, and in the absence of a majority political base in the legislature, he found himself more and more dependent upon the support of the generals. This dependency gave the military direct access to the presidency. The military leaders were always in a position to veto any action or policy they considered detrimental to their interests or to the country's "national security."

Right-wing minority political parties adopted the same logic as the military. They felt their interests were better protected by a powerful President who in time of crisis could control the unpredictability of a popularly elected Congress. The military in conjunction with a strong President are the best guarantees for the interests of this group.

Two left-wing minority political parties were initially divided but closed ranks. PDT and the PT supported the presidential system for two reasons. First, both of these parties had potential presidential candidates with considerable chances of success—Brizola and Lula, respectively. Although their representation in the legislature was minimum—PDT had twenty-five members and PT had sixteen—they did enjoy popular appeal for a presidential race.[6] Second, these parties were frustrated with the legislative process. In their analysis, PDT and PT concluded that elections for legislative seats were often decided on the basis of family and parochial considerations; furthermore, they argued that the representation system was heavily skewed against the interests of the urban masses and highly populated states, in favor of rural localities and smaller states. Since PDT and PT were strong in large urban states and their appeal was toward the urban masses, they calculated that their chances of capturing the presidency, whose occupant is elected on a one-man, one-vote basis, were better than their chances of substantially increasing their representation in the legislature. In addition, a nationally waged presidential campaign, even if they did not win it, would give them the opportunity to extend their party organization to many states in which they were still not represented and thus transform their parties into truly national parties. Finally, a national presidential campaign would give them leverage to trade their votes as part of a coalition and influence the selection of the winning candidate.[7]

The bureaucrats viewed the presidential system favorably because it reserved for them the prerogative for making public policy. This system forces the President and his cabinet ministers to spend most of their time orchestrating legislative majorities through the distribution of favors. Therefore, the bureaucrats are given great discretion in running everyday chores. It allows them self-aggrandizement, and outright corruption. Throughout the last half of this century, Brazilian bureaucracy has been the major beneficiary of whatever economic progress the country has achieved.[8] Most social legislation such as health, education, housing, transportation, insurance, social securities, and labor legislation benefits the bureaucrats. This state of affairs has been referred to as corporatist and, since 1964, as "bureaucratic-authoritarian," with the bureaucracy playing a central political role. It was not surprising, therefore, that the bureaucracy, both in its military and civilian manifestations, strongly supported the presidential system.

Since Brazil began its transition to civilian rule in 1985, special interest groups have organized and set up well-financed lobby operations. Groups such as the Rural Democratic Union (UDR), which represents big landlords and agricultural businesses, the Federation of Brazilian Industrialists, which represents the industrialists, and others have become major actors on the political scene. These groups supported a presidential system of government because of their long familiarity with the system. They have historically developed an excellent rapport with the bureaucrats and the technocrats who were supposed to regulate their affairs. It was easier to influence one center of power than to sail the murky and turbulent waters of Brazilian legislative politics, where the policy-making process would be in great flux. These special interests needed stability, and the permanent bureaucracy under a presidential system was their best bet, notwithstanding the instability of presidential politics itself.

State governors, as chief executives of the states, controlled state patronage from both state and federal resources. Because of their dependency on federal largess, they were closely tied to the presidency and the federal bureaucracy that controlled these resources. Although twenty-one of the twenty-three state governors belonged to PMDB—the party whose leadership[9] in the legislature was spearheading the campaign for parliamentarism—most of the PMDB governors came out in support of the presidential system of government. Some did so because they did not want to risk the wrath of the executive which controlled significant resources that were being channeled to various state projects. Others feared that a parliamentary system, if adopted at the federal level, would be imposed at the state level, thus weakening the position of the governorship. Since state governors have played an important role in controlling their political party in their states, many of them used this influence to lobby state NCA delegations, in support of presidentialism.

Although all legislators in both the Senate and the Chamber were elected under the label of one of the dozen parties represented in the legislature, their allegiance to that party was a mere ephemeral convenience. Once elected, they were free to change parties, and often did, if it was in their personal interest. Because the legislature lacked any sort of "permanent" party or institutional leadership, each legislator was on his own in advancing his political and personal interests in and outside the legislature. Newly elected members often had the opportunity to acquire a temporary leadership position (such as membership in the Mesa, chairmanship or vice-chairmanship of committees, or even party leadership). The absence of well-established legislative leadership freed the members of any effective form of party pressure. Each member was free to maneuver in pursuit of his interests. Presidents trying to create a legislative majority in support of their programs targeted such members and showered them with patronage. These so-called "independent" members had a strong aversion toward strong party leadership and party discipline, since such discipline was likely to restrict their "entrepreneurial" activities. A presidential system afforded them ample opportunities to trade their votes for presidential favors in the continuous mini-battles of the legislative process. A parliamentary system, however, could strengthen party leadership and restrict their independent maneuvers. For this reason, many favored presidentialism.

Through the following three issues, we hope to illustrate how the authoritarian elites were able to negotiate a number of important issues in the constitutional debate.

The Role of the Armed Forces

The role of the armed forces in Brazilian history is controversial.[10] Some have argued that even before the Old Republic period (Constitution of 1889) the armed forces were viewed as arbitrators of internal conflict and guardians of the Constitution. Most military interventions in civilian affairs in times of crisis were viewed by the military and their supporters as legitimate protection of the Constitution that was in force. For the progressive forces, the proper role of the military was to defend the country against external threats. The military, according to the critics, should have no role in internal conflict. A constitutional provision to specifically prohibit the armed forces from intervening in the internal affairs of the country was therefore needed to assert this prohibition. On April 12, 1988, the NCA failed to uphold such a provision, with a vote of 326-102, and 5 abstentions (Table 8.1). The leftist parties voted as a block to support the prohibition, while most of the other parties voted against it in order to approve a substitute amendment that maintained the right of the armed forces to interfere in the internal affairs of the country with certain modifications. In accordance with the new Constitution, any of the three powers (the executive, the legislature, or the judiciary) could call upon the armed forces to intervene in internal affairs when necessary. This was intended to limit the authority of the executive to call upon the help of the armed forces in times of internal conflict, since any of the two other powers could issue a counter order. Authorizing the legislature and the judiciary to have the same right, it was felt, would place the armed forces under a sort of joint leadership when it came to internal security. In effect, this compromise provision was intended to provide each of the powers with a veto over the use of the armed forces in internal conflict. For the armed forces to be acting constitutionally, the three powers would have to agree on the same action. If not, the armed forces could be cited for disregarding the authority of one of the powers, which is unconstitutional. How this complex and ambiguous provision will actually be implemented, and what will happen in case the three powers disagree with one another, is still uncertain.

Critics of this provision have argued that this would put the armed forces under conflicting loyalties. By definition, a conflict situation occurs when the three powers do not have the same position. If the armed forces, for example, received an order from the executive to intervene, and another order from the legislature not to intervene, they would be placed under conflicting orders. How would such a conflict be resolved? Would it lead to intervention, nonintervention, or to one military group accepting to intervened in support of one branch while the other intervened in support of the other branch? Judging from the previous behavior of the armed forces in similar situations, it is likely that they would take matters into their own hands and suspend the whole constitutional order under the pretext of defending the Constitution.

Two other points of interest to the military were resolved in their favor. First, a proposal offered by the Left with the purpose of limiting the use of nuclear energy to peaceful affairs was defeated by a vote of 223-168, with 8 abstentions. With the exception of PDT, the leftist forces voted for the limitation, while the other parties were divided. This was a victory for the military, since they always advocated unrestricted use of nuclear technology. Brazil was then one of the few countries that had not signed the Nuclear Proliferation Treaty.

The second point involved the question of amnesty and the rights of the hundreds of individuals in the armed services who were affected by the various repressive institutional and complementary acts issued during the military regime in the late 1960s and early 1970s.[11] Many individuals were dismissed from their jobs and denied employment in other places.[12] Members of the armed forces, especially those who were in the air force, lost their jobs and could not find alternate work in the civilian sector, since the latter was also run by the military. The Congress had previously issued limited amnesty with retroactive compensation for specific groups, such as those professors who were dismissed from their jobs at various universities. The NCA was considering issuing a comprehensive amnesty for all those individuals who were affected during the military regime. The military and their supporters argued against such a blanket opening of the old records. Such a move, especially with regard to members of the armed forces, they argued, would be considered undue interference in the internal affairs of the military and would necessarily affect morale and discipline. Furthermore, opening the door to the barrage of retroactive claims of compensation would place the government under financial obligations it could not possibly meet. The military therefore pushed for a limited amnesty with rights of compensation also limited to those who were dismissed for purely political reasons and were denied alternate work also for political reasons. Several transitory articles in the new Constitution articulated a compromise solution regarding this sensitive issue to the satisfaction of the military.[13] The details of how the amnesty procedure would actually work were left to legislation, to be elaborated by the Congress. The military was assured that the new Constitution would not permit any form of retribution against those who committed the acts in question.

Land Reform

In 1985 the Congress began debating the implementation of the military land reform law of 1965. During the debates to legally enable squatters to own the agricultural land they had occupied, reports of massacres against the squatters, committed by roving armed bands, began to surface in various states in the North and Northeast. Like the issue of the form of government, land reform has long been at the center of political debates in Brazil.[14] The military takeover in 1964 was motivated in large part by the impasse that had developed between the executive and the legislature over this issue. Although the issue of land reform was not directly relevant to the military, it had special importance to their landlord supporters. During the 1980s, the latter became well organized in an association called *União Democrática Ruralista* (UDR, Rural Democratic Union). This organization was well financed (mostly by auctioning thousands of cattle donated by the landlords) and mobilized for political actions.

The question of land distribution produced the most intensive lobbying efforts by UDR. For days, representatives of this organization visited every member of the NCA and tried to persuade them to vote against proposals submitted by the Progressive Front, which would subject all land, private and public, productive and nonproductive, to possible expropriation, if it did not meet the legal requirements, with unspecified due compensation. Members of *Centrão* waged a successful campaign to exclude productive, private land from expropriation for the purpose of land reform. On July 20, 1988, by a vote of 233-180, with 11 abstentions, the NCA denied inclusion of productive, private land in the scope of land reform. As expected, all of the leftist parties voted for inclusion; PMDB, which by that time had lost many of its progressive members to the newly founded PSDB, or Brazilian Social Democratic Party, voted 85 in favor of expropriation, 83 against, with 8 abstentions. PSDB, on the other hand, voted 41 for expropriation, 1 against and 1 abstention. The *Centrão* coalition also won assurances that in case of expropriation of any private land, the owners would receive market-value monetary compensation rather than the promissory notes that were advocated by the progressive forces. In addition, further legislation in complementation of the constitutional provision has to be approved by the Congress in order to implement land reform.

Absolute Job Security

The new Constitution registered many gains for the labor classes in both the public and private sectors.[15] One measure, however, was particularly opposed by the urban and industrial elites who were represented by the *Centrão*. It was the attempt by the progressive forces to pass a constitutional article assuring employees in the private sector of absolute job security rights, similar to those enjoyed by employees in the public sector. The compromise that was worked out protected workers against arbitrary dismissals without granting them a permanent right in the job they occupied. It assured the owners some flexibility in managing their business by granting them the right to dismiss employees under specific conditions to be specified under the laws, such as when the business was operating at a loss.

We can see from Tables 8.1 and 8.2 that the unity of the major parties in the center and the right (PMDB, PFL, PDS, and PTB) proved to be elusive, revealing the weak coalition nature of these parties. By casting a split vote on many of the controversial articles of the Constitution, they facilitated the formation of an across-parties coalition, called *Centrão*, which endeavored to work out compromises that enjoyed wide-based support. Indeed, an informal group of leaders representing the major parties emerged as the focal point in hammering out agreements. The role of the formally constituted Systematization Committee was superseded by the informal meetings carried out by this group of leaders, a process that was not mentioned in the internal rules of the NCA.

On the other hand, the extreme discipline in the voting behavior of the small leftist parties can also be observed. Parties such as PDT, PT, PSB, PC do B, and PCB consistently voted on a party line. Within the Brazilian context, party discipline was viewed positively by the general public. It was therefore expected that in future elections those parties were likely to benefit from the favorable image they projected during the constitutional debate.

AGENDA OF THE EMERGING ELITES

Until now, we have discussed some of the issues that the *Centrão* coalition was able to win or negotiate. Their victories, however, were achieved at a price. *Centrão* was a diverse group of urban and rural elites and professionals, each with its own agenda and priorities. Only by agreeing to mutually support the other members' priorities was the coalition able to hold together. On a large number of issues, *Centrão* members had very little in common. Furthermore, having won election to the NCA under a variety of labels, and quite often having advocated for progressive political, social, and economic programs during their campaigns, they were acutely aware that, unless they fulfilled some of those promises, their political futures and the futures of their parties would be endangered.

The open process designed to draft the Constitution, which was devised by the progressive leadership of the NCA, unleashed a media campaign of great magnitude and gave impetus to the mobilization of significant groups in society to lobby for their own favored vision of what the new constitutional order should be. Members of the NCA were quite aware of the forces that were unleashed and the demands that these forces began to articulate. It was no accident, therefore, that the *Centrão* coalition realized its limitations and adopted a conciliatory and compromising position with regard to most of the provisions of the Constitution, especially in the political, social, and economic areas.

Their strategy was that of damage control. Often, this meant adopting minimal demands on most issues in order to keep their members together, combating strongly only the most extremists positions of the leftist forces, or, as in many cases, accepting compromises that had the solid support of the moderate progressive forces. By holding their members together and isolating the extremists, they were able to forge a working alliance with the moderate progressive forces, which enabled the NCA to make most of its important decisions by an overwhelming majority, often arriving at unanimous consent. As a price for its success (in areas mentioned previously), *Centrão* had to accept, though with minor changes, the agenda of the progressive forces within the NCA.

Some of the most important items in the agenda of the emerging elites were division of power among government institutions, political and human rights, labor and other social provisions, and economic issues. Table 8.2 illustrates party voting behavior on some of these constitutional issues.

Division of Power among Government Institutions

Although presidentialism, as a system of government, eventually won, the power and prerogatives of the President were drastically reduced, while the powers and prerogatives of the Congress, and of the states and municipalities, were enhanced.

One way in which the power of the presidency was undermined was through decree laws. This legislative instrument was created during the military regime and had been resorted to, quite frequently, by the various presidents to bypass legislative scrutiny. Sarney, for example, enacted some of his most important legislation in the economic field—such as the Cruzado Plan, the Bresser Plan, and the supplementary budget for the remaining part of 1988—through decree laws. With the new Constitution, in the few cases in which the President is allowed the use of provisional measures, he is obligated to submit his action to Congress for approval. Unless approved by the Congress within thirty days, the law is automatically null and void. If the decree law was issued under circumstances not allowed by the Constitution, the President can be held responsible for any obligations or damages generated. Those affected by the measures instituted by invalidated decree laws are entitled to sue the government for damages.[16]

The President's powers to reorganize the administration and to grant licenses and permits were also severely restricted. All administrative reorganization has to be voted on by the Congress; therefore, executive reorganization can be subjected to a congressional veto. The powerful instrument of distributing radio and television concessions to supporters and friends was placed under congressional control. Furthermore, the power to decide on economic and budgetary matters was restored to the Congress. Several key positions in the public economic domain that had previously been filled through presidential appointment are now also shared with the Congress. To ensure that all of these provisions and others stipulated in the Constitution, plus future legislation, are properly implemented, the executive was put under a permanent injunction, that is, the executive is responsible for all the decisions and directives that it issues in the exercise of its powers. Rules and regulations promulgated by the executive that are found to be unconstitutional or illegal are considered null and void, and those who promulgate them can be held responsible and can be sued. Such measures were intended to prevent the reemergence of the imperial presidency, characteristic of the Authoritarian period.

A newly rejuvenated federal system, under which the states and municipalities regained some degree of functional and fiscal autonomy, was established to further restrict the power of the presidency. Through sweeping tax provisions and new formulas for revenue sharing, the new Constitution grants the states and municipalities the power to have their own tax bases, to have their augmented share of the Union's revenues defined in the Constitution rather than depending on the favors and predilection of the executive agencies, and to be entrusted with the delivery of several services previously provided by the federal government. By redefining the powers of the states and localities, the framers of the Constitution sought to restrict the central power of the Union and deny the President one of the most powerful instruments by which he could curry favors and distribute the spoils to his supporters and allies.

Table 8.2

Agenda of the National Democratic Coalition

Issues:	Political Parties:	PCDOB	PCB	PDC	PDS	PDT	PFL	PJ	PL	PMB	PMDB	PSB	PSDB	PT	PTB	PTR	W/P	TOTAL
Strengthening Congress	Y	5	3	3	22	21	65	-	2	1	176	3	-	15	15	1	2	334
	N	0	8	0	2	0	22	-	0	0	42	0	-	0	1	0	0	75
	A	0	0	0	0	0	0	-	2	0	10	0	-	0	1	0	0	13
	T	5	11	3	24	21	87	0	4	1	228	3	0	15	17	1	2	422
Direct Democracy	Y	5	3	2	20	26	48	-	3	1	218	4	-	16	21	-	2	369
	N	0	0	2	4	0	44	-	2	0	29	0	-	0	8	-	0	89
	A	0	0	0	2	0	4	-	0	0	5	0	-	0	0	0	0	11
	T	5	3	4	26	26	96	0	5	1	252	4	0	16	29	0	2	469
Voting Rights to Citizens 16 Years of Age and Above	Y	5	3	3	13	19	47	-	3	1	140	5	43	15	15	1	3	316
	N	0	0	0	15	1	44	-	1	0	33	0	1	0	3	0	1	99
	A	0	0	0	0	0	2	-	0	0	3	0	0	0	1	0	0	6
	T	5	3	3	28	20	93	0	4	1	176	5	44	15	19	1	4	421
Freedom of Information	Y	5	3	4	25	20	78	-	7	-	223	3	-	16	19	-	3	406
	N	0	0	0	0	0	0	-	0	-	0	0	-	0	0	-	0	0
	A	0	0	0	0	0	2	-	0	-	1	0	-	0	0	-	0	3
	T	5	3	4	25	20	80	0	7	0	224	3	0	16	19	0	3	409
Mandate of Collective Security	Y	5	3	3	9	22	46	-	6	1	199	4	-	16	11	-	1	326
	N	0	0	1	15	1	41	-	0	0	35	0	-	0	9	-	1	103
	A	0	0	0	1	0	3	-	0	0	6	0	-	0	0	-	0	10
	T	5	3	4	25	23	90	0	6	1	240	4	0	16	20	0	2	439
Death Penalty	Y	0	0	0	17	0	35	-	1	0	31	0	0	0	8	0	1	93
	N	5	3	3	11	17	44	-	4	1	123	4	45	15	12	1	1	289
	A	0	0	0	1	0	5	-	0	0	5	0	0	0	0	0	0	11
	T	5	3	3	29	17	84	0	5	1	159	4	45	15	20	1	2	393
End of Censorship	Y	5	3	1	7	23	29	-	1	1	203	5	-	16	17	0	2	313
	N	0	0	2	20	0	64	-	3	0	30	0	-	0	6	1	1	127
	A	0	0	3	1	0	13	-	1	0	19	0	-	0	0	0	0	37
	T	5	3	6	28	23	106	0	5	1	252	5	0	16	23	1	3	477

Another provision of the new Constitution endeavored to limit the arbitrary power of the executive in controlling the formation and operations of the political parties. The process of establishing new political parties was simplified, and the parties are now allowed to operate autonomously—free of government control. Furthermore, to ensure that future presidents and governors are elected with some degree of consensus, the new Constitution stipulates that a candidate must receive 50 percent plus one of the votes in order to be declared a winner. If a presidential candidate fails to receive an absolute majority of the votes in the first round of ballots, the two candidates who receive the highest percentage of votes face each other in a run-off election. To further democratize the electoral process, the new Constitution grants voting rights to citizens at age sixteen, and confirms the right of illiterates to vote. Voting is obligatory for those between eighteen and sixty-five years of age, but is voluntary for those under eighteen and above 65 years old, and for those who are illiterate.

The electoral provisions in the Constitution were meant to empower the youth and the underprivileged of Brazil, which, as in many developing countries, constitutes a large percentage of the population. Finally, in an attempt to keep all government actions under constant popular scrutiny, the new Constitution establishes a moderate form of direct democracy in which citizens, through plebiscites, referendums, and popularly initiated campaigns can force the government to follow or abstain from following certain policies.

With all of these changes, the presidency had its powers severely restricted, while the Congress had its powers widely expanded, as the following section will continue to illustrate.

The Powers of the Super-Congress

The new Constitution strengthened the Congress in many ways and extended its jurisdiction to many areas that had previously been the exclusive prerogative of the President.[17]

The Congress regained the power to elaborate and approve the whole budget of the Union, through the budgetary authorization law. In accordance with the new Constitution, the Congress was empowered to determine expenditure priorities, specify investment policies and the priorities of the government, and review the budget of state-run corporations and utilities. The Joint Budget Committee, representing the Senate and the Chamber, became a permanent committee, now able to hold sessions all year round to follow the development and execution of the budget. Furthermore, during the congressional recess, a committee representing both houses will continue working to monitor executive initiatives and operations.

All initiatives of the executive in the nuclear area, including the determination of nuclear waste sites, are to be submitted for congressional approval.

The *Tribunal de Contas da União* (TCU)—an important arm of the federal government charged with the responsibility for audit, control, and other types of program evaluation—now has two-thirds of its ministers selected by the Congress, and one-third nominated by the President, but confirmed by the Senate. Foreign companies were excluded from participating in mineral exploration. Exploration of mineral resources can only be undertaken with congressional authorization. The expropriation of land, of more than 2,500 hectares, for public use or whatever other reason can only be done with congressional approval. The creation of state enterprises, including their participation in private ventures or the creation of subsidiaries, can only be done in accordance with congressional approval. The attorney general and the board of directors of Central Bank have to be approved by the Congress. The imposition of new taxes or compulsory loans (such as when the federal government forces one of its state enterprises to lend it money), as well as the use of the receipts of such loans (all of the above used to be done through a decree law), requires the approval of the Congress. At the beginning of each legislative session, the Congress is required to examine the fiscal effects of all legal executive orders and administrative directives to determine whether unfair exemptions from taxes and other duties were created. The President is required to submit to the Congress a bimonthly report on how the budget is being implemented. The Congress was now empowered to determine salaries and other benefits, including procurements and armaments for the armed forces, not only during peace time, but also during wars.

The permanent subject-matter committees were also strengthened. They can study and approve certain proposed legislation, in accordance with the internal rules of each house, without the need to refer these laws to the whole house. Once approved in committee, these measures will be submitted to the whole house only if one-tenth of the members so request; otherwise, they are considered approved. Permanent committees are also empowered to call for state ministers' testimony, without the need for approval of such a request by the Mesa. They are also empowered to pass all authorization bills in their sphere of jurisdiction before they are submitted for appropriation. Finally, they are authorized to approve all public works projects and national, regional, and sectorial development plans.

Comissões Parlamentares de Inquérito (CPIs, Parliamentary Inquiry Committees) now enjoy judicial investigatory powers. They are also free to determine the duration of the investigation, and their findings can be forwarded directly to the proper authorities for action.

These provisions and many others were at the top of the Left's agenda. Through these provisions, it sought to address some of the many abuses of power perpetrated by the executive during the Authoritarian period. Although these demands were championed by the Left and the progressive forces of the NCA, many of whom had been victimized by the authoritarian regime, the Left were able to moderate their demands and put them in a language that could be supported by a majority of the NCA, with minimal opposition. The provisions to strengthen the Congress were passed by a majority of 334 votes in favor, only 67 against, and 17 abstentions. The provisions allowing for the exercise of direct democracy by the people were passed by a majority of 360 votes in favor, 89 against, and 12 abstentions. The provision extending the voting rights to sixteen-year-old was approved by 316 in favor, 99 against, and 6 abstentions. Finally, the approval of the provisions expanding the rights and prerogatives of the states and localities were approved by 290 votes in favor, 39 against, and 8 abstentions. As Table 8.2 in this chapter shows, the leftist parties maintained their voting discipline in favor of all these issues. The centrist and rightist parties of PMDB, PFL, PDS, and PTB, as in all other instances, caste a split vote, confirming once again the coalition nature of these parties and their ideological heterogeneity.

Human and Individual Rights

Brazil's new Constitution charted new horizons in guaranteeing to its citizens individual and collective rights known only in the most advanced industrial democracies of the world. Legislation to protect political and individual rights had long been proposed by members of the Congress, political activists, human rights advocates, and the Catholic church, but the authoritarian regime managed to stifle those initiatives, citing its concern with law and order. While human rights concerns were feverishly championed by the progressive forces, the commitment of the NCA to institute a comprehensive and strict bill of rights for all citizens enjoyed a widespread support that transcended all political parties and ideologies. The security-conscious authoritarian elites were able to wage only rear guard actions, for the purpose of ensuring that the human rights provisions of the Constitution would not be used retroactively against those of its members who committed willful crimes against innocent citizens in the name of national security. The NCA approved by a vote of 325-98, with 14 abstentions, a provision prohibiting any form of political or religious censorship. According to the Constitution of 1988, all citizens are equal before the law, regardless of any type of difference. Life, liberty, and the right to private property are considered inviolable. Freedom of thought, conscience, belief, assembly, and expression are also affirmed for all. Any form of discrimination is considered a crime, and racism is considered an abominable offense.

Furthermore, the bill of rights went into some detail in spelling out the actions on the part of the government that would be considered a violation of individual rights, such as torture, intimidation, discrimination, or violation of due process. All of these rights and guarantees are also extended to legal non-Brazilian residents in the country. As soon as the Constitution was promulgated, the impact of these measures was felt immediately throughout the country. Many inmates who had been arrested and sent to prison under previous legal procedures became eligible for release, because their constitutional rights, as seen through the lens of the new Constitution, had been violated. The judiciary had to scramble for answers as to who should be released and who should remain in prison.

Three provisions received a lot of attention and extensive media coverage during the constitutional debate: the *habeas-data*—the right to information; the *mandado de segurança coletivo*—the mandate of collective security; and the *mandado de injunção*— the mandate of injunction. These provisions raised possible implications for the authoritarian elites, and, therefore, were very sensitive.

Habeas Data

The *habeas-data* guarantees the citizen and the legal resident the right to have access to any information that the government holds on him or her, and provides remedies for any harm done to the individual as a result of false information. It also guarantees the individual access to data banks of general information, whether in the public or private sector, such as credit-rating information by banks and credit cards, employment records, confidential files, and others. Furthermore, in order to help individuals who lack the financial means to secure these rights in court, the Constitution of 1988 authorizes that, if necessary, they receive free public assistance, so as to oblige the concerned entity to comply with the constitutional provisions. It also imposes penalties against violators and compensation for those adversely affected. Supporters of the authoritarian elites were concerned that such wide-ranging guarantees might endanger national security. The departing elite was especially concerned that sensitive information, collected about individuals who had committed abuses of power during the authoritarian regime, would be accessible to those affected, and would prove to be an embarrassment to the national security and intelligence community. Some congressmen themselves, those who had held government or military positions during the regime, were worried about being exposed. Before this provision could be endorsed, there had to be an assurance that it would not lead to retroactive criminal prosecution for those who had abused their official power in the past by falsely levying on innocent citizens unsubstantiated accusations. Its only application would be to clear the names of innocent citizens who were denied their rights on the basis of allegations and information collected about them, of which they had no opportunity to defend themselves from, since they had no access to the records.

Mandate of Collective Security

In an attempt to make the attainment of individual rights more realistic, the framers of the Constitution approved a provision that permitted groups, associations, and organizations to enter into litigation on behalf of its members. Thus, unions, professional associations, clubs, and political parties acting on behalf of an aggrieved member (or members) can go to court in a class-action suit. Given the time and money burden that individuals normally face when suing the state, the mandate of collective security allows for the feasibility of pursuing those rights and also contributes to the economy of time and resources by allowing the courts to establish rights for a whole class of individuals, instead of on a case-by-case basis.

Mandate of Injunction

The mandate of injunction translates into yet another way of guaranteeing that the machinery of government, entrusted with implementing or providing the rights granted under the Constitution, shall develop and promulgate the necessary procedures and policies to do so.[18] It is an answer to those who argue that while the Constitution grants many rights, it is the day-to-day practice of the administration, with its rules, policies, and programs, that ensures whether these rights are translated into reality. The mandate of injunction authorizes a citizen whose constitutional rights are not met, because of existing administrative regulations and practices to go to court against the administrative agency. The enactment of the mandate of injunction demands that the administration review all of its existing rules and procedures developed under the authoritarian regime, and requires the administration to undertake the necessary modifications and revisions to bring them into compliance with the provisions of the Constitution.

Although these three provisions were extensively discussed and hotly contested, the NCA, after removing provisions that would be threatening to the authoritarian elite, approved them almost unanimously. The *habeas-data* was approved by a vote of 406-0, with only three abstentions. The provision for the mandate of injunction was also approved, by a vote of 424-1, with 4 abstentions. The mandate of collective security was more controversial; nonetheless, it was approved, 326-103, with 10 abstentions.

Labor and Social Rights

Labor and social rights were a primary item on the agenda of the progressive forces within the NCA.[19] Many critics of the economic model followed during the authoritarian regime had long maintained that economic policies of state capitalism ignored the needs of the poor and working classes. The economic progress that Brazil attained under the military-dominated regime, they argued, was based on the suffering and misfortunes of the poor and the workers. To alleviate the harsh social and economic realities under which the poor and the workers of Brazil survive, the Constitution of 1988 provides for a number of benefits, such as free education, national health insurance, and special assistance to the disabled, the handicapped, the young, and the old. Labor rights, working conditions, and job security became a central topic during the constitutional debates. The NCA adopted provisions granting workers the right to form unions for both the private and the public sector and granted them an unrestricted right to strike. Working hours are not to exceed forty-four hours per week, and in those industries using the shift system, the Constitution provides that the working shift is six hours long. Other articles granted women maternity leave of 120 days, and men paternity leave of five days. Finally, workers were entitled to receive 33 percent above their regular salary during their annual vacation.

All of these provisions were controversial and were approved after certain qualifying language was incorporated. The unrestricted right to strike was one such highly controversial article that was hotly debated and criticized. It was approved by a vote of 288-112, with 4 abstentions. Similarly, the provision of six-hours working shifts was approved by a vote of 324-125, with 6 abstentions, only after the word "maximum" was deleted from the article. The six-hour shift became the norm; however, labor unions and management are allowed to negotiate. Paternity leave was reduced from nine to five days before it was approved by a 337-67 vote, with 28 abstentions. Maternity leave was approved by an overwhelming majority of 429 votes for and 11 against, with 6 abstentions (Brazil's legislation already had a maternity leave of ninety days; the new Constitution merely added another thirty days of paid leave). The 33 percent extra payment for workers during vacations and holidays was approved by 373 votes in favor and 36 against, with 15 abstentions. Again, the leftist parties maintained a unified front on all of these issues, while the rightist and centrist parties displayed their usual fragility, divisiveness, and indecision.

The Economic Order

Traditionally, in Brazil, the state has played a very active role in the economy. The Brazilian economy is a mixture of a dominant public sector working in tandem with a private sector—until recently, both operating within a pronounced ideology of development and a doctrine of national security. The development ideology, at the theoretical and academic level, was dominated by a mixture of Marxist logic and its various derivatives of dependency theories. At the governmental bureaucratic level, the development ideology was dominated by a group of pragmatic technocrats and politicians who, while realizing the importance of the international market for Brazil's development, were able to pursue nationalistic economic policies. Opposed to the nationalists—both the theoretical and the pragmatic—were the internationalists, who were also found in the private sector, the government financial and monetary institutions, and certain segments of the armed forces. Thus, when the NCA came to define the future economic order, the conflict was not merely a conflict between the Left and the Right, but also between the nationalists and the internationalists.

The nationalists (see Chapter 6) viewed the presence of multinational corporations with suspicion. They advocated strong state-national private joint ventures; the establishment of temporary preferences and privileges for national capital for the purpose of acquiring the needed technology; and the creation of the necessary infrastructure in the country to enable economic competitiveness both domestically and internationally. Although not disagreeing on the end product of a technologically strong and economically advanced Brazil, the internationalists, on the other hand, differed on the methods to achieve those objectives. The internationalists advocated an open economic system, where foreign capital and technology would be welcomed and encouraged. They argued that, within the context of the existing international order and its interrelated parts, any attempt at protectionism would be counterproductive. In addition to being expensive and wasteful (since it protected inefficiency), it would also be archaic because it would discourage the acquisition of new technology. They argued that if Brazil was to attain economic development and technological progress, all restrictions on foreign capital and technology should be removed and joint ventures without any preferences or discrimination should be encouraged. The constitutional articles dealing with the economic order were a resounding victory for the nationalistic forces. The Constitution differentiated between national and foreign enterprises, called upon the government to encourage national enterprises, and reserved the right of mineral, oil, and other underground explorations to national enterprises. Three areas in the economic order deserve some elaboration: the definition of national enterprises, preferential treatment of those enterprises, and the exploration of minerals and other natural resources.

Defining the National Enterprise

The economic order of the Constitution of 1988 emphasizes the value of human labor and free initiative in securing a dignified existence, in accordance with the principles of national sovereignty, private property, the social function of property, free competition, preservation of the environment, reduction of regional and social inequalities, full employment, and a "favorable treatment for Brazilian enterprises with national capital by small investors" (Article 170). Since the Constitution granted preferential treatment to national enterprises in many areas of the economy, the controversy during the constitutional debate centered on what constitutes a national enterprise. The strategy of the internationalists was to expand the definition as much as possible and make it as ambiguous as possible, so that many joint ventures or local operations of multinational enterprises could qualify for preferential treatment. On the other hand, the nationalists wanted a definition as restrictive as possible. Brazilian enterprises with national capital were defined as those registered in Brazil according to the law and effectively and permanently under the direct or indirect control of persons who live and reside in Brazil, or those controlled by public enterprises with majoritarian national capital and control (Article 171). This restrictive definition excluded many foreign subsidiaries and joint ventures whose control and majority capital were not in national hands, as well as nonphysical entities (trusts and others). The provision defining national enterprise generated a lot of polemic and was approved by 290 votes in favor (only 10 votes above the minimum) and 126 against, with 4 abstentions. The leftist parties were solidly behind this provision, while the rightist and centrist parties were divided.

Preferential Treatment for National Enterprises

While the previous provision, with all the contradictory principles it enunciated, established the principle of two categories of enterprises and firms, the preferential treatment provisions spelled out in some detail the kind of preferences that the national firms would be entitled to. Among other things, national firms would be entitled to better credit, special tax incentives, benefits from government investment in research and development, investment in training, and, most important, in the case of certain strategic sectors, such as the computer industry, domestic market protection against foreign competition for specified periods of time, and preference in government purchases. This last provision was approved by 288 votes in favor, 103 against, with 12 abstentions.

Mineral Exploration

Another hotly debated provision of the Constitution affecting the economic order dealt with the preference given to national enterprises in the area of exploration of mineral and other natural resources. The article reserving mineral exploration to national firms was approved by 343 votes in favor, 126 against, with 17 abstentions.

There is no doubt that the nationalist forces, favoring the curbing of the competition of the multinationals, scored a major victory, even with all the contradictions and ambiguities of the various provisions. Future governments were empowered to undertake a whole series of preferential treatment for the national sector. On the other hand, the ambiguities and contradictions should help provide the government with a degree of flexibility, which is needed in dealing with foreign firms and governments. Many of these future economic policies will ultimately be decided on political grounds rather than constitutional mandates.

NOTES

1. The Constitution of 1967-1969 defined the term of the President as six years. Sarney and his supporters wanted five years. Those who favored a four-year term for Sarney cited the proposal made by Tancredo Neves in February 1985 which was seconded by Sarney in May 1985. Both promised that their term in office would be for only a period of four years. A shorter term would allow the transition period to be completed earlier, permitting the direct election of the President.

2. In accordance with the 1967-1969 Constitution, the term of President was for six years. Sarney's supporters argued that the President had agreed to a five-year term in an effort to speed up the transition process. They threatened that unless this was adopted, they would push for a six-year term as stipulated by the Constitution that was in force.

3. For a coherent defense of presidentialism, see Marco Maciel, "Por um Novo Presidencialismo" (Brasília: Senado Federal, 1988).

4. According to the electoral laws, a state, regardless its population size, is entitled to three senators and, at least, eight deputies. Smaller states feared that in a parliamentary system these advantages would disappear and the government would be dominated by the Southeastern states. See Antonio Carlos Pojo do Rego, "O Lobby Nordestino: Novos Padrões de Atuação Política no Congresso Brasileiro," *Revista de Informação Legislativa*, no. 21 (January/March 1984); David Fleischer, "O Regionalismo na Política Brasileira: as Bancadas Nordestinas na Câmara Federal 1983," *Revista de Ciência Política*, 28, no. 1 (1985), pp. 3-25.

5. The 1947 state Constitution of Rio Grande do Sul stipulated a parliamentary system of government. It was struck down as unconstitutional by the Federal Supreme Court.

6. In fact, in the 1989 presidential race, Lula came in second and Brizola came in third in the number of votes received.

7. According to the new Constitution, the presidential candidate must get 50 percent plus one of the votes to be declared a winner, as is the case in the French presidential system.

8. See Samuel A. Morley, *Labor Markets and Inequitable Growth: The Case of Authoritarian Capitalism in Brazil* (Cambridge: Cambridge University Press, 1982).

9. Ulysses Guimarães was the exception by not openly advocating parliamentarism. Indeed, many PMDB members broke with PMDB because they were disenchanted with the position of Guimarães on this and other critical issues.

10. See Alfred Stepan, *Rethinking Military Politics: Brazil and the Southern Cone* (Princeton, N.j.: Princeton University Press, 1988); and Eliézer Rizzo de Oliveira et al., *As Forças Armadas no Brasil* (Rio de Janeiro: Espaço e Tempo, 1987).

11. Civilians affected by these measures received amnesty in 1985. The questions still to be resolved were (1) retroactive pay and (2) reinstatement to previous positions.

12. The story of those tortured and exiled has been highlighted and debated throughout the rule of the authoritarian regime. See Alberto Venâncio Filho, *Notícia Histórica da Ordem dos Advogados do Brasil: 1930-1980* (Rio de Janeiro: OAB, 1982); Alípio de Freitas, *Resistir é Preciso: Memória do Tempo da Morte Civil do Brasil* (Rio de Janeiro: Record, 1981); José Alvaro Moisés, *Greve de Massa e Crise Política* (São Paulo: Polis, 1978); Márcio Moreira Alves, *A Grain of Mustard Seed: The Awakening of the Brazilian Revolution* (Garden City, N.Y.:

Anchor Books, 1973); João Quartim, *Dictatorship and Armed Struggle in Brazil* (New York: Monthly Review Press, 1971); and Márcio Moreira Alves, *Torturas e Torturados* (Rio de Janeiro: Idade Nova, 1966).

13. It should be mentioned that the military had the best organized lobby in the NCA.

14. For the controversies surrounding land reform, see Carlos Minc, *A Reconquista da Terra: Lutas no Campo e Reforma Agrária* (Rio de Janeiro: Zahar, 1985); Vilma Figueiredo, "A Questão Agrária e as 'Estratégias' do Governo," Trindade (ed.), *Brasil em Perspectiva*, op. cit. (1982); *Brazil: A Review of Agricultural Policies* (Washington: World Bank, 1982); and Marta Cehelsky, *Land Reform in Brazil: The Management of Social Change* (Boulder, Colo.: Westview Press, 1979).

15. For a review of labor problems and their relationship to the state, see Octávio Bueno Magano, *Organização Sindical Brasileira* (São Paulo: Revista dos Tribunais, 1982); Heloísa Helena Teixeira de Souza Martins, *O Estado e a Burocratização do Sindicato no Brasil* (São Paulo: Hucitec, 1979); Kenneth S. Mericle, "Corporatist Control of the Working Class: Authoritarian Brazil since 1964," Malloy (ed.), *Authoritarianism and Corporatism*, op. cit. (1977), pp. 303-38; and Evaristo de Moraes Filho, *O Problema do Sindicato Único no Brasil* (Rio de Janeiro: A Noite, 1952).

16. In spite of this constitutional provision, normally the Congress either ratifies the provisional measures, or when it rejects those measures, it makes sure that neither the President nor the state is liable for actions undertaken under the provisional measures. President Collor has excessively used provisional measures to pass and enact many of his legislative proposals, thereby forcing the Congress to consider passing legislation restricting and defining the use of the provisional method.

17. Regarding the problems that the new Congress is likely to face, see Antonio Carlos Pojo do Rego, "Institutional Advance and Retreat: Obstacles to the Emerging Role of the Federal Legislature in the 'New Republic'," *Secolas Annals*, no. 28 (March 1987). Some of the reforms were advocated as far back as the mid-1960s; see José Bonifácio, "A Reforma do Poder Legislativo," *Revista Brasileira de Estudos Políticos*, no. 20 (January 1966), pp. 23-28. See also Ronald M. Schneider, "Brazil's Political Future," Selcher (ed.), *Political Liberalization*, op. cit. (1986), pp. 217-60.

18. This is a constitutional right without teeth, since the courts have refused to accept it.

19. See Hélio Jaguaribe et al., *Brasil, 2000: Para um Novo Pacto Social* (Rio de Janeiro: Paz e Terra, 1986).

Chapter 9

Conclusion. Congressional Performance and the Presidential System: Brazil 1964-1988

When I began my research more than a decade ago, I had a single purpose: to investigate the role a legislature plays under an authoritarian regime. In the 1970s, I had been a participant in and contributor to the literature on legislatures in Third World countries. My mission and task, therefore, appeared to be simple and straightforward, and Brazil seemed the ideal subject for such a research undertaking. Between 1964 and 1986, Brazil had an authoritarian regime that allowed the Congress to function in what most assumed was a minimal role. The joint legislative development program between the Brazilian Congress and the University at Albany, State University of New York, which I directed, provided unusual opportunities for observing the Congress from within. For close to two decades, many of the main congressional actors had maintained a close association with me, both as students and colleagues.

Yet in the course of undertaking this study, in spite of its apparent simplicity, something unsettling kept complicating my mission. The phenomena I was studying and my interpretation of it in accordance with the available literature proved difficult to reconcile. The behavior of the Congress did not fit any of the roles identified in the literature. It was neither minimal, maximal, nor in between. It was different. The question then became, How do you interpret these differences?

In reviewing the literature on the political system of Brazil, and on other authoritarian societies in transition, a recurring theme kept emerging. Regardless of which institution was being studied, whether the political parties, the bureaucracy, or the military, the political system failed to provide a modicum of stability so that the pressing issues of the country could be met. The research emphasis, therefore, could no longer be limited to the role of the Congress in the political system. Rather, the emphasis had to be shifted to the nature of the system itself, and how the various institutions in that system interact. It was then that new conceptual categories emerged, shedding light on the role of the Congress, how that role was discharged, and the significance of congressional actions.

Brazil's presidential system has oscillated between being open and restrictive, oppressive and liberal, legitimate and illegitimate, and orderly and in disarray. It has failed to provide a mechanism where legitimacy and governability can be combined, or order and progress can be achieved, within a democratic environment. The 1964 coup d'état, among other things, was an attempt to resolve the contradictions inherent in such a presidential system.

The contradictions associated with the presidential system in Brazil have permeated all the political relationships between the presidency and the other institutions in society, including that of the Congress. The President found himself playing irreconcilable roles and meeting inherently contradictory expectations. His role as chief of state collided with his role as a chief of his political party. As chief of state, he was expected to be fair, impartial, and a symbol of unity in a country faced with division and diversity. As chief of his political party, he was called upon to reward his supporters and isolate and undermine his opponents. As chief of state, he expected support and reverence. As chief of his political party, he received criticism and opposition. His role as arbitrator was undermined by his role as partisan.

Presidents in Brazil have been very strong and very weak at the same time. To limit presidential power, successive Brazilian constitutions imposed restrictions on the ability of presidents to succeed themselves. The presidential system also adhered to the principle of separation of powers. Thus, although the President was supposed to be all powerful, he found himself opposed by entrenched opposition forces within the Congress, the bureaucracy, and the judiciary that constitutionally he could do little about. At the same time, the principle of separation of powers prevented the opposition from mounting any serious challenge to the powers of the President. It could only exercise a veto power; it could not remove an unpopular President or force him to change his policies. Oftentimes, this impasse led the presidents to use unconstitutional or extra-constitutional mechanisms to break the opposition groups within the Congress, the bureaucracy, or the judiciary.

The presidential system in Brazil also suffered from what is called the "winner-take-all" syndrome. Since there is only one position being contested, the winner takes all, while the losers are left with little power to mount a credible comeback. Opposition forces have no political space in which to engage in constructive battle. Instead, they can only mount guerrilla warfare and ambushes. Finally, political parties, instead of uniting to unseat a President, which is constitutionally prohibited, find themselves fighting each other in search of presidential favors to keep them alive until the next election. The solidarity of political parties is, therefore, undermined and fractured.

These weaknesses in the presidential system permeated the relationship between the President and the other political institutions, such as political parties, the bureaucracy, the judiciary, and especially the Congress.

For a President to be popularly elected, he needs to appeal to the unorganized urban masses. He also needs to put together a winning coalition that will support him. To do so, a candidate accumulates political debts, which he finds himself unable to settle once elected. The expectations of the poor collide with the interests of the veto groups within the Congress, the bureaucracy, or the judiciary. Without the acquiescence of these groups, the President finds himself helpless. Winning the support of these groups becomes his principal preoccupation. Since he lacks the constitutional means or the political strength to force any discipline on these well-entrenched groups, he engages in continuous pitched battles, using whatever means under his control. Often this involves divide-and-conquer strategies, the granting of favors, and, when all else fails, the threat and use of force and other unconstitutional and extra-constitutional mechanism to force compliance.

The bureaucracy, which is supposed to be neutral and career- and merit-oriented, becomes the only means available to ensure that the President's programs and priorities are followed. Thus, the President often has to resort to political appointments to the bureaucracy, not only to gain support for his agenda, but also to obtain the bureaucracy's services and pay off his political debts. Hence the politicization of the bureaucracy, the undermining of its merit, and the abuse of its resources and power in the service of immediate political gains. Political appointees, instead of being transients in their jobs, become permanent, even when their political mentors have departed and the need for their services have disappeared. The merit bureaucracy is transformed into the welfare, corrupt, and career bureaucracy. Newly elected presidents keep those political appointees, but to neutralize their power and possible sabotage, the presidents add their own political appointees—thus the uncontrolled expansion and demoralization of the bureaucracy.

Under the presidential system of government in Brazil, political parties do not fair any better. The universal election of the President does not lead to the creation and consolidation of national parties, as is the case of the United States. The coalition that brought the President to power disintegrated as soon as the election was over. Presidents found it in their political interest to weaken organized political parties, even their own, in order to minimize the veto powers that those parties may come to exercise over the President's legislative agenda. Influential groups, representing geographic or sectorial interests, on the other hand, found it more profitable to organize in a separate party to extract favors from a President in return for temporary support.

Thus the relationship between the President and the Congress became dominated by the exchange of temporary favors, rather than a fight over priorities and alternative public policies. Since the President cannot constitutionally dissolve a recalcitrant Congress and call for a new election, nor can the Congress withdraw a vote of confidence from an unpopular President, an impasse can only be resolved through the distribution of favors. But there is a limit to the extent the President can disburse favors without bankrupting the state or forfeiting a coherent public policy. When state resources are depleted and the conflict becomes unmanageable, the veto groups must be suppressed, hence the resort to coercion and unconstitutionality. From this perspective, the role of the Congress must be conceived as a veto group and not as a public policy-making institution. In exercising its veto, the Congress uses many mechanisms and strategies, one of which may be the participation in the public policy-making process.

After assuming power, the leaders of the 1964 coup d'état were faced with these very same contradictions, which are inherent in the Brazilian presidential system. Their goal became the resolution of these contradictions so that order and progress could be attained constitutionally and peacefully. This book concentrated on the attempts of the military regime to transform this relationship between the presidency and the Congress, how the Congress adapted to those attempts, what role the Congress played under the authoritarian presidential system imposed by the military, and finally, how the Congress reemerged and returned to its classical role under the liberal presidential system enshrined in the 1988 Constitution.

To restrict the veto power of the Congress, the military after 1964 institutionalized a series of new structures and procedures. Since the military in Brazil has traditionally conceived of its role as guardians of the constitutional order against "subversive" elements in society, it tried to achieve this change in the executive-legislative relationship within the constitutional framework of the presidential system. To transform the system and eliminate its contradictions, however, assumed the acquiescence of the veto groups, including the Congress. Since these veto groups were not willing to acquiesce, the resort to political, legal, and constitutional manipulation using coercion and unconstitutional means became necessary to reshape the presidential system, so that it could become constitutionally functional. The more the military persisted in its goal, the more it found it had to resort to unconstitutional means and coercion. The more the regime resorted to coercion and unconstitutional means to achieve its goals, the less legitimacy it enjoyed. The less the legitimacy of the regime, the stronger the role of the veto groups.

Thus the main role of the Congress during the authoritarian regime was to undermine the legitimacy of the regime and strengthen Congressional veto power. Even when the Congress, willingly or unwillingly, ratified presidential decisions, it managed to undermine the legitimacy of those decisions. The Congress, which under the manipula tion of the military became politically illegitimate, was in no position to bestow legitimacy on the regime.

To eliminate the veto power of the Congress, the regime created by administrative fiat two political parties, which were supposed to channel all political life. The pro-government party was supposed to lend unquestionable support to presidential programs, while the opposition party was to act as a loyal opposition with no realistic hopes of becoming a majority party. To ensure that the pro-government party maintained its majority status in the Congress, elections had to be waged and won. This could be done only through the manipulation of electoral laws and the distribution of favors to supporters, and restrictions and denials of services to opponents. Thus the elections, which were supposed to legitimize the regime, institutionalized a two-party system and transformed the Congress into a compliant supporter of the policies of the regime, undermined the legitimacy of the regime, discredited political parties, and further alienated the Congress from the regime.

Winning elections was not the only preoccupation of the regime. Once elections were won, there also existed the need to ensure that the majority party remained compliant and subservient to the authority and directions of the military. To prevent members of the government party from voting against the government, the party fidelity law was passed. Leadership of the Congress and the parties was centralized, marginalized, and made accountable to the President. The primary function of the leaders of the government party was to ensure that members supported the President's programs. Rotation of leadership within the Congress, which preceded the military regime, was further institutionalized and extended to cover even party leadership. Party leadership was separated from Congressional leadership. Institutional resources were all centralized under the Mesa of each chamber of the Congress, thus denying opposition members or recalcitrant members of the government party any chance of meaningful opposition. Committee leadership became rotational as well, preventing the emergence of strong and specialized leadership that might challenge the expertise of the President's men or hold them accountable for their actions.

It is important to point out that the fracturing of congressional and party leadership and its bureaucratization was not the sole doings of the military regime. Party and congressional leaders have always been weak and fractured. Such a phenomenon must therefore be conceived of as an outcome of the presidential system and the tenuous executive-legislative relationship. What the military regime did was to capitalize on and exploit this relationship to annul the veto power of the Congress.

The bureaucratizing, marginalizing, and depoliticizing of Congressional leadership was coupled with a series of measures that robbed the Congress of its budgetary powers and restricted its ability to debate public policy. Congress was required to create a joint budgetary committee and to debate the budget in a joint session. Its power to alter the budget was reduced to internal alterations. Unless the Congress completed the budget within ninety days, it was considered approved and the President was able to promulgate it into law. Laws forwarded by the President to the Congress as urgent had to be acted upon within a limited period, otherwise the President could also promulgate them as decree laws. Finally, the President, when necessary, can promulgate provisional laws and then request the Congress to ratify them after the fact. This practice was by no means restricted to the military regime. It is indeed a permanent feature of the Presidential system. It was more often resorted to by presidents during the liberal periods than by presidents during the Authoritarian periods. President Sarney and more recently President Fernando Collor employed this method more frequently than their military predecessors to pass their legislation and bypass the veto power of the Congress.

Although the power of the Congress was curtailed and its leadership muzzled or co-opted, its ability to delegitimize the regime and on occasions to veto or subvert presidential initiatives was never completely eliminated. On occasion, politics may have been controlled and contained, but rarely was it ever extinguished. Against the onslaught of the military regime to eliminate the congressional veto power, the Congress undertook a series of adaptations to ensure its survival.

This book also detailed the survival strategies of the Congress and the mechanisms it used to fight its battles vis-à-vis the President. It also discussed the effectiveness of those adaption strategies and mechanisms in succeeding to delegitimize the regime and in ushering in Brazil's peaceful transition to the liberal democratic presidential system as embodied in the 1988 Constitution.

The Congress was able to counter the instability of its leadership by rotating its leaders. Influential members of the Congress, having been limited to one nonrenewable term in the same leadership position, conveniently rotated among the different leadership positions within the Congress, between the Congress and each members own party, and on occasions, between the Congress and other elected or appointed positions within the executive at the federal, state, and local levels, thus assuring their survivability and power base. This rotation, while denying them the opportunity to develop specialization and a power base in one area, gave them the opportunity both to circulate and establish general expertise and power in more than one area and at more than one level. Instead of the leader having one overriding public policy concern, his interests covered several public policy concerns. The rotation among different levels and powers of government expanded the leaders' horizons and enriched their access to information. Thus while the intention of the regime was to depoliticize the Congress and its leadership, it unwittingly succeeded in expanding their political horizons. A senator who has served as a governor, a mayor of a large urban area, or a cabinet minister becomes more aware of the operations of the executive, develops local and national credentials, and receives training in areas of public policy that the executive denies to the Congress.

Another successful adaption was in the area of information and staffing. In a regime whose motto is order and progress, high technology, especially in the information area, receives special priority. The Senate successfully maneuvered to establish a sophisticated and comprehensive information center. The establishment of Prodasen gave the Senate and the Congress access to a unified legislative and legal data base and enabled it to modernize all its administrative, personnel, and financial operations. Prodasen spearheaded modernization in other areas of legislative operations, from the recording of debate minutes to printing operations.

Most important, Prodasen, as a leader in information technology, allowed the Congress to improve its political image. Prodasen became a source of legal and legislative information not only for the Congress, but also for the executive and judicial branches of government at both the federal and state levels. Even private institutions for a fee were able to tap its rich data bases. The election data bases Prodasen developed in the early 1980s attracted the political attention of both the executive and the Congress. The development and operations of Prodasen enabled the Congress to resort to "scientific and objective" rationality to justify political choices.

Beginning in the early 1970s, the Congress launched a comprehensive administrative reform project to equip itself with needed staff help. It established new staff units, modernized existing ones, and recruited a large number of staff. The additional staff streamlined legislative operations and provided support to the members. Following the nonpolitical and centralized organizational pattern of the Congress, the staff were also bureaucratically centralized and were expected to be politically neutral. This bureaucratic organization coincided with the military regime's vision of the most appropriate administrative structure for running the affairs of the state. Their nonpartisan structure and operations were more tolerable to the regime.

In time, the centralized bureaucratic structure of the staff lent itself to many abuses. Successive congressional leaders and their principal aids and supporters exploited their positions by adding staff to the rosters of the Congress. Quite often these staff were added with no regard to their qualifications or need. Congressional employment became one of the few perks that the Congress could use to reward supporters and relatives.

Unfortunately, the contribution of the staff to the political and legislative role of the Congress during the 1970s and early 1980s was limited and had no relationship to the number or qualification of the staff. The return to a multiparty system and the repoliticization of the Congress managed to develop informal staff-legislator relationships that enhanced their political and legislative utilization. Certainly the technical and professional capabilities the staff had developed enabled the Congress to play a central role in the drafting of the 1988 Constitution.

Nonetheless, the formalistic and centralized structure of the staff continues to limit their utilization. The return to the liberal presidential system after 1988 did not adequately address the political and administrative structure of the Congress. Instead, the political and administrative structures developed in the past two decades were adopted with minor modifications. If the way a legislative body organizes itself influences the functions it performs and the manner in which it performs those functions, then the present organization and structure of the Congress fall short of what is needed.

During the military regime the ability of the Congress to exercise its veto function was curtailed, but not eliminated. The various measures undertaken by the regime proved temporarily effective, until the Congress discovered more subtle ways to play its delegitimizing and, eventually, its veto role. This book has provided a detailed analysis of what the Congress did during this period, the mechanism and strategies it utilized, and the impact of congressional actions in selected areas.

Although the military regime was able to limit congressional veto power, the Congress during this period continued to perform a number of functions and its veto power was not totally eliminated. Instead of frontal confrontations, the Congress adopted guerrilla warfare and limited engagement strategies in its confrontations with the President.

Although the floor of the plenary sessions remained the arena of congressional actions, committees continued to function and perform a number of activities. The proliferation of congressional committees kept pace with the proliferation of new governmental functions. Committees continued to review proposed legislation initiated by the executive, the individual members, the committees themselves, and the other Chamber.

Because of their sheer size and the socioeconomic representation within the Chamber of Deputies, committees in the lower house displayed more vigor and more energy than those in the Senate. Yet committees in both houses reviewed hundreds and then, with the gradual political opening, thousands of draft bills each year. Most of these bills originated from individual members and ranged from the specific and trivial to the comprehensive and profound. Some came from the committees, while others came from the executive or the judiciary.

Many of the legislative bills presented by the members were screened out at the committee level in each house. Those that were reported out were mostly rejected by the plenary session of the house where they originated. Those few that were approved by one house were rejected by the other house. House-originated bills usually were rejected by the Senate. Yet some that made it all the way had to be vetoed by the President. Over the years, the number of member-sponsored bills was progressively increasing, and a higher number of them were being approved, forcing the executive to use its veto power.

Bills sponsored by committees had a better chance of being reported out and approved by the plenary session. Yet many of the bills either died in the other chamber or were vetoed by the executive. Bills presented by the judiciary were always reported out by the committees and normally approved by both houses. Executive-sponsored bills were always reported out by the committees and normally approved on time by both houses.

At the plenary session, the Congress had few options but to approve executive-sponsored bills. In this sense, the military regime, at least until the late 1970s, was able to eliminate the veto power of the Congress. The restrictions the military imposed and the prerogatives it arrogated to the presidency ensured approval of its sponsored legislation. Yet while the majority of the Congress as a whole complied with these restrictions, a vocal minority engaged in guerrilla tactics to embarrass and delegitimize the regime. Defiant speeches were made criticizing government actions and policies and were reported in the press, bypassing the military censors. Embarrassing questions and requests for information were asked of the executive about government actions and policies with regard to security matters, human rights violations, and other abuses. Supporters of the government in the Congress were questioned, and the policies they advocated on behalf of the executive were repudiated and critiqued. All of these tactics, while not producing alternative public policies, sowed suspicions, innuendoes, and mobilized opposition to the regime.

On occasion, the Congress managed to pass legislation contrary to presidential priorities, or introduced amendments not sanctioned by the President, thus forcing him to exercise his full or partial veto power. In such a case, even the facade of political legitimacy was denied to the executive, further undermining the regime. On other occasions, the pressure in the Congress against executive-sponsored bills reached a high level, thereby forcing postponement of the debate and causing delays which enabled the President to pass legislation into law under the time-limitation provision. On other occasions, when he anticipated congressional resistance, the President opted for the provisional method to pass his legislation. In all of these cases, by forcing the President to resort to exceptional means to pass his legislation, the Congress managed to withhold legitimacy from the regime.

These maneuvers and tactics were a reaction to the restrictions and limitations imposed on the Congress and an attempt to assert the congressional veto power, all characteristic of the Brazilian presidential system. On the one hand, they negatively impacted the presidency, by undermining its political legitimacy. On the positive side, they contributed to the peaceful transition to democracy. Both the opposition members and the government supporters developed a working relationship and a certain level of personal trust. When it was time, they were able to arrive at agreements and compromises, thereby facilitating the shift to civilian, freely elected institutions. Familiarity with the dilemmas of public policy moderated the opposition's political agenda. In time, this same familiarity enabled the opposition to assume power, fully prepared to the tasks ahead. It enabled the regime to extricate itself from power without permanent scars in the body politic. Finally, congressional debates, seminars, and publications educated the concerned public and occasionally the executive as well to important issues and priorities that were embodied in the various articles of the 1988 Constitution. Periodic electoral campaigns gave opposition parties excellent opportunities to advocate their programs and priorities. At the same time the regime became sensitive to popular concerns and dissatisfactions. Quite often programs advocated by the opposition in the Congress were co-opted or preempted and presented as part of the priorities of the President.

The Congress, on occasion, successfully arbitrated bureaucratic conflict within the executive. When conflict within the bureaucracy became internally unmanageable, as the debate on the informatics policy showed, the various protagonists sought allies outside.

The Congress became the arena where those battles were fought. On those occasions, the Congress was given the opportunity to participate in the debate and to some extent shape the direction of the policy. In those public policy debates, the Congress showed concern for the distributive impact of the policy, as well as sensitivity to environmental concerns and the impact of technology on individual well-being and basic human rights.

The full potential of congressional actions was manifested during the constitutional debate. Operating as a forum for the formulation of public policy—more akin to a parliamentary system of government than a Congress reacting to a presidential system—the Congress was challenged to draft a new constitution under very difficult political and economic conditions. It successfully met that challenge.

The ascendancy of Sarney to the presidency propelled the Congress into the prominent role of policymaker. Sarney's lack of political legitimacy and an independent power base forced him to rely more on the support of the Congress. He found this support in the Democratic Alliance under the leadership of Ulysses Guimarães. The informal relationship that developed between Sarney and Guimarães was that of a President to a prime minister. Guimarães as the leader of the majority party was put in charge to articulate government policies and build congressional majorities in support of those policies. The honeymoon between Sarney and the Democratic Alliance continued only until after the election of 1986, which elevated PMDB to the status of dominant party at the national, state, and local levels.

The division between Sarney and a significant segment of the Democratic Alliance came over the issue of the form of government. Sarney and a diverse assortment of political parties favored a presidential system. Influential members of PMDB and other supporters favored a parliamentary system. When the Constitutional Drafting Commission headed by Senator Afonso Arinos recommended a parliamentary form of government, Sarney decided to reject its recommendation and throw the issue wide open to the NCA. Drafting a constitution and deciding on the form of government became the sole prerogative of the NCA. The main challenge facing Guimarães as the leader of the NCA was how to create a majority coalition that would adopt the various articles of the constitution. The Congress in a sense was asked to act as a policy-making body rather than a veto group since the President had no veto power over its work.

The work of the Congress during this period—though Congress was still formally functioning under a presidential system—was informally akin to a parliamentary system. Guimarães and his chief lieutenants acted more like a cabinet in a parliamentary system than as congressional leaders. Their primary task was to build internal agreement within the coalition and then negotiate with the *Centrão* over the final disposition of each of the provisions of the constitution. In spite of the formal structure within the NCA, which was supposed to lead the process, an informal process emerged and took over. An informal group of leaders on both sides emerged whose main function was to hammer out agreements over controversial issues outside the formal work of the NCA plenary sessions. Immediately the work of party leaders reasserted itself and overshadowed the work of the formal congressional leaders. In the case of Guimarães, there was a fusion of his roles as the national leader of the major party, the president of the Chamber of Deputies, and the president of the NCA. All of a sudden politics permeated the congressional halls, and Congress regained its identity as a political institution.

Even the staff while operating under the formalistic, bureaucratic, and neutral structure of the Congress became involved in a public policy and support role. Energetic members of the staff attached themselves to various political leaders and committees and became involved in the design and articulation of the public policy strategy of their political bosses. The work of the NCA was recorded, systematized, and packaged for distribution to the media. Extended working hours in support of the NCA both inside and outside the Congress became the norm rather than the exception. A sense of esprit de corps and accomplishment prevailed, replacing the apathy noted in their previous attitudes. A major constitutional document was drafted, debated, amended, and, in a relatively short time, adopted and ratified, allowing the transition to liberal democracy to proceed on schedule.

It should be noted that the Congress acting informally as a parliamentary institution was able to accomplish this important feat in spite of the odds it was facing. Many of the obstacles normally cited as detrimental to the success of a parliamentary system of government were present. Political parties within the NCA were fragile and of recent vintage. Party leaders were yet to develop their leadership credentials and their power base. Close to half of the 559 members of the NCA were newcomers. Within the NCA, close to a dozen political parties were represented with a similar number of informal political groups with cross-party affiliations. Even within PMDB many opportunists, fellow travelers and formal supporters and collaborators of the military regime, who had jumped ship at the last moment, were abundant. The economic crises was crippling the country. Unemployment, labor strikes, and unrest, including the public sector, were prevalent. And, more important, at least at the formal level, presidentialism was still the form of government, and its future fate was yet to be decided. Yet the Congress succeeded in its mission and was able to transform itself from a veto group to a public policy-making institution.

On March 22, 1988, supporters of the presidential system of government in the NCA won a stunning victory. By a narrow margin, the presidential system of government was adopted in the proposed constitution, and the prospect of parliamentarism began to fade into the background. As soon as the presidential system was adopted, presidential politics began to reassert itself.

President Sarney reemerged as a power center and began contesting the power of Guimarães. Against the objection of the national leader of PFL, Senator Marco Maciel, Sarney engineered the appointment of Senator Marcondes Gadelha from the state of Paraíba as the Senate leader of PFL. Against the objection of PMDB and its leadership in the Congress, Sarney appointed Senator Saldanha Derzi, a recent convert to PMDB from the state of Mato Grosso, as the leader of the government in the Senate. He discredited and rejected the work of a Senate investigatory committee chaired by Senator Carlos Chiarelli of the PFL from the state of Rio Grande do Sul. Finally, Sarney reclaimed his presidential prerogatives of promulgating major economic and budgetary laws through the use of a provisional measure imposed on the Congress after the fact.

Presidential politics reasserted itself in the NCA and the political parties. Ratification of the main articles of the Constitution slowed down and agreements became more difficult to reach. The fragile unity of PMDB, which had been maintained through the prospect of the advent of parliamentarism, began to disintegrate. The recent converts found affinity with the *Centrão*. The founders and authentic elements of PMDB found themselves squeezed and saw no electoral benefit in continued association with the coalition that PMDB had become and built. In June 1988 they formally severed their ties and formulated their own separate party, PSDB. Minor political parties from both the Left and the Right realized that their only chance to join the government was through winning the presidential race. Consequently, their voting behavior within the NCA was being orchestrated to build a political profile that promoted their presidential aspirations. Reaching agreements and joining coalitions became politically less attractive than maintaining ideological purity and integrity in preparing for the next presidential election where the winner takes all, irrespective of either national or congressional party strength.

Since the Constitution was promulgated on October 5, 1988, Brazil has undergone three national elections, a local election, a presidential election in 1989, and congressional, gubernatorial, and state legislative elections in 1990. Multiparty, liberal, presidential democracy returned to Brazil in full force.

During the 1989 presidential election, a young photogenic governor from the small, northeastern state of Alagoas won the election. What is significant about the election of Fernando Collor de Melo is that until the presidential campaign Collor had been only loosely identified with an established political party, first PMDB and later PFL. And he had not participated in the NCA. Candidate Collor established his own party (PRN) a few days before the presidential campaign, ran a populist campaign, and effectively used the media against both the government and the opposition parties and emerged victorious.

The presidential campaign was contested by close to a dozen candidates, representing the entire political spectrum. The candidates of the parties that had played a leading role in the NCA, such as PMDB, PFL, PDS, and PSDB, had a poor showing in the first round. The candidates of PT, Luis Inácio "Lula" da Silva, and PDT, Leonel Brizola came in second and third, respectively, after Collor. The second round of elections pitted Collor against Lula. As expected, two established, left-of-center parties with small representation in the NCA polled the most votes in the presidential election. Both PT and PDT were rewarded on many of the social and economic issues for the uncompromising positions they had adopted during the constitutional debates. Compromising parties that conjured up the various agreements that gave birth to the Constitution fared poorly in the election. Presidential politics, once again, penalized those who played a constructive public policy role and rewarded the puritan and the demagogue.

In the 1990 congressional and state elections, Collor's PRN had a poor showing at both the federal and state levels. PMDB, while still the largest party, lost the majority status it had initially enjoyed after the 1986 election. With the creation of PSDB and the defection of many members to other parties, PMDB representation in the 1990 Congress was reduced to half its 1986 number. PFL, PDS, PDT, and PT all managed to increase slightly their numerical representation. The country was back to its pre-1964 coup status—a Congress splintered among a dozen political parties, with no one enjoying a majority status, and a President who won popular majority, but lost in the Congress and the states. To pass his legislative program President Collor had to deal with a splintered and polarized Congress. Constructing congressional majorities required a return to the classical tactics of the politics of the liberal presidential model, and the utilization of state resources including favoritism, perks, and similar incentives to forge the needed majorities. The closer the election, the higher becomes the price of these coalitions. The closer the end of the President's term, the more difficult the task becomes. It is no surprise, therefore, that Collor has utilized the provisional method to pass his legislation in the first year of his term, more than his predecessors resorted to it in their full term, prompting the Congress to consider passing legislation restricting its use.

Many of the forces and personalities that opposed the parliamentary form of government in Brazil have now reversed their position, such as Ulysses Guimarães and even Collor himself. Whether parliamentarism will resolve Brazil's institutional and political instability is still to be seen. This study only dealt with the problems associated with the presidential model of government, as it has manifested itself in recent Brazilian history. To some extent the Brazilian presidential system reflects the weaknesses of the presidential system in Third World countries in general. During the brief period under President Sarney when the Congress functioned, at least at the informal level, as a parliamentary system, Brazil saw that such a system was able to build parliamentary majorities, transform the Congress into a public policy-making body, and, for that short period, maintain the solidarity of the political parties. In 1993 Brazil will again decide what system of government it will follow.

Bibliography

BOOKS

Abreu, Hugo. *O Outro Lado do Poder*. Rio de Janeiro: Nova Fronteira, 1979.

Adler, Emanuel. *The Power of Ideology: The Quest for Technological Authonomy in Argentina and Brazil*. Berkeley and Los Angeles: University of California Press, 1987.

Agor, Weston (ed.). *Latin American Legislatures: Their Role and Influence*. New York: Praeger, 1971.

Almino, Affonso. *Raízes do Golpe: Da Crise da Legalidade ao Parlamentarismo, 1961-1963*. São Paulo: Marco Zero, 1988.

Almino, João. *Democracias Autoritárias*. São Paulo: Brasiliense, 1980.

Alves, Márcio Moreira. *Torturas e Torturados*. Rio de Janeiro: Idade Nova, 1966.

Alves, Márcio Moreira. *A Grain of Mustard Seed: The Awakening of the Brazilian Revolution*. Garden City, N.Y.: Anchor Books, 1973.

Alves, Maria Helena Moreira. *State and Opposition in Military Brazil*. Austin: University of Texas Press, 1985.

Andrade, Auro Soares de Moura. *Political Survival: Politicians and Public Policy in Latin America*. Berkeley and Los Angeles: University of California Press, 1987.

Andrade, Auro Soares de Moura. *Um Congresso Contra o Arbítrio: Diários e Memórias, 1961-1967*. Rio de Janeiro: Nova Fronteira, 1985.

Assis, José Carlos de. *A Chave do Tesouro: Anatomia dos Escândalos Financeiros, Brasil 1974-1983*. Rio de Janeiro: Paz e Terra, 1983.

Baaklini, Abdo I. *Legislative and Political Development: Lebanon, 1842-1972*. Durham, N. C.: Duke University Press, 1976.

Baaklini, Abdo I., and James J. Heaphey. *Legislative Institution Building in Brazil, Costa Rica, and Lebanon*. Beverly Hills: Sage Publications, 1976.

Baaklini, Abdo I., and James J. Heaphey (eds.). *Comparative Legislative Reforms and Innovations*. Albany: State University of New York, 1977.

Bacha, Edmar. *Os Mitos de uma Década: Ensaios de Economia Brasileira*. Rio de Janeiro: Paz e Terra, 1976.

Baer, Werner. *The Brazilian Economy: Growth and Development*. New York: Praeger, 1983.

Bandeira, Moniz. *O Governo João Goulart: As Lutas Sociais no Brasil, 1961-1964*. Rio de Janeiro: Civilização Brasileira, 1977.

Baptista, Lourival. *Atuação Parlamentar: Atividades no Senado Federal*. Brasília: Senado Federal, 1980.

Barão de Javary. *Câmara dos Deputados: Organizações e Programas Ministeriais desde 1822 a 1889*. Rio de Janeiro: Imprensa Nacional, 1889.

Barbosa, Rui. *A Ditadura de 1893*. Rio de Janeiro: Ministério da Educação e Saúde, 1949.

Barbosa, Waldemar de Almeida. *A Câmara dos Deputados como Fator de Unidade Nacional*. Rio de Janeiro: José Olympio, 1977.

Barbosa, Waldemar de Almeida. *A Câmara dos Deputados e o Sistema Parlamentar de Governo no Brasil*. Brasília: Câmara dos Deputados, 1977.

Bello, José Maria. *História da República: 1889-1954*. Stanford, California: Stanford University Press, 1966.

Benakouche, Rabah (ed.). *A Questão da Informática no Brasil*. São Paulo: Brasiliense, 1985.

Benevides, Maria Victória de Mesquita. *A UDN e o Udenismo: Ambiguidades do Liberalismo Brasileiro, 1945-1965*. Rio de Janeiro: Paz e Terra, 1981.

Biato, F., and M.A. Figueiredo. *Transferência de Tecnologia no Brasil*. Brasília: Ipea, Série Estudos para o Planejamento, No. 4, 1973.

Bierrenbach, Flávio Flores da Cunha. *Quem Tem Medo da Constituinte?* Rio de Janeiro: Paz e Terra, 1986.

Blondel, Jean. *Comparative Legislatures*. Englewood Cliffs, N. J.: Prentice Hall, 1973.

Boynton, G.R., and Chong Lim Kim (eds.). *Legislative Systems in Developing Countries*. Durham, N. C.: Duke University Press, 1975.

Bresser Pereira, Luiz Carlos. *Desenvolvimento e Crise no Brasil, entre 1930-1967*. Rio de Janeiro: Zahar, 1968.

Bresser Pereira, Luiz Carlos. *O PMDB e as Eleições de 1986*. São Paulo: Fundação Pedroso Horta, 1987.

Cabral, Milton. *Ação Parlamentar*. Brasília: Senado Federal, 1976.

Cachel, Julian M., Pamela S. Falk, and David V. Fleischer. *Brazil's Economic and Political Future*. Boulder, Colo.: Westview Press, 1988.

Campos, Roberto. *Reflections on Latin American Development*. Austin: University of Texas Press, 1968.

Campos, Roberto. *Temas e Sistemas*. Rio de Janeiro: Apec, 1969.

Campos, Roberto. *Além do Cotidiano*. 2d ed. Rio de Janeiro: Record, 1985.

Cardoso, Fernando Henrique, and Enzo Faletto. *Dependency and Development in Latin America*. Berkeley and Los Angeles: University of California Press, 1979.

Carone, Edgar. *A República Velha*. São Paulo: Difel,1983.

Carone, Edgar. *Revoluções do Brasil Contemporâneo, 1922-1938*. São Paulo: 1965.

Branco, Carlos Castello. *Os Militares no Poder*. Rio de Janeiro: Nova Fronteira, 1976.

Castro, Antônio Barros de, and Francisco Eduardo Pires de Souza. *A Economia Brasileira em Marcha Forçada*. Rio de Janeiro: Paz e Terra, 1985.

Cehelsky, Marta. *Land Reform in Brazil: The Management of Social Change*. Boulder, Colo.: Westview Press, 1979.

Chacon, Vamireh. *Estado e Povo no Brasil: As Experiências do Estado Novo e da Democracia Populista, 1937-1964*. Brasília: Câmara dos Deputados, 1977.

Chacon, Vamireh. *O Novo Parlamentarismo*. Brasília: Fundação Milton Campos, 1979.

Chacon, Vamireh. *História dos Partidos Brasileiros*. Brasília: Universidade de Brasília, 1981.

Chacon, Vamireh. *Parlamento e Parlamentarismo: O Congresso Nacional na História do Brasil*. Brasília: Câmara dos Deputados, 1982.

Chacon, Vamireh. *Vida e Morte das Constituições Brasileiras*. Rio de Janeiro: Forense, 1987.

Chagas, Carlos. *113 Dias de Angústia: Impedimento e Morte de um Presidente*. Porto Alegre: L&PM, 1979.

Chagas, Carlos. *A Guerra das Estrelas, 1964-1984: Os Bastidores das Sucessões Presidenciais*. Porto Alegre: L&PM, 1985.

Chilcote, Ronald H. *The Brazilian Communist Party: Conflict and Integration, 1922-1972*. New York: Oxford University Press, 1974.

Cohen, Youssef. *Popular Support for Authoritarian Regimes: Brazil under Médici*. Ann Arbor: University of Michigan Press, 1979.

Collier, David (ed.). *The New Authoritarianism in Latin America*. Princeton, N.J.: Princeton University Press, 1979.

Cruz, Adelina Maria Alves Novaes et al (eds.). *Impasse na Democracia Brasileira, 1951-1955: Coletânea de Documentos*. Rio de Janeiro: Fundação Getúlio Vargas, 1983.

Daland, Robert T. *Brazilian Planning: Development Politics and Administration*. Chapel Hill: University of North Carolina Press, 1967.

Dassin, Joan (ed.). *Torture in Brazil*. New York: Random House, 1986.

Dimas, Nelson, Filho. *Costa e Silva: O Homem e o Líder*. Rio de Janeiro: Edições O Cruzeiro, 1966.

Dimenstein, Gilberto et al. *O Complô que Elegeu Tancredo*. Rio de Janeiro: JB, 1985.

Dines, Alberto et al. *Os Idos de Março e a Queda em Abril*. Rio de Janeiro: José Alvaro, 1964.

Diniz, Eli. *Voto e Máquina Política: Patronagem e Clientelismo no Rio de Janeiro*. Rio de Janeiro: Paz e Terra, 1982.

Diniz, Eli, and Renato Boschi. *Empresariado Nacional e Estado no Brasil*. Rio de Janeiro: Forense-Universitária, 1978.

Drake, Paul W. and Eduardo Silva (eds.). *Elections and Democratization in Latin America, 1980-1985*. San Diego: University of California Press, 1986.

Dreifuss, René Armand. *1964: A Conquista do Estado*. Petrópolis: Vozes, 1981.

Dulles, John W. F. *Castelo Branco: The Making of a Brazilian President*. College Station: Texas A&M University Press, 1978.

Dulles, John W. F. *President Castelo Branco: Brazilian Reformer*. College Station: Texas A&M University Press, 1980.

Eldridge, Albert (ed.). *Legislatures in Plural Societies*. Durham, N.C.: Duke University Press, 1977.

Erickson, Kenneth Paul. *The Brazilian Corporative State and Working-Class Politics*. Berkeley and Los Angeles: University of California Press, 1977.

Evans, Peter. *Dependent Development*. Princeton, N.J.: Princeton University Press, 1979.

Faoro, Raymundo. *Os Donos do Poder*. Porto Alegre: Globo, 1958.

Felizardo, Joaquim José, and Mateus Schmidt. *Partidos Políticos e Eleições no Brasil*. Petrópolis: Vozes, 1982.

Fenno, Richard F. Jr. *The Power of the Purse: Appropriation Politics in Congress*. Boston: Little, Brown and Co., 1966.

Fenno, Richard F. Jr. *Congressmen in Committees*. Boston: Little, Brown and Co., 1973.

Ferreira, Oliveiros S. *As Forças Armadas e o Desafio da Revolução*. Rio de Janeiro: Edição GRD, 1964.

Fiechter, Georges-André. *Brazil since 1964: Modernization under a Military Regime*. New York: John Wiley & Sons, 1975.

Figueiredo, Eurico de Lima. *Os Militares e a Democracia: Análise Estrutural da Ideologia do Presidente Castelo Branco*. Rio de Janeiro: Graal, 1980.

Fleischer, David V. (ed.). *Os Partidos Políticos no Brasil*. 2. vol. Brasília: Universidade de Brasília, 1981.

Fleischer, David V. (ed.). *Da Distensão à Abertura: As Eleicões de Novembro de 1982*. Brasília: Universidade de Brasília, 1988.

Fleischer, David, with Antonio de Pádua Gurgel. *O Brasil Vai às Urnas: Retrato da Campanha Presidencial*. Brasilia: Ed. Thesaurus, 1990.

Flynn, Peter. *Brazil: A Political Analysis*. Boulder, Colo: Westview Press, 1978.

Fox, Harrison W. Jr., and Susan Webb Hammond. *Congressional Staffs: The Invisible Force in American Lawmaking*. New York: The Free Press, 1977.

Franco, Afonso Arinos de Mello. *Evolução da Crise Brasileira*. São Paulo: Companhia Editora Nacional, 1965.

Franco, Afonso Arinos de Mello. *A Câmara dos Deputados: Síntese Histórica*. Brasília: Câmara dos Deputados, 1976.

Franco, Afonso Arinos de Mello, and Raul Pilla. *Presidencialismo ou Parlamentarismo?* Rio de Janeiro: José Olympio, 1958.

Freire, Felisbelo. *História Constitucional da República dos Estados Unidos do Brasil*. 2d ed. Rio de Janeiro: Aldina, 1894.

Freire, Marcos. *Oposição no Brasil, Hoje*. Rio de Janeiro: Paz e Terra, 1974.

Freitas, Alípio de. *Resistir é Preciso: Memória do Tempo da Morte Civil do Brasil*. Rio de Janeiro: Record, 1981.

Furtado, Celso. *The Economic Growth of Brazil*. Berkeley and Los Angeles: University of California Press, 1963.

Furtado, Celso. *Um Projeto para o Brasil*. Rio de Janeiro: Saga, 1968.

Furtado, Celso. *Análise do 'Modelo' Brasileiro*. Rio de Janeiro: Civilização Brasileira, 1972.

Furtado, Celso. *O Mito do Desenvolvimento Econômico*. Rio de Janeiro: Paz e Terra, 1974.

Gasparian, Fernando. *Em Defesa da Economia Nacional*. Rio de Janeiro: Saga, 1966.

Goes, Walter de, and Aspásia Camargo. *O Drama da Sucessão e a Crise do Regime*. Rio de Janeiro: Nova Fronteira, 1984.

Graham, Laurence S. *Civil Service Reform in Brazil*. Austin: University of Texas Press, 1968.

Graham, Laurance and Robert Wilson. *The Political Economy of Brazil*. Austin: University of Texas Press, 1990.

Guedes, Geraldo. *As Bases da Reforma*. Brasília: Cegraf, 1971.

Hambloch, Ernest. *Sua Majestade, o Presidente do Brasil: Um Estudo do Brasil Constitucional: 1889-1934*. Brasília: Universidade de Brasília, 1981.

Hartlyn, Jonathan, and Samuel A. Morley (eds.). *Latin American Political Economy*. Boulder, Colo.: Westview Press, 1986.

Heaphey, James J. and Alan P. Balutis (eds.). *Legislative Staffing: A Comparative Perspective*. New York: Sage Publishing, 1975.

Hippólito, Lúcia. *De Raposas e Reformistas: O PSD e a Experiência Democrática Brasileira, 1945-64*. Rio de Janeiro: Paz e Terra, 1985.

Hirsch, Herbert, and M. Donald Hancock (eds.). *Comparative Legislative Systems: A Reader in Theory and Research*. New York: The Free Press, 1971.

Hughes, Steven W., and Kenneth J. Mijeski. *Politics and Public Policy in Latin America*. Boulder, Colo.: Westwiew Press, 1984.

Huntington, Samuel P. *Political Order in Changing Societies*. New Haven: Yale University Press, 1968.

Ianni, Octávio. *Crisis in Brazil*. New York: Columbia University Press, 1970.

Iglesias, Francisco. *Constitutintes e Constituições Brasileiras*. São Paulo: Brasiliense, 1986.

Jaguaribe, Hélio, et al. *Brasil, 2000: Para um Novo Pacto Social*. Rio de Janeiro: Paz e Terra, 1986.

Kinzo, Maria D'Alva Gil. *Representação Política e Sistema Eleitoral no Brasil*. São Paulo: Símbolo, 1980.

Knight, Peter T. *Economic Policy and Planning*. Boston: Northeastern University, 1985.

Kofmehl, Kenneth. *Professional Staff of the Congress*. West Lafayette: Purdue University Press, 1962.

Kornberg, Alan (ed.). *Legislatures in Comparative Perspective*. New York: David McKay, 1973.

Kornberg, Alan, and Lloyd D. Musolf (eds.). *Legislatures in Developmental Perspective*. Durham, N. C.: Duke University Press, 1970.

Koutzii, Flávio (ed.). *Nova República: Um Balanço*. Porto Alegre: L&PM, 1986.

Kucinski, Bernardo. *Abertura, A História de uma Crise*. São Paulo: Brasil Debates, 1982.

Lamounier, Bolivar (org.). *Voto de Desconfiança, Eleições e Mudança Política no Brasil: 1970-1979*. Petrópolis: Vozes, 1980.

Lamounier, Bolivar, and Fernando Henrique Cardoso. *Os Partidos e as Eleições no Brasil*. Rio de Janeiro: Paz e Terra, 1975.

Lamounier, Bolivar, and Maria D'Alva Gil Kinzo. *Partidos Políticos, Representação e Processo Eleitoral no Brasil: 1945-1978*. Rio de Janeiro: Associação Nacional de Pós-Graduação e Pesquisa em Ciências Sociais, 1978.

Lamounier, Bolivar, and Rachel Meneguello. *Partidos Políticos e Consolidação Democrática: O Caso Brasileiro*. São Paulo: Brasiliense, 1986.

Leal, Victor Nunes. *Coronelismo, Enxada e Voto: O Município e o Regime Representativo no Brasil*. 2d. ed. São Paulo: Alfa-Omega, 1975.

Lees, John D., and Malcolm Shaw (eds.). *Committees in Legislatures: A Comparative Approach*. Durham, N.C.: Duke University Press, 1979.

Leff, Nathanial. *Economic Policy-Making and Development in Brazil, 1947-1964*. New York: John Wiley and Sons. 1968.

Lima, Haroldo and Aldo Arantes. *História de Ação Popular da JUC ao PC do B*. São Paulo: Alfa-Omega, 1984.

Lima, Vicente Ferrer Correia. *O Congresso Nacional nos Períodos Presidenciais da República Brasileira*. 1984.

Lima, Olavo Brasil de. *Os Partidos Políticos Brasileiros: A Experiência Federal e Regional: 1945-1964*. Rio de Janeiro: Graal, 1983.

Loewenberg, Gerhard and Samuel Patterson. *Comparing Legislatures*. Boston: Little, Brown and Co., 1979.

Macêdo, Murillo. *Trabalho na Democracia: A Nova Fisionomia do Processo Político Brasileiro*. Brasília: Ministério do Trabalho, 1981.

Maciel, Marco. *Vocação e Compromisso*. Rio de Janeiro: José Olympio, 1982.

Maciel, Marco. *Liberalismo e Justiça Social*. Brasília: Senado Federal, 1987.

Magano, Octávio Bueno. *Organização Sindical Brasileira*. São Paulo: Revista dos Tribunais, 1982.

Mainwaring, Scott. *The Catholic Church and Politics in Brazil, 1916-1985*. Stanford, Calif.: Stanford University Press, 1986.

Malbin, Michael J. *Unelected Representatives: Congressional Staff and the Future of Representative Government*. New York: Basic Books Inc., 1979.

Malloy, James M. ed. *Authoritarianism and Corporatism in Latin America*. Pittsburgh: University of Pittsburgh Press, 1977.

Marcílio, Flávio Portela. *Atividades Parlamentares: Discursos, 1963-1982*. Brasília: Câmara dos Deputados, 1984.

Marcílio, Flávio Portela. *Atividades Parlamentares: Presidência da Câmara dos Deputados*. Brasília: Câmara dos Deputados, 1985.

Martins, Heloísa Helena Teixeira de Souza. *O Estado e a Burocratização do Sindicato no Brasil*. São Paulo: Hucitec, 1979.

Martins, Luciano. *Industrialização, Burguesia Nacional e Desenvolvimento*. Rio de Janeiro: Saga, 1968.

McDonough, Peter. *Power and Ideology in Brazil*. Princeton, N.J.: Princeton University Press, 1981.

Médici, Emílio Garrastazú. *O Jogo da Verdade*. Brasília: Secretaria de Imprensa da Presidência da República, 1971.

Mello, Jayme Portella de. *A Revolução e o Governo Costa e Silva*. Rio de Janeiro: Guavira Editores, 1979.

Mendes, Cândido de Almeida (ed.). *O Legislativo e a Tecnocracia*. Rio de Janeiro: Imago, 1975.

Meyers, Kenneth, and F. Desmond McCarthy. *Brazil: Medium-Term Policy Analysis*. Washington: World Bank, 1985.

Mezey, Michael L. *Comparative Legislatures*. Durham, N.C.: Duke University Press, 1979.

Minc, Carlos. *A Reconquista da Terra: Lutas no Campo e Reforma Agrária*. Rio de Janeiro: Zahar, 1985.

Moisés, José Álvaro. *Greve de Massa e Crise Política*. São Paulo: Polis, 1978.

Moraes, Evaristo de, Filho. *O Problema do Sindicato Único no Brasil*. Rio de Janeiro: A Noite, 1952.

Morel, Mário. *Lula, O Metalúrgico*. Rio de Janeiro: Nova Fronteira, 1981.

Morley, Samuel A. *Labor Markets and Inequitable Growth: The Case of Authoritarian Capitalism in Brazil*. Cambridge: Cambridge University Press, 1982.

Mota, Carlos Guilherme (ed.). *Brasil em Perspectiva.*, 3rd Ed. São Paulo: Difel, 1971.

Mota, Carlos Guilherme. *Estado e Partidos no Brasil, 1930-1964*. São Paulo: Alfa-Omega, 1976.

Motta, Paulo Roberto. *Movimentos Partidários no Brasil*. Rio de Janeiro: Fundação Getúlio Vargas, 1971.

Mourão Filho, Olympio. *Memórias: A Verdade de um Revolucionário*. Porto Alegre: L&PM, 1978.

O'Donnell, Guillermo A. *Modernization and Bureaucratic-Authoritarianism*. Berkeley and Los Angeles: University of California Press, 1967.

O'Donnell, Guillermo A. *Modernization and Bureaucratic-Authoritarianism: Studies in South American Politics*. Berkeley and Los Angeles: Institute of International Studies, 1973.

O'Donnell, Guillermo A., Philippe C. Schmitter, and Laurence Whitehead (eds.). *Transitions from Authoritarian Rule: Latin America*. Baltimore: Johns Hopkins University Press, 1986.

Oliveira, Eliézer Rizzo de et al. *As Forças Armadas no Brasil*. Rio de Janeiro: Espaço e Tempo, 1987.

Oliveira, Eliézer Rizzo de (ed.). *Militares: Pensamento e Ação Política*. Campinas: Papirus, 1987.

Paim, Gilberto. *Computador Faz Política*. Rio de Janeiro: Apec, 1985.

Peabody, Robert L. *Leadership in Congress*. Boston: Little, Brown, and Co., 1976.

Pedreira, Fernando. *Março 31: Civis e Militares no Processo de Crise Brasileira*. Rio de Janeiro: José Álvaro, 1964.

Pedrosa, Mário. *Sobre o PT*. São Paulo: Ched, 1980.

Pereira, Osny Duarte. *Constituinte: Anteprojeto da Comissão Afonso Arinos*. Brasília: Universidade de Brasília, 1987.

Pereira, Raimundo, Alvaro Caropreso, and José Carlos Ruy. *Eleições no Brasil Pós-64*. São Paulo: Global, 1984.

Portella, Petrônio. *Tempo de Congresso, II*. Brasília: Senado Federal, 1980.

Quartim, João. *Dictatorship and Armed Struggle in Brazil*. New York: Monthly Review Press, 1971.

Rainho, Luís Flávio, and Osvaldo Martines Bargas. *As Lutas Operárias e Sindicais dos Metalúrgicos em São Bernardo: 1977-1979*. São Bernardo: EG, 1983.

Ramos, Alberto Guerreiro. *A Crise do Poder no Brasil: Problemas da Revolução Nacional Brasileira*. Rio de Janeiro: Zahar, 1961.

Ramos, Alberto Guerreiro. *Administração e Estratégia do Desenvolvimento: Elementos de uma Sociologia Especial de Administração*. Rio de Janeiro: Fundação Getúlio Vargas, 1966.

Reale, Miguel. *Imperativos da Revolução de Março*. São Paulo: Livraria Martins Editora, 1965.

Redman, Eric. *The Dance of Legislation*. New York: Simon & Schuster, 1973.

Reis, Fábio Wanderley. *Os Partidos e o Regime: A Lógica do Processo Eleitoral Brasileiro*. São Paulo: Símbolo, 1978.

Rodrigues, José Honório. *Conciliação e Reforma no Brasil: Um Desafio Histórico-Político*. Rio de Janeiro: Civilização Brasileira, 1965.

Rodrigues, José Honório. *O Parlamento e a Consolidação do Império, 1940-1961*. Brasília: Câmara dos Deputados, 1982.

Rodrigues, Leôncio Martins. *Quem é Quem na Constituinte*. São Paulo: Oesp-Maltese, 1987.

Roett, Riordan. *Brazil: Politics in a Patrimonial Society*. New York: Praeger, 1984.

Rouquié, Alain et al (eds.). *Como Renascem as Democracias*. São Paulo: Brasiliense, 1985.

Santos, Wanderley Guilherme dos. *Estratégias de Descompressão Política*. Brasília: Instituto de Pesquisas, Estudos e Assessoria do Congresso, 1973.

Santos, Wanderley Guilherme dos. *Poder e Política: Crônica do Autoritarismo Brasileiro*. Rio de Janeiro: Forense, 1978.

Santos, Wanderley Guilherme dos. *Sessenta e Quatro: Anatomia da Crise*. São Paulo: Vértice, 1986.

Schmitter, Phillipe C. *Interest Groups, Conflict, and Political Change in Brazil*. Stanford, Calif.: Stanford University Press, 1971.

Schneider, Ronald M. *The Political System of Brazil: Emergence of a "Modernizing" Authoritarian Regime, 1964-1970*. New York: Columbia University Press, 1971.

Schneider, Ronald M. *Order and Progress: A Political History of Brazil*. Boulder, Colo.: Westview Press, 1991.

Selcher, Wayne A. (ed.). *Political Liberalization in Brazil*. Boulder, Colo.: Westview Press, 1986.

Silva, Golbery do Couto e. *Conjuntura Política Nacional, O Poder Executivo e a Geopolítica do Brasil*. Brasília: Universidade de Brasília, 1981.

Silva, Hélio, and Maria Cecília Ribas Carneiro. *Emílio de Médici: O Combate às Guerrilhas, 1969-1974*. São Paulo: Grupo de Comunicação Três, 1983.

Sinclair, Barbara. *Majority Leadership in the U.S. House*. Baltimore: Johns Hopkins University Press, 1983.

Skidmore, Thomas E. *Politics in Brazil: 1930-1964, An Experiment in Democracy*. New York: Oxford University Press, 1967.

Skidmore, Thomas E. *The Politics of Military Rule in Brazil, 1964-85*. New York: Oxford University Press, 1988.

Smith, Joel, and Lloyd D. Musolf (eds.). *Legislatures in Development: Dynamics of Change in New and Old States*. Durham: Duke University Press, 1979.

Smith, Steven, and Christopher J. Deering. *Committees in Congress*. Washington: Congressional Quarterly Press, 1984.

Soares, Gláucio Ary Dillon. *Colégio Eleitoral, Convenções Partidárias, e Eleições Diretas*. Petrópolis: Vozes, 1984.

Soares, Gláucio Ary Dillon. *Sociedade e Política no Brasil*. DIFEL, 1973.

Soares, Rosinethe Monteiro, and Abdo I. Baaklini. *O Poder Legislativo no Brasil*. Brasília: Câmara dos Deputados, 1975.

Souza, Maria do Carmo Carvalho Campello de. *Estados e Partidos Políticos no Brasil, 1930 a 1964*. São Paulo: Alfa-Omega, 1976.

Srour, Robert Henry. *A Política dos Anos 70 no Brasil: A Lição de Florianópolis*. São Paulo: Econômica, 1982.

Stepan, Alfred. *Military in Politics: Changing Patterns in Brazil*. Princeton: Princeton University Press, 1975.

Stepan, Alfred. *Os Militares: Da Abertura à Nova República*. Rio de Janeiro: Paz e Terra, 1986.

Stepan, Alfred. *Rethinking Military Politics: Brazil and the Southern Cone*. Princeton, N.J.: Princeton University Press, 1988.

Stepan, Alfred (ed.). *Authoritarian Brazil: Origins, Policies, and Future*. New Haven, Conn.: Yale University Press, 1973.

Stepan, Alfred (ed.). *Democratizing Brazil: Problems of Transition and Consolidation*. New York: Oxford University Press, 1988.

Syvrud, Donald E. *Foundations of Brazilian Economic Growth*. Stanford, Calif.: Hoover Institution Press, 1974.

Tavares, Cristina, and Milton Seligman, *Informática, A Batalha do Século XXI*. Rio de Janeiro: Paz e Terra, 1984.

Tavares, Maria da Conceição, and J. Carlos de Assis. *O Grande Salto para o Caos: A Economia Política e a Política Econômica do Regime Autoritário*. Rio de Janeiro: Zahar, 1985.

Távora, Virgílio. *Política Nacional de Informática*. Brasília: Senado Federal, 1985.

Tigre, Paulo B. *Technology and Competition in the Brazilian Computer Industry*. New York: St. Martins' Press, 1983.

Trindade, Hélgio (ed.) *Brasil em Perspectiva: Dilemas da Abertura Política*. Porto Alegre: Sulina, 1982.

Venancio, Alberto, Filho. *Notícia Histórica da Ordem dos Advogados do Brasil: 1930-1980*. Rio de Janeiro: OAB, 1982.

Viana, Cíbilis da Rocha. *Estratégia do Desenvolvimento Brasileiro: Uma Política Nacionalista para Vencer a Atual Crise Econômica*. Rio de Janeiro: Zahar, 1966.

Viana, Luiz, Filho. *O Governo Castelo Branco*. Rio de Janeiro: José Olympio, 1975.

Wahkle, John C., et al. *The Legislative System*. New York: John Wiley & Sons, 1962.

Weffort, Francisco C. *Por que Democracia?* São Paulo: Brasiliense, 1984.

Wesson, Robert (ed.). *New Military Politics in Latin America*. New York: Praeger, 1982.

Wesson, Robert, and David V. Fleischer. *Brazil in Transition*. New York: Praeger, 1983.

Wirth, John D., Edson Oliveira Nunes, and Thomas E. Bogenschild (eds.). *State and Society in Brazil*. Boulder: Westview Press, 1987.
Worthley, John A. *Public Administration and Legislatures*. New York: Nelson Hall Inc., 1976.
Worthley, John A. (ed.). *Comparative Legislative Information Systems*. Washington: National Science Foundation, 1976.

REPORTS AND GOVERNMENT DOCUMENTS

Centro de Estudos e Acompanhamento da Constituinte CEAC, *O Anteprojeto Constitucional e o Dia-a-Dia do Cidadão*. Brasília: Departamento de Imprensa Nacional, 1986.
Centro de Estudos e Acompanhamento da Constituinte CEAC, *Constituinte: Temas em Análise, Caderno CEAC/UnB.*, Ano 1, No. 1. Brasília: Gráfica Ipiranga Ltda, 1987.
Partido da Frente Liberal PFL, *Manifesto, Programa e Estatuto*. Brasília: PFL, 1985.
Partido da Frente Liberal PFL, *Carta Compromisso: Projeto*. Brasília: PFL, 1986.
SEI, *Transborder Data Flows and Brazil: Brazilian Case Study*. New York: United Nations Center on Transnational Corporations, 1983.
União Parlamentar Interestadual UPI and Associação Nacional para o Desenvolvimento das Atividades Legislativas ANDAL. *A Nova Constituição e as Contituições Estaduais: Seminário*. Brasília: Senado Federal, 1988.
A Informática e a Nova República. São Paulo: Hucitec, 1985.
Anais do Seminário sobre Modernização Legislativa e Desenvolvimento Político: 7 a 11 de Junho de 1976. Brasília: Senado Federal, 1976.
Boletim de Pessoal: 1987. Brasília: Senado Federal, 1987.
Boletim de Pessoal: 1988. Brasília: Senado Federal, 1988.
Boletim de Pessoal: 1989. Brasília: Senado Federal, 1989.
Brazil: A Review of Agricultural Policies. Washington: World Bank, 1982.
Comissões Parlamentares de Inquérito, 1946-1982. Brasília: Câmara dos Deputados, 1983.
Constituição da República Federativa do Brasil: Quadro Comparativo. 5th Ed. Brasília: Senado Federal, 1986.
Constituição: República Federativa do Brasil, 1988. Brasília: Senado Federal, 1988.
Constituições do Brasil. 2 Vols. Brasília: Senado Federal, 1986.
Legislação Constitucional e Complementar. Brasília: Senado Federal, 1972.
Legislação Eleitoral e Partidária: Instruções do TSE para as Eleições de 1982, 4th ed. Brasília: Senado Federal, 1982.
Legislação Interna da Câmara dos Deputados. Brasília: Câmara dos Deputados, 1987.
Organização Administrativa da Câmara dos Deputados: Resolução No. 20/71. Brasília: Câmara dos Deputados, 1976
Poder Legislativo: Prerrogativas. Brasília: Câmara dos Deputados, 1980.
Reforma Administrativa do Governo Federal. 10th ed. Atlas, 1977.
Reforma Administrativa: Organização da Administração Federal. 4th ed. Brasília: Senado Federal, 1984.
Regimento Interno. Brasília: Câmara dos Deputados, 1986.
Regimento Interno. Brasília: Senado Federal, 1986.
Regimento Interno. Brasília: Senado Federal, 1989.
Regulamento Administrativo do Senado Federal. Brasília: Senado Federal, 1983.
Relatório da Primeira Secretaria do Senado Federal. Brasília: Senado Federal, 1985.

Relatório da Primeira Secretaria do Senado Federal. Brasília: Senado Federal, 1986.
Relatório da Primeira Secretaria do Senado Federal. Brasília: Senado Federal, 1987.
Repertório Biográfico dos Membros da Assembléia Nacional Constituinte de 1987. Brasília: Câmara dos Deputados, 1987.
Resoluções da Câmara dos Deputados, 47ª Legislatura: 1983-1986. Vol. 10. Brasília: Câmara dos Deputados, 1987.
Seminário de Informática do Senado Federal. Brasília: Senado Federal, 1983.

CHAPTERS IN EDITED BOOKS

Astiz, Carlos A. "O Papel Atual do Congresso Brasileiro." In Mendes (ed.). *O Legislativo e a Tecnocracia,* op. cit. 1975.
Baaklini, Abdo I. "Legislative Staffing Patterns in Developing Countries: Problems and Prospects." In Heaphey and Balutis (eds.), *Legislative Staffing,* op. cit. 1975.
Baaklini, Abdo I. "Legislative Reforms in the Brazilian Chamber of Deputies." In Baaklini and Heaphey (eds.), *Comparative Legislative Reforms and Innovations,* op. cit. 1977.
Baloyra, Enrique A. "From Moment to Moment: The Political Transition in Brazil, 1977-1981." In Selcher (ed.), *Political Liberalization,* op. cit. 1986, pp. 9-53.
Cardoso, Fernando Henrique. "Partidos e Deputados em São Paulo: O Voto e a Representação Política." In Cardoso and Lamounier (eds.), *Partidos e Eleições,* op. cit. 1975.
Cardoso, Fernando Henrique. "On the Characterization of Authoritarian Regimes in Latin America." In Collier (ed.), *The New Authoritarianism,* op. cit. 1979, pp. 33-57.
Cardoso, Fernando Henrique. "Associate-Dependent Development in Democratic Theory." In Stepan (ed.), *Democratizing Brazil,* op. cit. 1988.
Collier, David. "Overview of the Bureaucratic-Authoritarian Model." In Collier (ed.), *The New Authoritarianism,* op. cit. 1979, pp. 19-32.
Collier, David. "The Bureaucratic-Authoritarian Model: Synthesis and Priorities for Future Research." In Collier (ed.), *The New Authoritarianism,* ibid., pp. 363-97.
Diniz, Eli. "O Empresariado e a Nova Conjuntura." In Trindade (ed.), *Brasil em Perspectiva,* op. cit. 1982.
Figueiredo, Vilma. "A Questão Agrária e as 'Estratégias' do Governo." In Trindade (ed.), *Brasil em Perspectiva,* ibid.
Fleischer, David V. "Parties, Elections, and 'Abertura' in Brazil." In Wesson (ed.), *New Military Politics,* op. cit. 1982, pp. 79-96.
Fleischer, David V. "Brazil at the Crossroads: The Elections of 1982 and 1985." In Drake and Silva (eds.), *Elections and Democratization,* op. cit. 1986, pp. 299-327.
Fleischer, David V. "The Brazilian Congress: From 'Abertura' to 'New Republic,'" In Selcher (ed.), *Political Liberalization,* op. cit. 1986, pp. 97-133.
Hirschman, Albert O. "The Turn to Authoritarianism in Latin America and the Search for its Economic Determinants." In Collier (ed.), *The New Authoritarianism,* op. cit. 1979, pp. 61-98.
Lamounier, Bolivar. "As Eleições de 1982 e a Abertura Política em Perspectiva." In Trindade (ed.), *Brasil em Perspectiva,* op. cit. 1982.
Lamounier, Bolivar. "Apontamentos sobre a Questão Democrática Brasileira." In Rouquié et al. (eds.), *Como Renascem as Democracias,* op. cit. 1985, pp. 104-40.

Lamounier, Bolivar, and Alkimar R. Moura. "Economic Policy and Political Opening in Brazil." In Hartlyn and Morley (eds.), *Latin American Political Economy*, op. cit. 1986, pp. 165-96.

Martins, Luciano. "The 'Liberalization' of Authoritarian Rule in Brazil." In O'Donnell, Schmitter, and Whitehead (eds.), *Transitions from Authoritarian Rule*, op. cit. 1986, pp. 72-94.

Mericle, Kenneth S. "Corporatist Control of the Working Class: Authoritarian Brazil since 1964." In Malloy (ed.), *Authoritarianism and Corporatism*, op. cit. 1977, pp. 303-38.

Packenham, Robert A. "Legislatures and Political Development." In Kornberg and Musolf (eds.), *Legislatures in Developmental Perspective*, op. cit. 1970.

Packenham, Robert A. "The Changing Political Discourse in Brazil, 1964-1985." In Selcher (ed.), *Political Liberalization*, op. cit. 1986, pp. 135-73.

Rezende, André Lara, Luciano Coutinho, Alkimar R. Moura, Pércio Arida, Walter de Goes, Maria do Carmo C. Souza, and Bolivar Lamounier. "A Crise Econômica e os Modelos Alternativos." In Trindade (ed.), *Brasil em Perspectiva*, op. cit. 1982, pp. 31-60.

Saldanha, Nelson "Separação de Poderes." Vol. 2 of *O Poder Legislativo*. Brasília: Departamento de Imprensa Nacional, 1981.

Nogueira, Octaciano "Poder Legislativo no Brasil." Vol 1 of *O Poder Legislativo*, Brasília: Departamento de Imprensa Nacional, 1981.

Schneider, Ronald M. "The Brazilian Military in Politics." In Wesson (ed.), *New Military Politics*, op. cit. 1982.

Schneider, Ronald M. "Brazil's Political Future." In Selcher (ed.), *Political Liberalization*, op. cit. 1986, pp. 217-60.

Serra, José. "Three Mistaken Theses Regarding the Connection between Industrialism and Authoritarian Regimes." In Collier (ed.), *The New Authoritarianism*, op. cit. 1979, pp. 99-163.

Share, Donald, and Scott Mainwaring. "Transitions through Transaction: Democratization in Brazil and Spain." In Selcher (ed.), *Political Liberalization*, op. cit. 1986, pp. 175-215.

Soares, Gláucio Ary Dillon. "Elections and the Redemocratization of Brazil." In Drake and Silva (eds.), *Elections and Democratization*, op. cit. 1986, pp. 273-98.

Souza, Maria do Carmo Campello de. "O Processo Político-Partidário na Primeira República." In Mota (ed.), *Brasil em Perspectiva*, op. cit. 1971.

Stepan, Alfred. "The New Professionalism of Internal Warfare and Military Role Expansion." In Stepan (ed.), *Authoritarian Brazil*, op. cit. 1973, pp. 47-68.

Wesson, Robert. "Populism and Military Coups." In Wesson (ed.), *New Military Politics*, op. cit. 1982, pp. 17-34.

ARTICLES

Abranches, Sérgio Henrique Hudson de, and Gláucio Ary Dillon Soares. "As Funções do Legislativo." *Revista de Administração Pública* 7, no. 1 (1973).

Adler, Emanuel. "Ideological Guerrillas and the Quest for Technological Autonomy: Development of a Domestic Computer Industry in Brazil." *International Organization* 40, no. 3 (1985).

Albuquerque, Medeiros de. "Parlamentarismo e Presidencialismo no Brasil." *Revista de Ciência Política* 27 (April 1984).

Ames, Barry. "Rhetoric and Reality in a Military Regime: Brazil since 1964." *Sage Professional Paper in Comparative Politics* 4, no. 01-042. Beverly Hills: Sage Publications, (1973).

Ames, Barry. "The Congressional Connection, the Structure of Politics, and the Distribution of Public Expenditures in Brazil's Competitive Period." *Comparative Politics* no. 19 (1987), pp. 147-71.

Baaklini, Abdo I. "Legislative Reform or the Bureaucratization of the Legislature?" *Administration Dublin, Ireland* 24, no. 2 (Summer 1976), pp. 138-58.

Baaklini, Abdo I. "Legislatures in New Nations: Toward a New Perspective." *Polity* no. 8 (1976), pp. 558-80.

Baaklini, Abdo I., and Antonio Carlos Pojo do Rego. "O Congresso e a Política Nacional de Informática." *Revista de Administração Pública* 22, no. 2 (1988), pp. 87-105.

Baaklini, Abdo I., and Antonio Carlos Pojo do Rego."O Presidencialismo na Política Brasileira." *Revista Brasileira de Ciência Política* 1, no. 2, (March 1989).

Bahia, Luiz H. Olavo B. Lima, and Cesar Guimarães. "Perfil Social e Político da Nona Legislatura." *Jornal do Brasil* (March 22, 23, and 24, 1979).

Black, Jan Knippers. "The Military and Political Decompression in Brazil." *Armed Forces and Society* no. 6 (Summer 1980), pp. 625-638.

Bolling, Richard. "The Management of Congress." *Public Administration Review* (September/October 1975), pp. 49-55.

Bones, Elmar. "Golbery: Silêncio e Poder." *Tribuna da Imprensa* (October 2 and 3, 1978), p. 9.

Bonifácio, José. "A Reforma do Poder Legislativo." *Revista Brasileira de Estudos Políticos* no. 20 (January 1966), pp. 23-8.

Britto, Luis Navarro de. "As Eleições Legislativas de 1978." *Revista Brasileira de Estudos Políticos* (July 1980), pp. 7-99.

Busey, James L. "Brazil's Reputation for Political Stability." *Western Political Science Quarterly* 18, no. 4 (December, 1964), pp. 866-80.

Campos, Milton, and Nelson Carneiro. "Organização dos Parlamentos Modernos." *Revista Brasileira de Estudos Políticos* 25, no. 6 (July 1968/January 1969), pp. 139-63.

Cardoso, Fernando Henrique. "Hegemonia Burguesa e Independência Econômica: Raízes Estruturais da Crise Política Brasileira." *Revista Civilização Brasileira* no. 17 (January/February 1968).

Carvalho, Getúlio. "Processo Decisório: A Fronteira Política e os Limites Econômicos." *Revista de Administração Pública* 7, no. 1 (January/March 1973), pp. 7-20.

Carvalho, Orlando de. "Os Partidos Políticos e a Legitimação do Processo Político Brasileiro." *Revista de Informação Legislativa*, no. 16 (October/December 1979), pp. 57-66.

Chartrand, Robert Lee. "Congressional Management and the Use of Information Technology." *Journal of System Management* (August 1978), pp. 10-5.

Coelho, Edmundo Campos. "A Instituição Militar no Brasil." *Boletim Informativo e Bibliográfico de Ciências Sociais BIB* no. 19 (1st Semester 1985), pp. 5-19.

Cooper, Joseph, and David W. Brady. "Institutional Context and Leadership Style: The House from Cannon to Rayburn." *American Political Science Review* no. 75 (June 1981), pp. 411-25.

Cotrim, Netto and Alberto Bitencourt. "Natureza Jurídica dos Partidos Políticos Brasileiros." *Revista de Informação Legislativa* no. 13 (January/March 1976), pp. 63-74.

Daland, Robert T. "Development Administration and the Brazilian Political System." *Western Political Science Quarterly* 12, no. 2 (June 1968), pp. 25-39.

Diniz, Eli. "A Transição Política no Brasil: Uma Reavaliação da Dinâmica da Abertura." *Dados* 28, no. 3 (1985), pp. 329-46.

Dutra, Yamil e Souza. "Automação e Formação de uma Rede de Informações Jurídico-Legislativa: Experiência no Senado Federal." *Informática Jurídica Fundação Petrônio Portella - Ministério da Justiça* no. 3 (1985), pp. 47-68.

Evans, Peter. "State, Capital, and the Transformation of Dependence: The Brazilian Computer Case." *World Development* 14, no. 7 (1966).

Faria, José Eduardo. "Constituinte: Seus Riscos e Seus Muitos Desafios." *Jornal da Tarde* (January 5, 12, and 19, 1985).

Figueiredo, Marcus Faria, and José Antônio Borges Cheibub. "A Abertura Política de 1973 a 1981: Quem Disse o Que, Quando - Inventário de um Debate." *BIB* no. 14 (1982), pp. 22-61.

Fleischer, David V. "A Evolução do Bipartidarismo Brasileiro, 1966-1979." *Revista Brasileira de Estudos Políticos* (July 1980), pp. 155-85.

Fleischer, David V. "Renovação Política - Brasil 1978: Eleições Parlamentares sob a Égide do 'Pacote de Abril.'" *Revista de Ciência Política* no. 32 (1982), pp. 57-82.

Fleischer, David V. "Constitutional and Electoral Engineering in Brazil: A Double Edged Sword, 1964-1982." *Interamerican Economic Affairs* no. 37 (1984), pp. 3-36.

Fleischer, David V. "Eleições e Democracia no Brasil: Transição ou Transformismo." *Humanidades* 3, no. 10 (August/October 1986), pp. 84-92.

Francis, Wayne. "Leadership, Party Caucuses, and Committees." *Legislative Studies Quarterly* 10, no. 2 (May 1985), pp. 243-58.

Franco, Afonso Arinos de Mello. "Ato Institucional no. 1: Considerações sobre os Artigos Nos. 3 e 4." *Revista de Informação Legislativa* 1, no. 2 (April/June 1964), pp. 13-17.

Frantzich, Stephen E. "Computerized Information Technology in the U.S. House of Representatives." *Legislative Studies Quarterly* 4, (May 1979), pp. 255-79.

Gomes, L. Maria Gaspar. "Cronologia do Governo Castelo Branco." *Dados* nos. 2/3 (1967), pp. 112-32.

Gomes, L. Maria Gaspar. "Cronologia do 1º Ano do Governo Costa e Silva." *Dados* no. 4 (1968), pp. 199-220.

Heaphey, James J. (ed.). "A Symposium: Public Administration and Legislatures." *Public Administration Review* 35, no. 5 (September/October 1975).

Helena, Silvia. "A Indústria de Computadores: Evolução das Decisões Governamentais." *Revista de Administração Pública* 14, no. 4 (1980).

Huntington, Samuel P. "Will More Countries become Democratic?" *Political Science Quarterly* 99, no. 2 (Summer 1984), pp. 193-218.

Jacques, Paulino. "Do Relacionamento dos Poderes Políticos na Constituição do Império." *Revista de Informação Legislativa* 11, no. 41 (January/March 1974), pp. 5-16.

Lamounier, Bolivar. "Opening through Elections: Will the Brazilian Case become a Paradigm?" *Government and Opposition* 19, no. 2 (Spring 1984), pp. 167-77.

Lima, Luiz Gonzaga de Souza. "A Transição no Brasil: Comentários e Reflexões." *Contexto Internacional* 1, no. 1 (January/June 1985), pp. 27-59.

Lima, Olavo Brasil de. "Evolução e Crise do Sistema Partidário Brasileiro: As Eleições Legislativas Estaduais de 1947 a 1962." *Dados* no. 17 (1978), pp. 29-52.

Magalhães, Irene Maria et al. "Segundo e Terceiro Ano do Governo Costa e Silva." *Dados* no. 8 (1971), pp. 152-233.

Mainwaring, Scott. "The Transition to Democracy in Brazil." *Journal of Inter-American Studies and World Affairs* 28, no. 1 (Spring 1986), pp. 149-79.

Markoff, John, and Silvio R. Duncan Baretta, "Professional Ideology and Military Activism in Brazil: Critique of a Thesis of Alfred Stepan." *Comparative Politics* 17, no. 2 (January 1985), pp. 175-91.

McDonough, Peter. "Repression and Representation in Brazil." *Comparative Politics* 15, no. 1 (October 1982).

Mendes, Cândido de Almeida. "Sistema Político e Modelos de Poder no Brasil." *Dados* no. 1 (2nd Semester 1966), pp. 7-41.

Mezey, Michael L. "The Functions of Legislatures in the Third World." *Legislative Studies Quarterly* no. 8 (November 1983), pp. 511-550.

Moreira, Collares. "A Câmara e o Regime Eleitoral no Império e na República." *Estudos Legislativos* 1, no. 1 (January/June 1973), pp. 71-133.

Munhoz, Dércio G. "A Política Salarial do Setor Público." *Folha de São Paulo* (February 14, 1978), p. 3.

Munoz, Blanca P. "Brazilian Elections 1982: The Ambivalent Legacy of Vargism." *Electoral Studies* no. 2 (December 1983), pp. 207-27.

Nunes, Edson de Oliveira. "Legislativo, Política e Recrutamento de Elites no Brasil." *Dados* no. 17 (1978), pp. 53-78.

Patterson, Sammuel. "The Professional Staff on Congressional Committees." *Administrative Science Quarterly* no. 15 (March 1970).

Pereira, Jessé Torres. "Os Atos Institucionais em Face do Direito Administrativo." *Revista Brasileira de Estudos Políticos* no. 47 (July 1978), pp. 77-114.

Pimenta, Cornélio Octávio Pinheiro. "Parlamentarismo e Administração Pública." *Revista de Ciência Política* 27, no. 1 (April 1984), pp. 70-5.

Pimenta, Cornélio Octávio Pinheiro "Parlamentarismo, Presidencialismo e Interesse Público." *Revista de Ciência Política* 28, no. 1 (April 1985), pp. 32-8.

Pimenta, Cornélio Octávio Pinheiro. "Parlamentarismo e Profissionalização do Administrador Público." *Revista de Ciência Política* 29, no. 1 (1986), pp. 82-93.

Pitney, John. "Leaders and Rules in the New York Senate." *Legislative Studies Quarterly* 7, no. 4 (November 1982), pp. 491-506.

Pojo do Rego, Antonio Carlos. "O Lobby Nordestino: Novos Padrões de Atuação Política no Congresso Brasileiro." *Revista de Informação Legislativa* no. 21 (January/March 1984).

Pojo do Rego, Antonio Carlos. "Institutional Advance and Retreat: Obstacles to the Emerging Role of the Federal Legislature in the 'New Republic.'" *SECOLAS Annals* no. 28 (March 1987).

Polsby, Nelson W. "The Institutionalization of the U.S. House of Representatives." *American Political Science Review* no. 62 (1968), pp.144-68.

Reis, J. "Política de Pessoal do Serviço Público." *Ciência e Cultura* 31, no. 5 (May 1979), pp. 505-14.

Remmer, Karen. "Redemocratization and the Impact of Authoritarian Rule in Latin America." *Comparative Politics* 17, no. 3 (April 1985), pp. 253-75.

Remmer, Karen. "The Politics of Economic Stabilization: IMF Standby Programs in Latin America, 1954-1985." *Comparative Politics* 19, no. 1 (October 1986), pp. 1-24.

Riggs, Fred. "Bureaucratic Politics in the U.S.: Benchmarks for Comparison." *Governance* 6, no. 4 (October 1988), pp. 343-79.

Rios, José Arthur. "As Eleições de 1982 e os Pequenos Partidos." *Revista Brasileira de Estudos Políticos* (July 1983), pp. 187-216.

Roett, Riordan. "The Transition to Democratic Government in Brazil." *World Politics* 38, no. 2 (January 1986), pp. 371-82.

Roett, Riordan, and Scott D. Tollefson, "The Transition to Democracy in Brazil." *Current History* (January 1986), pp. 21-4.

Romero, Sylvio. "Parlamentarismo e Presidencialismo na República Brasileira." *Revista de Ciência Política* 27, no. 3 (December 1984), pp. 129-72.

Sampaio, Nelson de Sousa. "O Poder Legislativo no Brasil." *Política* no. 5 (July/September 1977), pp. 39-88.

Santos, Wanderley Guilhermo dos. "Eleição, Representação, Política Substantiva." *Dados* no. 8 (1971).

Sarles, Margaret J. "Maintaining Political Control through Parties: The Brazilian Strategy." *Comparative Politics* 15, no. 1 (October 1982), pp. 41-72.

Sarmento, Cléa. "Estabilidade Governamental e Rotatividade de Elites Políticas no Brasil Imperial." *Dados* 29, no. 2 (1986), pp. 139-75.

Sarney, José. "Brazil: A President's Story." *Foreign Affairs* 65, no. 1 (Fall 1986), pp. 105-6.

Schwartzman, Simon. "As Eleições e o Problema Institucional." *Dados* no. 14 (1977), pp. 447-72.

Silva, Helena. "A Indústria de Computadores: Evolução das Decisões Governamentais." *Revista de Administração Pública* 14, no. 4 (October/December 1980), pp. 73-109.

Smith, Steven. "The Central Concepts in Fenno's Committee Studies." *Legislative Studies Quarterly* 11, no. 1 (February 1986), pp. 5-18.

Soares, Gláucio Ary Dillon. "Military Authoritarianism and Executive Absolutism in Brasil." *Studies in Comparative International Development* 14, nos. 3/4 (Fall/Winter 1979), pp. 104-26.

Soares, Gláucio Ary Dillon. "La Cancelación de los Mandatos de Parlamentarios en Brasil." *Revista Mexicana de Sociologia* 42, no. 1 (January/March 1980), pp. 267-86.

Trigueiro, Oswaldo. "Os Poderes do Presidente da República." *Revista de Direito Administrativo* 29 (July/September 1952), pp. 22-37; and *Revista Forense* 148, nos. 601/602 (July/August 1953), pp. 36-45.

Trigueiro, Oswaldo. "A Representação Proporcional no Sistema Eleitoral Brasileiro." *Revista Forense* 153, no. 611/612 (May/June 1954), pp. 7-17.

Trigueiro, Oswaldo. "A Crise do Sistema Eleitoral Brasileiro." *Revista Brasileira de Estudos Políticos* no. 6 (July 1959), pp. 102-10.

Trigueiro, Oswaldo. "A Crise Legislativa e o Regime Presidencial." *Revista Brasileira de Estudos Políticos* no. 7 (November 1959), pp. 45-74; and *Revista Forense* 192, nos. 689/690 (November/December 1960), pp. 7-19.

Trigueiro, Oswaldo. "A Crise do Federalismo." *Revista Brasileira de Estudos Políticos* no. 11 (June 1961), pp. 39-56.

Trigueiro, Oswaldo. "A Revolução Americana e o Constitucionalismo Moderno." *Revista da Ordem dos Avogados do Brasil* 7, no. 19 (May/August 1976), pp. 215-32.

Trigueiro, Oswaldo. "A Federação na Nova Constituição do Brasil." *Revista Brasileira de Estudos Políticos* nos. 60/61 (January/July 1985), pp. 147-75.

Wahrlich, Beatriz M. de Souza. "Reforma Administrativa Federal Brasileira: Passado e Presente." *Revista de Administração Pública* 2, no. 8 (April/June 1974), pp. 27-75.

Wallerstein, Michael. "The Collapse of Democracy in Brazil: Its Economic Determinants." *Latin American Research Review* 15, no. 3 (1980), pp. 3-40.

Zeler, Robert. "The Search for Information: Specialists and Non-specialists in the U.S. House of Representatives." *Legislative Studies Quarterly* 4 (February 1979), pp. 31-42.

DISSERTATIONS, PAPERS AND SPEECHES

Abranches, Sérgio Henrique Hudson de. "O Processo Legislativo: Conflito e Conciliação na Política Brasileira." Master's thesis, University of Brasília, 1973.

Barros, Alexandre de Souza Costa. "The Brazilian Military: Professional Socialization, Political Performance, and State Building." Ph.D. diss., University of Chicago, 1978.

Brigagão, Clóvis. "Poder Legislativo no Brasil: Análise Política da Produção Legal de 1959 a 1966." Master thesis, Instituto Universitário de Pesquisas do Rio de Janeiro - IUPERJ, 1971.

Camargo, Margarida Maria. "A Escolha do Presidencialismo." Paper presented at the annual meeting of ANPOCS, Águas de São Pedro, 1988.

Campos, Roberto. "Address to the Federal Senate on June 8, 1983." Brasília: Senado Federal, 1983.

Carvalho, Maria Isabel Valladão de. "A Colaboração do Legislativo para o Desenvolvimento do Executivo durante o Governo JK." Master's thesis, Instituto Universitário de Pesquisas do Rio de Janeiro - IUPERJ, 1977.

Elonge, Henry Akwo. "A Political and Administrative History of the Cameroon National Assembly, 1946-1986." Ph.D. diss., State University of New York at Albany, 1989.

Figueiredo, Angelina Maria Cheibub. "Política Governamental e Funções Sindicais." Master thesis, Department of Social Sciences of the Universidade de São Paulo, October 1975.

Fleischer, David V. "Um Perfil Sócioeconômico, Político e Ideológico da Assambléia Nacional Constituinte de 1987." Paper presented at the annual meeting of ANPOCS, Águas de São Pedro, 1988.

Guimarães, Ulysses. "Estatuto do Homem, da Liberdade, da Democracia." Brasília: Câmara dos Deputados, 1988.

Hartlyn, Jonathan. "Presidentialism and Columbian Politics." Paper presented at the International Political Science Association meeting in Washington, D.C., August 1988.

Jenks, Margaret S. "Political Parties in Authoritarian Brazil." Ph.D. diss., Duke University, 1979.

Khalaf, Jassim M. "The Kuwait National Assembly: A Study of Its Structure and Function." Ph.D. diss., State University of New York at Albany, 1984.

Khatib, Abdullal al. "The Jordanian Legislature in Political Development Perspective." Ph.D. diss., State University of New York at Albany, 1975.

Linz, Juan. "Democracy: Presidential or Parlamentary? Does it Make a Difference?" Paper presented at the International Political Science Association meeting in Washington, D.C., August 1988.

Maciel, Marco. "Constituição para o Futuro." Brasília: Senado Federal, 1987.

Maciel, Marco. "Por que a Crise é Contemporânea?" Brasília: Senado Federal, 1987.

Maciel, Marco. "Por um Novo Presidencialismo." Brasília: Senado Federal, 1988.

Marcílio, Flávio Portela. "Conjuntura Política Nacional: O Poder Legislativo." Brasília: Câmara dos Deputados, 1979.

Molinelli, N. Guillermo. "President-Congress Relations in Argentina: 1960-1980." Paper presented at the International Political Science Association meeting in Washington, D.C., August 1988.

Riggs, Fred. "The American Presidentialist Case." Paper presented at the International Political Science Association meeting in Washington, D.C., August 1988.

Santos, Wanderley Guilhermo dos. "The Calculus of Conflict: Impasse in Brazilian Politics and the Crisis of 1964." Ph.D. diss., Stanford University, March 1979.

Valenzuela, Arturo. "Party Politics and the Failure of Presidentialism in Chile: A Proposal for Parliamentary Form of Government." Paper presented at the International Political Science Association meeting in Washington, D.C., August 1988.

Index

ABOUT THE AUTHOR

Abdo I. Baaklini is Director of the Center for Legislative Development and a professor in the Department of Public Administration and Policy, Nelson A. Rockefeller College of Public Affairs and Policy, University at Albany, State University of New York. He is the author of *Comparative Legislative Reforms and Innovations* (1977) and has been long engaged in research about legislatures in South America and Eastern Europe.